# REVITALISED URBAN ADMINISTRATION IN INDIA

# REVITALISED URBAN ADMINISTRATION IN INDIA

(Strategies and Experiences)

*Editor*
**U.B. Singh**

KALPAZ PUBLICATIONS
Delhi–110 052

**REVITALISED URBAN ADMINISTRATION IN INDIA**
*(Public Administration)*

Rs. 750



ISBN: 81-7835-077-7



Published in 2002 in India by
Kalpaz Publications
C–30, Satyawati Nagar
Ashok Vihar Phase–III
Delhi–110 052
E-mail: Kalpaz@hotmail.com

*Lasertypesetting at:* VARSHA GRAPHICS, Delhi
*Printed at:* Mehra Offset Printers, New Delhi

# Contents

# Preface

Last decade of the 20th century witnessed a revolutionary trend in local administration in the country. The seventy-third and seventy-fourth amendments to the Indian Constitution reinvented the federal structure of the country. For the first time Panchayats and Municipalities (tools for local governance) were incorporated in the Constitution. New Chapters were added. New Schedules were annexed. Democracy was decentralised. It was provided a stable life. All sections of society were got associated with the local administration. Administration was made accountable to people. Planning was initiated at the grassroot level. The higher echelons of administration are forced to devolve more and more functional and financial powers to local units of governance.

Although a period of five years is not sufficient to measure the impact of any new system in any organisation, it is essentially a trend indicator, a path setter and a goal determinator. With this sole aim in sight an attempt was made to overview the initial implementation process of this revolutionary step. The endeavour is confined to the urban administration only.

Prior to this, I studied conformity legislations in different states in the country. As a sequel this work is presented before the awakened readers. The venture, probably a pioneer one, aims to present holistic experiences across the country in connection with the actual implementation of the Constitution (74th) Amendment Act, 1992. I hope the success story presented here will act as an eye opener to decision makers and implementors at different levels.

**U.B. Singh**

# Acknowledgements

Creating a book involves many people, those who are actively involved in its design and writing, and many more who provide vision, guidance and inspiration. In this endeavour, I got overwhelming response from my friends and colleagues across the country. At the outset, I would like to express my deepest sense of gratitude to all the experts and scholars who obliged me by contributing these papers. I am indebted to Prof. S.K. Singh who went through the manuscript and provided guidance in enriching the volume. I am fully conscious about the assistance provided by Dr. R.K. Trivedi and Sri K.D. Pandey. I thank them all. I am especially thankful to my family and friends who provided love, support and understanding during the arduous task of creating and editing the manuscript. I am grateful to Kalpaz Publications, Delhi for publishing the book in the record time.

# List of Contributors

1. Hoshiar Singh, Ph.D. is Professor of Public Administration, Kurukshetra University, Kurukshetra.
2. H.M. Golandaz, Ph.D. is former Professor and Director of the Regional Centre for Urban and Environmental Studies, Mumbai.
3. S.M.Y. Sastry is the former Deputy Commissioner of the Mumbai Municipal Corporation, Mumbai.
4. S.K. Banerjee is the former Joint Secretary to the Government of Uttar Pradesh, Lucknow.
5. K. Deva Manikyam is Associate Professor and Head of Department of Public Administration and MHRM at Kakatiya University, Warangal.
6. T.V. Sujatha, Ph.D. is associated with the Department of Public Administration and HRM at the Kakatiya University, Warangal.
7. B. Venkatachalapati, Ph.D. is Assistant Professor and Head of the Public Administration in the S.V. University, P.G. Centre, Cuddapah.
8. S.K. Sinha is the former Chief Town Planner to the Government of Bihar, Patna.
9. Ashok Kumar, Ph.D. is Assistant Professor of Planning in the School of Planning and Architecture, New Delhi.
10. S.A. Javed, Ph.D. is Lecturer in Political Science in the Kuvempu University, Shimoga.
11. P. Surendran, Ph.D. is Sr. Lecturer in Economics at K.M.M. Government Women's College, Kannur.
12. Lcy K. John, M.Phil is Lecturer in Economics at the Marthoma College, Tiruvalla, Kerala.
13. Kailash, Ph.D. is Lecturer in Urban Studies Unit of the Tata Institute of Social Sciences, Mumbai.
14. Bijoyini Mohanty, Ph.D. is Reader and Chairperson in the Department of Public Administration at Utkal University, Bhuvaneswar.
15. Bhagabata Patro, Ph.D. is Reader in Economics at the Berhampur University, Berhampur.

16. Preyasi Nayak, is associated with the Department of Economics at Berhampur University, Berhampur.
17. K.S. Saxena, D. Litt., is the Director of Academic Staff College, J.N. Vyas University, Jodhpur.
18. K.P. Subramanian, B.E., Ph.D. is Assistant Professor in Urban Systems Engineering at the Anna University, Chennai.
19. Subramaniam Chandran, Ph.D. is Lecturer in Public Administration in the Department of Politics and Public Administration at the University of Madras, Chennai.
20. H.D. Dwarakanath, Ph.D. is Head of the Department of Political Science in SAP P.G. College, Vikarabad.
21. Gagan Deep, is Associate Fellow at the M.G. State Institute of Public Administration, Punjab, Chandigarh.
22. A.C. Mohapatra, Ph.D. is Professor of Geography and Dean of School of Humanities and Environmental Sciences, Shillong.
23. Awadhesh Kumar Singh, Ph.D. is Faculty Member at the Institute of Development Studies in the University of Lucknow, Lucknow.
24. S. Srikrishna, Ph.D. is Reader in Political Science and Public Administration at Sri Venkateswara University, Tirupati.
25. S. Anil Kumar Associated with the Department of Political Science and Public Administration at Sri Venkateswara University, Tirupati.
26. U.C. Dasgupta is the former Chief Town Planner to the Government of Uttar Pradesh, Lucknow.
27. P.K. Banta is in the Department of Public Administration, Summer Hill University, Shimla.

# Introduction

India is likely to enter the 21st century with an urban population of about 30 crores, thus adding approximately 80 million persons to the present urban population of 21.79 million (1991 Census). At least 3 to 5 of its cities will have crossed the 10 million mark by then and approximately 50 cities will have population in excess of one million. Such a huge concentration of population in urban areas will present needs of unprecedented scales. It is in this context that the city governance has to be reviewed so that it can meet the emerging challenges of India's urbanisation in a responsive manner. The liberalisation of economy and the increasing emphasis on privatisation of services may also bring a competitive era in which the city administration has to survive and develop. It is felt more relevant and timely in view of having been progressively undermined the role of urban local bodies over the past five decades. Many functions performed hitherto by these grassroot institutions are now performed by urban development authorities and other agencies created for specific purposes. In recent years, even the obligatory functions of local bodies have been taken away and assigned to other institutions, in the name of specialisation and functional efficiency.

**Genesis of Local Government**

In the context of local self-government in India one basic point is the independent origin and development out of the social conditions whereas in the modern times it is the state, that creates autonomous centres by its conscious efforts. India since olden days has been a land of villages. The local institutions that made people essentially self-governing and enjoying the rights of administering themselves, their local affairs and interests have been in existence in rural areas. Thus, in rural India, the local body seems to have organised on every possible principles of formation and shows a flourishing growth of the local democracies.

Contrary to this, the modern urban local self-governing institutions in the country owe their genesis to Lord Ripon's Resolution of May 18, 1882 when for the first time an organised system of urban local bodies was constituted. Lord Ripon had devised the system at the local level with an avowed objective of making it a forum and an instrument of political and popular education. However, with the passage of time and change in political situation in the country, the municipal authorities declined tremendously and became static institutions.

By providing the urban infrastructure, they are required to act as instruments of economic activity and engines of economic development. They are in fact required to promote a sound tradition of democratic way of life at the grassroot to bring about social development and to initiate and enhance economic development by strategic planning and administration. Unfortunately the decline has led them to lose their legitimacy to a very large extent. As a consequence of this, they have miserably failed to deal with the dynamic growth created by the process of urbanisation and urban growth. In years to come, their task is expected to become much more complex and difficult.

Many factors are responsible for this trend. To mention, a few of them may be the organisational incapacity of the local bodies in the face of severe services deficits, the problems assigning out of the haphazard and unplanned peripheral growth of towns and cities and, the continuing image of these institutions as having lost the motivation to face the challenges of growing urbanisation. In sharp contrast of the political prestige and influence that many of the municipal bodies engaged in earlier days enjoyed, the very existence of the municipal system has become vulnerable in recent years. The urban local self-government units in the country were frequently superceded, many for more than a decade or so.

The multi-dimensional decline in urban local government has always highlighted the importance and urgency of reform in the system. As a result, post-independence era has witnessed numerous impressive attempts for reform at the level of urban government. What is more, a surprisingly more number of proposals for reform have been repeated by successive committees and forums, indicating a consensus on specific measures of reforms in the realm of urban government as well as the urgency of the issues involved. Yet, most of the thinking on municipal reforms has remained confined to paper only. This demonstrates absence of sustained will and determination at the higher level of governments, i.e., Union and State, to respond to the problems of municipal government.

In spite of the apathetic attitude of the government in considering the local government as their youngest sister, the problems of urban areas as well as the structure and composition of municipal bodies, their functions and duties, and their resources have been the subject of discussion and debate on various forums. For the first time the National Commission on

Urbanisation (1988) has given detailed recommendations about the measures required for strengthening the management and administration of urban government institutions in the country.

**Constitutional Status**

The status of urban local-government system in Indian Constitution is ambiguous. Article 40 of the Constitution directs the states to organise Panchayats and empower them adequately so that they become viable unit of self-government; but counterpart provisions regarding urban local government is absent. Entry 5 of List II (State List) places local government, including urban local government, within the legislative competence of the States.

The question of according constitutional status to local government in urban areas has been a subject of discussion in many countries, both unitary and federal, developed as well as developing. The need for according an independent status to urban local government in India has also been considered having taken into account the experiences of other federal countries as well as the consistent demand from Central Council of State Ministers and the All India Council of Mayors and also on the recommendations of the National Commission on Urbanisation.

Keeping in view the growing importance of urban local bodies, the Union Government introduced in the Lok Sabha the Constitution 65th Amendment Bill, 1989, which could not be passed and lapsed due to dissolution of the Lok Sabha. Again, another bill was introduced in 1991 and was passed in December 1992. It was ratified by majority of the States and after the Presidential assent came into force with effect from April 24, 1993 as the 74th Amendment Act.

The 74th Constitution Amendment Act prescribes for a uniform system of urban local government in the country. It facilitates the democratic decentralisation at the grassroot level and provides stability through the mandatory election within a stipulated period of five years. All sections of the society including women are guaranteed due representation in the city government. The Act provides for the setting up of a Finance Commission every five year to review, reserve the resources and help the urban as well as rural local bodies to strengthen financially. There would be a District Planning Committee to consolidate the plans prepared by the 'panchayats' and urban local bodies in the district and to prepare a draft development plan for the overall integrated development of the district. In addition, metro towns will have a Metropolitan Planning Committee. A new schedule enumerating a number of functions is also annexed. The mandatory provisions are discussed in succeeding pages.

### Constitution

The organisation and structure of local bodies do not correspond to the pattern of living and distribution of population. It is inadequate for planning development and regulation of coherent ideas. The organisation of local bodies should be based on interdependence of town and country. It should be able to provide rising standard of services and it must be a democratically viable unit in the sense that there should be a close contact between the citizen and the local administration.

The 74th Amendment Act provides to constitute three kinds of urban local bodies— 'Nagar Panchayat' for a transitional area, 'Municipal Council' for a smaller urban area and, 'Municipal Corporation' for a large urban area. This classification of areas would be specified by the Governor of a State on the basis of population, density, the revenue generated, the percentage of employment in non-agricultural activities, the economic importance or such other factors as he deems fit.

The effect of the reclassification has led a major shake-up in the structure of urban local bodies in most of the states, which previously had many types of institutions. The amalgamation into three may lead to the uniform salary structure, services and other factors. In addition, the local politicians may also show their resentment and unhappiness on their scope being made limited by reducing the number of local units.

### Composition

According to the Act, all seats in a municipality have to be filled by persons chosen by direct election. For the purpose, the city area is divided into wards. For giving municipality a representative character, persons having special knowledge or experience in municipal administration, Members of Parliament and State Legislature whose constituencies comprise wholly or partly the municipal area; the members of Rajya Sabha and the State Legislative Council registered as electors within the area; and the chairpersons of the different committees are included in the council.

This provision, more or less, was already present in the Acts. It would, however, be more fruitful if the Members of Parliament and State Legislature are not given the right to cast their vote (which presently is misused). Their attendance in meetings should be made mandatory. Many a State has excluded these higher level politicians.

### Decentralisation

One major issue with regard to the structure of municipal bodies in the country relates to the accessibility and responsiveness of the municipal government. It is an accepted fact that common citizen in a city does not have ready access to the municipal administration and its elected representatives. It is in this context that the National Commission on Urbanisation recommended a multi-tier system for bigger corporation and metropolitan areas.

In many States the administration in the corporation towns, had been decentralised since long and been yielding good results also. However, implementation of plans and schemes was not in its purview.

Keeping this aspect in mind, the Act provides for the creation of Ward Committees in the cities having population of 3 lakhs or more. The member representing the ward becomes the chairperson of the Committee. The other members, functions and responsibilities of the Committee are to be determined by the State Legislature. It would have been bitter if such committees are envisaged for smaller towns also.

**Duration and Election**

A major malady which needed remedy, unhesitatingly, has been attempted hereby. Most States and most parties in power, in the past displayed unconcern for periodic polls and with equal delinquency, had superceded local bodies to which they were allergic.

The Act makes mandatory to complete the election before expiry of the normal duration, i.e., five years. In case of a dissolved municipality the election has to be held within six months. The Act provides the elections to be held by State Election Commission. This provision may come as a boon to the local bodies against the uncalled for and self-motivated frequent supersession. The municipality cannot be dissolved without giving it opportunity of being heard.

**People's Participation**

The Indian Constitution accepts the representative parliamentary democracy in the country. The Act takes care of this provision at the grassroot level itself. It provides the reservation of seats for the Scheduled Castes and Scheduled Tribes based on their ratio in the population of the area. The Act further facilitates the representation of women to the extent of not less than one-third of the total number. Even the seats of chairpersons, mayors are reserved for these categories. This was a revolutionary decision and has certainly brought a social change in the country. This is in consonance with the commitment of the country to open opportunity to all irrespective of caste, creed, sex, religion, etc. Indian society is primarily traditional and man-dominated but the country has been a pioneer in giving the equal Constitutional and social status to the woman. Their provision further affirms the commitment of strengthening the vulnerable class of the society.

**Power, Authority and Responsibility**

Over the past five decades, the role of urban local bodies has been progressively undermined. Many functions performed hitherto by local government are now performed by other functional and specialised agencies created for the purpose. In recent years, even the obligatory functions of local bodies have been taken away and assigned to other institutions. This has happened at all levels of cities and towns.

The Act attempts to reconsolidate and restrengthen the urban local bodies. It empowers the municipalities to prepare the plans for economic development and social justice and to perform the functions and implementation of schemes entrusted to them including 18 items appended in the Constitution as the Twelfth Schedule. Most of the listed functions are already in the existing Acts, but have been transferred, temporarily, to other institutions.

Only enlisting the functions will not yield any fruitful result. There is a need to restrengthen—politically, financially, personnel-wise and technically—to the urban local government. Besides, attitudinal change on the part of personnel, people's civic consciousness and participation is also a must for discharging functions satisfactorily.

**Financial Powers**

For a developing economy, decentralised federal system has been conceived as an ideal system of financial management. In this way the financial performance of a local body in providing local services and their financing has been very crucial for the success of a federal system. The importance of role of state governments in the working of local governments is very important. At the same time the role of urban local bodies is also important for proper functioning of a federal system.

On the basis of the findings of various Commissions/Committees, it is found that the urban local bodies in the country have always been in hot water and have faced a resource crunch. A good number of municipalities in many States have not been in a position even to pay salary to their staff regularly, what to talk of development work or maintaining minimum level of civic services.

Despite having been empowered to levy, collect and appropriate the local taxes, the local bodies have not been able to initiate without a clearance from the State Government. Even the local councillors do not intend favourably. Every politician keeps vote in mind while dealing with local taxation.

The Act, keeping the weak financial base in view, prescribes for constituting a Finance Commission every five years. It would review the financial position of the municipalities and make recommendations to the Governor regarding the distribution of taxes between the state and local bodies, the determination of taxes, etc. It would also suggest the measures to improve the financial position of urban local bodies besides other matters reflected in the interest of sound finance of the municipalities. However, the recommendations made by the Commission are not mandatory on the State Government who may dilute them at its liberty.

**Integrated Planning**

The planning system in the country has always been a sectoral in nature. However, the Act initiates a historical approach to local planning. It provides for constituting at the district level a District Planning Committee which will consolidate the plans prepared by the rural as well as urban local units in the district and to repare a draft development plan for the district as a whole. Not less than four-fifths of the total members would be elected by, and from amongst the elected members of both the local governments in proportion to the ratio of the population of the rural and of the urban areas in the district.

In addition, the Act also provides for constituting in every metropolitan area, having a population of 10 lakhs or more, a Metropolitan Planning Committee to prepare a draft development plan for the area. Not less than two-thirds of the members of the Committee shall be elected by, and from amongst the elected members of the municipalities and chairpersons of the rural local bodies in the metropolitan area in proportion to the ratio between the population covered by both types of local bodies. However, in most of the States these Committees are not made functional as yet.

It is clear from the fore-gone discussion that the principal aim of the 74th Amendment Act is to facilitate the democratic decentralisation in the country. The Government recognises the importance of these grassroot level institutions and intends to strengthen them. However, the urban local institutions have been left totally on the mercy of the State Governments, which are short of political will to strengthen these local units of government. If the government realised the importance of the urban local government, they should be recognised as a constituent unit of the whole federal system. Their relationship of superior and subordinate has to be changed as partner in the whole system. However, this is a good beginning and time is not far off when these grassroot institutions would be recognised as a constituent, after Union and State Governments, of the federal system in the country. They would act as a 'nursery' of democracy and be able to produce mature, outstanding, devoted and committed patriot and national leaders like Nehru, Subhash, Patel and many others who saw their rise in the soil of urban local bodies only.

In this historical backdrop, the status of implementation of the 74th Amendment to the Constitution in different states is at different stages. The abstract of the various papers, discussing the status in different States follows.

Prof. Hoshiar Singh in his paper identifies the heterogeneity in the formation, creation and composition of municipalities in different states. The apathetic attitude of the State Governments and the callousness on the part of urban local bodies has led to a deteriorating environment and lack of civic services and facilities in urban centres. The finances were also not found in good health. The Seventy Fourth Amendment to the Constitution, according to Prof. Singh, is a step in the right direction to revitalise the municipal institutions. But he is apprehensive about its implementation and impact. Prof. Singh raises a number of genuine questions about the relationship of local executives with that of the State and Union Governments, between the District Planning Committee and National State Planning Commission and the Metropolitan Planning Committee, about the devolution of powers and functions to these grassroot institutions, the sanctity of creating agencies for discharging local functions, etc.

Dr. H.M. Golandaz in her paper focuses upon the main provisions of the 74th Amendment to the Constitution. She welcomes the Constitution of District Planning and Metropolitan Planning Committees, State Finance Commission, Election Commission and Ward Committees but is apprehensive about the composition and effectiveness of these bodies. Dr. Golandaz suggests the composition and a set of functions to be given to these bodies. She feels the need of amending the other Acts as well, in consonance with the mandatory provisions of the 74th CAA. Dr. Golandaz emphasises that instead of annexing a schedule of functions to be given to urban local bodies, it would have been better for their autonomy to create a separate list of local functions in the Constitution. She wonders whether the State Governments would be prepared to devolve administrative and fiscal powers to these grassroot institutions as envisaged in the Constitution. Dr. Golandaz apprehends that the State Finance Commission would be treated by the State Government as advisory body thus diluting the impact of its recommendations related to widen the municipal resource base. Despite all these apprehensions, Dr. Golandaz finds the 74th CAA as 'harbinger of democratic decentralisation' in the country, besides provider of 'right to exist' to these local institutions.

Sri S.M.Y. Sastry explains extensively the problems of resource mobilisation of urban local bodies. He welcomes the decision of constituting State Finance Commission every five years as envisaged in the Constitution but is apprehensive about the implementation of its recommendations. However, he sees a ray of hope in the role as assigned to the Central Finance Commission. Sri Sastry feels that amendment to Art. 280 will necessarily better the situation and enhance the effectiveness of the State Finance Commission and the Central Finance Commission. He discusses comprehensively the recommendations made, time and again, by the various Commissions/Committees set up by the Union and State Governments for strengthening the financial situation of urban local bodies. He favours the identification of local taxes as having been recommended by the Taxation Enquiry Commission. These taxes should, he argues, be allowed to be levied as municipal taxes. Sri Sastry further observes that the octroi should not be abolished and if it has to be, it should be substituted by an equally flexible tax rather than being compensated. He emphasises upon the proper exploitation of the allotted taxes by the municipalities. He feels the need of making the services self-sufficient and exhorts municipality to ensure cost-recovery of major services. He advocates the award of two types of grants-in-aid, one essential to ensure a certain standard of requirements and the other, to induce better performance.

Sri S.K. Banerjee in his paper discusses at length the main provisions of the Amendment Act. He details out the background of framing this historical legislation. Sri Banerjee describes the importance of planning at lower level and emphasises upon the new emerging role of urban local bodies in the context of the Central enactment. While discussing the impact of the 74th CAA, Sri Banerjee identifies a number of critical areas having emerged out of the implementation of the 74th CAA. He talks about the functions incorporated in the Twelfth Schedule. He analyses the new challenges before the local bodies and the future of the town planners. He feels the need of amending the Town Planning Act in consonance with the emerging scenario and functions entrusted to the municipalities. Sri Banerjee underlines the importance of strengthening the urban local bodies financially, in absence of which these grassroot level democratic institutions would not be able to bear the new burden.

Dr. K. Deva Manikyam and Dr. T.V. Sujatha elaborate the trends of urbanisation in the country, in general and Andhra Pradesh in particular. They feel urbanisation as a *sine qua non* for progress and prosperity and an important social characteristic. The problems of housing, educational facilities and other basic civic services are arisen as a result of haphazard urbanisation. The authors find lacking inter-dependence between the process of urbanisation and regional development. The cities have been accepted as an evolution by accident. The cities, according to them, hardly be designated as 'generative cities'. The city's ability to serve as the growth centre is greatly hindered. The authors identify acute scarcity of finance as the most serious problem facing the urban local bodies. Because of inadequate finances, the local bodies are not able to fulfil even their obligatory functions. They feel unemployment and political interference as the major problems for urban development. They find that the forces controlling urban local government do not identify themselves with the goals of urban development.

Dr. Manikyam and Dr. Sujatha, discussing the Andhra Pradesh status, explain the major provisions of the State Municipal Acts pre- and post-74th Amendment to the Constitution. They discuss the criteria for classifying the municipal boards and the strength of the council, reservation of seats and the provisions for constituting various committees.

Adjudging the implications, the authors find the enactment in Andhra Pradesh made 'in haste'. They point out certain anomalies and problems. The basis of classification is not practical and integrated. The implications of reservations are quite complicated. The authors express lack of sincerity in devolution of functions to local bodies. According to them, nine functions of the Twelfth Schedule are being performed by different state level departments. The municipal bodies are not able to perform these tasks. Paradoxical to the 74th CAA, according to authors, the powers earlier enjoyed by the elected wing are withdrawn and transferred to the executive wing. They feel the role of the State Finance Commission important in view of the problematic areas in the financial dimension of local bodies.

The duo high-light certain mandatory provisions of the 74th Amendment to the Constitution yet to be incorporated in the State Municipal Acts. They advocate restoration of powers to the elected wing and debureaucratise the local government. They express the need of involving local community in planning, management and revenue collection. The function-finance match is the crux of the problem and the authors emphasise upon it.

Dr. B. Venkatachalapathi presents, in brief, the salient features of the Central enactment. He explains the disadvantages as well. Dr. Venkatachalapathi examines the state of affairs in different municipalities in Andhra Pradesh. He presents a situation analysis of civic services in various municipal areas. He identifies the principal reasons of such a deplorable situation of urban services and not so sound the financial health of municipalities in the State. He discusses the realities and challenges before the municipalities all over the State and urges early measures to improve the situation. A new comprehensive legislation, in his opinion, is the need of the hour for better provision of services in urban areas.

Sri S.K. Sinha presents a wholistic scenario of urban management in Bihar. He explains the various authorities and agencies involved in discharging local functions in urban state. Sri Sinha discusses at length the salient features of all the legislations having been practised in urban sector. According to him, the State Government has since amended the Municipal Acts in consonance with the Constitution 74th Amendment Act, but the implementation part is still missing. The functions mentioned in the Twelfth Schedule are made obligatory in Acts, but other agencies are still discharging those responsibilities. Despite the creation of a State Election Commission, the elections are still awaited. The Finance Commission is set up but not active as yet. Sri Sinha depicts a comprehensive picture of urban management in the State and finds the State lagging behind in implementation of the Constitutional provisions.

Dr. Ashok Kumar traces the history of governance in Delhi Region. Presenting a historical overview, Dr. Kumar explains the history of governance of Delhi from feudal past and centralised administration to post-Independence practices. According to him, National Capital Territory of Delhi is governed by more than 20 large and about 200 medium and small organisations as Delhi consists of 205 villages, 29 census towns, 3 municipal bodies and two tehsils. He elaborates the major authorities active in urban sector and the functions assigned them. The different administrative boundaries in Delhi have created the mess of administration. The functioning of Delhi Municipal Corporation has been merged because of the frequent dissolution of the Corporation. Moreover, the Government of India has delegated limited legislative powers to the city government but the administrative control clearly vests in the President. Even the Metropolitan Council did not have the executive powers. The administration of Delhi has been a victim of fragmentation. Dr. Kumar discusses the various mechanisms of coordination and supervision of other Government Departments and also the impediments to effective governance of Delhi.

Dealing with the situation as arisen as a result of the 73rd and 74th Amendments to the Constitution, Dr. Kumar finds the picture anything but clear. This has led to conflicts between the Chief Minister and Mayor, on one hand, and the Union Government and the Lt. Governor, on the other. All the provisions are implemented half-heartedly. Various mandatory provisions are still missing.

Dr. Kumar advocates a case for consolidating and integrating the basic services. He talks about the need of infrastructure and discusses at length the role of Infrastructure Development Finance Corporation of India to be set up by the Government of India for providing better infrastructure. In Delhi power and public transport have been identified as the thrust areas. The Government has allocated funds for setting up the Delhi Infrastructure Development and Finance Corporation. Dr. Kumar is optimistic that the Corporation would be able to provide more than one service including water, electricity, sewerage, drainage and solid waste. However, he is apprehensive about the measures taken in the name of decentralisation. Dr. Kumar suggests that the Corporation should not indulge in producing any service but should organise their provision. Its objective should be to serve the people and not a selected group of people. This should be a citizen's Corporation.

Dr. S.A. Javeed explains at length the urban governance in Karnataka in pre and post-74th CAA situation. He critically examines the hurdles in effective urban administration. Emphasising upon the need of checking migration from rural areas, he feels that the solution to the problems of urban areas lies outside the urban centres. He calls upon to improve the rural areas on a priority basis and develop them at par with the urban areas. The developed rural areas may be able to absorb people therein thus curbing the migration to urban areas. Another important problem area baffling the city administration, according to the author, is lack of coordination between various authorities responsible for local services and identifies the areas of lacking coordination. Dr. Javeed emphasises upon the need of trained and competent municipal personnel. He describes the practice of hiring officers from State Government departments to urban local bodies not good for their sound administration and brings out the shortcomings emanated therefrom. He necessitates the improvement in motivation and training and development programmes to the municipal officials. Dr. Javeed feels the need of political will to get the benefits of the new enactment.

Dr. P. Surendran exhaustively explains the changing profile of urban local government in Kerala. The state has not only witnessed the increase in literacy but has also recorded a large increase in urban population. According to him, the state is differently categorised so far as the urbanisation is concerned. Urban living in Kerala is only an extension of the rural inhabitation. There is a deep-rooted rural-urban continuum in the State.

Comparing Panchayat Raj Institutions with the Urban Local Bodies, Dr. Surendran says that unlike Panchayats Nagar Palika is a single-tier system. Nagar Palikas are designed at par with the Urban Panchayats. The lowest unit in urban governance is Ward Sabha, a nominated body with the elected member as its convener. In all, 29 departments of the State Administration are transferred to the urban local bodies in the State as a resultant to the powers and functions as devolved on the basis of new enactment. The Nagar Palikas have a broad tax base. These grassroot institutions are taken as a nodal unit to draft bottom level plan projects in touch with the felt needs of the people.

Dr. Surendran concludes his paper with a few suggestions. He emphasises upon more plan allocation to these bodies for strengthening the connecting process in industry and agriculture. The allocation should consider geographical conditions as well. He emphasises upon further devolution of powers and resources to the urban local units.

Dr. Lcy K. John discusses at length the impact of the 74th Constitution Amendment Act in Kerala. He lists out the functions transferred to the urban local bodies as a consequence of the Amendment. Dr. John details out the institutions transferred to urban bodies in conformity with the devolution of functions to them. He appreciates that in order to galvanize the decentralisation process, besides transferring the institutions, schemes and projects, the State Government has initiated the devolution of funds as well. The government employees have been shifted to urban government. A separate budget account for the local bodies has been framed. The Government has also appointed an Expert Committee to suggest other administrative and necessary measures to strengthen the local bodies. In pursuance of the Act, the Standing Committee has been found. In addition to political impact, according to Dr. John, an administrative impact is also seen on the local bodies. Evolution of a new development culture is a pointer to social impact as well. The planning process in the state is totally decentralised. In between urban local bodies and the District Planning Committee, a Voluntary Technical Core or the Municipal Local Expert Committee is set up for evaluating the plans prepared before finally submitting them to the District Planning Committee. Thus, the total planning process in the State has become the people's planning. Dr. John substantiates his observation by discussing an empirical situation analysis of three urban local bodies. He concludes his paper with an optimistic note of the experiment turning out to be the most successful in Kerala.

Dr. Kailash in his paper traces the historical development of local self-government in the country, in general, and in Maharashtra state, in particular. According to him, about 40 per cent of State's population lives in different urban centres. The Mumbai Metropolis contains majority of the urban population. The big towns have shown a remarkable growth over the years and the smaller centres have been facing stagnation. Dr. Kailash presents districtwise urban scenario. As regards the formation of municipalities, the first attempt was made through the direction of King George III to the Governor-General of Bengal to constitute Bombay Municipal Corporation and appoint the Justices of Peace in 1792. However, the first municipal government came into existence in 1865. He elaborately explains the main provisions of the Mumbai Municipal Corporation and the Nagpur Municipal Corporation Acts, the Maharashtra Provincial Municipal Corporation Act and the Maharashtra Municipalities Act. Dr. Kailash examines the provisions of different State municipal Acts as modified in commensurate to the 74th CAA. He describes the provisions relating to the Wards Committees, the Finance Commission and the State Election Commission and also the main focus of the laws enacted for planning purposes as envisaged in the Amendment. He feels that the Act ensures a better participation by people at grassroot level, social and gender justice, decentralisation of municipal administration and the role of urban local bodies in the planning and development at local and regional levels. Dr. Kailash also comprehends the newly introduced Mayor-in-Council system of municipal governance in two Corporations. He is optimistic about the increase in effectiveness of municipal administration as a result of the new system (the system was discontinued later on).

Dr. Bijoyini Mohanti successfully traces the historical development of urban governance in Orissa. She presents an exhaustive evolutionary study of municipal administration in this eastern part of the country. Dr. Mohanty, while discussing the administrative system goes back to the olden days, much before the creation of the modern state of Orissa. She analyses legal framework in the historical perspective. The trend of urbanisation in the State is also discussed at length by her. Dr. Mohanty establishes a linkage-organisational, structural, legal, administrative over different periods of development. She explains an interesting picture of municipal administration in Orissa consequent upon the 74th CAA. Dr. Mohanty illustrates the planning—fiscal and functional—and electoral reforms having been introduced in the post—74th CAA era. Although a good beginning has been initiated in the field of urban governance in Orissa, according to her, a much more in the form of the constitution of District Planning Committees, outcome of the State Finance Commission, etc. are still awaited. The full implementation of the provisions can only facilitate a better urban governance in the State.

Dr. B. Patro and Ms. Preyasi Nayak in their joint paper discuss at length the trend of urbanisation in Orissa. They elaborate the objectives of urban development policy and the administrative machinery for accomplishing the development of urban areas in the state. They examine different developmental schemes undertaken by the urban local bodies and depict the present status of urban infrastructure in Orissa and also the pattern of public expenditure thereon. The authors establish relationship between the improvement and the expenditure made for the specific purposes in the post–74th CAA period. They feel the inadequacy and availability of codified statistical information relating to urban governance. They apprehend the outcome of the State Finance Commission constituted in pursuance of the 74th CAA. They express doubt about the tax revenue yield of urban local bodies. The authors advocate the need to formulate a realistic and scientific budget in order of priority of demand for different urban services.

Explaining urban government in Rajasthan, Dr. K.S. Saxena emphasises upon the importance of city government in the Indian federation. Politics and political awareness, according to Dr. Saxena, are the critical factors in the municipal administration. He feels that the Constitution 74th Amendment Act, 1992 has infused a new blood in the city governance in the country. The elections to all the three types of municipalities in Rajasthan were fought on party basis which has led to 'politicisation' of municipal administration in the State. This has created a 'political confusion' also. He advocates us municipal elections to be held on non-party basis. The reservation of seats for women is bound to uplift the status of women in Rajasthan, which is considered a backward state. Dr. Saxena is, however, apprehensive that most of the women candidates are almost "illiterate, have no experience and are prisoners of age-old social traditions of *parda pratha*. This has resulted into "menfolk virtually running the administration". Dr. Saxena is, however, optimistic that in coming years "women will realise their hidden strength and will come out with more courage and vigour". He concludes that "in coming years, these bodies will be more strengthened by giving more financial powers and would contribute in strengthening the roots of democracy" in the country.

Dr. K.P. Subramanian examines the amendments made into various local Acts dealing with urban affairs in Tamil Nadu. As regards devolution of functions, he feels the need of redefining the role of specialised functional agencies vis-a-vis the local bodies. Discussing the role and responsibilities assigned to the District/Metropolitan Planning Committees, Dr. Subramanian apprehends the role of the District Planning Committees. He describes the various interfaces between the functional agencies like Metropolitan Development Authority, Water Supply and Sewerage Board, Housing Board, Slum Clearance Board, Pollution Control Board and Transport Corporation and the City Municipal Corporation. Dr. Subramanian highlights the areas of functional conflicts between these local agencies. He appreciates the attempts made by the government in balancing the relationship. Critically analysing the situation, Dr. Subramanian explains the complexities arisen as a result of powers having been transferred to the local bodies and the technical expertise been available with the functional agencies. He apprehends a tussel between the 'democratically elected local bodies' and 'nominated bureaucratic functional agencies'. He discusses the measures taken by the government in the form of Joint Administrative Committees to bring all the agencies under the purview of the Corporation. Dr. Subramanian examines the fiscal devolutions to local bodies as recommended by the State Finance Commission. Explaining the people's perception, he finds the people ridiculed with the elected council. Despite rating the devolution of powers not complete, Dr. Subramanian finds it a good beginning.

Dr. S. Chandran traces the history of urban local government in the country, in general and in Tamil Nadu, in particular. He discusses at length the various enactments made during British regime for effective urban administration in the city of Madras (now Chennai). Dr. Chandran explains the growth of municipal administration in Tamil Nadu since the year of establishment of first modern municipality in Madras, the creation of office of Sheriff and that of the Mayor and of the President. He highlights the changing character of local administration from nominated to coopted for making it more representative and participative, to voluntary system of self-government.

Although the State is bestowed with first municipality having come into existence in 1687, according to Dr. Chandran, urban administration in Tamil Nadu began with the enactment of the Town Improvement Act of 1850, and municipalities were constituted under the Act of 1865. All sorts of local functions were assigned to these bodies under the presidentship of the District Magistrate. Dr. Chandran also discusses in brief electoral scenario in Madras Municipality.

After a historical perspective, Dr. Chandran elaborately explains the provisions made and implemented as a consequence of the 74th Amendment Act to the Constitution. He feels that the Amendment has placed greater responsibilities of urban governance in the hands of urban local bodies. A large number of functions have been entrusted to them. The municipalities have to meet simultaneously the infrastructure needs of rapidly increasing population. This all poses a challenge before the local bodies. Dr. Chandran also talks of some vagueness in the Nagar Palika Act, which in his opinion, may add to certain doubts about the strength of this legislation. However, he feels satisfied and seems optimistic to the elected members providing an expansion of public realm of interaction. He concludes his paper with the hope that, in one way, the people's participation in local governance is strengthened.

Dr. H.D. Dwarakanath presents a situation analysis of women in the country and discusses their status in different areas. Although the Constitution of the country guarantees to women equality in political participation, in practice, their voice, according to him, is hardly given any weightage. This situation is attributed to the ignorance, illiteracy and poor representation of this vulnerable class of society. Dr. Dwarakanath describes the women's entry into politics and their situation in the Parliament has been an eyewash. He is optimistic that the political and economic reservation of seats as provided under the 73rd and 74th Amendments to the Constitution may help women to develop and also link them to the national mainstream in managing the resources and governing the local community. The process of women empowerment, according to him, is expected to open the whole vista of human resources development. He substantiates his views by illustrating data from various states. Dr. Dwarakanath concludes his paper with an urgent requirement of training to women in administration. He is optimistic about the role women can play in the development of the country, whether rural or urban.

Dr. Gagan deep examines the role and importance of octroi in the financial condition of urban local bodies in the country. He traces the history of octroi in India and establishes it as a major source of income to urban local bodies. Making out a strong case, Dr. Deep analyses the strength and weaknesses of octroi and impact of its abolition. In Punjab, large part of income in most of the urban local bodies is accrued through octroi only. In his opinion, octroi is an indicator of development and industrial advancement of a city. He advocates its continuance but cautions against leakage and emphasises on plugging the loopholes in its administration to get a maximum of this major source of income.

Prof. A.C. Mahapatra described the trend of urbanisation and its economic impact on the people of the North East Region. He illustrates a clear picture of urbanisation and urban poverty in seven sister-states of the Region. Prof. Mahapatra explains that steady increase in the level of urbanisation has resulted into inadequate infrastructure which is the main cause of urban poverty in the Region. The Region records a low level of urbanisation in comparison to national level, but a very high growth of population concentration in urban areas. Prof. Mahapatra emphasises upon the effective implementation of urban poverty alleviation programme. He feels the need of making the people aware and develop them to participate in the programmes. He reiterates the need of widening the non-formal and adult education programmes for the people at large. Prof. Mahapatra underlines the importance and need of associating the existing local community groups with the programmes instead of creating new community based organisations as envisaged in the various programmes.

Dr. A.K. Singh in his paper analyses the finances of urban local bodies in Uttar Pradesh, in general, and of municipal corporations in particular. Dr. Singh explains the sources of municipal revenue and also underlines the main recommendations of the State Finance Commission. He presents the statistical analysis since 1959–60 (formation of the municipal corporations in the State) and projects the income pattern upto 2000–01. Dr. Singh examines the expenditure pattern as well as the provision of major services also. He concludes his paper with certain valuable suggestions regarding reforming the property taxes, licence fees, tax collection and fiscal administration.

Dr. S. Srikrishna and Mr. S. Anil Kumar in their joint paper evaluate the functioning and achievement of Tirupati Urban Development Authority. The authors discuss the process of urbanisation in this holy city, the seat of Lord Venkateshwara, presently the richest deity on the earth. They explain the roles and responsibilities of the Municipality, Authority and Tirupati Devasthanam in providing basic physical infrastructure in the Tirupati Development area. The duo examine the impact of a number of housing schemes and sites and services programmes having been undertaken to match with the increasing demands of this holy town. They advocate the hide scope of expanding the existing schemes of water supply and feel the need of initiating new ones as well. Various projects of road widening and laying out of new link roads have also discussed by them. They describe a number of measures taken up for augmenting the financial resources of municipality as well as Tirupati Development Authority, the organisation responsible for developing this town.

Mr. U.C. Dasgupta examines the trend of urbanisation in Uttar Pradesh. He explains that the growth in agricultural sector leads an expected high rate of urbanisation. Mr. Dasgupta analyses the state of economy in Uttar Pradesh. He finds that the annual growth rate and per capita income of the State have always remained lower than the national average during different Plan periods. He classifies the ditricts on the basis of per capita net output and the rate of growth in total output. Mr. Dasgupta establishes a link between town development and rural growth strategies. He discusses the increase in urban population in different economic regions. Depicting the growth in urban population, he finds that the western region is more urbanised and is contained with majority of the urban centres. The industrial development is more in the western region than the other economic regions. Thus Mr. Dasgupta makes out a case before policy makers and planners for planning the overall integrated development of the State.

Sri P.K. Banta in his paper traces the history of Shimla city and evolution of the city administration. He establishes the setting up of city and its administration by the British. Shimla once recognised as summer capital of the country was the seat of Viceroy. It was the military headquarter as well. The city administration has travelled a lot from nominations to limited elections to universal franchise. Sri Banta links the present day city administration with the erstwhile local administration. He details out the functions being discharged by the Shimla Municipal Corporation. Sri Banta discusses at length the financial resources at the disposal of the Corporation. He concludes his paper with identifying a few drawbacks in the conforming municipal legislation and offers some suggestions to remedy them.

# 1

# Revitalisation of Municipal Government Through 74th Constitution Amendment Act, 1992

*—Hoshiar Singh*

The municipal institutions in India have evolved over the past one century as an exclusive system having jurisdiction over specific urban areas. The social and economic changes due to developmental efforts and the problems created by rapid urbanisation imposed new responsibilities upon municipal government. Urban centres attracted industries and the consequent industrialisation led to a rapid increase in the population. This rapid urbanisation created the problem of housing, public utilities and community facilities. As a result, the urban environment has deteriorated giving rise to shanty towns and slums, heavy population concentrations, uncontrolled land use, unauthorised constructions, inadequate urban services such as water supply, sewerage, and transport facilities and deficient educational, recreational, health and welfare facilities. It has become essential to plan and control urban growth; adequate public utilities and community facilities have to be provided if haphazard urbanisation is designed to be checked. It is understandable, therefore, that municipal institutions have been created in large number to solve the problems of urban population.

The municipalities are set up in cities and larger towns and are generally governed by respective State enactments. The territorial unit of a municipal body in a local area, the limits of which are determined by the State Government who have power to vary these limits or abolish the municipality altogether. The term 'municipality' means a municipal council or committee.

In most of the States no statutory criteria for determination of municipality have been laid down. A city must have a certain minimum population in order to qualify for the establishment of a municipality. But what should be the minimum population? There is, obviously, no uniform standard. In West Bengal, Bihar and Orissa, population and density have been laid down as criteria for constitution of a municipality. In Bengal, municipalities are established in those towns which contain not less than 1,000 inhabitants to the square miles of area and a population of 20,000. In Bihar and Orissa minimum population for the establishment of a municipality is 5,000. In Rajasthan the population required is 8,000, in Maharashtra, Punjab and Haryana it is 10,000 while in Tamil Nadu it is 20,000 and in U.P., it is 20,000 with an annual income of Rs. 40,000. In Andhra Pradesh it is 25,000 and in Gujarat it is 30,000. However, no uniform criteria in terms of population and income are laid down for constituting a municipality in all States. By and large, population, income and other relevant factors are taken into account for constituting a municipality.

The income criteria assumes significance only when a locality having a small population has been permitted to get a municipality. When population exceeds a particular size, it automatically assures a certain income. The income criterion is thus not of primary importance in the granting of a municipal status but it is decisive in determining the class or grade in which a municipality may be placed. According to the Rural-Urban Relationship Committee, "a categorisation of municipal bodies into suitable grades is inescapable, if any homogeneity in administrative service, civic facilities is to be introduced."[1]

In States, municipalities are classified on one or more of the three bases: population, income, and other relevant factors. Thus, in Punjab, municipalities are divided into three classes; in M.P. they are divided into four classes on the basis of population; in Andhra Pradesh there are five grades of municipalities on the basis of their annual income; in Rajasthan municipalities are divided into four categories on the basis of population and income. In Maharashtra and Gujarat there are three categories of municipalities. In Bihar and Kerala there are four categories of municipality according to their income.

Presently, the organization of municipal government in India seems to be at cross-roads. No doubt, the introduction of an executive officer has been a salutary departure from the earlier practice of leaving executive administration to the president and councillors. There is thus a conscious attempt to evolve an integrate administration through the municipal executive officer. At the same time, however, a consistent trend has been to parcel out statutory powers among a number of authorities, such as the whole council, the executive officer, and the standing committee or committees. Structurally, the municipalities are resembling more and more to the organizational model of corporation government. But the difficulties involved in the latter are now percolating down to other municipal bodies also. Apart from statutory fragmentation of powers, as in the case of southern municipalities, the current trend towards provincialization of municipal service[2], will have the effect of diverting the municipal councils of their ultimate controlling powers over municipal personnel and driving a wedge between the council and the municipal officers born on the provincialized cadres. The separate personnel system which was almost universal throughout India is gradually giving way to unified or integrated cadres of municipal services controlled by the State Governments. The demand of municipal staff for better pay scales and security and service benefits, general inability of the municipalities to evolve progressive personnel policies and attract qualified staff, and the eagerness of State Governments to extend the radius of State control, are primarily responsible for hastening the trend towards the provincialization of municipal services. This is going to gather momentum in the years to come and unified or integrated cadres at least for key municipal personnel will, in all probability, be universally accepted.

The Central as well as State Governments have been aware about the weakness and problems of urban governments, therefore, they have tried through appointing commission and committees to look into the problems of urban governments and suggest the ways to improve their working. A major step in this direction was taken by amending the Constitution through 74th Constitution Amendment Act, 1992. The main characteristics of the Act are:

(i) The Act provides for three categories of urban areas, Nagar Panchayat for a transitional area which is turning from a rural to an urban area; a municipal council for a smaller urban area; and a municipal corporation for a larger urban area, decided on the basis of population of the area, the density of the population in that area, income and percentage of employment in non-agricultural activities by the Governor of the State. The term of municipalities shall be five years.

(ii) Wards committee for one or more wards in towns with a population of three lakhs or more. Elected members of the wards in the area shall be members of the committee and from amongst them they will elect their chairman.

(iii) Reservation of seats in municipal bodies for SC and ST in proportion to their population to total population in municipal area. Out of these seats one-third shall be reserved for SC/ST women. These reserved seats will rotate among the various constituencies in the Municipality.

(iv) One-third of total number of seats shall be reserved for women (including the number of seats reserved for SC and ST women) and for election purposes these seats will rotate among the different constituencies in a municipality.

(v) A State Election Commission for the superintendence, direction, control and mandatory periodic elections every five years for municipal bodies.

(vi) State legislatures, for sound financial positions of municipal bodies may authorise them to levy, collect and appropriate taxes, duties, tolls, fees and grants-in-aid from the Consolidated Fund of the State.

(vii) A Finance Commission to review the finances of the municipalities and recommend principles on the basis of which funds should be distributed to them.

(viii) The procedure for maintenance of accounts and audit of such accounts would be decided by the State government.

(ix) District Planning Committee, for consolidation of plans prepared by Panchayats and municipalities in the district and preparation of district plans as a whole, has been created by the Act. The four-fifths members of the committee shall be elected from the members of the Panchayats of the district level and of the municipalities in the district in proportion to their population.

(x) For Metropolitan area a Metropolitan Planning Committee has been created for the preparation of development plans.

(xi) The State governments would also devolve power to the municipalities to prepare plans for economic development and social justice. Significantly, a whole new schedule called Twelfth Schedule has been added containing functional areas. The Schedule contains 18 items mentioning many functions for the municipalities.

Some of the provisions of the 74th Amendment Act are good, such as regular elections for municipal bodies after expiry of their term, making municipal bodies financially viable involving municipal bodies into micro-level planning and creation of a District Planning Committee for preparation of the composite district plans, State Election Commission for their elections and appointment of Finance Commissions for distribution of finances between the States and Municipalities. These are all welcome provisions.

But there are certain shortcomings in the Act, such as, the functions listed in Twelfth Schedule show that most of these items are taken from the State List and States are asked to frame rules to devolve these functions to municipal bodies, which is not feasible. This task has been left to each State legislature to determine and past experience has shown that States are always reluctant to part with their powers. The Act has made the District Planning Committee a Constitutional body, while Planning Commission at National level is just a creation of the Executive Order. The implication of such a provision would be that can a body created just by executive order override the decisions of a Constitutional body? Theoretically no, but in practice, Planning Commission would finalise the plans making appropriate changes in the State and district plans. The Act failed to define the relationship between the local level bureaucracy and municipal bodies. Over-domination of bureaucracy in these institutions was a major factor for their failure and this problem again has not been dealt with by the Act. Secondly, the role of political parties in municipal elections has not been spelt out in the Act, which is very essential for domestic process. Lastly, the Act created a three-tier administration, i.e., the Centre, the State and the municipalities. What would be the relationship of third tier, the municipalities, with the Centre and the State? The working of our Constitution shows, so far as the relations between the Centre and the States are concerned, the tilt towards the Centre is quite visible. As a corollary in this case the tilt would be in favour of States making the municipalities subordinate entities and State administration, in the name of development, will perform all the non-plan activities in urban areas.

**Conclusion**

The numerous problems faced by the city governments at present arise out of lack of financial resources; general feeling in the government and public is that these are not competent and able to perform their function; adequate attention devoted to urban development in the process of national planning and dysfunctional activities of existing structures. The creation of additional parallel authorities proves municipal inefficiency. The fact of poor performance on the part of municipal authorities cannot be denied. But, is it a solution that these be completely replaced by other urban development agencies? What is needed, therefore, is to create both a climate and an institution of genuine self-government in each town or city whereby the people can participate in the management of their affairs.[3]

The working of municipal bodies in the country was not upto the expectations of the people. They failed to perform their duties efficiently due to various reasons, therefore, it was felt that these nurseries of democracy should be revamped. The Constitution Seventy-fourth Amendment Act is a step in the right direction to revitalise the urban government units for better civic services and amenities in these areas.

## REFERENCES

1. Report of the Rural-Urban Relationship Committee, Vol. 1, Ministry of Health and Family Planning, 1966, para 4, 12.

2. Report of the Committee on the Service Conditions of Municipal Employees, Ministry of Health, Family Planning and Urban Development, Government of India, 1968.

3. See, Ali Ashraf, *Government and Politics of Big Cities: An Indian Case Study,* Delhi: Concept Publishing Company, 1977, p. 183.

# 2

# Empowerment of Urban Local Government in India

*—H.M. Golandaz*

In recent years, most of the governments in developing countries have realised that one of the primary obstacles to meet the challenges of urbanization and implementation of national development policies and programmes has been the absence of capacity and skills, whether financial, managerial or technical at the urban local government level. These deficiencies have been, more often than not a consequence of the Constitutional status of urban local bodies and the extent of political, administrative, and financial autonomy enjoyed by them.

Urban local government is an integral part of the system of government of a country. As such, it is subordinate to the Central and the State governments with respect to legislation, policies and other matters of national interest. However, urban local government can function effectively as a vibrant democratic unit only when it is bestowed with political, administrative and financial autonomy. What is needed is to find the optimum balance in the distribution of functions and powers between various levels of government.

Two and a half decades ago the Rural Urban Relationship Committee (RURC) pointed out that local government can no longer remain merely instruments of political education and civic conscience, but have to become institution for promotion of social and economic development of local community as well as an integral part of the National Government.

The Constitution Amendment Act (CAA) has enabled to realise the essence of RURC recommendation. It has ushered a new era in the history of urban local government in India. It is indeed a first serious attempt to ensure the estabilization of democratic municipal government through constitutional provisions.

In this paper an attempt has been made to discuss provisions relating to functions of different local bodies/committees and finances of municipal bodies made under the Seventy-Fourth Constitution Amendment Act, 1992 (CAA).

The CAA with provisions such as municipal organisation and its structure, formal procedures for municipal election, supersession, functions, devolution of funds through the State Finance Commission, transfer of administrative and planning functions to the municipal bodies, has been welcomed by all segments of the society. It is envisaged that the CAA will enable people to participate in development process at ward, municipal, district and metropolitan regional level. The empirical evidence of such optimism could be realised only after the incorporation of the various provisions of CAA in the existing Municipal Acts.

The structure and the composition of the municipality today varies widely in different parts of the country. There is generally no accepted set of criteria with reference to urban agglomeration resulting in discrepancies between one state to another. The CAA has brought out uniform constitution of municipal bodies by classifying them as (a) Nagar Panchayat for transitional area, (b) Municipal Council for a smaller urban area, and (c) Municipal Corporation of a larger urban area. Subsection 2 of Article 243 Q has listed the parameters for classifying the urban local bodies into above-mentioned categories. The application of these parameters for classification of urban local bodies is, however, left to the discretion of State Government.

**Functions of Municipal Bodies and of the Planning and Implementation Agencies**

All the Municipal Acts in India provide for functions/duties and responsibilities to be carried out by the municipal government. Some of the Acts demarcate these duties and responsibilities as obligatory and discretionary. Potable water supply, sanitation and sewerage, drainage, street lighting, street cleaning and refuse collection, street paving, health services etc. are obligatory functions whereas urban transport, construction and maintenance of parks, playgrounds etc. are some of the discretionary functions/duties.

CAA provides for the Twelfth Schedule listing the function of municipal bodies. The functions of the municipality, including those listed in the Twelfth Schedule are left to the discretion of the State Government, but these local bodies have to be bestowed with sufficient powers, authority and responsibility to discharge the functions entrusted to them to enable them to prepare plans for economic development and social justice and undertake implementation of schemes. However, the

Construction Amendment has not specified any powers directly to the municipalities and it has left it to the discretion of the State Government.

Some of these functions mentioned in the Twelfth Schedule of CAA are of highly technical nature which is likely to render municipal bodies ineffective. The CAA has provision regarding devolution of powers and responsibilities. However, the devolution of powers commensurate with such responsibilities is left to the discretion of the concerned State Government.

Thus, local governments are required to provide for services irrespective of their administrative capacity to do so, and have to face unexpected new terms of their own as consequence of new sets of standards.

In pursuing decentralization objectives, it is important to ensure that existing municipal structures are updated to undertake added responsibilities. Where, the administrative functions of State Government for development of urban infrastructure are transferred to the local level, it will become necessary to examine whether local government is capable of handling such responsibilities. If such capacity is not existing, it will have to be created or where it is inadequate it needs to be strengthened.

The State governments need to be more specific and definite about assigning functions to municipal bodies. In the absence of a set of assigned functions to the municipal bodies, it would be difficult for the State Finance Commission to assess the fiscal needs and required resource allocation. Significance of the planning function could not be contended, hence in the interest of a rational integration between spatial (urban and regional) and socio-economic planning and development need to be on the mandatory cost. Recognizing that these two types of planning are complementary and interdependent, first three functions related to planning mentioned in the Twelfth Schedule (Article 243-W) should be included in the obligatory list of the Constitution. These are:

(i) Urban planning including town planning,
(ii) Regulation of land uses and construction of buildings,
(iii) Planning for economic and social development, should now form part of the obligatory functions since spatial planning has now been recognized as a municipal function and these functions no longer be derived from the State Town Planning Acts.

Accordingly, under Article 243-R-2(a)(i) it would be advisable to provide representation of experts in the following disciplines; (i) Municipal

Administration, (ii) Town Planning, (iii) Finance, (iv) Engineering and (v) Health.

**Functions of the Ward Committees**

The 74th Amendment does not specify the functions to be entrusted to the Ward Committees. It is desirable that a set of functions are assigned to these Committees. The basic purpose of having such Committees is to provide limited deliberative and executive powers to the citizens of different wards, having more than three lakhs population, to deal with problems and issues related to their respective areas. The functions of these Ward Committees among others could be to;

(i) make the municipal bodies responsive to the aspirations of the residents of the ward,

(ii) identify problems and remedial measures in implementation/ provision of,

(a) municipal amentities, services and facilities call upon the concerned departments/agencies for action,

(b) building code and local components of development plan and development rules,

(iii) ensure greater citizen participation in development of their respective local area,

(iv) serve as a medium for the execution of local works through allocated funds and contributions,

(v) provide common platform for residents to express their views, grievances about the municipal services and functions.

There has been increasing gaps in quality and quantity of services in rich and poor areas of the cities. The process is backed–up by market forces as well as government programmes. Even in programmes such as UPA it has been noticed that more vocal and power groups within the community get benefits of 'Community Empowerment'. The formation of Ward Committees vested with certain powers and responsibilities for resource mobilization and planning is likely to widen the gap between the 'rich' and the 'poor'. High income colonies capable of generating resources from their residential and economic bases could get better services. The equity principle is likely to be compromised with the involvement of private sector in provision of municipal services.

Although elaborate provisions have been made in CAA about induction of planning process in the Panchayats and urban settlements and the consolidation of the plans into a District Plan, the Seventy–third

Amendment Act pertaining to Panchayat Raj institutions does not have any reference about this. Without the authority base for formation of plans, how Panchayat Raj institutions be involved in consolidation of planning process at the district level.

**District Planning Committee (DPC)**

Article 243 ZD (i) of the CAA provides for constitution of District Planning Committees (DPC) to consolidate the plans prepared by the municipalities and panchayats in the district and to prepare a draft development plan for the district as a whole.

With this provision the integrated regional planning has been recognized by the Constitution where investment, its spatial impact and development are to be considered and realized.

The Constitution of DPC as per the CAA will have bearing on the Regional and Town Planning Act and other Acts in which planning, land use related provisions have been made. The CAA does not have any provision about the urban development authorities. The DPC as envisaged in the CAA is a permanent Statutory Committee and will be largely responsible for co-ordination of development activities in the area; the existing development authorities in the DPC area may provide necessary technical input and thus contribute to the effective functioning of the DPC.

Article 243–ZD(2)(a): The composition of membership of DPC is suggested as under:

- 20–25 members to be elected from amongst the elected members of Panchayat and Municipalities in the district in proportion to the ratio of rural urban population in the district.
- Chairpersons to be elected from amongst the members.
- Seven members to be nominated by the state government having special knowledge, expertise in the following fields:
- Finance
- Spatial Planning
- Economic Planning
- Health
- Engineering
- Environment
- Administration
- Member-Secretary as may be decided by the members of the Committee.

The functions of DPC as provided in the CAA include aggregation of fiscal and investment plan for Annual/Five-Year Planning. Article 243-ZD(3a) elaborates the scope of DPC to include spatial planning, sharing of water and other physical and natural resources, integrated development of infrastructure and environmental conservation. Sub-para (ii) of the article provides for discharging of these functions as per the extent and type of available resources.

**Following Functions could be Assigned to the DPC**

(i) Preparation of Draft Development Plan including spatial and economic planning of the district with reference to the common interest between the panchayats and municipalities.
(ii) Rationalization of investment allocation on an annual basis for the district.
(iii) Approval of guidelines for planning and building controls.
(iv) Decision about sharing of resources including water between different bodies urban and rural within the district.
(v) Resolution of conflicts regarding peripheral area and hinterland.
(vi) Matters relating to sources of water supply, sites of disposal of sewage, solid waste, etc.
(vii) Formulating plans for development of integrated infrastructure for scheme of water supply to enable peripheral village areas and the main city.
(viii) Formulating operation guidelines to minimize overlapping of functions between panchayats and urban local bodies and also for planning and location of agricultural markets and mandies.

**Metropolitan Planning Committee (MPC)**

Article 243–ZE of CAA provides for constitution of Metropolitan Planning Committee (MPC) in every metropolitan area as defined by the Constitution as an area having a population of 10 lakhs or more comprised in one or more districts and/or consisting of two or more municipalities or panchayats or any other contiguous area as specified by the Governor. The Constitution of MPC provides a democratic and responsible institution in a metropolitan area.

The CAA provides for Constitution of the MPC within the Metropolitan areas. However, it is not clear whether the DPC and the MPC would be constituted in a case where the district has acquired the status of a metropolitan district. In the interest of better co-ordinated planning, implementation, monitoring and development in a Metropolitan district, only Metropolitan Planning Committee should be constituted.

In cases where the metropolitan areas cut across the boundaries of a state and cover areas of one or more states, the MPC would require to follow the procedure laid down in the Constitution of India. The procedure provides for passing Resolution by the participating states authorizing the Central Government to legislate in this matter.

**Composition of MPC Article 243–ZE(2)(a)**

The Metropolitan Planning may consist of :

(i) Chairman—Minister of Urban Development in the State.
(ii) Vice-chairman—to be elected from amongst members, who will also be a full time chief executive of the Committee.
(iii) 15–20 members to be elected by and from amongst the elected members of municipalities and chairpersons of the panchayats in the Metropolitan area in proportion to population of the municipalities and panchayats.
(iv) Secretary, Urban Development Department of the concerned State government.
(v) Representative from the Ministry of Urban Development, Government of India.
(vi) Secretary, Environment Department of the concerned State government.
(vii) Secretary, Industries Department of the concerned State government.
(viii) Director of Town Planning/Chief Town Planner of the concerned State government.
(ix) Municipal Commissioner of the Corporation of the concerned Metropolitan area.
(x) Member (Finance) full-time.
(xi) Member (Administration) full-time.
(xii) Member (Engineering) full-time.
(xiii) Member-Secretary may be nominated by the Members of the Committee.

**The Functions of Metropolitan Planning Committee**

Under Article 243–ZE(2)(d) the suggested functions to be assigned to MPC by the State Governments are:

(i) Preparation of Draft Development Plan of Metropolitan area.

(ii) Study of dynamics of urbanization and preparation of a perspective plan with long-term development objectives, policies and priorities.

(iii) To prepare and co-ordinate investment plans for metropolitan regional infrastructural development involving more than one local body or agencies of central and State governments.

(iv) To resolve conflicts related to (a) sharing of resources water, physical, natural among various local bodies and (b) overlapping of functions.

**Role of Town Planning Department**

The Plans formulated by the Municipalities, Panchayats, DPC and MPC will have to be scrutinized by the State Town Planning Department/ Directorate of Town Planning and assist the State governments in making these development plans legally enforceable. It may also assist in preparation of plans by all these statutory bodies and advise the State on all matters relating to towns, districts and metropolitan planning and development within the State. The district development plans will have to be consolidated into regional plan to ensure over-all development of the State.

The provision for setting up of Metropolitan Planning Committee is likely to create tension about the role, responsibilities and relationship with a number of development and multifunctional agencies. The fate of the existing development authorities does not get any reference in the CAA.

**Municipal Finances and Constitution Amendment Act**

Municipal Acts in India provide for sources of revenue. Municipal revenues are generated from property tax, octroi, other services taxes, fees and grants-in-aid. In addition to these, certain schemes/programmes, such as Integrated Development of Small and Medium Towns (IDSMT) scheme are often financed with loans/grants.

It is well-established fact that the structure of local-government finance and deficiencies in the revenue collection affect their capacity to meet routine obligations and to generate resources.

The effective financial management of local governments requires adequate resources to operate and maintain public service. Given that local government revenues are generally constrained, new measures will need to be devised to supplement existing resources.

Article 243 X and Article 243 Y of the CAA envisage that the Legislature of a State may confer such powers and authorities including the power to levy, collect and appropriate taxes/duties. However, the Act has been silent about taxes to be assigned to the local bodies and power to tax. Similarly, sharing of such taxes as entertainment tax, vehicle tax, sales tax, etc. also does not find any place in the Act. Municipal Councils can borrow beyond a certain limit subject to approval by the State legislature. There are no specifications about borrowing powers of Municipalities in the CAA. The said provision needs empirical verification on the following ground of hard reality:

(i) Will the provisions relating to the Municipal Finance be able to improve the existing resources and resource base of the Municipal Bodies?

(ii) Will it be possible to have equitable distribution of resources across different size class of Municipalities?

It is known fact that urban decision-making is not confined to the urban areas. If the town is taken as a conglomeration of a large population in a given area, the motivating factors for such congregation are responsible for determining not only its size but also its character. Such motivating factors can be operated in single or multiple order and their presence, so also their influence, will fluctuate overtime. Generally, towns are created for trade, industry, administration and political purposes. Some towns acquire more than one strength in time to come, whereas some other may loose some of their strengths. The political process at the local level is not free from 'inter' and 'intra' pressures and counter pressures.

The pattern of urban growth in India shows a significant variation across size classes urban areas, districts, states and the regions. In comparatively backward states, small and medium towns with population with 50,000 have experienced rapid growth during seventies and eighties. In developed states, the rate of growth was rapid in larger towns. The growth of small and medium towns was largely on account of 'Push' factors. With the decline in State and Central financial assistance and after initial financial assistance by the Central Government in implementation of the schemes, such as IDSMT (soft loan) and UBSP (grant), the decline in financial assistance, most of these, small and medium towns are not able to make investment for improving basic services and infrastructure. The abolition of octroi being the progressive tax, in a number of states has already reduced the resource-base and resource of the municipalities, leading them to heavily depend on grants-in-aid. Poor economic base and inability to mobilize tax-and non-tax resources make these "Self-Government" bodies heavily dependent on the State Governments.

The provision has been made in the Act about the establishment of state finance commission to review finances of Municipality and to recommend principles for (i) determining the taxes which may be assigned to the Municipalities; (ii) Sharing of taxes and (iii) Grants-in-aid and it may recommend to the Governor the measures to improve the financial position of the Municipality. However, the Finance Commission would have the status and powers of an advisory body and hence the recommendations would not be obligatory.

Despite lack of specification and infirmities, the Constitution Amendment Act is a harbinger for democratic decentralization at the local level. It gives municipal government 'right to exist' by providing measures to hold election within six months of dissolution of a municipal body. It also empowers weaker sections and women by providing for the reservation of seats. It also provides for the constitution of finance commission to contribute to the strengthening of fiscal capabilities of the municipal authorities.

**Twelfth Schedule of the Constitution (Seventy-Fourth Amendment) Act, 1992**

**(Article 243 W)**

1. Urban planning including town planning.
2. Regulation of land-use and construction of buildings.
3. Planning for economic and social development.
4. Roads and bridges.
5. Water supply for domestic, industrial and commercial purposes.
6. Public health, sanitation, conservancy and solid waste management.
7. Fire services.
8. Urban forestry and promotion of ecological aspects.
9. Safeguarding the interests of weaker sections of society.
10. Slum improvement and upgradation.
11. Urban poverty alleviation.
12. Provision of urban amenities and facilities, such as parks, gardens, playgrounds.

13. Promotion of cultural, educational and aesthetic aspects.
14. Burials and burial grounds; cremations and cremation grounds and electric crematoriums.
15. Cattle Ponds; preventation of cruelty to animals.
16. Vital statistics including registration of birth and deaths.
17. Public amenities including street lighting, parking lots, bus stops and public conveniences.
18. Regulation of slaughter houses and tanneries.

# 3

# 74th Amendment Act 1992: An Approach Towards Strengthening of the Local Bodies

*—S.K. Banerjee*

Government of India's effort to appoint a National Commission on Urbanisation for identifying the major and crucial issues of urbanisation and the related issues with urban development activities at grass-root, sub-state, and state levels and the National Housing Policy along with State Housing Policy has been a sincere and practical approach for giving a meaningful direction to urban development activity for the 21st century.

On the heels of these efforts the Constitution Amendment Act, 1992 has also been another landmark in an effort to make the Municipalities Democratic Institutions and not to remain merely as a service-oriented institutions.

The Constitution Amendment Act, 1992 envisages a planning process whereby the Municipal Bodies are to be empowered to act and discharge their municipal functions in the field of Urban Planning as a democratic institution and also to encourage the involvement and active participation of the local people through their elected representatives.

**Need for 74th Amendment Act 1992**

Serious thinking and deliberations at various forums have been in progress as early as 1968 for restructuring and revitalising the local bodies in the form of democratic institutions. At these forums it has also been a point of discussion as to how best to make the local bodies function more freely without much and excessive interference from the top governing body and how to empower them with enough constitutional rights and jurisdictional powers.

Against the background of these thinking and discussions at various forums, an intensive desire was expressed by our Late Prime Minister Sri

Rajiv Gandhi to work out a methodology in the form of an Act so as to empower the Nagar Panchayats, Municipal Councils and Corporations with enough constitutional and jurisdictional powers so as to make them capable to function as Democratic Institutions and not to discharge functions merely as a service-oriented municipal body. This desire of Sri Rajiv Gandhi saw the light of the day in the form of 74th Amendment Act 1992.

**Basic Concept of the Amendment Act**

The basic concept of the Amendment Act is to democratise the local bodies by giving them more constitutional and jurisdictional powers, to encourage the participation of local people through their elected representatives and thus to ensure implementation of the functions related with urban development as has been incorporated in the Twelfth Schedule under Article 243 W.

The Twelfth Schedule incorporates items on urban development like Urban Planning including Town Planning, Regulations of Land Use, and construction of buildings, Planning for Economic and Social Development, Water Supply for domestic, industrial and commercial purposes, urban forestry, protection of the environment and promotions of ecological aspects, slum improvement and upgradation.

**Mechanism for Implementation of Urban Development Items**

The items of Urban Development as identified in the Twelfth Schedule have been suggested in the Act to be implemented at two levels.

(i) District Level.
(ii) Metropolitan Area Level.

Along with the suggested levels at which the functions to be implemented as identified in the Twelfth Schedule, the Act has further suggested constitution of district committees who shall be responsible to see the preparation of plans. These committees at the above two identified levels will be responsible for preparation of plans. These will be:

(a) District Planning Committee.
(b) Metropolitan Planning Committee.

The Act has suggested that the District Planning Committee and the Metropolitan Planning Committee shall prepare District Plans and Area Plans for the respective categories of Urban settlements.

District Planning Committee while preparing plans shall see that the plans prepared by Nagar Panchayats for the transitional area have to be incorporated with the plans prepared for small urban area existing in the form of a town with a population of 50,000 and population density of 2,400 persons per sq. km. with 80 per cent non-agricultural workers and revenue generation to be Rs. 35 lakh.

The Metropolitan Area Committee has to ensure the preparation of a draft development plan incorporating urban areas each having a population of 3,00,000 and above, population density 6000 persons per sq. km., non-agricultural workers in each municipal corporation to be 95 per cent and the revenue generation should be Rs. 150 lakh.

**Salient Features of Amendment Act 1992**

The Amendment Act, besides recommending the creation of Planning Committees at District and Metropolitan Area Level, governed by the elected members of the local bodies, identified at 3-levels certain other features have also been suggested to make the urban development activity more meaningful and practical. These features in brief are as follows:

1. *New Role for Elected Bodies for City Management.* It has been proposed in the Amendment Act that local bodies should actively discharge their obligatory and multifarious functions through the elected members meaningfully. Till now the functions related with urban development activities as identified in the Twelfth Schedule are mostly discharged by Government and through semi-government bodies like Development Authorities, Housing Board, Prescribed Authorities and Special Area Development Authorities. In these authorities the representation of local people through the elected members is rather very insignificant. The Amendment Act vide Article 243-ZD (2) (a) has suggested 24 members to be elected in District Planning Committee from amongst the elected members of the Panchayats and Municipalities in the district and only 6 members to be appointed by State Government who will be expert in their field of Technical/Administrative functions.

In case of Metropolitan Planning Committee, the Act advises for a 30-member Committee of which 20 members to be elected by and from amongst the elected members of municipalities and Chairpersons of Panchayats in the Metropolitan area.

2. To make the urban local bodies more democratic in character and purpose. This will help in reducing and minimising the accessibility gap between citizens and government.

3. To set certain parameters and criteria for functioning of local bodies. This will help in minimising the frequent interferences by the top administrative bodies in the day-to-day functioning of municipalities.

4. To enable the Local Bodies to freely perform their multifunctional urban development activities. If the Local Bodies can accordingly work freely then they will not only function merely as service-oriented institutions but rather a decision making institution in performing their multi-functional urban activities for which they have committed themselves to the public through its elected representatives.

5. To create confidence among the City Councillors that their active participation is highly desired and needed in the urban development process of the town for which they are very indispensible.

6. To restructure and simplify the existing assessment and Property Taxation System.

7. To evolve a system so as to help in the smooth and unobstructed transfer of resources for urban development purposes from State Government to city government.

8. Creation of a Directorate of Local Body for giving a direction to every body for discharging their urban development functions.

9. To widen the field of public participation.

10. To find out ways and methods for fiscal support from State and Central Governments.

11. To evolve a management system headed by a political executive in place of Chief Executive Officer.

12. Technical Expertise.

The Amendment Act has proposed 18 functions in the "Twelfth Schedule" under Article 243 W, number of these functions like urban planning including town planning, regulation of land use and construction of buildings, slum improvement and upgradation, urban poverty alleviation and many others are urban-oriented in character. There arises a need for technical personnels well qualified and highly experienced in the fields for the implementation of the above functions. It is through such technical expertise that District Planning Committee and Metropolitan Planning Committee will be able to get the District Plans and Metropolitan Area Development Plans prepared and implemented. Therefore, there is a need to create a State cadre of Town Planning professionals.

13. To make the objectives of the provisions of the Amendment Act realistic and meaningful, creation of a dynamic political will is necessary at all levels for coordinating the technical and management responses with the political will and capacity.

**Impact**

In the context of the provision of 74th Amendment Act, 1992 as outlined in this paper, its impact on the urban scenario which is likely to appear with new urban development dimensions has to be assessed. This assessment is likely to raise certain issues which are to be discussed and viable solutions are to be worked out. Unless the Municipal Bodies address themselves to the new problems and challenges, they cannot be true to qualify as democratic institutions and they will simply remain service-oriented institutions.

**Urban Scenario and India's Urban Future**

Correct assessment of the urban scenario and the likely impacts of the provisions of the Amendment Act will remain incomplete unless a brief and passing review of the findings and recommendations as proposed by the National Commission on Urbanisation is made. The findings of the Commission have projected India's urban future in 21st century which calls for a sincere and serious effort on the Indian planners and administrators.

**Urban Scenario—21st Century**

With the advent of 21st century, India will have an urban population somewhere between 34 and 35 crores. Cities with one million population will increase from 12 (1981) to 40 in 2001, thus showing an increase of 267 per cent within a time span of 20 years. Urban problems of tremendous magnitude will be knocking at the doors of urban India. It is in the context of this urban scenario that the functions of the Twelfth Schedule are to be implemented by the local bodies.

The Commission on Urbanisation has identified 600 cities which will be generating Economic Momentum all over the country. Out of these 600 urban centres 329 centres has been finally selected for development. The Commission has further grouped these cities into two major categories of Priority Towns.

(i) ***National Priority Cities.*** With population of 1 million and above, by 2001, nearly 27 urban centres will be heading towards million plus cities besides 30 cities already existing as State and Union Territory Capitals and have qualified for being defined as National Priority Cities. The Commission is of the opinion that 57 cities of the National Priority do show evidences of economic and demographic momentum, therefore, the municipal councils and corporations must be careful to see that the existing infrastructure does not collapse. Rather, it should be strengthened to create more employment.

(ii) ***State Priority Cities.*** In this category a total of 212 cities of State Priority Status existing in the country have been identified which include mostly headquarters of Districts with 30 per cent urban population. This category also includes district headquarters of such districts where 90 per cent of the district population is rural. State Priority Cities mostly represent the districts which are less urbanised and economically poor. Out migration is higher. Therefore, employment and economic growth should be generated at regional and sub-regional level by promoting the rural-urban centres and urban centres with one lakh population as Medium and Small Towns. Thus the local bodies for such municipal areas will have more responsibilities to function as democratic institutions.

**Major Issues**

Municipal Bodies will have to address themselves, to the new urban problems and its magnitude as emerging out of the urban scenario in the context of the findings of the Commission on Urbanisation. The functioning of the Municipalities as per the urban scenario will depend much on their capability of implementing the provisions of the Amendment Act 1992 and the major urban development functions as have been identified in the Twelfth Schedule.

Implementation of the provisions of the Amendment Act will be practical and meaningful only when the local bodies will ensure that the major issues have been properly addressed and a solution has been worked out. These issues towards which the Municipal Councils/Corporations have to address themselves are as given below:

1. Need for a comprehensive Town Planning Act which takes care of the urban development functions as per Twelfth Schedule. There is a need to restructure the Town Planning Act so as to make legal provisions for preparation of District Plans, and Metropolitan Area Plans. The Town Planning Act should also make sure that the District Planning Committees and Metropolitan Planning Committees are legally empowered to prepare plans and their functions should be defined.
2. Need for a structural change in the administrative set up of the municipal organisations so as to make enough scope for town planners, and to physical planners so that the urban development functions as defined in the Act can be properly discharged by the respective municipality.

3. To ensure that the local bodies, are capable enough to discharge the functions of urban planning, regulations of land uses, planning for social and economic development.
4. Local Bodies shall have to address themselves to the aspirations of the people for providing a healthy and liveable urban environment because of the fast changing urban scenario of the million and million plus cities.
5. Need for improvement in the working of Municipalities so as to increase their level of efficiency.
6. Need for adequate and necessary urban oriented administrative and technical manpower and expertise.
7. Need for amendment of Municipal Acts so as to incorporate and provisions of Amendment Act, 1992 and making provisions for the meaningful functioning of functions as suggested and proposed in the Twelfth Schedule.

**Role of State Town Planning Body**

One of the most important issues that arises out of the Amendment Act, 1992 is that urban development activity which at present is being performed by State Town Planning Department has been vested in Municipalities. In such circumstances the functions of existing government and semi-government agencies which are associated with Town Planning activities have to be re-defined. In many states of India town planning activities are implemented through Development Authorities, Special Area Development Authorities, Regulated Areas/Committees. The major question which is to be debated now is that when Municipal Councils/ Corporations have been empowered to prepare Master Plans and District Plans then what role the other agencies will play. Will they merge with the Municipal Council/Corporation and function as a wing for urban planning or they will function on pattern as Pollution Control Board.

The 74th Amendment Act, 1992 has thus highlighted the importance and role to be played by Town Planners in the preparation and implementation of District Plans and Metropolitan Area Plans. Since the city councils have been defined as the apex body for the management of urban development activities and its implementation, it therefore needs to be ensured by the urban local bodies that town planners are involved in the developmental works of the urban areas ranging from transitional areas to metropolitan area development plans. Therefore, it becomes necessary to debate this point of Town Planners' and Town Planning Organisations' role in the perspective of the Amendment Act and to impress upon the government of the viewpoints emerging out of the debate.

To sum up the whole matter regarding the Amendment Act, 1992, one very important issue still remains to be properly and seriously discussed about. The issues pertains to effectiveness of the Amendment Act, 1992 in rendering the Local Bodies financially operative. This issue has been raised by the National Institute of Public Finance many times in their different studies and discussion. In their opinion, the Act has not empowered the Local Bodies with sharp teeth so as to overcome all the financial difficulties. As a result of which the financial enactment of the Act, a very glaring example of this ineffectiveness of the Act, is the Supreme Court's Order (1996) as appeared in *The Pioneer* (dated 22.11.1996) in which it has been clearly stated that maintenance of a clean environment in the city is the complete responsibility of the Mayor. According to the Mayors, the Corporation/Council has neither the manpower nor the funds to keep the basic environmental and sanitary conditions in order. All these problems are nothing but due to financial crunch of the local bodies. Therefore, one of the main and most important issues is that how best the local bodies can function when financially they are *crippling*. Once such issues are resolved then other matters regarding the preparation of integrated plan and the structural and procedural changes can be examined further in the context of the 74th Constitution Amendment Act, 1992.

# 4

# Problems of Resource Mobilization of Urban Local Bodies

*—S.M.Y. SASTRY*

While the 74th Constitution Amendment Act has provided for the compulsory constitution of a State Finance Commission every five years, that by itself does not assure a greater flow of resources to the local bodies. Though not compulsorily and every five years, a few States have been constituting Finance Commissions to determine what taxes should be allowed to be levied by the local bodies, what shares of States's taxes, if any, should be distributed to local bodies and even what grants should be given. The decisions have been somewhat ad-hoc on the recommendations made but, by and large, a generally accepted framework already exists. Can the newly constituted finance commissions bring any real fresh thinking or attitude in assessing the requirements of the local bodies and the resources that should be assigned to them? There is, of course, one real change from the previous scenario and that is not the constitution of a Finance Commission by the State but the provision made under Art. 243 amending Article 280 of the Constitution enjoining of the Central Finance Commission to consider "measures needed to augment the consolidated fund of the State to supplement the resources of the municipalities in the State on the basis of recommendations made by the Finance Commission of the State. It is assumed that this will enable the Central Finance Commission to make a specific allocation of the amount that must be earmarked for augmentation of the resources of local bodies only. Otherwise, if the Central Finance Commission merely takes into account this need also along with other needs and makes a generalised increased allotment to the States, it is likely that it will be used up by the State in its various schemes and the increased allotment for the augmentation of municipal resources may not really reach them. In the circumstances, I feel that the first emphasis should be on securing an earmarked specific allotment to the States for augmenting municipal resources to fulfil the recommendations made by the State Finance Commissions.

The second requirement would be to revive the sanctity of what may be identified as "Local Taxes". It is well to remember in this connection the recommendations made by the Taxation Enquiry Commission of 1952–54. They have after mature consideration identified some taxes as local taxes that must be allowed (empowered) to be levied as municipal taxes and some taxes that should be treated as shared taxes, i.e., taxes levied by the State Government but distributed to the local bodies on some well designed principles. It may be worthwhile recapturing that recommendation.

**Taxes to be Levied by the Local Bodies**

1. Taxes on lands and buildings.
2. Taxes on vehicles, boats and animals other than those mechanically propelled vehicles e.g. motor vehicles.
3. Octroi.
4. Taxes on Profession, Trades, Callings and Employment.
5. Taxes on advertisements other than advertisements in newspapers.
6. Theatre Tax.
7. A surcharge on the Duty of Transfer of Property.

**Taxes to be Shared**

1. Motor Vehicles Tax.
2. Entertainment Tax.
3. If it is not feasible to allow a surcharge on the transfer of property, then some share to represent that charge from what is collected by the State.

While almost every committee appointed by the Centre, e.g., Rural-Urban Relationship, Zakaria; or by the States have endorsed this fundamental recommendation and identification of local taxes, there have been innumerable breaches. Maharashtra has appropriated for State Revenues the Profession Tax. Nor is entertainment tax uniformly shared in full. In respect of sharing Motor Vehicle Tax, too, there is laxity.

The second emphasis should accordingly be to ensure that the recommendations of the Taxation Enquiry Commission should be treated as the foundation and every breach plugged.

In this connection, for various reasons octroi abolition may get treated as inevitable. If so, some specific alternative tax must be identified and levied which would prove equally elastic and productive. The local bodies should not be "compensated for loss" but be substituted, and must be treated as a "replacement tax". If it is levied and collected by the State for the sake of convenience, the entire proceeds minus collection expenses should be distributed at not less than monthly intervals.

Similarly it should be one of their essential tasks to enquire whether the allotted tax resources are being properly exploited by the local bodies. Even a cursory examination reveals that in respect of property taxes... taxes on lands and buildings... there is a lot of scope for improvement, in fixing the annual value—rateable value—on which the rates are levied, in ensuring that all properties are promptly brought under the tax net, periodical revisions are undertaken, etc. This will be an opportunity also to take appropriate decisions regarding the baleful influence of rent control acts and how they can be rectified, at least to the extent of removal of their effect on the fixation of the annual value.

Similarly in respect of octroi too, there are complaints of evasion and malpractices which is one of the reasons why its abolition is being stridently voiced. Maharashtra which has come to the conclusion that it is not presently, in a position to abolish octroi, has to curb the malpractices, etc., adopted a worse remedy than the disease. It has made legal provision and is encouraging local bodies to contract out the collection of octroi. Contracting out or privatisation of tax collection will surely make the administration a deplorable one. It should not be difficult to find remedies and rectifications within the system. Special attention must be paid to this aspect of levy of the taxes and their administration.

Along with the rectification and streamlining of the imposition and administration of the taxes, the problem of making as many of the services as possible self-sufficient should be looked into. Notwithstanding the conditions attached to World Bank loans for Water Supply Schemes, etc., almost every water supply scheme except in Mumbai is running at a loss. Mumbai has become self sufficient because it levies two—water and sewage—benefit taxes as also because its tariff is being adjusted to secure cost recovery. Financing a service through the levy of a land and building-based service tax should be reviewed and replaced by a user charges tariff structure. Some subsidy may be considered inevitable but there should be strict vigilance, as also the subsidy should be openly disclosed. As far as possible, the subsidy must be generated from the service itself and not tagged to general revenues. This entire restructuring need not, perhaps should not, be attempted to be achieved at one go but gradualness can be introduced so that over a period, self sufficiency coupled with equity can be achieved. Apart from the taxes indicated by the Taxation Enquiry Commission as taxes to be shared, the Finance Commission should inquire whether there are any other taxes being levied by the State which can be treated as forming part of the divisible pool. In Maharashtra, for example, the State levies a tax on Urban Transport Passengers (the tax is collected in Mumbai through the B.E.S.T. bus tickets by an addition). This is a tax collection in which surely the urban local body must get a share. In this identification of divisible shares, each state will have to be separately examined but the general guidelines could be that if any tax is exclusively collected from the urban residents or users of an urban facility a share should go to the urban local bodies.

Grants-in-aid can be divided into two categories, one essential to ensure a certain standard requirement and the other to induce better performance. In every State, the local bodies receive a grant towards payment of dearness allowance to the staff. It is an essential requirement for entertaining any staff. There can not be strings attached to such a grant based on performance. If owing to low performance there is cut in such a grant, it will have a deleterious effect in making the local body since it cuts the essential support. But there can be some grants specially designed to encourage better performance, the quantum increasing with improved performance.

In undertaking some essential capital works, e.g., water scheme, a grant composed of part loan and part pure grant on condition of a part contribution from the local body has been in force in some states. If the local body has not been able to raise the initial contribution, the entire scheme fell through nullifying the entire essential scheme. It may have to be redesigned somewhat eliminating the initial contribution. This, however, should not be based on ad hoc decisions on consideration of patronage, but on well developed principles.

A part of the sharing the proceeds of a tax on the grants, as mentioned earlier is based on the principle of encouraging efficiency by better performance. Gujarat has experimented with elaborate criteria besides setting apart some money for improving the infrastructure, e.g., purchase of a computer etc. while the advance (grant) for infrastructure improvement has succeeded, setting up too many criteria for evaluating performance and basing the grant/share on that evaluation has not become a success and they had to revise the formula by simplifying it. Evaluation of performance is quite a complete operation and the simpler it is designed the greater response will it evoke.

# 5

# Administrative Implications of 74th Constitution Amendment Act in Andhra Pradesh

*—K. Deva Manikyam, T.V. Sujatha*

Urbanisation is an outstanding and inescapable factor of modern life. In the history of makind the growth of urban life has given rise to striking developments. The pace of urbanisation and the technological changes following it have brought transformations in the way of living of the people, specially in urban areas. Rapid growth of urbanisation is a phenomenon which has markedly characterised the twentieth century. Of course, it is true that cities had unprecedented growth during the last two or three centuries. But the fact remains that those trends which led to increased urban growth in the past, merely have their intensification in the present century. Futurologists fully agree that there is to be no looking back whatsoever with regard to urbanisation.

Urbanisation is the *sine qua non* for progress and prosperity. The degree of urbanisation in a country is an important social characteristic. The state which has more of urban population is considered to be more advanced. Certain facilities and services are available in cities and towns which are not provided to the people in rural areas. Urbanisation is an increase in the proportion of city as well as in a population which implies an absorption of peasants and rural people into a modern state. Urbanisation implies a change to an impersonal style in social relationship and an increase in the range of alternatives for individuals in most aspects of life without losing the old community pattern. Thus urbanisation represents the way of life. As such, it is primarily, although not entirely associated with living in towns and cities. It differs from ruralism mainly in ways of work, habits of thought and with the tempo of life and work is fasten. Urbanisation is more dynamic than ruralism.

**Problems of Urbanisation**

According to 1991 census, India had 25.72 per cent or 217.18 million people living in areas classified as urban; which means that every fourth Indian is now living in urban communities. By the year 2001, India's population is likely to be around a thousand million and it is probable that as much as one–third of it could be urban, that is, around 335 million.

Urbanisation gives rise to a number of problems due to the inability of the city and its environs to grow as fast as the growth of urban population and human activity. This holds equally good in India as in other developing countries of South-West Asia. There is a fast increase of the population. Such rapid rise in population growth has resulted in the increase in their urban population. All States in India have registered significant increase in their urban population. During 1901-1981, the population of 12 cities increased to 10 lakhs. As a result of this there have arisen problems of housing, educational facilities and other basic civic services.

The main problem with regard to urbanisation in India is that there is no interdependence between the process of urbanisation and regional development. The national policies also lack sound basis of economic develoment. There is a lack of serious comprehension of the distorted nature of urbanisation both in terms of over concentration of population in a few large urban centres and in terms of unintegrated development of the lagging regions. There is no effective land-use planning and control. Moreover, there is haphazard growth of cities which has been accepted as an evolution by accident.

Socio-cultural issues also cut at the root of India's urbanisation, Indian cities could hardly be designated as generative cities. It is the peculiar socio-cultural system of the Indian society which could be held mainly responsible for lack of creative influence of cities. It may be apt to describe the Indian society as plural in nature. Caste and cultural distinctions mark the basis of a number of hereditary groups which comprise the Indian society. On the one hand due to the differential caste composition of the rural and urban areas people from one area are indifferent to the interests of the people of the other. This greatly hinders the city's ability to serve as the growth centre of its region. On the other hand, there is increase of the economic gap between the people of the higher and the lower castes. This gives a general impression that in India, the gap between the rich and the poor is increasing along with development.

The most serious problem facing the urban local bodies is the acute scarcity of finance. Generally their sources of income are inadequate as compared to their functions. Their chief sources of income are the varied types of taxes. However most of the income generating taxes are levied by the Union and State Governments, and the taxes collected by the urban bodies are not sufficient to cover the expenses of the services provided. Though they can impose certain new taxes, the elected members of these urban bodies hesitate in doing so for fear of displeasing their electorate. The administrative machinery, at the disposal of these local bodies, is insufficient and ineffective. The staff, which is often underpaid, indulges in corrupt practices which leads to loss of income. Quite often, failure in collecting taxes leads to accumulation of arrears running into crores of rupees. As a result, many urban bodies are on the brink of bankruptcy. Financial stringency has become the biggest hurdle for almost all municipal bodies on account of the ever increasing expenditure on establishment which has gone up to about 60 per cent of the income. Virtually no money is available for development work. Municipal committees of many small towns find it difficult ever to disburse salaries to their employees on time. Many civic bodies have not been able to provide even the basic civic humanities in the areas which have been included in their jurisdiction during the last couple of decades.

Because of inadequate finances, the local bodies have not been able to fulfil their obligatory functions. As a result, they suffer a constant outcry from the public as well as the government. The most basic necessity, water, is not supplied properly, drainage facilities do not cover the entire city, unplanned colonies and slums develop fast, menace of stray cattle on the road continues, traffic is hazardous, roads are not properly maintained and unsafe buildings are allowed to continue to exist despite the obvious threat to the inmates and the inhabitants of the area. In short, poor sanitation, poor hygiene and shortage of basic necessities make cities unsafe.

Unemployment is another problem of urbanisation. It is education through which the creativity of the people could be heightened at the city level. Lack of any innovative educational system and educational planning in India has resulted in the problem of educated unemployed who are mostly concentrated in urban areas. The educated youth who are either unemployed or underemployed while hindering the development of production create further problems for the urban authorities. It is, therefore, needless to say that there is the need for proper educational planning to augment production and to eradicate the problem of educated unemployed.

The urban authorities in India are confronted with the challenges of restricting the haphazard urban growth and to make available extra facilities to the growing urban population. However, a number of difficulties surround the city managers and planners in India in dealing with the problems. These are: financial, administrative, technical and legal.

Normally, the city in India is a municipality or a corporation with limited boundaries and infrastructure. Due to expansion of population, the city also has expanded both its boundaries and infrastructure. The difficulty in administrative and legal problems which the city faces is clear from the following statement made by the Justice Wanchoo, former Chief Justice of India, "The administrative structure which would carry through the schemes of urbanisation to meet the expansion of population, the problem of administering the complex urban laws, is to strike a delicate balance between the rights of the individual and the necessities of public good".

Political interference is another problem for urban development. The local political system at the urban level in most parts of the country suffered from skew power structure and lack of public spirit. Studies of municipal bodies and experiences of municipal administrators demonstrate that the urban local authorities are exploited by the political actors of their own advantage. The character of urban politics becomes evident when certain particular aspects are taken into account. Improvement of civic services and urban environment in general presuppose progressive legislation, and suitable administrative organisation and procedures. Adoption of new taxes, required allocation of resources and administrative changes are sure to cause redistribution of benefits and burdens among different segments of the society. Numerous conflicting interests are being touched upon by such measures which evoke opposition by such elements as may have to lose and bear the burden of development. The fundamental issue which stems is who controls the local governments and for what ends. Thus, control over local government becomes either an end in itself, or an aid to political ends not necessarily related to civic improvement. Sometimes, such controls are used to serve and promote different social and economic interests such as jobs, contracts, privileges and political power. The stronger motivation for participating in a local government is pursuit of benefits and advantages, other than the idealised goals of education for citizenship or service to the community. Thus, the forces controlling urban local government do not identify themselves with the goals of urban development and have a stake in these goals.

Vested interests tend to emerge in the maintenance of status quo from the control of the social groups and classes and their power resources. As such, they lose their innovative capacity and the political system is unable to reflect the public demands, instead, the administration becomes a hindrance to the achievement of new goals. It is observed that the municipal politics in India is not functionally oriented towards civic improvement. It does not seem to permit political mobilisation conducive to such development. Moreover, the values and interests of decision makers are not compatible with the requirements of development. The local regime under such conditions of political control and accountability seems to lose the capacity to adopt itself to the challenges of urban growth and development. Thus, urbanisation in India poses certain special types of problems unknown to other countries of the world.

**74th Amendment Act**

Keeping in view the above problems, Government of India passed many Acts for urban development. Municipal Government in India in its present form was introduced by British. After 1947 urbanisation proceeded at a more quickened pace. This was largely the result of the process of industrialisation on which Five Year Plans embarked. The rate of urbanisation is influenced by the policies of the Government and the population distribution by economic activities based on the several developmental programmes in the successive Five Year Plans. The enactment of the 74th Constitution Amendment has brought a new life in the urban local bodies. Besides strengthening these grass–root institutions and decentralising the democracy, the Act has provided a legal entity and ensured stability to the urban local government in the country.

The Central as well as state governments have been aware about the weaknesses and problems of urban government. Therefore, they have tried through appointing commissions and committees to look into the problems of urban governments and suggest the ways to improve their working. A major step in this direction was taken by amending the Constitution through 74th Amendment Act, 1992. The main characteristics of the Act are:

1. The Act provides regular and fair conduct of municipal elections by statutorily constituted State Election Commission.
2. Limiting the state power to do away with democratically elected municipal governments.
3. Adequate representations to weaker sections and women in municipal bodies through reservation of seats.
4. Constitution of wards committees in municipalities with a population of three lakhs or more, with no bar on such committees in cities having lesser population, to ensure people participation in civic affairs at the gross–root level.
5. Specification by Law, through the state legislatures, of

the powers and functional responsibilities to be entrusted to municipalities and wards committees.

6. Placing relationship of state government and urban local bodies on firm footing with respect to local taxation powers and revenue-sharing between state and local authorities through statutory State Finance Commission to be set up every five years.
7. Involvement of elected representatives in planning at district and metropolitan levels, and
8. One-third of total number of seats shall be reserved for women (including the number of seats reserved for SC and ST women) and for election purposes these seats will rotate among the different constituencies in a municipality.

All states in the country were expected to make appropriate Amendments in the state Acts within a period of one year. Most of the states completed this progress. Most of the states have also constituted State Finance Commissions.

**Andhra Pradesh Scenario**

The state of Andhra Pradesh came into existence on 1st November 1956 with the merger of 11 districts of Andhra state, which itself was carved out from the Madras state in 1953, and 9 districts of Telangana region of the old Hyderabad state. Later, three more districts were carved out, making the total number of districts in the state to twenty three. The state is the fifth largest and populous state in the country. It is also fifth largest urbanised state in the country with 8.2 per cent of India's urban population in 1991. In the state, 26.89 per cent people live in urban areas. The state experienced a decadal growth rate of 42.64 per cent during 1981-91. About 67 per cent of urban population in the state live in Class I towns whereas only 12.6 per cent live in class II towns. The number of Class I towns increased from 20 in 1981 to 32 in 1991, whereas the Class II towns increased just by four during the same period.

In Andhra Pradesh, there were two Acts governing the municipal administration namely: The Andhra Pradesh (Andhra area) District Municipalities Act, 1920 and Andhra Pradesh (Telangana region) Districts Municipalities Act, 1956. The APM act was amended several times during the last three decades incorporating changes on various aspects of governance like elections, political and administrative executives, committee system and taxation. There are two Acts that govern the municipal corporations. The earlier one is the Hyderabad Municipal Corporations

Act, 1955 (HMC Act) which is applicable to the Hyderabad, Vishakhapatnam and Vijayawada Corporations. In 1934, Andhra Pradesh Municipal Corporation Act, 1994 (APMC Act) was passed by the legislature which is applicable to the rest of the municipal corporations in the state. This Act came into effect from July, 1994, and incorporates provisions of the 74th Constitution Amendment Act, 1992 (hereinafter 74th CAA) and all the provisions of the HMC Act, 1955, were construed as forming part of this Act. The amendments in 1994 were basically in the form of conforming legislation aimed at giving effect to the 74th CAA.

In Andhra Pradesh, there were three types of urban local bodies viz., municipalities, municipal corporations and notified area committees. There were 108 municipalities, four municipal corporations and three notified area committees before the 74th CAA. Besides, there is a Cantonment Board in Secunderabad. To constitute a municipality, for any local area, a minimum of 25,000 population is prescribed in the APM Act. There are three municipal authorities in respect of the municipalities, viz., council, chair person and commissioner. In corporations, corporation standing committee and commissioner are the municipal authorities. Elections of councillors and chairpersons/mayors were on party basis since 1981. But, in the municipalities, this provision was deleted by Act 4 of 1993 that came into effect on 6-11-1992.

In every municipality, constitution of two committees, viz., appointment committee and constracts committee is mandatory. The council is however, free to constitute any committee for specific purposes. In case of municipal corporation, the standing committee is one of the municipal authorities. Major executive decisions of the corporation are taken by the standing committee.

**74th CAA: Conformity Legislation**

The APM Act, 1965 and the HMC Act, 1955 were amended in conformity with 74th CAA before 31st May 1994, as stipulated. The CAA provides for three types of municipal bodies, viz., Nagar Panchayats for transitional areas, Municipal Councils for smaller urban areas and Municipal Corporations for larger urban areas. In Andhra Pradesh, the following criteria were fixed to constitute different categories of municipal bodies according to 74th CAA.

The Act also provides that if a local area acquires urban characters, these criteria can be released, especially in terms of density of population and municipal revenues. At present, there are 94 municipalities, 14 Nagar Panchayats and seven Municipal Corporations.

**TABLE 1**
**Criteria for Classification of Municipal Bodies**

| *Sl. No.* | *Criteria* | *Category of Municipal Body* | | |
|---|---|---|---|---|
| | | *Nagar Panchayat* | *Municipal Council* | *Municipal Corporation* |
| 1. | Population | 25,000 to 40,000 | Above 40,000 | 4 lakhs and above |
| 2. | Density of Population (in sq. kms.) | 1000 and above | 1000 and above | 1000 and above |
| 3. | Percentage of Employment in Non-agricultural Activities | 50 per cent and above | 60 per cent and above | 85 per cent and above |
| 4. | Economic Importance | Availability of market facilities | Availability of market facilities and Potential for Industrial Dept. | Availability of markets, civic infrastructure, etc. |
| 5. | Revenue of local body | Rs. 40 lakh and above | Rs. 60 lakh and above | Rs. 4 crore and above |

The 74th CAA provides that all the seats in the municipal councils must be filled only by elections. In Andhra Pradesh, the strength of the council was marginally changed based upon population ranges. The minimum and maximum strength excluding the ex-officio and co-opted members was changed from 20 and 50 to 21 and 45 respectively.

Ex-officio members already exist in state. As per the 74th CAA, the provision for co-opted members was also made. One person, in case of municipalities, and two persons, in case of municipal corporations, belonging to minorities will be co-opted by the council and they have voting rights. This provision is a feature which can bring strength to municipal governments provided it is properly utilized.

The manner of election of chairpersons was left to the discretion of the state government. Before 74th CAA the Mayor/Chairpersons were elected directly by the voters. The direct elections were introduced as a result of the 74th CAA. The elections were also held on this basis to the municipalities and municipal corporations in 1995.

**TABLE 2**
**Strength of Council**

| *Sl. No.* | *Population range at the last census* | *No. of elected members* |
|---|---|---|
| 1. | Less than 40,000 | 21 |
| 2. | 40,000 to 1,00,000 | 21 plus one additional member for every 10,000 population above 40,000 |
| 3. | 1,00,000 to 2,00,000 | 27 plus one additional member for every 15,000 population above 1,00,000 |
| 4. | More than 2,00,000 | 33 plus one additional member for every 20,000 population above 20,000, maximum strength however, is 45 |

In India, the issue of reservation is becoming complex. In recent years, the demand for reservations for weaker sections is increasing which has become a major political issue. While recognizing this vital issue, the 74th CAA provided for reservation of seats for Scheduled Castes, Scheduled Tribes and women as mandatory. In Andhra Pradesh, reservations already exist for Scheduled Castes, Scheduled Tribes, Other backward Castes and women. But their percentages are 15, 6, 10 and 9 respectively. However, these provisions were amended to bring parity with the CAA. The features of amended provision are:

(i) Reservation of seats to the Scheduled Castes and Scheduled Tribes in proportion to the population of these categories to the total population of the municipality concerned and such seats may be allotted by rotation to different wards.

(ii) One-third of the total number of seats are reserved for Other Backward Castes and allotment to different wards is by rotation.

(iii) One-third of the seats reserved for Scheduled Castes, Scheduled Tribes and Other Backward Castes are again reserved for women of these categories.

(iv) Not less than one third of the total number of seats (including reservations for SC, ST and BC categories) are reserved for women.

In the 74th CAA, the issue of reservation for the Backward Castes was left to the discretion of the state governments. In Andhra Pradesh, reservation for Backward Castes already existed and it is being continued in the amended Municipal Acts with an increase in their percentage.

Adopting the provisions of the 74th CAA along with reservation for Backward Castes had increased the total percentage of reservations from fifty to more than sixty in the municipalities and corporations. This is also true of reservations to the chairpersons. It is because the percentage of reservation for Backward Castes and women increased from 20 and 9 to 33¹/₃. Earlier certain percentages were fixed for Scheduled Castes and Scheduled Tribes, but in the amended Acts, it was changed to the proportion of respective population to total population of the town or city.

Committees play a significant role in the decision-making process in modern governments. The 74th CAA make provision for wards committees in larger cities of three lakhs or more population. In Andhra Pradesh, provision for constitution of wards committees was made in the conformity legislation. The Act provided for the constitution of these wards committees in the municipalities whose population is three lakhs and more and in case of other smaller municipalities it is left to the discretion of the Commissioner and Director of Municipal Administration. Though the 74th CAA has not assigned any specific role to the wards committees, in Andhra Pradesh, they are interpreted in terms of decentralization of municipal administration, overtime, they may become truly decentralized unit relieving the burden on the standing committees or councils in case of the municipalities.

**Implications and Perspectives**

The 74th CAA has no doubt, ushered a new era in urban governance in India. In Andhra Pradesh, the conformity legislation was formulated in haste mainly to adhere to the time limits fixed for operationalising the Act. Provisions relating to structures received much importance and the crucial aspect of bringing out amendments in other relevant Acts like A.P. Town Planning Act and A.P. Urban Areas Development Act, did not receive any attention. Many provisions were incorporated without changes. Consequently, it led to certain anomalies and problems. The representation for Scheduled Castes and Scheduled Tribes population are taken into consideration for fixing their number of reserved seats while a fixed percentage was made for Backward Castes. Though, an increased percentage is fixed for Backward Castes, it appears to be a discriminatory provision. The implications of reservation are quite complicated and need thorough review.

The existing gradation of municipalities which is based on criterion was not changed, but another category of Nagar Panchayat was introduced. The two types of classification create confusion and problems, if the present gradation is purely based upon the income criteria. The other classification as per the 74th CAA has many factors like density, urban characters and economic growth potential. Ideally, the existing gradation could have been integrated with the classification of CAA which is broad-based and reflects dimensions of urban development. The financial needs, personnel requirements and administrative powers can be better assessed, based upon the broader criterion than the mere revenue based classification.

Another significant aspect which has been left-out is the functional area. The Acts are silent on the functions as listed in the Twelfth Schedule of the 74th CAA. In Andhra Pradesh, municipalities' and corporations, Acts already provide for a majority of these functions. The municipal bodies are performing these functions within their limited resources. The remaining functions listed in the CAA are being performed by the state level departments as listed on the next page:

| Functions | Department |
|---|---|
| 1. Planning of economic and social development | Social welfare and other departments like industries |
| 2. Fire services | Fire services department |
| 3. Urban forestry, protection of environment and promotion of ecological aspect. | Forest and environment department |
| 4. Promotion of cultural and aesthetic activities | Cultural Affairs Deptartment |
| 5. Prevention of cruelty to animals | Food and Agriculture Department |
| 6. Bus stops/shelters | Road Transport Corporation |
| 7. Regulation of Tanneries | Industries Department |
| 8. Urban poverty alleviation | Municipal Administration and Urban Development under sponsored schemes. |
| 9. Safeguarding the interests of weaker sections of society including the handicapped. | Weaker sections Housing Corporation and Social Welfare Department |

*Source:* D. Ravindra Prasad and V. Gnaneshwar, 74th Constitution Amendment Act conformity legislation in Andhra Pradesh.

Basic issue relating to the municipal functions is that they are not in a position to carry out the existing responsibilities in face of rapid urban growth and increasing demands. Some of the functions listed above, viz., urban poverty alleviation, planning for socio-economic development and environment protection are very broad-based. Their effect spills over a wider area cutting across the existing municipal administrative jurisdiction. In this respect, municipalities can play a key role in planning, implementing, monitoring and co-ordinating development programmes in conjunction with several departments and agencies. To perform these tasks, municipal bodies must be strengthened in terms of expertise and financial resources.

It is paradoxical, that, while the CAA and the conformity legislation stresses the democratic functioning of the urban local bodies, at the same time, the bureaucratic elements being strengthened in Andhra Pradesh. Some of the powers of the chairpersons were withdrawn and were given to the commissioners. Interestingly, these changes were made when the councils were dissolved in the state after the expiry of their terms in 1992. Ironically, the conformity legislation and the amendments withdrawing some of the powers of the chairpersons and conferring them on the Commissioners were introduced in the legislature simultaneously. The following changes were brought through the Act 3 of 1994 which undermines the importance of the chairpersons in municipalities:

1. The power of signing contracts on behalf of the council (up to Rs. 3,000) in case of grade I and II and (up to Rs. 5,000) in case of others which was with the chairpersons was withdrawn and was given to the Commissioner, while enhancing the monetary limits (upto Rs. 50,000 in the case of grade II and III, Rs. 10,000 in case of grade I and Rs. 25,000 in case of special and selection grades).

2. Earlier, every contract exceeding Rs. 500 was to be signed by the chairperson. Through the amendment, the Commissioner was empowered to sign the contracts on behalf of the council.

3. The chairpersons were the appointing authority for all the posts sanctioned by the council. But this power has been conferred on the Commissioner.

4. The appointments to the posts sanctioned by the council were to be made from a panel prepared by a municipal committee consisting of commissioner, chairperson and 3 to 7 councillors. But now, this power is to be exercised by a committee constituted by the state government for the purpose.

5. While the controlling powers of the commissioner over the employees of the council were enhanced to the extent of removal or

dismissal, the powers of the chairperson to take disciplinary action over the municipal employees have been removed.

The dual attitude is detrimental to strengthen local democracy in India. In fact, there have already been demands from the newly elected chairpersons of municipalities and corporations to restore their powers especially, in the light of their direct election.

The financial dimension reveals some more problematic areas. In fact, the basic problem of the municipal bodies is their shrinking financial resource base as against the fast increasing demands. The 74th CAA specified that adequate resources must be provided by the state government to municipal bodies to make them strong enough to perform their functions efficiently. The State Finance Commission should examine these issues. It is in this context that the role of the State Finance Commission (SFC) becomes significant. The SFC so must formulate principles that govern sharing of certain taxes, duties, tools etc., levied by the state government with municipalities, determination of taxes, toll etc., that may be assigned or appropriated by municipalities; and the grant-in-aid to the municipalities.

In the absence of substantive provisions in the 74th CAA, the issue of sharing of certain taxes with the municipalities may remain debatable issue.

**Conclusion**

The enactment of the 74th Constitution Amendment has brought a new life in the urban local bodies. Besides strengthening these grass-root institutions and decentralising the democracy, the Act has provided a legal entity and ensured stability to the urban local government in the country. The 74th Constitution Amendment Act created three tiers of municipal bodies and accordingly, most of the states in the country have amended their Municipal Legislation. Thus, independent State Election Commission, State Finance Commission have been set-up. Similarly, elections to the Municipal Bodies have been completed after making appropriate provisions for reservation of seats for women, scheduled castes, scheduled tribes and other backward classes of the society.

In Andhra Pradesh, most of the provisions of the CAA were incorporated in the Municipal Acts. The conformity legislation incorporates the provisions relating to constitution of municipalities, elections. The state finance commission and the state election commission, provisions relating to district and metropolitan planning committees and functions included in the Twelfth schedule are yet to be incorporated. Reservation for Backward Castes in the municipal councils which is already in existence in the state is being continued with changes. The Government of Andhra Pradesh introduced the system of direct election. The party-based elections were also introduced. One significant aspect of reforms in Andhra Pradesh has been curtailing the powers of the chairpersons in certain vital areas like contracts, appointments and control over municipal staff at a time when the conformity legislation was made with a view to strengthen local democracy. The role of the chairpersons in the municipal corporations and municipalities in the state is thus undermined. Weakening of the political executive and introducing party politics may put the urban governments under pressure. It may strain the relations between the deliberative and administrative wings further. Introducing the direct election and curtailing the powers certainly is a negative step which needs to be corrected. Democratic governance must be based on mutual trust and confidence between the political and administrative wings and the governing system must provide proper checks and balances rather than moving towards bureaucratisation and centralisation. Another area that needs attention is function-finance balance. Though the 74th CAA provided for a host of municipal functions, it must be examined in terms of the resources allocated to perform these functions. Each state can adopt its own pattern and this exercise has just been initiated in Andhra Pradesh, both by the state finance commission and the government. Recognising the importance of decentralisation for sustainable development, more decision making power and resources should be transferred to regional and municipal bodies. Local Communities need to have more involvement in planning, management and revenue collection. The complexity of management, services and infrastructure in large urban agglomeration necessitates greater cooperation between various administrative areas and levels.

To cope with rapid urbanization, government should create a favourable climate for private sector investment in smaller towns and cities and provide for the required support mechanism, such as fiscal and social infrastructure, and favourable fiscal and monetary policies.

## REFERENCES

### Books

1. Amruth Rao, A.: *Personnel Management and Municipal Administration in India,* Ashish Publishing House, New Delhi, 1985.
2. Apurba Kumar Basiston: *Urban Local Administration,* B.R. Publishing Corporation, Delhi, 1986.

3. Arthur W. Bromage: *Introduction to Municipal Government and Administration,* Appleton Century-Crofts, Inc, New York.
4. Kamaldeo Narain Singh: *Urban Development in India,* Abinav Publishers, New Delhi.
5. Mohit Bhattacharya: *Municipal Government; Problems and Prospects,* Delhi.
6. Omprie Srivastava: *Municipal Government and Administration in India*, Chug Publication, Allahabad, 1980
7. Ramesh K. Arora, Rajani Goyal: *India Public Administration Institutions and Issues,* Wishwa Prakashan, New Delhi, 1995.

## Articles

1. Bernd Hamm: Thinking Globally and Acting Locally; Global Arguments for local reform; *Quarterly Journal of the AII of Local Self-Government,* B. Vol. LXII, No. 1, Jan–March, 1992.
2. Davis, Kinglsley and Hilda H. Golden: "Urbanisation and the Development of pre-Industrial Areas", *Economic Development and Cultural Change,* Princeton University Press, Vol. III, No. I, October 1954, p. 6.
3. Harnam Singh Azad: 74th Constitutional Amendment and District Development Planning with Special Reference to Rajasthan, quarterly Journal of the All of Local Self-government, Bombay, Vol. LXV. No. 1, Jan–Mar. 1994.
4. Hosiar Singh: "Revitalisation of Municipal Govt. through 74th Constitutional Amendment Act 1992. *Quarterly Journal of the All India Institute* of Local Self-government, Bombay, Vol. LXV No. 1, Jan-Mar. 1994.
5. Madhukar: Municipal Administration in Mumbai, *QJ AIILSG,* Vol. LXVII No. 3, July-Sept. 1996.
6. Patil, N.S.: Difficulties Experienced in Municipal Administration in Maharashtra, *QJ AIILSG,* Vol. LXVIII, No. 1, Jan–Mar. 1992.
7. Ravindra Prasad D. and Gnaneshwar V.: 74th Constitutional Amendment Act conformity legislation in Andhra Pradesh.
8. Sastry, S.M.Y., Amendments to Municipal Laws to implement the 74th Constitutional Amendment Maharashtra, Vol. LXVI No. 1, Jan-Mar. 1995.
9. Sastry, S.M.Y: Amendments to Municipal Acts to implement the 74th, Constitutional Amendment *QJ AIILSG,* Vol. LXVI No. 1, Jan–Mar. 1995.
10. Subha Kashelikar: Aspects of Establishment of Municipal Council, *QJAIILSG,* Vol. LXIII, No. I, Jan–Mar. 1992.

# 6

# Post-74th Constitution Amendment Act—Andhra Pradesh Municipalities—Review

*—B. Venkatachalapathi*

Mahatma Gandhi said that the development of the village is the corner stone of Rama Rajya and the key-stone of democracy. The representatives of the local bodies like the municipalities should not aspire to power for selfish reasons but seek office as an opportunity to contribute to the development of society in the spirit of love and service. However, it is very unfortunate that no such selfless motive has prompted the initiation of development over the past fifty-one years.

Under such circumstances, Parliament brought about the 74th Amendment to the Constitution in 1992. As per this Act, local bodies are given a free hand to do as they think fit for the development of society. The salient features of the Constitution Amendment Act are as under:

1. Municipalities to be categorised according to the size of the area administered.
2. Direct elections to the municipalities.
3. Reservation of seats for Scheduled Castes and Scheduled Tribes according to their population and one-third reservation of seats for Backward Classes rests with the State Government.
4. The tenure of elected representatives is five years.
5. The municipalities can levy tax and take other decisions from time to time with the concurrence of the State Government.
6. A Finance Commission will be constituted to review the financial position of the municipalities once in five years.
7. The municipal elections will be conducted by the State Election Commission which will be appointed by the State Governor.
8. A Committee will be specially appointed to scrutinize the development activities in the municipalities.

9. As per the recommendations of the State Finance Commission, a consolidated fund releases funds as per the requirements of the municipalities. This has been made possible as per the amendment to Article 280 which is a part of this Act.

According to this Act, the State Government should not postpone municipal elections indefinitely. It should also release funds to local bodies without any prejudice or partiality.

**Disadvantages**

The Members of Parliament and Members of the Legislative Assembly are also members of the municipalities. As they are usually busy with problems concerning their own constituencies, they cannot really concentrate on the working of the municipalities, and their contribution to the smooth functioning of the municipalities is doubtful.

Similarly, the experts who are nominated to the Ward-Committees contribute to practically nothing except to the increase in the number of meeting and consequent paper work. As the Act has already given financial powers to the municipalities, the municipalities, if they so wish, can raise finances through the issue of bonds and loans to the public.

Like other states, the municipalities in Andhra Pradesh also face various problems including financial crunch. It is amazing that about seventy per cent of the income goes towards salaries and only the remaining 30 per cent is left for developmental activities. Hence, the Rambhupal Committee recommended the following steps to strengthen the financial position of the municipalities:

1. The municipalities should be given the right to impose surcharge on commercial taxes.

2. They should also be given the right to collect vehicle tax.

3. The professional tax should be raised from Rs. 250 to Rs. 500 and 75 per cent of this amount should be allotted to the municipalities.

4. The municipalities should be given their due share of the entertainment tax, vehicle tax and professional tax from the government without hindrance.

If these recommendations are followed, the financial burden of the municipalities will be lessened to a great extent.

In spite of the provisions given under Constitution Amendment Act of 1992, the municipalities in Andhra Pradesh are in a very deplorable condition. During his recent visit to different places, the Chief Minister observed that the conditions of the roads, drainage and sanitary conditions in general were the same everywhere. Roads are full of pot-holes and they are often used as refuse dumps. In the rainy season, the condition worsens. The proliferation of mosquitoes and swarms of flies gives ride to the spread of diseases among the public.

In the district of Adilabad, authorities in the Adilabad, Manchirial, Kagaznagar, Bellampalli, Nirmal, Biampar and Mandamarri municipalities have failed to provide even the minimum amenities to the public. In Adilabad, the District Headquarter which has a population of 1,20,000, there is only one road which is tarred. All the other roads in the town remain untarred.

In the Karimnagar, Ramagundam, Jagatial, Sircilla and Koratal municipalities of Karimnagar District, the sanitary conditions are deplorable. Although 10 to 15 per cent of the annual budget is allocated for development, the sanitary conditions have not improved and the drainage system is conspicuous by its absence.

Again in the District of Nizamabad, the sanitary condition prevailing in the municipalities of Nizamabad, Kamareddy, Bodhan, are no different. The lack of adequate staff and finances have made the situation worse. To date, no development has been possible. As recently as in 1998, no less than forty person succumbed to Cholera.

In the District of Warangal, the Warangal Municipal Corporation, the Janagama Nagara Panchayati and the major grama panchayatis of Mahaboobnagar, Saimpeta and Narasannapeta there is total absence of sanitary development. The only drainage existing is that which was constructed during the British days and it has become inadequate due to the growth of the population and expansion of the town. The lack of staff is another factor that has prevented the Warangal Municipal Corporation from much needed development in the sanitary conditions of the town.

Mention may be made specially of two municipalities in Mahaboobnagar District which are extremely unhygeinic. The overbridges in these two municipalities are in very bad shape. All the roads usually submerged by drainage water overflowing onto them in all seasons. The situation becomes unbearable during the monsoons.

In Medak District, three municipalities have been facing multifarious problems related to general sanitation and drainage. Again, inadequate staff and finances make the municipalities helpless. In the monsoon season, all these municipalities become vast slum areas.

In the district of Kurnool, the Nandyal, Adoni and Yammiganur municipalities have been facing similar problems. Sanitary, drainage and welfare activities have been neglected. The Kurnool municipality, however, is comparatively somewhat better.

In the six districts of coastal Andhra, there are thirty-three municipalities and three corporations. In these districts also, there are problems pertaining to water supply, sanitary conditions and roads. The little financial resources at their disposal are not being utilized properly. The public become the victims and are made to face a lot of inconvenience. In the Prakasam District, for example, all the four municipalities are lacking in basic sanitary facilities. Due to lack of adequate sanitary staff, drains are clogged and remain uncleaned and rubbish dumps grow into mountains as they are not cleaned regularly.

In the Ongole Municipality also, the sanitary conditions are grossly inadequate. More often than not, the roads have become dwelling places of pigs and cattle. In Chirala, the lack of inadequate municipal staff is reflected in the complete absence of lavatories. During the rainy season, the roads are covered by rain and drainage water, forcing the public to shift for themselves and exposing them to such unhygienic conditions resulting in epidemic diseases from time to time. In the Kandukur and Markapur municipalities also, the same conditions prevail.

In the Krishna District, the Vijayawada Municipal Corporation, the Machilipatnam Gudiwada and Nuzvid municipalities suffer from shortage of sanitary staff. The two main arteries of Vijayawada town, the Eluru road and the Bandar road, in addition to the Ring road, have become refuse and litter dumps to such an extent that they cause obstruction to the free flow of vehicular traffic and pedestrians. According to the local public, inadequate funds from the government, insufficient powers of the authorities are factors responsible for such extreme conditions. The Machilipatam municipality also has not seen any development due to lack of financial resources. It has become impossible to meet the expenditure towards salaries and electricity bills. The same problems are faced by the Gudivada and Nuzvid municipalities also.

The municipalities in Khammam District such as the Khammam, Kothagudem and Palvaocha municipalities, the circumstances are somewhat peculiar. Even though the income of these municipalities is in crores, no interest is taken in developmental activities. Although elaborate plans were drawn up for the proposed underground drainage system, it did not materialize for some reason or the other. Here too, shortage of staff plagues the municipality. Tractors used for removing rubbish dumps are in bad repair and there has been no sanction for the purchase of new tractors. Government bottlenecks and red-tape are responsible in no small measure to holding up regular payments of salaries.

In the eight municipalities of West Godavari even the minimum facilities are not being provided. The Eluru Municipality is in a state of complete collapse. The attempt to provide underground drainage was a failure, and conditions have become a hell to the local public. In the absence of any drainage, either underground or overground, filthy water overflows onto the roads.

In the North Andhra area also, the municipalities are in a bad state of affairs and the public have to face severe odds. In Vijayanagaram, Srikakulam and Visakhapatnam districts, there are twelve municipalities and one corporation. These municipalities are also no different from the others in the rest of the State with only slight differences. Drainage and sanitary problems seem to have no solution. While the population has been increasing by leaps and bounds, there has been no corresponding increase in the strength of the municipal staff. In Srikakulam District also, shortage of staff and vehicles prevent the removal and disposal of rubbish dumps, thus creating much inconvenience to the public.

In Vijayanagaram and Visakhapatnam, the municipalities seem to be vying with each other in maintaining unhygienic and insanitary conditions. The suburbs of these towns are facing the brunt of overflowing drains. The Gajuvakka Municipality also is in the same sorry plight.

In the Rayalaseema and Nellore districts, public health is in a hazardous condition. The rapid growth of population in these areas has materialized all the efforts of the municipalities in development even though funding is liberal. In the last two years, due to release in finances and official supervision, some beginning was made to ameliorate the harsh circumstances prevailing, but this too proved to be unsatisfactory.

As a result of recent decisions and effective measures taken, the sanitary conditions in the Anantapur, Tadipatri, Nellore, Tirupati and Chittor municipalities have been improved to a better extent than before but in contrast, the Guntakal, Rayadurg, Hindupur, Cuddapah, Proddatur, Gudur, Srikalahasti, Mandanapalle and Punganur municipalities are in an extremely bad shape. The Nellore Municipality, in comparison to the Kavali and Gudur Municipalities, is far better. In the Kavali and Gudur areas, flies, mosquitoes, coupled with contaminated water leading to cholera, typhoid, jaundice and malaria are rampant causing much suffering to the public in those areas.

In the Kavali municipality, the situation is so bad that there are no funds even to pay the salaries of the municipal staff. In Chittoor district, there are four municipalities. In Tirupati, besides a local population of 2.5 lakhs, a floating population of thousands of pilgrims regularly visit Tirupati and Tirumala. In consequence of this, the problems are so immense that the municipality is not able to cope with the same in spite of recent decisions to ameliorate the conditions of the public. In the Chittoor municipality, the situation today is slightly better than it was two years ago.

**Conclusion**

It has been observed that more or less, similar conditions prevailing all over the State are due to the following main reasons:

(i) Unwarranted Government interference has led to the lack of leadership, lack of autonomy and lack of stability.

(ii) A number of MPs and MLAs who are members of the municipal councils and corporations, usually assume the powers that should rightfully be held by the municipal authorities.

If the municipalities throughout the State are to function efficiently and effectively, in providing a clean and healthy atmosphere for its tax-paying citizens, new legislature should be instituted to remove the drawbacks of political interference in the functioning of the municipalities.

# 7
# Urban Development Management in Bihar State

*—S.K. Sinha*

**I. Bihar State: A Profile**

Bihar is named after Buddhistic "Viharas" or monasteries for which it was famous during the Buddhist period. It has seen the rise and fall of many dynasties dating back to the Vedic days. During the current century, it was carved out as a separate province in 1912 from Bengal, by the British administration and Patna was made its capital. During 1936, the portion of present Orissa state was carved out as a separate province from the then Bihar province.

Physically Bihar state is a land-locked state, squeezed in between West Bengal, Orissa, Madhya Pradesh, Uttar Pradesh and reaching upto the Himalayas in the north. The State is bounded on the north by Nepal, on the south by Orissa and Madhya Pradesh, on the east by West Bengal and on the west by Uttar Pradesh.

However, in respect of urban population, the state ranks ninth in the country and contains 5.23 per cent of the national urban population (113.69 lakhs). Secondly, the state has only 13.17 per cent population living in the urban areas, as compared to the All-India percentage of 25.72. The remaining 86.83 per cent of the state's population lives in the rural areas, as compared to the All-India percentage of 74.28.

For administrative purposes, the state has been divided into Divisions, Districts, Sub-Divisions and Community-Development Blocks (C.D. Blocks). As during November 1997, there were thirteen (13) Divisions, fifty-five (55) Districts and one-hundred and thirty (130) Sub-Divisions.

In terms of absolute figures, the situation in respect of Bihar state, as per the 1991 census, is as under:

| | | |
|---|---|---|
| (i) | Total area | 173,877 sq. kms. |
| (ii) | Total population | 86.34 million |

| | | |
|---|---|---|
| (iii) | Urban population | 11.35 million (13.17 % of total) |
| (iv) | Rural population | 74.99 million (86.85% of total) |
| (v) | No. of urban settlements | 271 |
| (vi) | Number of habited villages | 67,503 |
| (vii) | Number of urban local bodies | 170 |

(Municipal Corporation—6, Municipalities—70 and Notified Area Committees—94)

**II. Urban Development Administration**

The Urban Development Department of Government of Bihar is the administrative department for all urban development activities in the state, and is responsible for the following:

(i) administrative control over all personnel associated with urban development within the department and statutory bodies;
(ii) management of budgetary funds of the department;
(iii) administrative control and approval of budget of the urban local bodies; Bihar Urban Development Agency and District Urban Development Agency;
(iv) Urban planning and development control managed/regulated through the various categories of statutory bodies and legislative Acts and Ordinances; and,
(v) monitoring of centrally sponsored schemes of Integrated Development of Small and Medium Towns (IDSMT) and Urban Poverty Alleviation (UPA).

The following three important wings within the department assist the department in the discharge of the various functions mentioned above.

The state Town and Country Planning Organisation (TCPO) headed by the Chief Town Planner, Bihar is responsible for assisting the department in all matters pertaining to Regional and Urban Planning, Preparation and Monitoring of Projects of Centrally Sponsored schemes of IDSMT.

The TCPO also assists the various urban local bodies, development authorities and various departments of government, in preparation of regional plans, master plans, zonal development plans and other development schemes. The Chief Town Planner is an ex-officio member of all development authorities, Bihar State Housing Board, Bihar State Agricultural Marketing Board and nominated member/special invitee to Bihar State Tourism Development Corporation and Industrial Area

Development Authorities.

The Directorate of Local Bodies, headed by a Director (generally of the rank of Deputy Secretary) is responsible for ensuring effective administration of the legislative provisions for local bodies, management of budgetary funds earmarked for the various urban local bodies, and approval of their annual budget.

The Directorate is also responsible for administrative control over the local bodies and the Executive Officers posted in these local bodies.

The Directorate of Urban Poverty Alleviation Programmes (UPAP), headed by a Director (generally a senior level I.A.S. officer), which is responsible for administration and budgetary control of funds as well as monitoring of the centrally sponsored schemes of urban poverty alleviation.

The above functions are discharged through Registered Societies, namely Bihar Urban Development Agency (BUDA) as the apex body for the entire State and District Urban Development Agency (DUDA) for each district.

The budget allocations of the Urban Development Department in various Five Year Plans and the annual plans have been/are made under three main heads, as under:—

1. ***Urban Water Supply and Sanitation Sector***
   Under it funds are budgeted and released to urban local bodies as well as the district magistrates for implementation of water supply schemes, drainage and sewerage schemes and schemes of low cost sanitation, comprising of conversion of service latrines into septic latrines and construction of community toilets.
2. ***Urban Roads Sector***
   Under it, funds are released to urban local bodies, development authorities and district magistrates for improvement and upgradation of roads and construction of culverts.
3. ***Urban Development Sector***
   Under it, funds are released to urban local bodies, development authorities and district magistrates for implementation of the following schemes and programmes:

   (i) Civic amenities comprising of municipal markets, street lighting, community/town halls, bathing ghats, etc;
   (ii) Grants-in-aid to Regional Development Authorities;
   (iii) Master plan and training;
   (iv) Environmental improvement of urban slums (EIUS);

(v) Centrally sponsored scheme of IDSMT;
(vi) Centrally sponsored schemes under the Urban Poverty Alleviation Programmes (UPAP) and UNICEF funded activities;
(vii) Rickshaw pullers welfare scheme; and
(viii) Administrative and Operational expenses.

All the funds released out of the annual plans are in the form of grant. The Central assistance is generally in the form of loan with interest to be repaid in accordance with the terms and conditions spelled out by the Government of India.

In addition to the urban development department, the following departments and statutory boards of the State government are also associated with the development activities in the urban area of Bihar State:—

(i) Road Construction Department
(ii) Building Construction and Housing Department
(iii) Public Health Engineering Department
(iv) Health and Family Welfare Department
(v) Human Resources Department
(vi) Welfare Department
(vii) Forest and Environment Department
(viii) Industries Department and Industrial Area Development Authorities
(ix) Bihar State Housing Board
(x) Bihar State Electricity Board
(xi) Bihar State Agricultural Marketing Board
(xii) Bihar State Pollution Control Board.

Since the Sixth Five Year Plan (1980-1985), the International organisation, UNICEF, has also been assisting the Urban Development Department in cash and equipment required for urban poverty alleviation programmes with focus on women and children, as well as for organising orientation and awareness programmes for UPAP personnel and beneficiaries.

**III. Urban Statutory Bodies**

The State has three-tier system of Urban Local Body (ULB), namely:

(i) Municipal Corporation for urban settlements having an urban population of 2,00,000 persons and above;
(ii) Municipality for such towns which contain not less than forty thousand inhabitants; and

(iii) Notified Area Committee (NAC) for such urban settlements which contain not less than 20,000 inhabitants.

The above three categories of urban local bodies are constituted and notified, under the provisions of two Acts:

(i) The Bihar and Orissa Municipal Act, 1922, and
(ii) The Patna Municipal Corporation Act, 1951.

These two Acts have since been amended as follows through two separate ordinances, during May, 1994 to incorporate the provisions contained in the Constitution 74th Amendment Act, 1994:

(i) The Bihar Municipal (Amendment) Ordinance, 1994, (Bihar Ordinance No. 13, 1994)
(ii) The Bihar Municipal Corporation (Amendment) Ordinance, 1994 (Bihar Ordinance No. 12, 1994).

The main functions of the urban local bodies are maintenance and provision of civic amenities, ensuring public health safety, water-supply, roads, drainage, creation of assets through markets, dharmasalas, offices, and creation of municipal fund through taxes and levies.

Before the enactment of the Bihar Regional Development Authority Act, 1981 (Ordinance of 1975), the local bodies had the power to sanction/ approve building and land development plan.

These powers have since ceased for the six Municipal Corporations where development authorities have been notified.

As during November 1997, the state had only 170 urban local bodies as follows:—

(i) Six Municipal Corporations for the Divisional Headquarter Cities of Patna, Ranchi, Gaya, Bhagalpur, Muzaffarpur and Darbhanga;
(ii) Seventy (70) Municipalities and Ninety four (94) Notified Area Committees.

Thus, the remaining 101 towns have no urban local body. The second category of urban statutory body in Bihar state is of three types, as follows:—

(i) Regional Development Authorities (RDA) constituted and notified under the provisions of the Bihar Regional Development Authority Act, 1981 (Ordinance of 1975). As during November 1997, there are six Regional Authorities functioning for the Divisional Headquarter Cities of Patna, Ranchi, Gaya, Bhagalpur, Muzaffarpur and Darbhanga. A senior level I.A.S. Officer is the Chief Executive of these Authorities and is designated as Vice-Chairman.

(ii) Coal Mining Area Development Authority (CMADA) constituted and notified under the provisions of the Coal Mining Area Development Authority Act, 1986 (Ordinance of 1984). This Authority has been renamed as Mineral Area Development Authority (MADA) during August 1992, through on Ordinance.

Presently, this Authority has been set-up and functioning for the integrated development of the urban and rural settlements of the entire coal mining districts of Dhanbad and Bokaro. A senior level I.A.S. officer is the Chief Executive of this Authority and is designated as Managing Director.

The Minister of Urban Development or a person nominated by the State Government, is the Chairman of both types of Authorities and there is a Board of Directors constituted under the provisions of both the Acts.

(iii) The single-member Authority, named as Town Planning Authority (TPA), is set up and notified under the provisions of the Bihar Town Planning and Improvement Trust Act, 1951. This category of Authority is generally headed by the Divisional Commissioner of the District Magistrate of the area, within whose jurisdiction the Authority exists. The Chief Executive is notified as the Town Planning Authority. There is an Advisory Committee constituted under the provisions of the Act.

As during November, 1997, there are ten Authorities notified for the following areas :—

(a) Divisional Headquarter towns of Hazaribagh, Daltonganj, Dhumka and Saharsa;
(b) District Headquarter towns of Biharsharif, Begusarai, Gopalganj and Bettiah; and
(c) Tourist centres of Rajgir and Maner.

The main statutory functions and responsibilities of the above three categories of Authorities are briefly as follows:—

(i) The Regional Development Authorities with the approval of the Board of Directors are statutorily charged with the following responsibilities:—

(a) Preparation and enforcement of Regional Plans, Master Plans and Zonal Development Plans, to ensure planned development of the areas under their control;

(b) Preparation and implementation of urban development schemes, including land development, roads, drainage, sewerage and water supply, commercial schemes, and schemes of urban poverty alleviation.

(c) Control of land use, and architectural buildings, land and building development in accordance with the provisions of the Planning Standards and Building Bye-Laws framed within the framework of this Act.

They hand over the urban development schemes after their implementation to the concerned urban local bodies for maintenance.

(ii) The Mineral Area Development Authority with the approval of the Board of Directors is statutorily charged with the following responsibilities:

(a) Preparation and enforcement of Development plan and Zonal Development plan for integrated development of the rural and urban settlements within the jurisdiction.

(b) Preparation and implementation of development schemes, including development, housing, infrastructure like roads, drainage, sewerage, pollution control, reclamation of the land subject to dereliction due to mining activities, and development of commercial areas, industrial areas, etc.

(c) Preparation and maintenance of water-supply schemes including supply of water to users, and collection of charges for the water supply system.

(d) Control of land use and land building development in accordance with the provisions of the Planning Standards and Building Bye-laws framed within the framework of the Act/ordinance.

(e) Preparation and implementation of Urban Poverty Alleviation Programmes.

(iii) The Town Planning Authorities with the approval of the Advisory Committee are statutorily charged with the following responsibilities:

(a) Preparation and enforcement of Master Plan, to ensure planned development of the area under their control.
(b) Control of land use and land and building development in accordance with the provisions of the Bihar Restriction of Uses of Land Act, 1948, as also Planning Standards and Building Bye-Laws framed within the Act.
(c) Preparation and implementation of urban development schemes and ensure their proper maintenance, through funds created out of disposal of assets.

The third category of urban statutory body is the Bihar Jal Parishad (originally named as Bihar State Water and Sewerage Board) set up under the provisions of the Bihar State and Sewerage Board Act, 1982. The salient features of the Jal Parishad are as under:—

1. A person nominated by the State Government is the Chairman and the Chief Executive is a senior level I.A.S. officer who is designated as Managing Director.

2. The functions of the "Parishad", comprise of the following:—

(a) Preparation and implementation of schemes of major water-supply systems, drainage and sewerage schemes and schemes of garbage disposal and reclamation.
(b) Preparation and implementation of schemes under the Ganga Action Plan, initiated during the Seventh Five Year Plan (1985–1990).
(c) Preparation of Feasibility and Study Reports for control of river-water pollution of such rivers identified by the Government from time to time.

There exists a fourth category of urban statutory body known as water board, which are administratively under the control of the urban local bodies within whose jurisdiction Board exists.

At present, there exist three Water Boards at Patna, Manager and Bhagalpur, and their main functions are:—

(a) preparation and implementation of schemes of water-supply system and their maintenance,
(b) collection of charges for supply of water from beneficiaries.

**IV. Legislation for Urban Areas**

The following legislation in the form of Acts and Ordinances are operative at present in Bihar State for urban management, planning and development, under the administration of urban development department:

*(i) For Urban Management*

1. The Bihar and Orissa Municipal Act, 1922.
2. The Patna Municipal Corporation Act, 1951.

These two Acts have since been amended, as follows, through two separate Ordinances, during May 1994, to incorporate the provisions of the Constitution 74th Amendment Act, 1992:

1. The Bihar Municipal (Amendment) Ordinance, 1994
2. The Bihar Municipal Corporation (Amendment) Ordinance, 1994.

Both the ordinances became Acts in 1995.

*(ii) For Planning and Development*

1. The Bihar Restriction of Uses of Land Act, 1948.
2. The Bihar Town Planning and Improvement Trust Act, 1951.
3. The Bihar Regional Development Authority Act, 1981 (promulgated as an Ordinance in 1975).
4. The Bihar Coal Mining Area Development Authority Act, 1986 (promulgated as an Ordinance in 1984).
   This Act has now been re-enacted as Mineral Area Development Authority Ordinance during August 1992.
5. The Bihar State Water and Sewerage Board Act, 1982.
6. The Bihar Cinema Regulations Act, 1954.

In addition to the above eight Acts/Ordinances, the following six legislations are also operative in the urban areas of Bihar State, but under the administration of other Departments of the Government:

(a) The Bihar State Housing Board Act, 1982 (promulgated as an Ordinance in 1971) under the administration of building Construction and Housing Department. Through this legislation, the State Housing Board, after approval of the Board of Directors, plans, develops and maintains housing areas in the urban areas of the state.

A person nominated by the State Government functions as Chairman of the Board and a full-time senior-level I.A.S. Officer is the Chief Executive of the Board designated as Managing Director.

(b) The Bihar Agricultural Produce Market Act, 1960 (amended by the Bihar Agricultural Produce Market Ordinance, 1974) under the administration of the Agriculture Department. Through this legislation, the State Marketing Board, after approval of the Board of Directors, plans, develops and manages marketing yards in the urban areas of the state.

A person nominated by the State Government functions as the Chairman of the Board and a full-time senior-level I.A.S. Officer is the Chief Executive of the Board designated as Managing Director.

(c) The Bihar Industrial Area Development Act, 1974 under the administration of the Department of Industrial Development. Through this legislation, the Industrial Areas are set up, who after approval of their Board of Directors, plans develops and manages the assets created within the industrial area.

A person nominated by the state government functions as the chairman for each Industrial Area and a full-time senior level I.A.S. officer is the chief executive for each industrial area, and designated as Managing Director.

(d) The Central Act of Urban Land (Ceiling and Regulation) Act, 1976 is under the administrative control of Department of Revenue and Land Reforms. Through this legislation the provisions and controls as spelled out in the Act are enforced, after scrutiny of each proposal of Ceiling and Regulation, within the frame-work of the master plan for the concerned urban area, approved by the Urban Development Department.

(e) The Department of Forest and Environment is the administrative Department for enforcement of the provisions of the following two Acts, enacted basically to regulate and enforce pollution:

(i) The Water (Prevention and Control of Pollution) Act, 1974.
(ii) The Environment (Protection) Act, 1986.

### V. Post-constitution 74th Amendment Act, 1992 Status

In Bihar State, *consequential amendments* have been made in the existing legislation, through two Ordinances notified on May 30, 1994. The detailed modalities of operationalising the Construction of 74th Amendment Act, 1992 are yet to be worked out.

In Bihar there exists two Acts, relating to constitution of urban local bodies and containing their powers and functions, sources of finance and structure and composition of the local bodies.

These two Acts have been amended through two separate Ordinances, during May 1994, to incorporate the provisions contained in the Constitution 74th Amendment Act, 1992 as follows:

1. The Bihar and Orissa Municipal Act, 1992 has been amended and ordered as the Bihar Municipal (Amendment) Ordinance, 1994. (Bihar Ordinance No. 13, 1994).

2. The Patna Municipal Corporation Act, 1951, has been amended and enacted as the Bihar Municipal Corporation (Amendment) Ordinance, 1994, (Bihar Ordinance No. 12, 1994).

The two Amendment Ordinances provide for setting up of local bodies at *three levels* as follows:

(i) Municipal Corporations for large urban areas with population of 3,00,000 and above;
(ii) Municipal Councils for smaller urban areas with population of 50,000 and above; and
(iii) Nagar Panchayats for "transitional areas", that is to say an area in transition from a rural area to an urban area.

While notifying these local bodies, the State Government will give regard to the population of the settlement, the density of population therein, the revenue generated for local administration, the percentage of employment in non-agricultural activities, economic importance or such other factors as deemed fit.

The duration of the local bodies has been provided for a term of five years from the date appointed for the first meeting and no longer, in the two Amendment Ordinances. An election to constitute a local body shall be completed;

(a) before the expiry of its duration, namely, before five years term; and,
(b) in case of dissolution before the expiration of the duration, i.e., five years, before the expiration of a period of six months from the date of its dissolution.

As regards **"Reservation of Seats"**, the two Amendment Ordinances have made the following provisions:—

(i) Reservation of seats for SC, ST and Backward Classes in every local body, in the same proportion to the total number of seats to be filled in by direct election, as the population of the SC, ST and Backward Classes.
(ii) It has also provided that such seats may be totally allotted by rotation to different constituencies in a local body, in such manner as may be prescribed by the State Election Commission.
(iii) It has also been provided that not less than one-third of the total number of seats to be filled in by direct election in every local body, shall be *reserved for women.*

(iv) It has further been provided that not less than one-third of the total number of seats reserved for SC, ST and Backward Classes, shall be reserved for women belonging to SC, ST and Backward Classes.

The two Amendment Ordinances have provided that the State Election Commission constituted under the Bihar Panchayati Raj Act, 1993 (Bihar Act 19 of 1993), shall also function as the State Election Commission for the superintendence, direction and control of elections to the urban local bodies.

Provision has also been made to frame Rules for the above activities related to the elections.

The two Amendment Ordinance have provided that the State Finance Commission constituted under the Bihar Panchayati Raj Act, 1993 shall also function as the State Finance Commission for urban local bodies constituted under these two Ordinances.

The two Ordinances have also provided that this Finance Commission will make recommendations to the State Government in respect of the principles and procedures for assignment and sharing of taxes, grants-in-aid and measures needed to improve the financial position of the local bodies.

Regarding "Augmentation of the Finances" of the urban local bodies, new sections have added in these Ordinances enacted by Bihar Government.

The two Amendment Ordinances have inserted new sections relating to the Powers, Authority, Responsibility and Functions of the local bodies, as provided in the Constitution 74th Amendment Act, 1992 and its Twelfth Schedule.

For planning at the District and Metropolitan levels, the two Amendment Ordinances have inserted new Sections relating to:

(a) Constitution of two separate committees, namely, committee for district planning and committee for metropolitan planning as provided in the Constitution 74th Amendment Act, 1992.

(b) Composition, functions, duties, etc. and election of chairperson for each of the two Committees which shall be according to provisions of section 134 of the Bihar Panchayati Raj Act, 1993.

Thus, the Bihar State has not fully implemented the provisions of the Constitution 74th Amendment Act, 1992 as has been done in other States.

# 8

# Governance of Delhi–A Case for Streamlined Administration for the Organisation of Infrastructure

—*Ashok Kumar*

"...given its present political organisation and decision making processes, the city is fundamentally ungovernable. By ungovernable I mean that the urban policy making system is incapable of producing coherent decisions, developing effective policies, or implementing state federal programmes" (Yates, 1977 : 5).

**Introduction**

Governance means "the arena where politicians and administrators manage and organise the city by articulating and translating political philosophies into programmes of action" (Davoudi, 1995:225). But McCarney (1996) argues that governance is more than just government and its actions. A comprehensive view of governance provides for the identification of major actors and their involvement in governing relationships. Other than centre, state and local government, major actors also include people as individuals, people as interest groups, the NGOs and CBOs, and other government bodies. This still precludes the influence and resultant pressures on the governing relations exerted by the multinational and transnational corporations. An understanding of corporations on governing relations is equally important for it is these corporations which pressurize for better infrastructure which surely leads to prioritisation of policies and actions directly in favour of corporations rather than people. It is, however, not necessarily true that infrastructure priorities of the coroporations will be always at odds with the peoples' priorities.

After defining governance, it is pertinent to note what government might be required to do in the near future. Whatever may be the predominant form of government, in the next century state and local governments in metropolitan areas are likely to perform two major functions. Organising rather than the provision of infrastructure is likely to become the top priority of governments. Secondly, enforcement of laws for the control of pollution consequent to tremendous increase in the population of human beings and motor vehicles would become another major responsibility of governments. Therefore, governments may be called upon to specialize in organising as well as in managing the participatory decision making processes. Empowering by enabling populations to take part in decision making process will become the cornerstone of successful governance.

The paper strongly argues for a more streamlined and consolidated but at the same time decentralised administrative structure for better governance of the National Capital Territory of Delhi. It contends that one way of achieving this is by abolishing the large number of infrastructure providing organisations such as Delhi Vidyut Board etc. and creating a new Delhi Infrastructure Development and Finance Corporation. This will reduce fragmentation but retain status quo as far as centralisation is concerned. To change that decentralisation is proposed within this consolidated framework. After this brief introduction, the second section traces the history of the governance of Delhi and finds that it had feudal system of governance till 1947. This system was extremely centralized and decisions were taken by Central Government. People and other actors were not involved in governance. The third section reviews the post-independence history of governance of Delhi. The third section also contains an analysis of the major hindrances to streamlined administration of Delhi. Governments after 1947 also effectively excluded people from participation in decision making by erecting centralized and quite often confused organisational structures. It is in the last section that the concept of the integrated planning and development corporation is introduced and developed. The integrated planning and development corporation will be strongly supported by a regime of district and ward committees of elected members. In order to complete the process of peoples' administration, community organisations are proposed to constantly interact, participate and decide at ward level. This proposal does not preclude the possibility of an increased role of government but at the same time the role of local people and the third sector will be enhanced.

## History of Governance of Delhi: Feudal Past and Centralized Administration

Delhi had a long history of feudal administration beginning with the birth of the First Delhi otherwise known as Indraprastha (see Table 1 for details). Feudal administration of Delhi continued till the neneteenth century when it was taken over by the East India Company in 1805. But it was only after the building of the city of New Delhi that a local authority in the form of New Delhi Municipal Committee was created in 1911. But even after the establishment of the Municipal Committee, the executive powers were still exercised by the Governor General in Council through the Chief Commissioner. All the Municipal Committee had was five appointed members of Central Government who worked as executive officers to the Chief Commissioner.

**TABLE 1**
**Pre-War Governance of Delhi**

| *Time* | *Ruler(s)* | *City* | *Type of Governance* |
|---|---|---|---|
| 1450 B.C. | Pandava | I.P. | Feudal |
| 1060 A.D. | Anangpal | Lal Kot | Feudal |
| 1303 A.D. | Alauddin Khilji | Siri | Feudal |
| 1320 A.D. | Ghiyas-ud-Tughlaq | Tughlaqabad | Feudal |
| — | Muhammad Tughlaq | Jahanpanah | Feudal |
| 1354 A.D. | Feroz Shah Tughlaq | Ferozabad | Feudal |
| — | Dinpanah | Humayun | Feudal |
| 1638 A.D. | Shahjahanabad | Shahjahan | Feudal |
| 1805 A.D. | East India Co. | Delhi | Feudal |
| 1911 A.D. | British India Government | New Delhi | Foreign Yoke |
| 1911 | British India Government | New Delhi | New Delhi Municipal Committee |
| 1938 | British India Government | Delhi Cantonment | Delhi Cantonment Board |
| 1911-1947 | British India of India | New Delhi | Governor General in Council |

*Source: Compiled from Goyal (1993 : 1– 7).*

Imperial government of the city of Delhi had two clear areas of concern—the military requirements and the civil requirements (King, 1976 : 236-237). The military requirements produced regimented structures and processes of governance in the form of Cantonment Board leading to a closed system of governance with full military control of the British India Government through the Station Commander. The Board had 14 members on it.

However, the civil requirements of government created an organisation called the New Delhi Municipal Committee which was also largely composed of nominated members of the Empire. These officers represented the interests of the ruling elite and bureaucracy. The New Delhi Municipal Committee provided for the Raj, and controlled for the Raj. Openness in government was allowed to the extent it helped the Raj and not the people of the city. According to King (1976) the New Delhi Municipal Committee never made any discernible effort to create industrial and commercial areas for local residents. Not only that the city administration was devoid of any form of people's participation, the planning committees established for the building of the city of New Delhi were more autocratic. With hindsight, one can say that the nature of planning policies and processes clearly established autocratic regimes for the next 50 years to come.

**Governance of Delhi after Independence**

Although most recent elections to elect 134 municipal councillors for the Municipal Corporation of Delhi were held in February 1997 after a gap of more than 15 years, Delhi had been governed by elected governments in short spells after 1947 (see Table 2). For instance, Delhi was declared as the self governing Part C state with a Legislative Assembly of 48 members in 1952. However, the Legislative Assembly was abolished in 1956. After 11 years, i.e., in 1967, elections were held to elect members to the Metropolitan Council which was created only a year before. But the Metropolitan Council was dissolved by the Indira Gandhi Government in 1980. The Metropolitan Council was, however, revived in 1983 but only to be dissolved in 1990 again, this time by the National Front Government.

**TABLE 2**
**Governance of Delhi between 1947 to 1997**

| | |
|---|---|
| 1947-1952 | Government of India |
| 1952-56 | Self Governing Part C State with the Legislative Assembly of 48 Members |
| 1956 | Delhi Legislative Assembly abolished |
| 1956-1966 | Directly Administered Union Territory and Birth of the Delhi Administration |
| 1957 | Delhi Municipal Corporation created |

| | |
|---|---|
| 1966 | Metropolitan Council set up under the Delhi Administration Act |
| 1967 | First Elections held to the Metropolitan Council of 56 elected and 5 Nominated Members |
| 1980 | Metropolitan Council dissolved by the Indira Gandhi Government |
| 1983 | Metropolitan Council revived |
| 1990 | National Front Government dissolved Metropolitan Council |
| 1992 Onwards | Elected Government of the National Territory of Delhi with 70 Members' Legislative Assembly headed by the Chief Minister |

*Source: Compiled from Kumar (1996a : 24) and Goyal (1993 : 16–39).*

Local government of New Delhi has also remained nominated and unelected and therefore largely unrepresentative. For example, the Presidential Ordinance promulgated on 25 May 1994 provides that three MLAs, 5 Union Government officers, 2 nominated members such as lawyers, etc. and the MPs of New Delhi will oversee the working of the renamed New Delhi Municipal Council. But the Chairperson of the Council will be still an IAS Officer appointed by Central Government. Similarly the Municipal Corporation of Delhi has been primarily run by the unelected bureaucrats. Infrastructure such as roads, drains, etc. in "development areas" is provided by the Delhi Development Authority which operates under the direct control of Central Government. Major urban development projects have been undertaken by a central agency called the Delhi Development Authority.

Government of India had delegated limited legislative powers to the city government but all administrative control was clearly vested in the President through the Chief Commissioner. In 1966, Delhi Administration was born whereby governance through appointed directorates through the direct administrative control of the President of India was exercised. In spite of periodic elections to the Municipal Corporation of Delhi, the appointed Commissioner remained the principle executive. Even the Metropolitan Council did not have the executive powers. Even today Delhi's Chief Minister has less powers than the Lieutenant Governor. Powers of the Government of the National Capital Territory of Delhi are severely curtailed. For example, the Act which created the state, reads:

"Provided that in the case of difference of opinion between the Lieutenant Governor and his ministers on any matter, the Lieutenant Governor shall refer it to the President for decision and act according to the decision given thereon by the President and pending such decision it shall be competent for the Lieutenant Governor in any case where the matter, in his opinion, is so urgent, that it is necessary for him to take immediate action, or give such direction in the matter as he deems necessary" (Government of India, 1991 : Article 4).

Unlike other states, the National Capital Territory of Delhi is much less than a full state, although the special status under the Government of the National Capital Territory of Delhi Act, 1992 has been accorded to Delhi (Goyal, 1993). Since 1992 a seventy member Legislative Assembly and seven member Council of Ministers has been created. The Legislative Council is led by the Chief Minister. However, the Legislative Council has no powers to legislate on various important issues including public order, police, land and matters on the State List particularly Entry 1, 2 and 18 (also refer Table 2).

Major arguments for not according the full status of a state to Delhi has been repeatedly outlined. Firstly, it is contended that since New Delhi hosts important national and international offices, its governance can not be left to the sole administrative control of local authorities of the state government. This underscores the lack of faith in the administrative capacity of local governments. Secondly, it is argued that since 80 per cent of the property in the National Capital Territory of Delhi is owned by Central Government, it is only pertinent that Central Government or its own civil service agents look after and develop these lands. Lastly, it is argued that it would be appropriate if Central Government is involved in the administration of Delhi in order to provide efficient services for country's image. The Delhi Chief Minister came quite close to achieving the full status of state during the thirteen days BJP government led by Atal Behari Vajpayee. But as Central Government could not secure vote of confidence, Chief Minister's dreams shattered.

**Who Governs Delhi?—A problem Centred View Maze of Organisations**

Governance of the National Capital Territory of Delhi is a stupendous task for it is governed by more than 20 large and about 200 medium and small organisations. All these organisations look after the total area of 1,483 sq. km out of which 685.34 sq. kms. is rural and the remaining 797.66 sq. kms. is classified as urban area. Delhi has 209 villages, 29 census towns, 3 municipal bodies and two tehsils. Further, it is heartening to note that more than 10 million people now reside in Delhi. Therefore, the governance of Delhi has become an administration of the impossible with the present administrative structures.

The authority of the state of Delhi is further curtailed by minimizing its financial powers. Whereas other states have their public accounts in the Reserve Bank of India, Delhi Government does not have any such account. Unlike other states Delhi government is also not allowed to borrow from the market. Nor can it dip into the safer provident fund. Nonetheless, a plethora of organisations has emerged in the National Capital Territory of Delhi (see Table 3). In addition to these organisations, numerous technical colleges and hospitals are run by the Delhi Government. Each of these organisations is as big as a medium size (in terms of number of employees and the extent of operations) private company.

**TABLE 3**

**Major Organisations Providing Various Services in the NCT of Delhi, 1996**

| *Name of the Service* | *Organisation providing the service* | *Administrative Control* |
|---|---|---|
| Urban Planning and Development | Delhi Development Authority | Ministry of Urban Affairs and Employment |
| Water and Sewerage | Delhi Water Supply and Sewerage Disposal Undertaking | Ministry of Water Resources and the MCD |
| Electricity | Delhi Vidyut Board* | Delhi Government |
| Transport | Delhi Transport Corporation | Delhi Government |
| Drainage | Irrigation Department of Delhi Administration | Delhi Government |
| Fire | Delhi Fire Service | Delhi Government |
| Telephone | Mahanagar Telephone Nigam Limited | Ministry of Communications |
| Milk | Delhi Milk Scheme | Delhi Government |
| Law and Order | Delhi Police | Home Ministry |
| Slum and Squatter Improvement | Slums Department | Delhi Government |
| Enforcement of Planing Controls | Special Task Force | Home Ministry |

| *Name of the Service* | *Organisation providing the service* | *Administrative Control* |
|---|---|---|
| Urban Form and Aesthtics | Delhi Urban Arts Commission | Delhi Government |
| Finance for Industry and the Business | Delhi Finance and Development Corporation | Delhi Government |

*Source:* Compiled by the author from various sources (1997).
*Note:* DVB was known as the Delhi Electric Supply Undertaking before early 1997.

Slums Improvement Board and Trans-Yamuna Development Board are yet to be accounted for. Both these boards are also headed by Bhartiya Janata Party MLAs and MPs. However, these are not statutory bodies.

**Centralisation, Decentralisation Versus Fragmentation**

Fragmentation simply does not mean counting the number of organisations in a metropolitan area for providing various services because this exercise simply names and measures the variables. However, it does not help in linking one variable with the other. "The relevant empirical question is the extent to which jurisdictional fragmentation leads to functional fragmentation, that is, a lack of necessary and useful coordination among jurisdictions with respect to specific functions" (Advisory Commission on Intergovernmental Relations 1988:2, also see Fogelson, 1967). Therefore, the existence of a large number of organisations in the National Capital Territory of Delhi in itself is not a bad situation of governance. But the fact that these organisations work without adequate coordination mechanisms to deal with difficult decision situations has led to chaos. According to Yates (1977) the city becomes ungovernable because

> "the city is too decentralized to permit coherent planning and policy making;
> it is too centralized to support a responsive, flexible relationship between the servers and the served in service delivery;
> it is too dependent on higher level government to take strong, independent policy initiatives;
> it is too independent of higher level government to ensure competence, control and fairness in the implementation of national programmes; and the principle actors in it have so little control over its governance" (Yates, 1977:6).

Let us now consider an illustration to understand the centralist but fragmented administration of the National Capital Territory of Delhi.

Centralisation implies that decision situations are controlled at state or central level and not at local level. Local authorities simply implement the policies and programmes of higher levels of government. For instance, prior to 1996, the Delhi Electric Supply Undertaking, now known as the Delhi Vidyut Board remained under the direct control of Union Power Ministry Water and sewerage, telephone, and law and order still remain largely the domain of Central Government. Significantly, urban planning and development is also looked after by Central Government through the Delhi Development Authority. This is significant because the Delhi Development Authority not only develops the state but also formulates policies about infrastructure. Another central agency called the Special Task Force is created in early 1997 which now looks after the enforcement of town planning controls. This is an area where the Municipal Corporation of Delhi and more particularly the Delhi Development Authority has failed to perform (Kumar, 1996a). Whereas the developed areas are handed over to the Municipal Corporation of Delhi for upkeep, the Municipal Corporation of Delhi plays only advisory role in shaping the form and content of developments.

Uncoordinated decentralisation also leads to fragmentation. For example, large scale privatisation of public transport in the late 1980s unleashed the phenomenon of decentralisation and fragmentation. Overnight individuals became owners of buses. No coordination and enforcement mechanisms were put in place. The result was catastrophic. Thousands of people died on the Delhi roads in eight years as a result of chaos created by the private bus operators (Kumar, 1996b).

**Overlapping Jurisdictions**

Take a look at the mess created by the different administrative boundaries in Delhi. According to new administrative set up (see below) Delhi has 27 revenue and police sub-divisions.

Delhi is also divided into 12 election zones but only 8 town planning zones. To further add to the confusion, one hundred and thirty-four unique election wards have been created. Moreover, there are unique boundaries of the slum and squatter areas.

**New Administration**

Chief Minister Sahib Singh Verma attempted to have established an effective new administrative set up which he claims will be transparent and impartial (also see Fig. 4). The Government of the National Capital Territory of Delhi now has nine Deputy Commissioners and 27 Sub Divisional Magistrates with a view to bringing the administration at the doorsteps of the people. The nine districts are West, South West, North East, New Delhi, Central, North, East, North East and South. The offices of the DCs and SDMs have started functioning since 1 January 1997. These offices will work as one window offices for all government departments at the district and sub-division level.

A Deputy Commissioner or Development Commissioner will head a district which will have more than one sub-division magistrate. Administrative districts will correspond to police districts. Administrative districts have been created to cover the entire geographical area of the National Capital Territory of Delhi. In all, Delhi will have nine administrative districts and police districts, and 23 sub-divisions (see Table 4).

The Development Commissioner is a civil servant who will be the incharge of new administration in a district. Each sub-division will have more than one police station. But Delhi Administration's 11 directorates and 24 departments still exist and nobody quite knows what to do with them. The problem of duplicity and coordination that they create remains unresolved.

**TABLE 4**
**Present District Administration of Delhi**

| *District* | *Police District* |
|---|---|
| **West District and its Sub-Divisions*** | **West Police District and its Police Stations** |
| I Punjabi Bagh | Punjabi Bagh, Paschim Vihar, Nangloi |
| II Rajouri Garden | Hari Nagar, Kirti Nagar, Rajouri Garden |
| III Patel Nagar | Patel Nagar, Moti Nagar, Anand Parvat, Tilak Nagar, Janak Puri, Vikas Puri |
| **South West District and its Sub-Divisions** | **South West Police District and its Police Stations** |
| I Vasant Vihar | Vasant Vihar, Sarojini Nagar, R.K. Puram |
| II Nazafgarh | Nazafgarh, Jagarpur Dabri, Delhi Cantonment, Vasant Kunj, Narayana, Mayapuri, Inderpuri |
| **North East District and its Sub-Divisions** | **North East Police District and its Police Stations** |
| I Seelampur/Seemapuri | Seelampur, Gokulpuri, Bhajanpura, Seemapuri, Nand Nagri |
| II Shahdara | Shahdara, Welcome, Mansarovar Park |
| **New Delhi and its Sub-Divisions** | **New Delhi Police District and its Police Stations** |
| I Connaught Place/ Parliament Street | Connaught Place, Tilak Marg, Parliament Street, Mandir Marg |
| II Chankya Puri | Chankya Puri, Tuglak Road |

| **Central District and its Sub-Divisions** | **Central Police District and its Police Stations** |
|---|---|
| I Darya Ganj | Darya Ganj, Chandni Mahal, Jama Masjid, Kamla Market, Hauz Quazi, I.P. Estate |
| II Pahar Ganj | Pahar Ganj, D.B.Gupta Road, Nabi Karim, Karol Bagh, Prasad Nagar, Rajinder Nagar |
| **North District and its Sub-Divisions** | **North Police District and its Police Stations** |
| I Sadar Bazar | Sadar Bazar, Kashmere Gate, Bara Hindu Rao |
| II Civil Lines | Civil Lines, Timarpur, Roop Nagar, Maurice Nagar, Subzi Mandi, Pratap Nagar, Sarai Rohilla |
| III Kotwali | Kotwali, Lahori Gate, Chandni Chowk |
| **East District and its Sub-Divisions** | **East Police District and its Police Stations** |
| I Vivek Vihar | Vivek Vihar, Anand Vihar |
| II Preet Vihar | Preet Vihar, Shakarpur, Kalyanpuri, Trilokpuri |
| III Gandhi Nagar | Gandhi Nagar, Krishna Nagar, Geeta Colony |
| **South District and its Sub-Divisions** | **South Police District and its Police Stations** |
| I Kalkaji | Kalkaji, Badarpur, Okhla |
| II Defence Colony | Defence Colony, Lodhi Colony, Kotla, Mubarakpur, Lajpat Nagar, Srinivaspuri, Hazrat Nazamuddin |
| III Hauz Khas | Hauz Khas, Malviya Nagar, Mehrauli, Greater Kailash, Chittaranjan Park, Aaya Nagar |
| **North East District and its Sub-Divisions** | **North West Police District and its Police Stations** |
| I Saraswati Vihar | Rohini, Jahangirpuri, Shalimar Bagh, Ashok Vihar, Saraswati Vihar, Keshav Puram, Sultanpuri, Kanjhawala, Mangolpuri |
| II Narela | Samaypur Badli, Narela, Alipur |
| III Model Town | Model Town, Mukherjee Nagar, Adarsh Nagar |

*Source :* Government of the National Capital Territory of Delhi (1997 : 8).

*Note:* * In all there are 27 revenue and police sub-divisions.

Delhi Cantonment, Karol Bagh, Seemapuri and Parliament Street are shown separately.

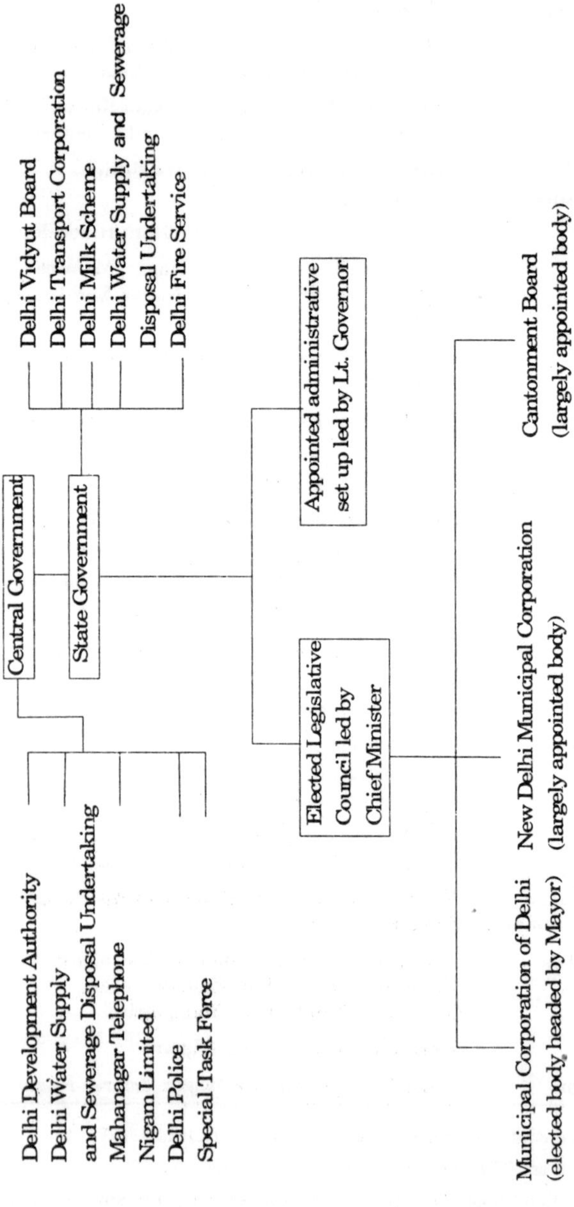


**Fig. 1. Existing Administrative Setup of the National Capital Terrtory of Delhi**

The functions of the DCs and SDMs include day-to-day administration, implementation of government programmes and schemes, and redressal of the public grievances.

**Magisterial Functions**

The officers will function as the Executive Magistrates as envisaged in the Criminal Penal Code in the context of Delhi in respect of Public Nuisance cases (section 133 Cr. P.C.), cases related to disputes over possession, apprehension of breach of peace (security proceedings), conduct of inquests (U/s 174 and 176 Cr. P.C.) with regard to dowry deaths, custody deaths and human rights cases.

**Revenue Functions**

All land matters which include mutation, land acquisition, consolidation, protection of Gaon Sabha land, notification, maintenance of land records and the revenue court cases under various revenue acts such as Urban Land Reforms Act and the Punjab Land Revenue Act.

**Issuance of Various Certificates**

The SDM's office will issue SC, ST, OBC, physically handicapped, Lal Dora, insolvency, birth, marriage, registration, income certificate, etc. to local residents.

**Registration Function**

Registration of various documents under Registration Act will be carried out by Sub-Registrar's office. Stamping as collector of stamps and functions under Indian Stamps Act as Chief Controlling Revenue Authority.

**Relief Work**

Distribution of relief and providing other facilities to the Punjab and, Jammu and Kashmir migrants of 1984 riot victims, relief to victims of natural calamities such as floods, fires, earthquakes and victims of terrorist activities, and payment of solatium to the victims of hit and run accident cases.

**Coordination and Supervision of other Government Departments**

The Development Commissioners and SDMs will be performing coordinating and supervising roles over all Departments whatsoever within their jurisdiction. They will also be performing certain statutory duties in respect of many departments such as cooperatives, employment and labour, excise, environment and forests, food and civil supplies, land and building, medical and health, and transport, etc. They will further have a broad supervisory role in respect of the other Departments in their jurisdiction such as DVB, MCD, Education, PWD, Social Welfare, Rural Development, Medical and Health, Irrigation and Floods, Fire Services, Industries, Food and Supplies, etc. The SDMs will carry out the raids to detect the electricity thefts all over Delhi. They will inspect all government offices, projects, schemes and institutions, and make efforts to redress the public grievances in their District and Sub Divisions. The SDMs shall ensure the registration of FIRs in their areas in the cases where public finds it difficult to do so.

**Miscellaneous Functions**

Supervision of Rajya Sabha Board, statutory functions as District Election Officer, Electoral Registration Officer, Returning Officer and Assistant Returning Officer for Parliamentary and Assembly Constituencies are also decentralised to district level.

**Impediments to Effective Governance of Delhi**

From the preceding analysis, the following major impediments to effective governance of Delhi can be highlighted.

***Lack of Coordination and Cooperation between Organisations***

The existence of a large number of small organisations providing the same or different services is not a problem by itself. However, their existence gives birth to the problem of fragmentation and centralisation. Fragmentation occurs when each provider organisation works on its own without understanding and addressing the implications of their operations. The case study of Delhi amply demonstrates this fact. For example, no coordination mechanisms exist between various directorates of Delhi Administration and the Delhi Development Authority other than the mechanism of communicating through files and occasional meetings between the top officials.

In fact, there is an extreme lack of inter-agency collaboration. Committees and Commissions are regularly formed to resolve conflicts and deliberate on issues of mutual interest, but most of these are advisory in nature. While there is a delegation of authority to look for solutions, these Committees and Commissions are unable to achieve any substantive objective for the want of perusal upto implementation stage. Furthermore, fragmentation without integration also hinders coordination and cooperation between organisations.

**Permanence of Organisations**

A large majority of the organisations serving and administering the National Capital Territory of Delhi are not only permanent but have acquired a statutory status. Permanence unleashes enormous organisational power of control without accountability for boards of all these organisations are also appointed and not elected. Shift of organisations from Centre to the National Capital Territory of Delhi is not particularly helpful if the power structures remain the same. This is particularly true about the transfer of the DTC and DESU to the Delhi Government. Staff remains demotivated and financial management regimes remain ineffective. Burden of debt continues to increase. Since there is no threat to job security and career enhancement, personnel in these organisations fail themselves and the organisations by non-performance.

***Political Bankruptcy and Bureaucratic Colonialism***

All major organisations such as the Delhi Development Authority, Delhi Transport Corporation, Delhi Vidyut Board, etc. are managed by the civil servants. Although they have inherited the British bureaucracy, which worked extremely efficiently for the attainment of the objectives of the imperial government, the present day bureaucrats lack of professionals. A gory nexus between the civil servants and their political masters leaves no room for accountability. Further, organisations do not have any coherent training policies for efficient administration and management. Trainings are often used as leisure trips abroad. Inside India a training programme is used by an employee to get an official off from the job. There are no programmes for integrated human resources development.

***Colonial Organisational Structures***

Organisational structures are centralized and employees operate them on the basis of secrecy and control. Since officers are unable to deliver in a reasonable time, most organisations lack credibility in the eyes of the citizen.

***Policy Direction and Leadership***

Top leadership whether elected or nominated or appointed completely lacks any policy direction. Even if good policies are formulated, implementation is thwarted by the lack of the commitment of the top leadership to serve the people. As far as appointed leadership is concerned, it is transferred on regular intervals resulting in the want of continuity of policy direction. Sometimes the civil servants are not even able to settle down before they are transferred to another place.

***Status Problems***

The status of Delhi as a state is everything but clear. This has led to conflicts between the Chief Minister and the Municipal Corporation of Delhi's Mayor on one hand and Central Government and Lt. Governor on the other. All important 73rd and 74th amendments to the Constitution of India have been implemented half-heartedly. For example, elections to the Municipal Corporation of Delhi were held recently. Whereas an important provision of reservation for women was applied as envisaged by the above mentioned Constitution amendments, the New Delhi Municipal Council remains unelected body. The establishment of the Finance Commission is not in sight as yet. Various other provisions of the Constitution amendments have been simply ignored.

***Breakdown in Communications***

There is complete breakdown in communications between the Government of the National Capital Territory of Delhi and the adjoining states. For example, the Uttar Pradesh Government impounded Delhi Transport Corporation's buses plying on the UP roads because the Delhi buses were exceeding the mileage allowed to them. In a retaliatory action the Delhi Government impounded UP Transport Corporation's buses. There were no conflict resolution mechanisms that could be used to resolve such conflicts. Talks between the two transport secretaries failed. It was only after the Delhi Chief Minister and the Governor of UP (elected government in UP was yet to be sworn in) held a meeting that the issue was sorted out. Communications between various organisations in Delhi also remains on the brink of a breakdown. For example, one of the major reasons why basic services in the slums and squatters of Delhi cannot be provided is the lack of communications between major providers such as the Municipal Corporation of Delhi, etc.

## Consolidation and Integration for Organizing the Basic Services

***The Infrastructure Development Finance Corporation of India***

The Infrastructure Development Finance Corporation will be set up with an authorized capital of Rs. 5,000 crore. Government of India expects that this capital will help to develop the capital market for infrastructure investment. With the help of Rs. 5,000 crore authorized capital, long-term bonds may be floated and guarantees could be provided for investment in the infrastructure sector. Further, new insurance and pension schemes will be used as ready sources of funds for infrastructure investment. Government also expects that the permission given to the Foreign

Institutional Investors (FIIs) to invest in the unlisted companies could act as a leverage for companies working in the field of infrastructure development. Additionally, the overseas companies with large funds to invest in infrastructure which in the past would have been given permission on case by case basis by the Foreign Investment Promotion Board (FIBP) can now directly come and invest in infrastructure in India as the Foreign Institutional Investors (FIIs). An FII can now invest upto 10 per cent subject to aggregate of 24 per cent for all the FIIs. Earlier this figure was only five per cent.

Funds meant for investment in infrastructure will be exempted from income tax. Further, any dividend, interest or long-term gains from investment in the form of shares or long term finance in any enterprise set up to develop, maintain and operate an infrastructure facility will not attract any income tax under Section 88. In such investments, the limit under Section 88 has been raised to Rs. 70,000 crore from Rs. 60,000. The capital base of the National Highways Authority (NHA) has been increased by Rs. 200 crore. The NHA will also be able to attract funds from within and outside India for highway development.

The Infrastructure Development Finance Corporation will receive contributions from Central government, the Reserve Bank of India and the financial institutions towards the share capital. The Finance Minister has already made a provision of Rs. 500 crore in the current financial year which will be matched by a similar contribution by the Reserve Bank of India (see Table 5).

**TABLE 5**

**Capital for the Infrastructure Development Finance Corporation**

| *Sector/Department* | *Rupees in Crores* | |
|---|---|---|
| Central Government | | 500 |
| Reserve Bank of India | | 500 |
| Special Customs Surcharge | 1,600 | |
| Seed Capital of IFDC | | 5,000 |

The allocation for the Ministry of Surface Transport has gone up from Rs. 240 crore in 1995-96 to Rs. 1,322 crore in 1996-97. The money, however will be primarily used for highway development. The budgetary support for the railways has been fixed at Rs. 1,269 crore in 1996-97. This may be increased.

There are income tax benefits for individuals investing in infrastructure projects. The 1996-97 budget has proposed a tax rebate of

20 per cent of the amount invested in equity shares or debentures issued by an infrastructure company. Such shares and debentures will have a lock-in period of three years.

Government has also levied a two per cent special customs duty on major imports to fund infrastructure sector. This estimated to yield an additional revenue of Rs. 1,600 crore in the financial year itself. This surcharge continued till 31 March, 1997.

The Infrastructure Development Finance Corporation will act as a direct lender, a refinancing institution and a provider of financial guarantees. This means that the Infrastructure Development Finance Corporation will be able to provide finance to other financial institutions like ILFS, IFCI, ICICI and IDBI for funding infrastructure projects. The Infrastructure Development Finance Corporation may also help in giving companies the necessary financial guarantees which are being viewed as an alternative to counter guarantees.

The Foreign Investment Promotion Board (FIPB) is in the process of framing standardized guidelines to clear foreign investment projects and for monitoring mega projects:

(a) The FIPB will grant automatic approval to power projects cleared by state governments, the Central Electricity Authority and the Pollution Control Boards.

(b) Consultations are going on with states to formulate unified guidelines on power, telecommunications and electronics.

The Infrastructure Development Finance Corporation will be a commercial firm and it will not be established under an Act of Parliament. It will be established by the end of this year or early 1998. It is likely that government will have a majority stake in the initial stages but that may be replaced by private enterprises at a later stage. The Company will finance all kinds of infrastructure projects but those will be company's commercial decisions and not political decisions.

Financial experts feel that the Infrastructure Development Finance Corporation should have professional set up to develop clear policies on sectors it would intend to finance. In the absence of a professional machinery to run the organisation, the Infrastructure Development Finance Corporation will also become another public-sector-like organisation which will be unable to take quick decisions and innovate ways of financing infrastructure projects. The Companies Act will be amended to provide that companies investing in the infrastructure sector are able to issue shares that are redeemable after 20 years.

Government projects that US $ 500 billion are required in the next ten years to fund the major transportation, telecommunications and power projects. Whereas the Infrastructure Development Finance Corporation will only have Rs. 5,000 crore of seed capital, it could attract upto Rs. 50,000 crore from the national and international markets. But that is possible only if the organisation is managed by professionals and not politicians turned policy makers.

The ball started rolling on 8 August 1996 when the Industry Minister approved foreign direct investment proposals worth Rs. 755 crore. The Infrastructure Leasing and Finance Services Limited has been given approval by the Ministry of Industry to establish a direct investment fund worth US$100 million for investment in infrastructure projects.

Sea-Land Services Inc. of USA has been given permission to establish wholly owned subsidiary with an investment of US$32 million. This company will invest in infrastructure related projects including ports, railways and highways.

The DCM Estates and Infrastructure Limited is allowed to develop roads, bridges, residential premises with a Foreign Direct Investment of Rs. 6 crore. The process to attract investment in the infrastructure sector has just begun.

**Delhi Infrastructure Development and Finance Corporation**

Presented immediately after the Union Budget, the Delhi Budget has also laid a greater emphasis on the provision of basic infrastructure including power and public transport. Power and public transport has been identified as the thrust areas.

The Delhi Government has allocated Rs. 309.49 crore on public transport against the revised estimates of Rs. 159.06 crore in 1995-96. This is an increase of 95 per cent over the previous year's allocation on public transport. Out of Rs. 309.49 crore, Rs. 90 crore is exclusively set aside for the Mass Rapid Transit System. The Delhi Government will also spend Rs. 418.21 crore on power, the highest amount on any sector. At present this money is simply allocated for the Delhi Electric Supply Undertaking budget and details are not provided:

**TABLE 6**
**Delhi Budget 1996–97**

| *Item(s)* | *Rs. in crores* | *Per cent* |
|---|---|---|
| Power, (DESU) | 418.21 | 20.52 |
| Transport | 309.49 | 15.19 |
| Urban Development | 362.83 | 17.80 |

| *Item(s)* | *Rs. in crores* | *Per cent* |
|---|---|---|
| Water Supply and Sewerage | 291.25 | 14.29 |
| Education | 168.88 | 8.29 |
| Medical and Public Health | 142.76 | 7.00 |
| Agriculture and Rural Development | 92.64 | 4.55 |
| Housing | 33.12 | 1.63 |
| Nutrition | 21.95 | 1.08 |
| SC/ST/OBC Welfare | 19.31 | 0.95 |
| Social Welfare | 17.60 | 0.86 |
| Other works | 159.67 | 7.85 |
| Total | 2,038.01 | 100.00 |

While the Union Budget has outlined plans to establish the Infrastructure Development Finance Corporation at the Central level, the state of Delhi made no mention of how it could benefit from the Infrastructure Development Finance Corporation. Delhi Government also did not indicate any plans to establish an infrastructure corporation for the state of Delhi. A great opportunity has been missed. Now we will discuss what kind of infrastructure development and finance corporation is needed for the state of Delhi.

The Delhi Infrastructure Development and Finance Corporation will combine the positive aspects of the special purpose and multipurpose authorities. Certain issues can not be contained within an organisation. There are other issues such as environmental issues which "do not fit into any conceivable structure of special purpose authorities" (Stewart and Clark, 1996 : 13). They are called the "wicked issues".

***Services to be Provided by the DIDFC***

The Delhi Infrastructure Development and Finance Corporation (DIDFC) will provide more than one service. It will provide water, electricity, and manage sewerage, drainage and solid waste. Transportation will not be provided by this corporation. This is done with a view to avoid fragmentation. "Fragmentation occurs where there is a differentiation without appropriate means of integration : Fragmentation as a problem almost certainly would be increased by replacing appointed authorities with elected authorities, since it would increase their perceived distinctive legitimacy and thus make integration even more difficult" (Stewart and Clark, 1996 : 12). Unlike a special purpose authority, the Delhi Infrastructure Development Finance Corporation will be a multipurpose authority with a potential to deal with wide ranging problems and issues.

At present, in the name of decentralisation "many special purpose organisations are tied into a set of vertical relationships leading back into

Central Government. Policy, finance and accountability are set within a national framework. This can make it difficult to take a 'horizontal' cut at local level—necessary for integration—even where there is a willingness to try and do so. Fragmentation is reinforced" (Stewart and Clark, 1996 : 12).

### *Directly Elected and Multipurpose Organisation*

This organisation will be a directly elected Corporation (Fig. 2). It will provide single window services and advice. For example, billing for water and electricity will be issued and collected by the same authority. This will further reduce chances of duplication and wastage of resources. Most importantly due to ever shrinking army of the demotivated staff, the Corporation will begin to enjoy some savings.

### *Self-financing*

The Delhi Infrastructure Development and Finance Corporation will be a self-financing company. However, it will be provided with an initial government equity of Rs. 1,000.00 at 1995-96 prices. It will be able to raise its resources through taxes and loans from the marketplace.

### *Lean Organisation of Managers*

All the technical departments will be overseen by the directly elected committees of ward councillors but without undue interference in the professional working of the Corporation. In order to achieve this, the statute will be put in place before the Corporation is established. Managers led Corporation will be lean and thin organisation.

### *Inputs from the Private Sector*

Private sector inputs will be allowed in many forms. Firstly, parts of the service/s may be privatised or jointly provided. Secondly, the private sector managers will be encouraged actively to work for the Corporation on short contract periods in order to introduce the competitive culture in the organisation.

### Market Pricing

Marketing pricing mechanisms (Foster and Plowden, 1996) will be adopted to better serve the people of Delhi. Therefore, like Mitlin, Sallerthwaite and Stephens (1996 : 3), this author does not believe that "all can join the market and those who cannot join the market cannot be helped effectively by intervention from either the state or from development assistance agenciese". (Mitlin, Sallerthwaite and Stephens, 1996 : 3). But wherever subsidies are necessary these will be provided directly and transparently.

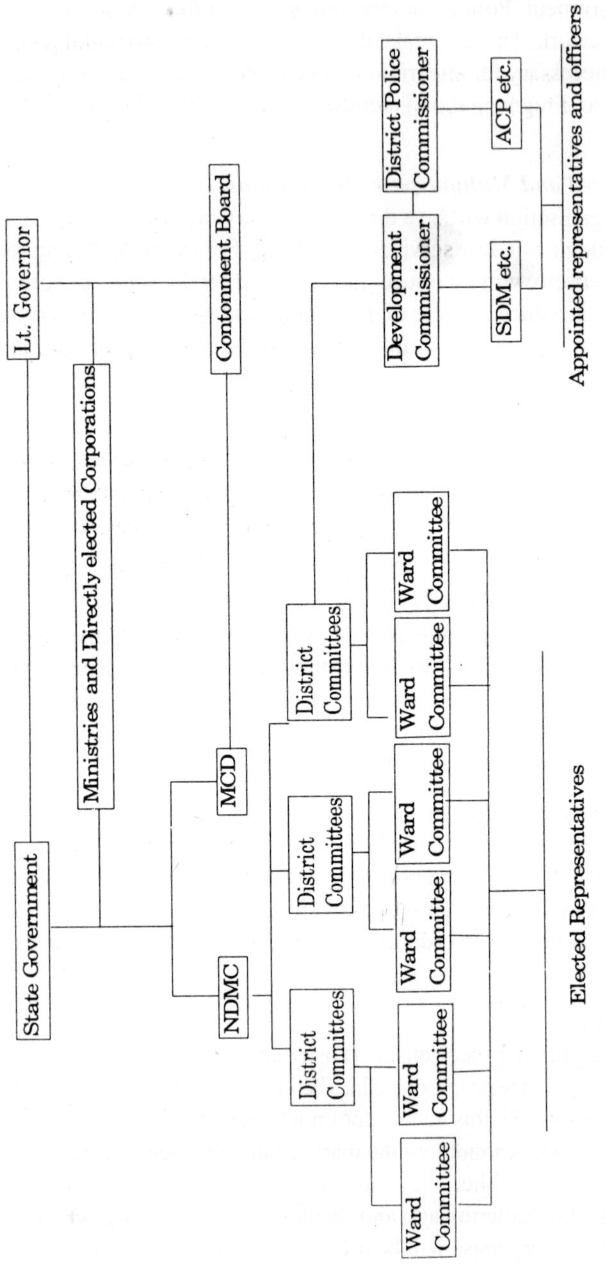


**Fig. 2. Proposed Organisational Structure of Government of Delhi.**

**Separating Purchasing Public Services from Production**

At present, there is no clear demarcation between purchasing and production of public services. It is proposed that the Delhi Infrastructure Development and Finance Corporation will not produce any of the services but organise their provision. Services will be provided by the private sector through the system of franchises for a stipulated period of time. As far as possible large providers, barring electricity and water, will be discouraged and provision will be decentralised. Administration and people's involvement will be geared towards controlling outputs rather than inputs.

***Whose Interests***

The Corporation will clearly state its objectives. One of the major objectives of the Corporation will be to serve the consumers rather than bureaucrats, political or producer interests. In practice, this would mean that this organisation will not act as factory for the provision of employment to all and sundry but a corporation created for the provision of services to the citizens.

## REFERENCES


Advisory Commission on Intergovernmental Relations (1988): *Metropolitan Organisation : the St. Louis case,* ACIR, Washington D.C.

Davoudi, S. (1995): *Dilemmas of Urban Governance,* in Healey, P. etal (eds.) 'Managing Cities, The New Urban Context', John Wiley and Sons, West Sussex.

Fogelson, R. (1967): *Fragmented Metropolis, Los Angeles,* Harvard University Press, Cambridge.

Foster, C.D. and Plowden, F.J. (1996): *The State Under Stress, Can the Hollow State be Good Government?*, Open University Press, Buckingham, Philadelphia.

Government of the National Capital Territory of Delhi (1997): Government of Delhi at your Doorsteps, *The Times of India,* Vol. CLIX, No. 38, p. 8.

Government of India (1991): *The Constitution (Sixty Ninth Amendment) Act 1991,* Government of India, New Delhi.

Goyal, P. (1993): *Delhi's March Towards Statehood,* UBSPD, New Delhi.

Held, D. (1996): *Models of Democracy,* Polity Press, Oxford.

King A.D. (1976): *Colonial Urban Development, Culture, social power and environment,* Routledge and Kegan Paul, London.

Kumar, A. (1996a): Does the Master Plan for Delhi has a Coherent Policy Framework?, Urban India, Forthcoming.

Kumar, A. (1996b): *Unified Metropolitan Transport Authority for Delhi,* in Vajpeyi, S.C. and Verma, S.P. (eds.) 'National Capital Territory of Delhi, a study on landmarks in state public administration since independence', IIPA, New Delhi.

Mc Carney, P.L. (ed.) (1996): *Cities and Governance : New Directions in Latin America,* Asia and Africa, Centre for Urban and Communities Studies, University of Tronto, Tronto.

Mitlin, D., Sallerthwaite, D, and Stephens, C. (1996): *Introduction, Environment and Urbanisation,* Vol. 8, No. 2, pp. 3-7.

Stewart, J. and Clark, M. (1996): Elected special-purpose Authorities : The cases considered, *Local Government Studies,* Vol. 22, No. 1, pp. 1-18.

Yates, D. (1977): *The Ungovernable City, the politics of Urban problems and policy making,* the MIT Press, Cambridge.

# 9

# Urban Administration in Karnataka: Problem Areas

*—S.A. Javeed*

If a question is asked to any person, whether you like to reside in a city or village and are you satisfied with the civic facilities in the city? The general answer would be they prefer to stay in a city. As for the second part of the question, the response would be they are not satisfied with the civic amenities. The nature of these two answers poses another question, why is it so? In fact, the whole of the paper deals with this.

When Karnataka emerged as a unified state after the linguistic reorganisations of states in 1956, there was no uniformity in the rules and regulations governing the urban government. The reorganised state of Mysore, incorporated not only the areas of former Mysore state, but also the entire area of Coorg and some areas from the states of Bombay, Madras presidencies and the Nizam's state of Hyderabad. To bring in a uniform type of urban government throughout the state of Karnataka, two new Acts were enacted by the Karnataka State Legislature:

(a) The Mysore Municipalities Act of 1964, and

(b) The Karnataka Municipal Corporations Act of 1976.

These Acts though supposed to be very systematic and elaborate, the urban governments were suffering from many problems like frequent supersession of the urban governments by the State Government, financial problems, structural defects, etc. Realising the gravity of these problems, three regional *sammelans* were organised at Bangalore, Cuttack and Delhi during June, 1989, by the Government of India when late Mr. Rajiv Gandhi was the Prime Minister of India.

These *Sammelans* were preceded by a Seminar of Municipal Officers from all over the country held in the first week of June, 1989 in Delhi. In all, 4500 delegates from all parts of the country attended these deliberations. Discussions were also held with the Chief Secretaries in a conference held on 27th June 1989 and with Ministers for Local Self-Government at a conference held on 30th June, 1989, both at Delhi. A conference of Chief Ministers was held on 7th July, 1989, where the issues relating to strengthening and proper functioning of urban local government were discussed. These issues were also discussed in two meetings of the Consultative Committee of Parliament relating to the Ministry of Urban Development. On the basis of these wide-ranging consultations, the Union Government introduced the Constitution (65th Amendment) Bill in Parliament in August, 1989. Unfortunately, the Bill was defeated in the Rajya Sabha. But when the Congress Government took charge once again in 1991 it was reintroduced and finally got the assent of the President on 20th April, 1993. It was notified in the Gazette of 20th April 1993 as the Constitution (74th Amendment) Act, 1992.

This amendment introduces a new part viz., Part-IX A, in the Constitution. This part deals with the issues relating to urban government. The provisions in this part can be grouped under the following heads:

(a) Structure and Composition of Municipalities.
(b) Reservation of seats.
(c) Elections to Municipalities.
(d) Powers and functions of Municipalities.
(e) Finances of Municipalities.
(f) Planning at the District and Metropolitan level.
(g) Miscellaneous provisions.[1]

In pursuance of the Amendment, the State Government has amended its Municipal Corporations Act of 1976. Despite the new changes that have been included in the Act, the city governments face certain administrative problems which need to be highlighted. Legally and formally, the corporation consists of three co-ordinate authorities viz., the Corporation itself, the standing committees and the Commissioner. The statutory and non-statutory relations obtaining between these authorities and the problems emanating out of it are to be described separately. In this paper the focus is on the problems arising from the overall defective framework of the city government. The administrative difficulties that follow from the existing defective structure will also be discussed. In executing most of the functions entrusted to the corporations like planning, drainage and sewerage, water supply, conservancy and garbage disposal, road maintenance, street lighting, there are many problems which demand attention.

"Municipal Government, may local goverment, has to be looked at as a whole and any effort to solve particular problem in a piece-meal fashion may not be helpful in putting the entire system on a sound footing. For instance, financial problems cannot be considered in isolation; functions have to be examined along with them. Again, functions are closely related to the problems of areas or territorial limits of the municipal authorities. Personnel problems and civic functions have to be considered together. All these would determine the scale of the municipal organisation in the light of which the internal management problems have to be discussed. It is no use discussing management problems, unless the functions to be managed are really important and challenging. Vital questions about functions and areas cannot be answered by examining the role of the municipal authorities only. Local government has to be considered as a whole, forgetting for the moment the traditional distinction between rural and urban local government. Special authorities such as improvement trusts, development authorities, housing boards, water and sanitation authorities, transport authorities and the like and even some of the State Government Departments have been operating at the local level. There are intimate linkages between their functions and those entrusted to the municipal authorities so much so that the operation of one virtually affects the other".[2] All said and done, it appears, that the very nature of municipal functions demand co-ordinated action, but, that is the element which is absent at present.

The statute divides the functions of the corporation into two categories, obligatory and discretionary. As for the former category is concerned, it is compulsory on the part of the corporation to carry it out. Section 58 of the Act specifies the obligatory functions as follows: "It shall be incumbent on the corporation to make reasonable and adequate provision by any means or measures which it is lawfully competent to use or to take, for each of the following matters". The discretionary functions can be carried at the will of the corporation.

There has been a hue and cry from all quarters that the migration of the rural folk into the city is creating many problems for the administration of the city. Prof. D.M. Nanjundappa, while delivering a lecture said that the urban citizens talk about preserving decent living conditions in urban areas which are being affected by the exodus of the rural population, mostly the poor, that come in search of shelter and employment to urban areas. Then he argued that the solution to the problems of cities and urban areas lay outside the cities and urban centres. In other words, if the rural areas and hinterlands are developed, the problem of migration to city can be checked.[3] Similar was the report of the Rural-Urban Relationship

Committee in India,[4] and the Redeliffe-Maud Commission in England. In fact, the Redeliffe-Maud Commission way back in 1969, observed that "the failure to recognise the interdependence of town and country is "the most fatal defect" in the structure of English local government".[5] On the basis of the foregone discussions it can be suggested that the best method of reducing the heavy migration from the rural areas to the cities, is to improve and develop the rural areas on a priority footing and develop them at a par with the urban areas.

Another great problem which is baffling the city administration is lack of co-ordination between the various authorities responsible for the administration of the city, directly or indirectly. The concept of co-ordination as one of the means of good management or administration has been discussed, and it is not regarded as the key function of the administrative process. Co-ordination is the syncronisation of efforts, in a given structure or set-up to achieve common objectives. To ensure harmonious and smooth working of an enterprise with a number of divisions, departments or units, the activities in all the areas should pull together, unified and blended so as to give them a commonness of purpose. Co-ordination implies the checking of all splintering efforts that may destroy the unity of action through purpose working.[6]

As living conditions grow more complex due to new technology and needs, there is tendency to break up what were simple activities into smaller fields of specialization for expert handling. At the same time the best results can be achieved only when there is a co-ordinated attack on the whole problem. Co-ordination becomes necessary only when the principle of specialization increases in any enterprise in its operations. This is because the total activities are divided into several units and sub-units on the basis of functional specialization or technical specialization. The greater the number of units and sub-units, the more difficult becomes the task of securing co-ordination of activities. Since very unit or department tends to concentrate its attention on activities and objectives of its own department, it may by-pass the other departments in realising its objectives. In view of the rapidly changing nature of the city, with its highly complex social and economic structures, the work of providing civic amenities has also assumed great and complex dimensions. This increased volume of responsibility has led inevitably to an expansion of the organisation as well as a division of labour between specialized departments and sections within them. This has led to a greater need for co-ordination.

It is the distrust of local government on the part of the State

Government, which has brought about a gradual proliferation of competitive special authorities in our local areas. Prof. Mohit Bhattacharya argues, that administrative fragmentation poses serious problems for effective co-ordination. But its effects on the citizens are far more harmful. He further observes that "it is small wonder that people in general have little attachment to weak municipal government... citizens awareness of civic problems cannot be generated in a vacuum. It is through available opportunities that consciousness grows".[7] Many other scholars in the field are of the same opinion.[8] Discussing this aspect at a seminar, held in 1974, Dr. C.S. Chandrashekara, observed that "this is a way in which the complete erosion of the local body's role has been successfully accomplished a process which started during the British rule. In this process the concept of local government at the local level has ceased to exist while this may not be serious in the case of function like law and order, revenue, judiciary, and such other fields, so far as planning and development is concerned, it is bound to be disasterous".[9] Important local functions such as housing, slum clearance/improvement, planning and development, electricity, water supply and sewerage have been entrusted to the special authorities or retained by the state government departments. Table 1 clearly illustrates the extent of fragmentation of authority at City government level. Apart from a general weakening of local government, it has resulted in an unco-ordinated administrativeness. Each function has been allowed to be administered in an insular fashion without regard for its repercussion on the allied services. One can imagine the amount of confusion in a situation where 'housing' is in general entrusted to the housing board, water supply and sewerage to Karnataka Urban Water Supply and Sewerage Board, Electricity to Karnataka Electricity Board, etc. In this case, the administration of the group of functions is not unified but fragmented. The improvement trusts and development authorities are supposed to undertake local development functions, while the municipal authorities, are mere maintenance agencies. When specific functions are assigned to special authorities, the pattern of different civic services is distorted. Thus, house construction may go on fast, but water supply, sewerage and electricity facilities may lag behind. For example, in the housing colony at Marakada, construction work by Karnataka Housing Board was over. Most of the allottees got into the houses. Later for months together, basic facilities like water supply, street lights and sewerage were not provided.[10] Special authorities and the State Government Departments have been operating at the local level. There are intimate linkages between their functions and those entrusted to the municipal authorities, so much so that the operation of one virtually affects the other. Especially, when we talk of planned areal development, the congeries of authorities should be made to move in concert.

In fact, in this situation, marked by discordant administration the overall needs of the local area are lost sight of, as there is no single authorities to look after the totality of the civic services of the local community. Arbitrary allotment of administrative responsibilities has tended to elevate functional administration above comprehensive area administration, and in consequence the local area has so many authorities but no single all-embracing local government. The following table illustrates the argument.

**TABLE 1**
**Administering Authorities for Local Services**

| | | | |
|---|---|---|---|
| 1. | Water Supply | Local government* | Special authority |
| 2. | Drainage and Sewage | Local government* | Special authority |
| 3. | Conservancy and garbage disposal | Local government | — |
| 4. | Public Works, Roads bridges, etc. | Local government | State government<br>Special Authority |
| 5. | Public health (inoculation, vaccination), prevention of food adulteration, burning ghats, etc. | Local government | — |
| 6. | Housing | — | Special authority |
| 7. | Slum clearance and improvement | Local government | Special authority |
| 8. | Parks and recreations | Local government | Special authority |
| 9. | Street lighting | Local government* | Special authority |
| 10. | Planning and development | Local government* | Special authority<br>State government |
| 11. | Hospitals | Local government* | State government |
| 12. | Electricity | — | Special authority |
| 13. | Regulatory activities, building regulations, licensing, etc. | Local government | State government. |

*This indicates divided responsibility between local government and special authority. To a large extent, the special authority administration.

The lack of a sense of a unified local government tends to alienate the citizens to some extent. But the alienated citizen is more a direct result of municipal administrative inefficiency. City administration works, no doubt, within many known constraints. Yet, the average citizen can be won ever through the efficient delivery of essential civic services. A good road, a good park, adequate water supply, a timely sanction of building plans, all these are the direct routes to the citizen's heart. But the fragmentation of administration of civic services and lack of co-ordination amongst the fragmented bodies stand as a hurdle in the effective execution of civic services. Instead of keeping a range of allied civic services in the hands of a single, compendious municipal government, the general tendency is to create a number of competitive local authorities, mostly without any popular base, each having control over a specific function. From the planning and administrative point of view, fragmentation gives rise to the serious problem of red-tapism. The effects of which on the citizens' mind are alienating. The fragmentation of local administration often leads to the weakening of popularly elected municipal institutions and inefficient execution of the civic functions. The above said argument can be proved with a few factual examples. For instance, if one goes round any city, one would find the road-cuts deeply here and there. This can be due to a mismanagement of roads. The situation arises only because of the absence of co-ordination between the Engineering department and the Water Supply department. The tearing up of a recently constructed road in order to lay water mains which could conveniently have been put into position before the road was finally asphalted, is a case in point. This unnecessary damage to the roads could have been avoided had the two departments acted in unison. In instances like these the city government suffers avoidable loss of time, energy and finance.

Another problem arising in the administration of the city because of poor co-ordination in the widening of narrow streets. The corporation most of the time, because of increase in human and vehicular traffic, takes up the programme of widening the narrow streets. As the roads would be widened, the electric poles come in the middle of the widened road. The corporation writes to the Karnataka Electricity Board to replace the poles to the edge of the road. In many cases till today the poles have not been disturbed. These poles have become hazardous for the traffic, certain times resulting in fatal and non-fatal accidents. Once again this is because of non-co-ordination between the corporation and the Karnataka Electricity Board.

Another issue is that of regulating vehicular traffic. The concerned authority to regulate traffic is the city's traffic police. On some roads, humps or speed breakers are erected. Erection of caution boards and painting of humps and roads with the help of white paint to direct the traffic is to be done by the city's traffic police. But the material involved like, the sign boards, white/yellow paint, etc., has to be supplied by the corporation. In most of the cities the humps carry neither the caution boards nor are they painted.

Blaming each other for this management has become a fashion. For example, when this researcher met the circle Inspector of Mangalore Traffic Police and interviewed him in this regard he said "the erection of sign boards at appropriate places, making on the roads is that work of the traffic police, but the materials are to be supplied by the corporation. I requested the corporation to arrange for the supply. I wrote to them for 1,605 litres of white paint in the first round and 1,000 litres once in every 3 months. But the corporation made available only 165 litres, i.e., only 10 per cent of what was required. So many accidents take place in the city due to this poor maintenance of roads. The blame has been shifted to the police. I suggest, it is better that we are linked to the corporation or we be given independent powers to purchase the material and execute the work". Whoever may be blamed, the ultimate sufferer are the citizens. Once again this is due to the absence of co-ordination between the agencies entrusted with parts of a single task.

Another issue which needs to be highlighted is the unevenness of the surface of the roads. The roads are maintained by the corporation, whereas the underground sewers cutting across the roads in the city are maintained by the Karnataka Urban Water Supply and Sewerage Board. At every intermittent distance an opening is constructed in the sewerage system called as "manholes". These manholes are constructed of cement and concrete and covered by an iron plate. The corporation while reasphalting the roads leaves such manholes untouched which leads to the formation of a pathole. Hence unevenness appears in the level of the road, posing a hurdle to the traffic. In certain spots the difference between the manhole and the road ranges between 6"-8".

Relatedly, in certain places the manholes are raised by the Board. These projected manholes are equally dangerous to the traffic. In other places, the manholes are covered with asphalt in the process of re-asphalting the roads, and the metal cover gets buried. Later on, in times of necessity, the Karnataka Urban Water Supply and Sewerage Board often faces trouble in locating the manholes. In the process of searching they tear up the surface of the roads and the damage persists till the time of remetalling the road once again, which might take two, three or even four years. When some junior engineers working in Karnataka Urban Water Supply and Sewerage Board were interviewed, they admitted, "if the corporation undertakes the road metalling work no information is given to the board". On the other hand, the Junior Engineers of the Engineering Section in the corporation blamed the Karnataka Urban Water Supply and Sewerage Board officials. This problem is only because of no interlink between the two departments. Though the execution of their function demands it.

Another problem in the administration of the city because of poor coordination between these two departments is, the maintenance and conservance of sewerage outflow. In the city there are two types of drainage: Underground Drainage System (UDS) and Open Drainage System (ODS). Whereas the former is maintained by the Karnataka Urban Water Supply and Sewerage Board, the latter is maintained by the corporation. Though the Karnataka Urban Water Supply and Sewerage Board maintains the Under Ground Drainage System, the cost of maintenance is met by the corporation. But, still the Underground Drainage System is found overflowing at certain areas, resulting in stagnation of sewage water. This has become hazardous to the health of the people residing in those areas. The stagnant sewerage water is the best breeding ground for a specie of mosquito called as 'Anopheles'. The bite from these mosquitoes gives rise to the disease of 'Micro Filaria'.

The corporation accuses the Board for the poor maintenance of the sewars, which is the cause for the spread of the disease. The Board, on its part, accuses the corporation for paying meagre sums of money for the maintenance of the Underground Drainage.

Another cause for the overflowing of the water is that the sewage water is collected in wet wells. Taking into consideration the topography of the areas, the city is divided into drainage districts. The sewage from each district is collected in the wet wells. From there it is pumped to the treatment plants. For pumping the sewage water electric pumps are installed. Intermittent interruption and low voltage of electricity supply during the peak hours of sewage water flow lead to accumulation of sewage water in the wells resulting in an overflow of the sewers.

Moreover, the Underground Drainage system is designed by considering the existing population, total water supply, expected sewerage flow, etc. Due to several reasons (few of them have been explained earlier) there has been a consistent increase in the city population. This leads to mismatch between the water supply, sewerage outflow, and the designed sewerage system. As a result, the system gets overloaded and functions improperly, the sufferers being the tax paying city dwellers.

This is also the case with street lighting. It is the corporation which has to maintain the street lights. The Act specifies that "it shall be incumbent on the corporation to make reasonable and adequate provision by any means or measures which it is lawfully competent to use or to take, the lighting of public streets, municipal markets and places of resort vested in the corporation". If any damaged or worn out light is to be replaced then it is the job of the corporation to supply the material, but, replacing it is the job of Karnataka Electricity Board. Many a time this has led to delay causing inconvenience to the public.

While interviewed, citizens answered negatively the question whether they had satisfaction in respect of street lighting. In many cases people write letters to the corporator of the Ward about this. Corporators in turn take it to the notice of the Electrical Section Officer. The officer has to see whether ready stock is available. If available, the Karnataka Electricity Board linemen are supposed to replace it. Such a simple job has become unnecessarily a complex one. In certain cases it takes months for replacement.

Another problem in the administration of the city government is the undue interference of the state government in relaxing the building bye-laws. According to the building bye-laws framed by the corporation, a new building or any housing or commercial construction, while being constructed, should leave a space called as the set back space, from the main road on its front or any side facing the road. This set-back space varies from area to area. Whatever be it, violation of this bye-law by constructors empowers the corporation to withhold the building licence and demolish the structure constructed over the set-back space. In many cases the corporation has withdrawn the building licence and issued demolition notice. The violators of the law appeal to the state government which is, of course, a superior authority to the corporation. To protect the interest of the law-violators and to pose themselves as protectors of the common people, the state government issues directions to the corporation. The directions are often in the form to relax the building bye-laws for those who have already commenced the construction work. Since the corporation is the creation of the state government and being subordinate to it, it has to accept the directions. As a result, the specified set-back space is reduced for example, from 20 feet to 10 feet or even 8 feet in certain cases. This results in narrow streets, narrow footpaths and thus congested traffic. There are many cases of this type.

No organisation can produce good results unless it is manned by trained and competent personnel. One of the main weaknesses of the civic body is the absence of a well-organised and effective system of qualified personnel. The key qualities of an effective personnel are competence, impartiality, contentment, integrity and devotion to duty. Though a majority of the personnel lack these ingredients, certain amount of competence, integrity and devotion to duty can be injected by motivating the personnel.

It has been assumed that the employees are motivated to perform better, if a system of rewards and penalties is directly linked to effective job performance. Motivation can be invoked by externally mediated rewards and penalties based on actual work performance. Employees do a job better if they have open promotional opportunities and are emotionally committed to the job. Freedom to work in the department one wishes and making a job challenging are likely to encourage the personnel to dedicate themselves to the job.

There is hardly any study on motivation among municipal personnel in Karnataka. The urban society depends almost exclusively on the municipal bureaucracy for essential civic amenities. It is, at the level of local government that the citizens can see government in actual operation. The way the citizens perceive the working of local government might be an important factor in conditioning their views about government in a much more general sense. From this angle of vision, motivation of municipal employees in their jobs is crucial not only for municipal administration but also for the image of government as a whole.

Of course, there are other factors which are responsible for low attachment to the work. One such is the system of deputation. For most of the posts in the corporation, the state government appoints the officers. As a matter of fact, most of the posts are occupied by officials who are deputed from other offices of the state. In many pamphlets brought and circulated by the municipal employees associations they have demanded the State Government to stop the practice of deputation, and they have alleged that it has intensified. As a consequence, the benefits of promotion which should have accrued to corporation employees have been denied to them. Consequently, the officials working in such a system find their position to be relatively stagnant in the official hierarchy. When interviewed, most of the officials admitted that if they got an opportunity to get into other services, State or Central, they would readily go. Efficient functioning of these officials would appear to be utopian with the existing service conditions.

It has been argued that "the system of deputation of top level municipal officials from state government to municipal bodies has posed several problems. It has invited charges that deputed personnel are birds of passage and hence do not work with full sense of involvement, that civic bodies are unable to elicit total compliance from them, the norms of municipal autonomy are often transgressed by this practice; deputed functionaries lack orientation necessary to work in the politico-administrative context peculiar to local bodies; and that the promotional prospects of lower level employees are marred on account of top level positions not being open to them and consequently posing the problem of low motivation for continuous good work."[11]

Even in regard to the training of the corporation employees, the system of deputation stands as a hurdle. One scholar has opined that preference may also be given to the opinion of the officials permanently appointed in the corporation who are dead against the practice of deputation of officials from other departments of the State Government to the corporation. Here it is useful to examine in brief the impact of the conditions in the urban government on training. Firstly, it should be stated that training in India, especially at municipal level, is still in a speculative stage. Secondly, the nomination of deputed employees for the training course does not find favour among municipal bodies. These have to be paid for by the municipal bodies and their transferability stands as a hurdle. It is argued that a given municipal body which pays the training bill may not get the benefit of the trained officer.[12]

Thus, to conclude, it is felt that all these problems and factors have reduced the efficient functioning of the system. There are ways and means by which this can be rectified. It is necessary to examine scientifically the municipal work situation and the mind of the executing authority. Only then it would be possible for us to diagnose more precisely the causes of inefficient functioning of the system. Accordingly, steps could be taken to find solutions to the problems. The nature of the problems faced by the urban local bodies is such that they call for special expertise. In this context, the training and orientation of personnel for efficient fulfilment of the duties is very essential. It is, therefore, only proper that training courses for such personnel should be suitably structured to expose them sharply to problems of urban administration and development planning, which is another crucial problem, can also be managed better. Physical planning, confined as it is now to the narrow legal limits of the city, has almost universally failed to check the urban growth at the periphery of the city, where its legal tools cannot be applied. Unless the city and its direct influence area are planned as one unit, planning becomes a futile exercise. The ability of the municipal government to solve these problems with the existing structure and system appears to be now limited. But we have also seen that there are hopeful possibilities. But their realization depends upon a political will prepared to act innovative imaginatively but without loosing the grip on the ground realities. For every problem there is a solution, provided, an attempt is made to solve them.

## REFERENCES


1. *Power to the People, the Nagarpalika Act,* Booklet Published by Ministry of Urban Development, Government of India, New Delhi, 1993.
2. Mohit Bhattacharya: "Re-organisation of Municipal Government", *Nagarlok,* Vol. II, No. 4, I.I.P.A., New Delhi, 1970, p. 6.
3. Lecture by Prof. D.M. Nanjundappa: Former Vice-Chancellor, Bangalore University on 19-10-1987 as a part of Sri A.B. Shetty Memorial Endowment Lecture, Mangalore.
4. Rural Urban Relationship Committee, Ministry of Health and Family Planning, Government of India, 1966.
5. Cited by Mohit Bhattacharya, *op. cit.,* p. 6.
6. Satya Sahan, Chatterjee: *An Introduction of Management: Its Principles and Techniques.* The World Press, Pvt. Ltd., Calcutta, 1980, p. 28.
7. Mohit Bhattacharya: *Civic Consciousness and Citizens Participation".* New Delhi, 1979, s. 11-12.
8. (a) K.S.R.N. Sharma: "Financing of Urban Service, Municipal Government Vs. Specialist agency", *Nagarlok,* Vol. XVII No. 3 I.I.P.A., New Delhi, 1985, p. 30.
   (b) William A. Robson and D.E. Regan(ed), *Great Cities of the World,* Vol. 1, George Allen and Unwin Ltd., London, 1972, p. 9.
   (c) "Municipal Governments in India, Problems and Prospects", Article by Hoshiar Singh in *Public Administration in India,* Emerging Trends ed. by Kaushik, S.L. and Pradeep Sahni, Kitab Mahal, Allahabad, 1983, p. 185.
   (d) "Challenges to Urban Government in India" Article by J.P. Gupta in, *Ibid.,* pp. 181-82.
9. C.S. Chandrashekhara: "Urban Planning and Development Authorities, Some basic issues", papers and proceedings of the seminar conducted by I.I.P.A. New Delhi, 1974.
10. Similar is the case of Housing Board Colony at Bondel. Mayor Sadashiva Bhandary had promised to immediately provide street lights to the residents of the colony who were deprived of civic amenities. Mr. Bhandary, who visited the colony said the corporation would hold discussion with the housing board commissioner for handing over the colony to the corporation. After this formality was done, more civic amenities could be provided to it. Source, *Deccan Herald* dated 31-7-1984.
11. G. Sreenivas and Veerashekarappa: "Urban Local Government in Karnataka", *Quarterly Journal of Self-Government Institute,* Vol. LV, No. 1, Bombay, 1984, p. 19.
12. Y. Raghaviah: "Training Municipal Administrators: Some Problems and Prospects", *Nagarlok,* Vol. VI, No. 4, 1974.

# 10

# The Changing Profile of the Urban Local Government in Kerala

*—P. Surendran*

Kerala, the southern most state of India, was formed on the basis of the Reorganisation Act of 1956 by unifying the former princely state of Travancore-Cochin and Malabar region of the erstwhile Madras state on 1st November 1956. Prior to it, the princely states of Travancore and Cochin were unified under a single government on 1st July 1949. The present Kerala State is a unification of three distinct administrative units on the basis of language-Malayalam.

The total population of the state, as per 1991 census, was 290.99 lakhs. Of this, the rural population was 214.18 lakhs and urban population 76.80 lakhs. The proportion of urban population had increased from 13.48 per cent in 1951 to 26.39 in 1991 and it was due to the re-classification of the villages as cities. During the decade 1981-91, as many as one hundred eleven new settlements were re-classified as urban settlements.

The Nagarpalika institutions are 58 in number in the state comprising three corporations and 55 municipalities and about 44 lakhs of population is residing in these areas.

The corporations, numbering three namely, Thiruvananthapuram, the Capital City of Kerala, Cochin and Kozhikode, vary greatly in geographical conditions viz. size, population, resources and other characteristics. They share 12.50 per cent, 13.47 per cent and 10.02 per cent of Nagarpalika population respectively. The combined share of Corporations is 36 per cent of Nagarpalika population. The Municipalities, 55 in number, cater 64 per cent of the Nagarpalika population spread over 14 districts of the state. The number of municipal institutions and the proportion of population thereunder is shown in Table 1.

**TABLE 1**
**District-wise Distribution of Nagarpalika Institutions and Population**

| *Sl. No.* | *Name of District* | *No. of Corporations* | *No. of Municipalities* | *Percentage of Nagarpalika Population* |
|---|---|---|---|---|
| 1. | Thiruvananthapuram | 1 | 4 | 16.13 |
| 2. | Kollam | — | 3 | 5.33 |
| 3. | Pathanamthitta | — | 3 | 2.80 |
| 4. | Alappuzha | — | 5 | 8.09 |
| 5. | Kottayam | — | 4 | 3.80 |
| 6. | Idukki | — | 1 | 0.97 |
| 7. | Ernakulam | 1 | 8 | 20.06 |
| 8. | Trichur | — | 7 | 6.11 |
| 9. | Palakkad | — | 4 | 5.69 |
| 10. | Malappuram | — | 5 | 6.19 |
| 11. | Kozhikode | 1 | 2 | 13.07 |
| 12. | Wayanad | — | 1 | 0.55 |
| 13. | Kannur | — | 6 | 8.65 |
| 14. | Kasaragod | — | 2 | 2.56 |
| | | 3 | 55 | 100.00 |

*Source:* Power to People: State Planning Board 1997.

## Settlement Pattern

The settlement pattern of the state is highly different from the rest of the country. In Kerala, urban living is only an extension of the rural inhabitation. There is a deep rooted rural-urban continuum and hence it is not easy to demarcate the social boundaries of the urban living from the rural. In addition to the permanent population, the Nagarpalikas entertain thousands of day birds like students, patients, traders and businessmen, employees who come over to cities in the dawn and return to their rural shelter at dusk.

The three Corporations of the state have a historical background and they were the seats of the erstwhile *Rajahs.* Thiruvananthapuram was the capital of the *Rajahs* of Travancore, Cochin related to the *Rajahs* of Cochin and Kozhikode was the palace city of the Zamorin. The post-independence period witnessed a geographical growth of these corporations due to the absorption of surrounding sub-urban areas in their fold.

**Nagarpalika Acts**

The local self-government institutions namely, Panchayat Raj, Municipalities and Corporations existed since 1959. They were endowed with such powers and authority as may be necessary to enable to function as units of self-government. The core lacuna of these local government units was the non-constitutional validity because they were constituted as per the Directive Principles of State Policy of Constitution of India. Later, it was found that the constitutional validity was an urgent requirement of these institutions to perform their functions and obligations according to the felt needs of the people. The Union Government made the 73rd Amendment to the Constitution on 24th April 1993 to organize Panchayat Raj institutions, as a fulfledged constitutional body of local self-government. It was followed by another amendment Act, the Constitution (Seventy four) Amendment Act to extend the same to organize Nagarpalika institutions namely, municipalities and corporations. In pursuance to the Central Acts, Kerala State Legislative Assembly enacted the Kerala Panchayat Raj Act, 1994 and the Nagarpalika Act, 1994 in 1994. These State Acts were amended in 1995 to endow some more powers and authority to them. These Acts replaced the existing Acts with regard to the Panchayat Rajs, Municipalities and Corporations and District Councils in the state.

**The Distinguishing Features**

The new Acts incorporate a number of distinguishing features over the earlier Acts. Some of them are:

1. It rendered Constitutional status to the three tier Panchayat Raj and Nagarpalika institutions.
2. It installed District Panchayat in the place of the District Council which shifted the dominance of urban governance over rural.
3. It reserved one-third of the total number of seats in every Nagarpalikas for women and such seats may be allotted by rotation to different constituencies.
4. It reserved the same proportion of the total number of seats to Scheduled Castes and Scheduled Tribes in proportion to their population and such seats may be rotated to different wards in a Municipality or Corporation.
5. It reserved not less than one-third of the total number of the chairpersons in Nagarpalikas for women and such office may be rotated to different constituencies of Nagarpalikas.

6. It also reserved for the same proportion to the total number of offices of chairpersons to SC/ST in proportion to their population in the state.
7. It aims to constitute a Finance Commission exclusively for Panchayat Raj and Nagarpalika institutions to review their financial position and for assignment of funds.

**Structure of Urban Local Government**

Kerala Panchayat Raj Act envisaged a three tier structure namely Gram Panchayat, Block Panchayat and District Panchayat institutions but Nagarpalika Acts visualised a single tier system for Nagar Palikas. There is a clear cut demaration of powers, authority and finance among the Panchayat Raj institutions. In a strict observation, Nagarpalikas are designed at par with Gram Panchayats and at the same time, the powers, authority and finances transferred for both Block Panchayats and District Panchayats are also entrusted to them.

The Ward Sabha, the lowest unit of Nagar Palika is also framed as equivalent to Gram Sabha; but in the constitution they are different. Gram Sabha constitutes the entire voters of the Panchayat ward: but the 'Ward Sabha' is a nominated body with the elected member as its convener. An exception noted here is that the Special Ward Sabha may be summoned with the entire voters of the concerned ward to discuss some particular issues.

**Devolution of Powers and Authority**

Kerala Nagarpalika Act aims to transfer 29 Departments of the State administration to urban local self-government. The wide range of powers are: (1) Planning, (2) Land use, (3) Socio-economic development, (4) Roads and bridges, (5) Water supply, (6) Public health, (7) Fire force, (8) Social forestry and environmental protection, (9) Social welfare including SC/ST, (10) Slum improvement, (11) Poverty eradication, (12) Parks and other public utilities, (13) Culture and education, (14) Cremation ground, (15) Cattle pound, (16) Registration of birth and deaths, (17) Public utility services, (18) Cattle slaughter houses, (19) Agriculture, (20) Animal Protection and milk development, (21) Minor irrigation, (22) Fisheries, (23) Small Scale industries, (24) Housing, (25) Electricity and non-conservative energy, (26) Public distribution system, (27) Labour, (28) Co-operation and (29) General.

The institutions of Panchayat Raj and Nagar Palika take its roots from the traditional Panchayat system that existed in the distant past. The traditional Panchayat which executed its powers and authority was bound to the regulations, customs, norms and taboos existed in the community.

The modern institutions of Panchayat Raj and Nagar Palika have to execute their powers and authority within the orbit of the legislations enacted by the State legislature. The powers devolved upon Nagar Palikas are spread over a number of operational areas namely, Compulsory and Regulatory powers, Development and Managerial powers and Agency functions. It fruitfully mixes the regulatory powers with development, extension and welfare since the regulatory powers lend support and authority for development administration. In addition to these, Nagar Palikas are expected to act as an agent of the State Government to identify the beneficiaries of the different development schemes of both state and Central Governments and also distribute pension funds meant for destitutes, widows, old agers, marriage grant to daughters of widows etc. The implementation of the Centrally sponsored schemes like Nehru Rozgar Yojana, Slum improvement schemes, Flood relief, Drought relief, DRDA, Trysem, Integrated Development of Small and Medium Towns, Urban Basic Services for the Poor Programmes etc. may be vested with the Nagar Palikas.

**Financial Resources**

The Acts aim to endorse the broad sources of finance to Nagar Palikas in addition to the constitution of a Finance Commission for Panchayat Raj and Nagar Palikas. The source of revenue may be two—taxes and non-taxes. The tax revenue may be three viz. own taxes, assigned taxes and shared taxes. The own taxes are the taxes levied by Nagar Palikas and they are: Building tax, Professional tax, Recreation tax including exhibitions, cultural meet, cinema and sports, Advertisement tax, Service tax, etc. The assigned taxes are those levied by State Government but shared between the State Government and Nagar Palikas. The main sources of non-taxes are the licence fees, income from assets owned by Nagar Palikas, contributions, grant from government, allocation from plan outlay, loans from government, semi-government corporations like LIC, HUDCO etc.

The Government of Kerala endowed substantial administrative, financial and legal powers to Panchayat Raj and Nagar Palika Institutions. They include Krishy Bhavan, Veterinary hospitals, Primary health centres, Government dispensaries, Primary schools and High Schools, Balavadi, Anganvadi, Village roads and district roads, small scale industries and co-operative institutions. The elected representatives of the grass root institutions are responsible for managing them and to supervise and control their staff right from Doctor to the Health workers and from Agricultural Officer to the Farm Labourers.

**People's Plan Experiment**

The Government of Kerala made an earnest attempt to make the Ninth Five Year Plan a People's Plan and this campaign was inaugurated on 17th August 1996. In the history of Kerala's Planning process, it is unique in the sense that it made an attempt to accommodate the participation of the people at the grass root level which was unknown to people. It is framed as a movement and celebrated as a festival all over the state covering the nook and corner by spreading over the Gram Panchayats, Municipalities and Corporations.

People's Plan is sponsored by the Government of Kerala under the leadership of a newly created Advanced Planning Supervisory Body which incorporated a few expert members.

The theory of People's Plan is mixed with statutory local government units like Panchayat Raj and Nagar Palika institutions and hence Gram Panchayats and Nagarpalikas are taken as nodal units to draft bottom level plan projects in touch with the felt needs of the people. In the first phase, Gram Sabhas and Ward Sabhas are summoned to identify felt needs of the people, indicate their priorities and suggest solutions. In the second phase, these felt needs of the people are discussed in a development seminar held at Gram Panchayat and Nagar Palika level to find out the solutions. In the third phase, the felt needs of the Gram Sabha or Ward Sabha level are integrated into an individual Gram Panchayat or Nagarpalika plan to be included in the Ninth Plan. In the fourth level, development seminars are conducted at the Block level and district level to codi-draft Block level plans into a District level plan.

As a movement it is celebrated as a festival all over the state covering the nook and corner by spreading over the Gram Panchayats, Municipalities and Corporations.

People's Plan is sponsored by the Government of Kerala under the leadership of a newly created Advanced Planning Supervisory Body which incorporated a few expert members.

The theory of People's Plan is mixed with statutory local government units like Panchayat Raj and Nagar Palika Institutions and hence Gram Panchayats and Nagarpalikas are units to draft bottom level plan projects in touch with the felt needs of the people. In the first phase, Gram Sabhas and Ward Sabhas are supposed to identify felt needs of the people, indicate their priorities and suggest solutions. In the second phase, those felt needs of the people are discussed in a development seminar held at Gram Panchayat and Nagar Palika to find out the solutions. In the third phase, the felt needs of the Gram Sabha or Ward Sabha level are integrated into an individual Gram Panchayat or Nagarpalika plan to be included in the Ninth Plan. In the fourth level, development seminars are conducted at the Block level and district level to codi-draft Block level plans into a District level plan.

In this situation, the state Planning Board felt the requirement of a technical expert committee to evaluate the projects prepared by local bodies. A new technical expert committee named Voluntary Technical Corps (VTC) consisting of professionals including retired personnel and scientists available at the local level is constituted. The corps is entrusted to evaluate the projects at block level to make these projects technically feasible and economically viable.

The district Panchayat code-drafts the Block level plans into a single District level plan which is placed before the District Planning Committee. The District Planning Committee consists of the elected representatives of both Panchayat Raj Institutions and Nagar Palika and some experts. It is headed by the District Panchayat President with the Revenue Collector as the officiating secretary. The District Planning Committee codi-drafts the plan of the District Panchayat, and the plans of the Municipalities and Corporations into one. The integrated plan may be submitted to the State Planning Board.

The task before the District Planning Committee is not an easy one. They have to fix priorities among the felt needs raised from the lower levels to be accommodated in the Ninth Plan. They cannot relegate or even postpone the needs raised by a region for the pleasure of another.

**Allocation of Funds**

On July 14, 1996, the State Government took a decision to earmark 35-40 per cent of the State plan outlay to Panchayat Raj institutions and Nagar Palikas. In the annual plan 1997-98, the Government decided to transfer 40 per cent of the plan funds to the local self government. The total outlay of the State Plan was fixed as Rs. 11,000 crore and the annual plan for 1997–98 was Rs. 2,400 crore. Later, making discussion with the Planning Commission, the state outlay for Ninth plan is raised Rs. 16,100 crore.

The Government took a decision to earmark 15 per cent of the annual plan fund earmarked for local governments towards Nagar Palikas and 85 per cent to the three tier Panchayats on the basis of the population in these areas. The criterion used to distribute the plan outlay was the population of the respective areas, and hence the share of the Nagar Palikas would be in accordance with the quantum of population and hence the amount earmarked for Nagar Palikas was distributed among 3 Corporations and 55 municipalities. The distribution is depicted in Table 2.

**TABLE 2**
**Distribution of Ninth Plan Funds among PRs and NPs**

*(in Rs. Crore)*

| *Category* | *1997-2002* | *1997-98* | *Percentage* |
|---|---|---|---|
| Nagarpalikas | 660 | 144 | 15 |
| Three tier Gram Panchayats | 3740 | 816 | 85 |
| Total | 4400 | 960 | 100 |

*Source:* Power to People, S.P.B. 1997.

A distinct criterion was adopted to distribute the respective shares of Panchayats. The Plan fund meant for the Institutions was distributed at a ratio of 15:15:70 respectively for the District Panchayats, Block Panchayats and Gram Panchayats.s The formula used for the allocation of funds among the units were (i) Population of the Scheduled Castes, (ii) The Population of Scheduled Tribes and (iii) Other population. The Combined population of the SC/ST were taken a criterion to determine the backwardness of the respective Panchayats. The allocation is collected in Table 3.

**TABLE 3**
**Distribution of Ninth Plan Fund among PRs**

*(in Rs. Crore)*

| *Class of Population* | *1997-2002* | *1997-98* | *Percentage* |
|---|---|---|---|
| 1. Scheduled Tribes | 187 | 40.80 | 5 |
| 2. Scheduled Castes | 935 | 204.00 | 25 |
| 3. Other population | 2618 | 571.20 | 70 |
| Total | 3740 | 816.00 | 100 |

*Source:* Power to People, S.P.B. 1997.

**Strategy of the People's Plan**

The Sponsors of the People's Plan are not committed to specify the strategy of Plan and sectoral priorities under local governments even if the state plan accorded high priority to productive sector. The crucial decision with regards the sectoral priority of the forty per cent of the state plan is left before the local governments under liberal stipulations. The stipulations state that the productive sector namely Agriculture, Minor irrigation, Animal husbandry, Fisheries and Small Scale industries may be accorded 40–50 per cent of the local government plans. The share of the Public utility services namely Education, Health care, Sanitation, Drinking Water, Welfare including SC/ST and Women and Housing may be between 30–40 per cent and other Service sectors like Transport and Public works etc. may be allotted 10–30 per cent according to the local requirements.

**Suggesions**

In the concluding part, some suggesions are put forward:

1. A 40–50 per cent outlay suggested for the already sluggish productive sector (Primary and Secondary) is highly inadequate to strengthen the correcting process in both industry and agriculture. Except Cochin Corporation, Thiruvananthapuram and Kozhikode corporations and majority of the Municipalities are characterised as service cum-primary functionaries. They may be motivated to enter into manufacturing sector to revamp industrial sector and to create employment opportunities to absorb the backlog of unemployment. The outlay proposed for manufacturing sector may be enhanced to atleast 40 per cent.

2. The criteria applied for the allocation of the resources to urban local government may be modified. In addition to population (including SC/ST population), the geographical conditions and size of the concerned bodies may be considered.

3. Since the urban local government caters the public utility services of the floating population like students, employees, patients, traders and businessmen, a special provision may be incorporated to them.

4. Migration of labourers and other categories of population is another area of concern. A special provision may be added to mitigate problems connected with migration.

5. Recently, disposal of urban garbage has emerged as a serious problem. The State government has to make special assistance to urban local government to install garbage processing units.

6. In the devolution of powers and authority, there should be a rigid demarcation between Panchayats and Nagar Palikas. Otherwise it may lead to the overlapping of powers and authority.

7. In the monitoring phase, the services of an independent Technical Expert Committee other than the Voluntary Technical Corps is highly appreciable and it may be ensured.

8. The basic unit of the Nagarpalika institution is 'Ward Sabha' or Ward. There is a possibility of neglect of some "Wards' for appeasing

other wards. It may lead to the concentration of development activities at a particular area at the cost of others. As per the present norms, the state government keeps 60 per cent of the State Plan outlay for state level plans and 40 per cent is transferred towards the local government. In the same way, 40 per cent of the Nagarpalika plan funds may be distributed among the 'Wards' on the basis of the criteria applied for upper layers and the remaining 60 per cent may be utilised for Municipality or Corporation level plans. It may be ensured to avoid the concentration of the plan funds in a few select areas and also to perculate the true spirit of development at grass root level. This suggession may be extended to Panchayat Raj too.

Devolution of powers, authority and finance is a continuous process. It was already started and naturally it will take some more time. In due course, it may attract dissent and consent. The success of the movement basically depend upon the 'will' to translate the dreams into reality by pooling the entire resources.

## REFERENCES


1. Clark, Colin, "The Conditions of Economic Progress", London, 1940.
2. Ghosh, Arun, "Decentralised Planning; West Bengal Experience" *Economic and Political Weekly,* Mumbai, March 1988.
3. Misra. K. Girish, *Block Level Planning* Rawat Publications, Jaipur, 1987.
4. Schumaches, E.F., *Small is Beautiful*, Vintage Book, London, 1973.
5. Sivadasa Menon, T, "Government System without Corruption" *Kerala Calling,* Thiruvananthapuram, June 1997.
6. Surendran, P. "Affinitization: A Process of Social Change", Man and Life, Calcutta, Jan.–June 1997.
7. Surendran, P. "People's Plan", Kerala Calling, Thiruvananthapuram, April 1997.
8. Surendran, P. "People's Plan of Kerala", Yojana, New Delhi, June 1997.
9. State Planning Board, "Power to People" (Mal). Thiruvanantpuram, 1997.
10. Thakur, Devendra, (Ed) "District Planning and Panchayat Raj", Deep and Deep Publications, New Delhi, 1991.

# 11

# Impact of the 74th Constitution Amendment–A Study in the Context of Kerala

—*Lcy K. John*

In the very long history of the transition of Indian society into a vibrant socio-economic framework the 74th Constitution Amendment brings in a new life to the polity and the economy of the nation. The spirit of the Amendment is the decentralisation of power which is the culmination of a very long theoretical process beginning with the First Five Year Plan itself. In the draft of the First Plan the Planning Commission had presented a strong case for the decentralisation. In the early seventies an attempt was made by a few states to translate this idea into practice. In the meantime, changes in the orientation and structure of planning were introduced more directly by launching the beneficiary oriented schemes and the area development programmes. But weak political will coincided with a number of constraints made the decentralisation a distant objective. While commenting upon this sorry state of affairs, Ashok Mehta Committee on Panchayati Raj Institutions (PRIs) states that decentralisation should not be treated as a political charity but a functional necessity.

In the early eighties, another attempt was made by the Yojana Bhavan to approach the decentralisation afresh and they brought out a report on District Level Planning in 1984. Yet we look one more decade to have the decentralisation a reality through the enactment of the Panchayati Raj and Nagarpalika bills. In strict conformity with the Central Act all State Governments have introduced the necessary legislation in their respective legislative bodies. Kerala is one of the first few states which moved along this line, where the Kerala Municipal Act (KMA), 1994 did come into existence with effect from 30th May, 1994.

In accordance with the Kerala Municipal Act, 1994, the urban bodies have been revitalised in Kerala. Election to the urban local self governments had been conducted way back in 1995. A time span of two years has been ever since the operation of Nagarpalika bill got underway in Kerala. Though this time span is too short to have a pros-cons analysis. It is interesting to look upon it at close range on account of the growing importance of the urban local self governments. An analysis of the implications of the Act and its immediate repercussions on socio-economic life will give us some inputs to derive the nature and trend of the decentralisation. The present study focussing on three urban local self governments in the Pathanamthitta district of the Kerala state has been taken up along this line.

**Functions Transferred**

The Government of Kerala has adopted the Kerala Municipality Act in May 1994 to facilitate the delegation of power to the elected urban bodies. In pursuance of the above Act, the Government had issued the necessary orders in September 1995 and the same has widely been acclaimed as a turning point in the nations story of decentralisaton. The following areas have been identified by the State Government for the devolution of power.

| *Major Areas* | *Functions Transferred* |
|---|---|
| 1. The formulation and the implementation of annual and perspective development plans for the urban area. | |
| 2. Regulation of constructions and land utilisation | |
| 3. Introduction of socio-economic programmes for the urban development | |
| 4. Roads and Bridges | construction and maintenance of those roads and bridges transferred by the government; construction of new ones subject to the availability of land. |
| 5. Water Supply | implementation of water supply scheme entrusted by the water authority; drinking water schemes. |

| | | |
|---|---|---|
| 6. | Public Health | supervision of the government hospital public health centres and clinics; independent schemes to promote public health, hygiene, vaccination, etc. |
| 7. | Social Forestry and Ecology | implementation of urban forestry schemes; popularisation of soft wood plantations; public awareness programmes on ecology, etc. |
| 8. | Social Welfare and SC/ST development | integrated Child Development Schemes, Anganwadis, Balawadies; Formulation and implementation of schemes for handicapped and retarded; various SC/ST development schemes both transferred and internally chalked out; slum improvement programmes. |
| 9. | Poverty Alleviation | implementation of NRY, urban basic services schemes. |
| 10. | Education and Culture | supervision of Lower Primary, Upper Primary and High Schools construction and maintenance of school buildings, Technical Training institutes, literacy programmes, library and reading rooms. |
| 11. | Public utility Services | street lights, parking places, etc. |
| 12. | Agriculture | different schemes |
| 13. | Dairy and Animal Husbandry | different schemes |
| 14. | Minor Irrigation | construction of canals, lift irrigation schemes, etc. |
| 15. | Fishing | promotion of inland fishing, coastal literacy, housing complex for fishermen etc. |
| 16. | Small Scale Industries | registration of S.S.I. units, promotion of village and cottage industries, small industrial estate, etc. |
| 17. | Housing | home for the homeless, construction of housing colonies and other schemes being transferred by the housing board. |
| 18. | Power and Non-conventional Energy | construction of micro-power projects schemes to generate power from non-conventional sources. |
| 19. | Public Distribution | supervision of public distribution outlets etc. |
| 20. | Co-operation | only minor functions. |
| 21. | Miscellaneous | |

In pursuance of the devolution of the above mentioned subjects, the Government of Kerala has transferred the following institutions along with its assets to the urban local bodies.

1. Agricultural offices called Krishi Bhavan,
2. Veterinary hospitals and polyclinics,
3. Industrial extension office,
4. Day care centres, Balawadis, Anganwadis, etc.
5. Community health centres, Government hospitals, etc.,
6. Lower primary, Upper primary and High schools,
7. Primary Co-operative Societies, and
8. Inland water fishing centres.

In order to galvanize the decentralisation process and also to enable the urban governments to chalk out development programmes, a number of administrative measures have been initiated by the government. The first and foremost among them was the transferring of institutions, schemes and projects amenable for decentralisation. The second step was devolution of funds to the urban local bodies. In this respect the relevant Government order reads that while transferring the institutions the balance fund available with them would automatically go to the urban local bodies. The next step was the shifting of Government employees. The employees, who were hitherto serving under the concerned State Government departments will now be under the urban government. The constitution of a separate budget account for the local bodies was the next step in this direction. Government has transferred the service of executive engineers to the local bodies to materialize the decentralisation. An expert committee has also been appointed to suggest other administrative and necessary measures to be initiated by the Government to strengthen the local self governments.

**Standing Committees—The Immediate Outcome**

Strategically a very important reflective outcome of the implementation of the Kerala Municipal Act, 1996 is the formation of standing committees. Among the urban bodies every municipality has three standing committees with specified functions–(i) Finance Committee (ii) Public Works Committee and (iii) Health Committee. With regard to urban corporations, standing committees are five. (i) Finance and Taxation (ii) Public Works (iii) Public Health (iv) Planning and Culture and (v) Appellate Committee.

Another notable outcome of the Act is the constitution of the metropolitan planning committee consisting of the people's representatives to chalk out the development plan for the metropolitan area within the following frameworks:

1. Co-ordination of spatial plans prepared by the local bodies in the metropolitan area;
2. Identification of the dynamics of urban growth and the preparation of a perspective plan thereon;
3. Identification of funding agencies as well as public and private sector promoters for the programmes;
4. Monitoring of the implementations of the approved plan by local bodies, etc.

**Power to People—The Political Impact**

The most striking impact, having wide political ramification of the new experiment is the switching over of power from brokers to people. The political system has undergone a drastic change through the revitalisation of the urban governments, which have now become the local points of administration. A number of areas amenable for decentralisation have been transferred to them and the urban governments can now exercise the administrative control over them. The political set up has been changed to the tune of eliciting people's opinion to guide the administration by the trickling down process through the ward sabhas. The ward sabhas turned out to be the lowest organs of the decision making in the new political framework.

Another political impact of the Act is the larger participation of women and weaker sections in the administration. As per the provision 6 (7) of the Kerala Municipal Act, 1994, 33 per cent seats in urban bodies have been reserved for women which has culminated to the representation of more than 480 women in the urban governments in Kerala. Similarly, proper reservation has also been given to the SC/ST population. In the higher echelon of political administration and decision making women come to have a say by presiding over one-third of the urban bodies in the State. The same criterion applies to women of weaker sections that they also have the chairpersonship of one-third urban local self bodies reserved for them. The political repercussion of the Act thus transcends the conceptual political framework of the society. The entry of more women into the active politics may have its own impact on the quality of pubic life.

**Executive Power—The Administrative Impact**

The decentralisation becomes effective and meaningful only when the decision making and implementation functions are being entrusted with the same body. It is the distinguishing feature of the the implementation of the 74th Constitution Amendment in Kerala. The executive power has been switched over from the urban corporation council secretaries to the chairperson. He may call for any records, he can verify anty files and he has to satisfy himself that the functions and duties are being discharged in order. The hitherto experience was the discharging of the executive functions by the commissioners, who could borne even contingent expenditure. But their powers were curbed. All payments falling under the purview of the body have to be passed by the chairperson and all expenditure are to be incurred by him.

**Evolution of a New Development Culture—The Social Impact**

The evolution of a new work culture having the following distinguishing feature is the social impact of the implementation of the Nagarpalika bill in Kerala:

1. The involvement of people, irrespective of their party affiliations, in the development process.
2. Voluntary work prone culture.
3. The enlarged role of bureaucracy.

Ward Sabhas, the lower tier of the vertical set up of grass root level democracy have been convened in all the urban bodies three or four times during this period. It is estimated that lakhs of people having varying political perspectives did attend the deliberations which itself is a manifestation of the involvement of people in the decision making process. A voluntary work prone culture is another outcome of the new experiment where both the organised and unorganised voluntary organisations extend their support to the development activities. A parallel incident that can be cited in this respect is the success of the total literacy campaign. The movement, launched to Kerala during the early 90s, did come off primarily because of the involvement of both formal and non-formal organisations in it. This involvement culture applies to the people planning too.

The new development culture brought about by the Nagarpalika bill caused to evolve an integration between bureaucracy and people on one hand, and academic and research institution and poeple, on the other. Since departmentalism and sectorism have no operational significance in the implementation of development schemes and programmes, the new experiment eliminates the gulf between bureaucracy and people as both of them have vertically and horizontally been tied up in introducing development programmes.

**Plan Preparation—The Striking Economic Impact**

The most dynamic impact of the application of the 74th Constitution Amendment in Kerala is the preparation of development plans by people themselves. Over the years the experience was one of pushing down the schemes and programmes finalised at the state or national headquarters for the implementation at the local level. It has finally been reversed in Kerala where people have become the masters to a great extent in introducing their development plan.

The mechanism of preparing development plans by people, called people's planning in Kerala carries through a number of stages beginning with the formal meeting of ward sabha. The first meeting of the ward sabha identifies the resource endowments and project the requirements through detailed deliberations under 4 to 16 working groups. Based on the data available from the ward sabhas development report of the concerned urban area has been prepared by an expert committee focussing on the potentialities and problems of urban development which in turn constitutes the prime input for the urban development seminar. The seminar priorities the schemes and programmes to be implemented in the plan period. The plan thus prepared by the action groups, chosen from the urban development seminar places before the Voluntary Technical Core or the Municipal Level Expert Committee for the evaluation and finally submitting to the District Planning Committee (DPC) for the approval. It is to be noted in this respect that if any proposal made by the ward sabhas found inconsistent with the set objectives of planning or having implementation constraints, it will not be set aside but modified by the Voluntary Technical Core.

The unique outcome of the application of 74th Constitution Amendment is the people's planning in Kerala and the state has now launched the 9th Plan along this direction. The state plan fund has now been divided into State's and Panchayati Raj Institutions (PRIs) and Nagarpalika funds. Nearly 40 per cent of the total state outlay has been given to the local self governments which comes to Rs. 1025.37 crore during the first year of the Ninth Plan itself. Of the outlay Rs. 276.57 crore (26.95 per cent) is for state sponsored schemes and the remaining Rs. 749 crore (73.05 per cent) for the projects of the local self governments. The urban bodies receive a sum of Rs. 95.87 crore on the basis of their absolute population and SC/ST population. A total of Rs. 6000 crore has been earmarked for the local self governments in the 9th Plan period. Thus local self governments are better placed in the new situation to prepare and implement their own development plan. What does it convey? People have been given the chance to work out their development programmes which will help to derive an interface between plan and resource mobilisation. The articulation of the people's aspirations is the greatest advantage of this movement and thereby the grass root level democracy gets revived.

With regard to the financing of the urban development plan, besides their collection of revenue, the following are the main sources of income:

1. State's outlay,
2. Funds for the centrally sponsored schemes,
3. Allocation for state sponsored schemes,
4. Co-operative fund,
5. Assistance from financial institutions,
6. Local contribution and voluntary work,
7. N.G.O.'s contribution, and
8. Contributions from the beneficiaries.

A State Finance Commission on line with the Finance Commission at the Centre has also been appointed to determine the modalities of sharing the resources between the state and local self governments. In short, the economic impact of the Nagarpalika bill has wide ramifications in the socio-economic framework of Kerala and the magnitude of the same can be assessed by the time.

**Empirical Study**

The Nagarpalika institutions have been in operation in Kerala for the last two years in accordance with the enacted Constitution Amendment. Though this time span is too short to have an objective analysis of the working of urban governments, it will enable us to have a preliminary reflection on the implementation and the leakages. The present study has been carried out by focussing on three urban bodies in the Pathanamthitta district of the State of Kerala Adoor, Thiruvalla and Pathanamthitta.

**TABLE 1**
**General Data**

| *Particulars* | *Adoor* | *Thiruvalla* | *Pathanamthitta* |
|---|---|---|---|
| Total population (91 census) | 23639 | 54745 | 35882 |
| Area (in sq. km.) | 20.42 | 27.5 | 23.5 |
| No. of Wards/Seats | 20 | 32 | 24 |
| No. of Women councillors | 6 | 11 | 8 |
| Women chairperson | — | Yes | |

The table depicts that of the total 76 seats 25 (32.89%) have been reserved for women and the Thiruvalla urban body has a women chairperson.

**TABLE 2**
**People's Response**

| *Particulars* | *Adoor* | *Thiruvalla* | *Pathanamthitta* |
|---|---|---|---|
| Percentage of people exercised their franchise in the urban election | 82 | 81.82 | 79.37 |
| No. of ward sabhas convened | 3 | 3 | 3 |
| Average no. of people participated in the ward sabhas | 177 | 145 | 270 |
| Peoples participation in percentage | 14.97 | 8.47 | 18.16 |
| People expressed expectation in the new mechanism (percentage) | 49.40 | 47.00 | 53.75 |
| Peoples having a cautious response (percentage) | 24.00 | | 21.00 |

In the first election to the restructured local self government, comparatively high percentage of voting had been recorded in all the three municipalities. Three ward sabhas have already been convened where the participation of the urbanites, as the table reveals was relatively low owing to the fact that the urbanites are mostly employed having very little time to spare and the ward sabhas were mostly held on working days. The discussions with the representatives of people and municipal functionaries did confirm this. As a new experiment in the changed circumstances nearly half of the urban population expressed their confidence in the workability of the new system and at the same time a good number of people have a cautious response in this regard.

**TABLE 3**
**Representations in the Urban Bodies**

| *Particulars* | *Adoor* | *Thiruvalla* | *Pathanamthitta* |
|---|---|---|---|
| No. of councillors | 20 | 32 | 24 |
| New entrants | 11 | 17 | 14 |

Of the 76 councillors in the above three urban bodies, 42 are new ones (55.26 per cent). The increased number of new faces in the urban bodies is the outcome of the 74th Constitution Amendment where 33 per cent seats have reserved for women.

**TABLE 4**
**Councillors Opinion**

*(Percentage Distribution)*

| *Particulars* | *Yes* | *No* | *Not much* |
|---|---|---|---|
| The new mechanism generated a positive response among the people | 74 | 9 | 17 |
| Only peripheral functions transferred | 58 | 42 | — |

**TABLE 5**
**Councillors Concern**

| | *Percentage* |
|---|---|
| In the new set-up responsibility increased and also power | 29 |
| Only responsibility and not power | 53 |
| Councillors role not clearly distinguished | 54 |
| New urban governments can become effective with some modifications | 83 |

In the restructured urban local self-governments, the representatives of people have a pivotal role. But the opinion of the councillors widely varies over a wide range of questions. Though there is a near unanimity among the councillors on the positive response generated by the movement among the people, many feel that only peripheral and minor functions have transferred to local bodies. It implies that several strategic functions are still centralised. They cite the example of the water supply and school management. Even now, the Kerala Water Authority is the final body in all matters relating to the supply of water to the urbanites. The urban bodies can make only suggestions, but implementation is still vested with Kerala Water Authority. Likewise in the case of schools, the urban bodies have only nominal functions to perform—the appointment power is still in the hands of the government.

The councillors have also voiced concern over the trend of entrusting more responsibility with absolutely marginal power. In this respect, they point to an example of land acquisition. Every constructive development activity requires land. But the local bodies have no power over the acquisition of land. It is still under the department of revenue and an urban body has to overcome a number of barricades in the form of fulfilling formalities to purchase or acquire land. Similarly in the case of street lights, the maintenance of the same has been entrusted with the urban bodies. They purchase all the required accessories including tube lights and bulbs, but they run from pillar to post to obtain the services of the Kerala State Electricity Board (KSEB) workers in installing it. Therefore the new mechanism has raised the responsibility of the people's representatives and also their accountability for they have to convene the ward Sabhes once in every six months.

A good number of people's representatives are also critical of the way of implementation of the development programmes under the new set-up. According to them, their role has not been clearly distinguished in the new framework. Apart from presiding over the ward meetings and conventions, what precise has there to be done by them is the question raised by them. But they are unequivocal in the capacity of the new mechanism in bringing about spatial development. They are of the view that it is a movement in tune with the requirements of the people at large.

**TABLE 6**
**Response of the Women Representatives**

| | *Percentage* |
|---|---|
| Women councillors having political experience | 42 |
| Women councillors stating lack of experience a constraint | 18 |
| Women councillors having confidence in their ability to discharge the functions | 84 |
| Women councillors willing to contest again | 68 |

Of the women councillors only less than half have the political experience which implies that majority are debutante in the public life but they have a strong confidence in their ability to discharge the functions. Another interesting finding, relates to the keenness of the women councillors is the participation of people in the ward sabhas of them. The survey in unquestioned terms revealed that the average number of people being participated in the ward sabhas of women councillors exceeds that of their counterparts in all the three municipalities. In a related discussion with them, they have disclosed that they were closely following the concerned officials in getting their projects prepared and works done. To a specific question of their willingness to contest again if another chance is made available, 68 per cent replied positively while a few conceded that it is tough for them to carry on both public life and family life simultaneously.

**TABLE 7**
**Attitude of Employees Shifted**

| | *Percentage* |
|---|---|
| Employees like to remain under the urban government | 24 |

Most of the employees have preferred to remain under their parent department, for according to them, they are now under a dual control. It is learnt that the new vigilance by the local self governments cause severe hardships for them that they need to be punctual and accountable.

**TABLE 8**
**Plan—Preparation**

| | *Adoor* | *Phiruvalla* | *Pathanamthitta* |
|---|---|---|---|
| Expert committee members (VTC) | 14 | 20 | 38 |
| State allocation (Rs. lakh) | 17.65 | 38.04 | 22.28 |
| Total plan outlay (Rs. lakh) | 236 | — | 290 |

**TABLE 9**
**Sectorwise Allocation**

| *Sector* | *Adoor* | *Thiruvalla* | *Pathanamthitta* |
|---|---|---|---|
| Production | 29.38 | 24.90 | 30 |
| Infrastructure | 31.86 | 36.48 | 35 |
| Tertiary | 38.76 | 38.62 | 35 |
| Total | 100.00 | 100.00 | 100.00 |

The table points to the gross estimated amount of the projects prepared by the urban bodies along with their sector wise break-up. In all the three municipalities, the priority has gone to the tertiary sector because of the steadfast development of the urban areas.

The above presented are the immediate impacts and response of the implementation of the 74th Constitution Amendment in Kerala.

**Constraints Identified**

In discussion with the various functionaries and the public, a number of constraints could be identified. Many had focussed on the delay in framing rules and regulations. Even the guidelines for preparing the budget has not been finalised. The municipal functionaries point to the lacuna in the Act as a major constraint. Similarly they are of the view that the interest so far taken by the councillors in the hitherto mechanism has not been forthcoming now as the major functions are being entrusted with the ward sabhas. The beneficiaries, for instance, are being chosen by the ward sabhas, where the role of an urban councillor confines to one of the supervision and co-ordination.

Another major constraint identified is the inability of the elected bodies in undertaking development activities within the strict stipulation of the Government that the urban bodies have to adhere to the existing rules and regulations. The urban bodies, for example, cannot even create an additional post in municipal/urban or subsidiary office. Likewise a limit has been set beyond which they cannot provide administrative sanctions for the urban works.

Infrastructure and essential services are the most sought after in the urban life. But the urban bodies have only nominal control over the departments which provide these services. Water supply, electricity, public distribution system, health, etc. are examples.

A number of other constraints like the dual control of the urban staff by both the municipal council and the secretary, problems in awarding works at the government determined rates, difficulties in getting voluntary works and mobilising local resources, etc. could also be traced by the preliminary analysis. It is worthwhile to note that many people stressed on the need to elect the chairperson directly as he represents the whole body and exercises the executive power. A change has also been suggested in determining the fund for the urban bodies to the tune that besides the present criteria of absolute population and Scheduled Castes and Scheduled Tribes concentration other factors like incidence of poverty, backwardness in agriculture and industrial development, infrastructural backwardness, etc. are also to be considered.

Despite the differences in opinion of the methodology of the decentralisation, nobody sets aside the dynamics of the new experiment. Many have suggested that the government should continue all the efforts to devolve the power to the lower strata of the administration so as to make decentralisation sound and meaningful. Since the process of decentralisation is under way in Kerala, a value judgement at this juncture is totally out of question and it is expected that the experiment will turn out to be most successful in Kerala.

## REFERENCES


1. Planning Commission: Draft of the First Five Year Plan, New Delhi.
2. Jooja Rakesh (1986): *District Planning: Concept, Setting and State level Application,* Aleakh Publications, Jaipur.
3. Planning Commmission (1984): Working Group's Report on District Planning, Vol. I.
4. Planning Commission (1978): Report of the Committee on Block level Planning.
5. Raj, K.N. (Dr.): *Planning from Below,* (Mimeo) CDS, Trivandrum, 1971.
6. Alagh, Y.K. (1973): "District Planning in India", *Journal of Lal Bahadur Sastri National Academy of Administration,* Vol. XX, No. 1.
7. Gadgi, I.D.R. (1971): "District Development Planning", In: *Some Problems of India's Economic Development* (ed.) C. Wadhawa, Tata McGraw Hill, New Delhi.
8. Kesavan, C.C. (1995): *Kerala Municipal Manual,* Kaveri Publications, Trivandrum.
9. State Planning Board, Trivandrum, Handbook on Project Evaluation, 1997.
10. Government of Kerala, Local Self Administration, Trivandrum, Handbook on Implementation of Schemes and Programmes, 1997.

# 12
# Urban Local Bodies in Maharashtra: The Post 74th CAA Scenario

*—Kailash*

**Introduction**

The fast growing metropolises, big cities and numerous medium and small urban centres function as growth centres for economic development over vast developing rural areas in our country. However, the regional and urban planners are of the opinion that cities and towns have always been ignored so far as the state and national level plannings are concerned. As a result these urban settlements are ailing with complex and weak internal structures. The complete restructuring of the various functional segments in a new democratic set up, their decentralised interlinkages and the complete autonomy with regards to the financial arrangements, etc. have been considered very vital steps to be taken to strengthen the urban local bodies so that they can work as a viable unit of economic development. The 74th Constitution Amendment Act, 1992 (74th CAA) is a revolutionary law in the sense that its various provisions together will help to revitalise the urban local bodies as the vibrant democratic unit of governance.

Objective of this study is to highlight the functioning of urban local bodies and their concern institutions in Maharashtra under various provisions of 74th CAA. Paper is divided into two parts. In the first part the distribution and growth of urban settlements and the history of the growth and development of the local bodies, under various municipal laws, have been discussed in brief. The second and the main part of this paper focuses on the nature and structure of the local self governments in Maharashtra after 74th CAA.

**Settlement Pattern and Urbanisation in Maharashtra**

Maharashtra is one of the highly urbanised states in India. About 40 per cent of its population is living in different urban centres ranging from metropolitan cities like Mumbai to smallest urban units (Class VI)

**Table 1**

**District-wise Level of Urbanisation in Maharashtra Year 1991**

| *Sl. No.* | *District* | *Total Population* | *Urban Population* | *Number of Towns* | | | *Degree of Urbanisation* | *Share in state urbanisation* |
|---|---|---|---|---|---|---|---|---|
| | | | | *Big Town* | *Medium Town* | *Small Town* | | |
| 1. | Greater Mumbai | 9925891 | 9925891 | 1 | — | — | 100.00 | 32.50 |
| 2. | Thane | 5249126 | 3393207 | 6 | 5 | 12 | 64.64 | 11.11 |
| 3. | Nagpur | 3287139 | 2030914 | 1 | 5 | 17 | 61.78 | 6.65 |
| 4. | Pune | 5532532 | 2807029 | 2 | 12 | 20 | 50.74 | 9.19 |
| 5. | Nashik | 3851352 | 1369085 | 2 | 8 | 7 | 35.55 | 4.48 |
| 6. | Aurangabad | 2213779 | 725143 | 1 | 6 | 4 | 32.76 | 2.37 |
| 7. | Amravati | 2200057 | 717129 | 1 | 3 | 4 | 32.60 | 2.35 |
| 8. | Solapur | 3231017 | 929483 | 1 | 5 | 7 | 28.77 | 3.00 |
| 9. | Akola | 2214271 | 634331 | 1 | 7 | 2 | 28.64 | 1.57 |
| 10. | Chandrapur | 1771994 | 496823 | 1 | 4 | 7 | 28.07 | 1.63 |
| 11. | Jalgaon | 3187634 | 874669 | 2 | 11 | 4 | 27.44 | 2.86 |
| 12. | Wardha | 1067357 | 283517 | 1 | 3 | 2 | 26.56 | 0.93 |
| 13. | Kolhapur | 2989507 | 787002 | 2 | 4 | 6 | 26.33 | 2.58 |
| 14. | Sangli | 2209488 | 502447 | 2 | 5 | 3 | 22.74 | 1.65 |
| 15. | Parbhani | 2117035 | 476599 | 1 | 8 | 2 | 22.56 | 1.56 |

*(contd.)*

| | | | | | | | | |
|---|---|---|---|---|---|---|---|---|
| 16. | Nanded | 2330374 | 506140 | 1 | 4 | 8 | 21.72 | 1.66 |
| 17. | Buldana | 1886299 | 388335 | — | 8 | 3 | 20.59 | 1.27 |
| 18. | Dhule | 2535715 | 519841 | 1 | 6 | 1 | 20.50 | 1.70 |
| 19. | Latur | 1676641 | 341868 | 1 | 4 | — | 20.40 | 1.12 |
| 20. | Raigarh | 1824816 | 328640 | — | 4 | 15 | 18.01 | 1.08 |
| 21. | Bid | 1822070 | 326968 | 1 | 6 | 3 | 17.94 | 1.07 |
| 22. | Yavatmal | 2077144 | 356931 | 1 | 6 | 3 | 17.18 | 1.67 |
| 23. | Jalna | 1364425 | 230728 | 1 | 1 | 2 | 16.91 | 0.73 |
| 24. | Ahmadnagar | 3372935 | 533481 | 1 | 7 | 5 | 15.82 | 1.75 |
| 25. | Osmanabad | 1276327 | 193880 | — | 3 | 5 | 15.20 | 0.63 |
| 26. | Bhandara | 2107629 | 275894 | 1 | 4 | 3 | 13.09 | 0.90 |
| 27. | Satara | 2451372 | 315840 | — | 4 | 7 | 12.88 | 1.03 |
| 28. | Ratnagiri | 1544057 | 138056 | — | 2 | 6 | 8.94 | 0.45 |
| 29. | Gadchiroli | 787010 | 68565 | — | 1 | 3 | 8.71 | 0.22 |
| 30. | Sindhudurg | 832152 | 63150 | — | 1 | 3 | 7.59 | 0.21 |
| | Maharashtra | 78937187 | 30541586 | 33 | 145 | 163 | 38.70 | 100.00 |

*Source*: Census of India, 1991 Series 14-Maharashtra: Part II-B (i) Primary Census Abstract (General Population).

situated in rural, hilly and tribal areas. During 1991 census enumeration more than 3 crores, out of total 7.87 crores population, found to be urban and they shared 14.04 per cent of the total urban population of our country. So far as the spatio-temporal pattern and growth of the urban settlement is concerned, Maharashtra experienced a downward trend in the total number of urban settlement between 1951–1961 decade. It happened not because of the disappearance of large number of towns in the state but because of the 'declassification' exercise adopted by the Indian Census for standardising the definitional criteria of urban areas in 1961 enumeration. Following this measure, more than 100 towns, mostly small urban centres, were debarred from their urban status and were put again in the category of village. The number of town increased gradually after 1961. However, this increase in not uniform across the various sizes of the towns. The big (Class I) and medium (Class II and III) size settlements have shown a remarkable growth over the years. For example, the number of Class I towns, which was 9 in 1951, increased to 33 in 1991. Similarly, Class II and III towns, also increased from 11 in 1951 to 28 in 1991 and from 29 in 1951, to 103 in 1991 respectively. On the contrary, the small urban settlements are facing the phenomenon of stagnation (Class IV) and sharp decline (Class IV and VI) in their numbers. This trend has affected the overall number of urban settlement in the state.

So far as the proportion of urban population by size class of settlement is concerned, the share of big towns has increased to about 78 per cent in 1991 from about 54 per cent in 1951. The medium towns show either the phenomenon of stagnation or a very marginal improvement. The proportion of small towns has declined over the years. Class IV, V and VI towns together had about 28 per cent share in the total urban population in 1951 but came down to about 5 per cent in 1991.

The district-wise pattern of urbanisation shows a wide ranging disparity in the degree of urbanisation as well as the share of the individual district in the state urbanisation in 1991. State has the credit to have district like Greater Bombay which has fully urbanised population. On the country, the districts like Gadchiroli and Sindhudurg have less than 10 per cent urban population.

Greater Bombay shares about one-third of the state urban population whereas there are seven districts viz. Ahmadnagar, Osmanabad, Bhandara, Satara, Ratnagiri, Gadchiroli and Sindhudurg with less than one per cent of state urban population. The spatial organisation of urbanisation favours the growth of metro towns like Greater Bombay, Nagpur, Pune and Thane.

These four metro towns share more than 50 per cent urban population of the state. The Bombay metropolitan town is spatially aligned with other metropolitan and big towns like Thane, Pune, Nashik, New Bombay, etc. The size and the number of the towns declines towards the peripheries of these towns.

**Brief History of Local Self Government in Maharashtra**

The first attempt to form the municipal government in Maharashtra was made through the direction of King George III to the Governor General of Bengal to constitute Bombay Municipal Corporation and appoint the Justices of Peace in 1792 (Watcha 1913). However, the first duly constituted municipal government came into existence on 1st July 1865 under Municipal Act II of 1865. Although this municipal government had 400 Justices of Peace, with majority from European community, all were nominated on the ad hoc basis. The municipal Act III of 1888 was the outcome of the reform Municipal Bill, 1887 in which the provisions like the elected representation and the independence of local bodies from outside interference were incorporated. For the first time the autonomy of corporation was enlarged including the deliberative and executive wings. The provision of elected representation was reaffirmed again through the Government of India Resolution dated 16th May 1918 which emphasised that the local bodies should be as representative as possible of the people whose affairs the local bodies deal. The Government of India Act, 1919 and Government of India Act, 1935 did not say much about the further improvement of local bodies but some important decisions were taken during this period. For the first time Municipal Districts were divided into wards in 1920 and in 1921 the principal of separate electorate for Muslims was accepted. Whereas the Harijan (Scheduled Castes) Backward Tribes and Women were given reservation of seats by the Bombay Act IX of 1938 (Thakore 1957).

The Bombay Municipal Corporation Act, 1888 was so comprehensive that it became the precedence for the enactment of other acts not only in Maharashtra but outside the state also. However, under this Act only the Bombay Municipal Corporation was formed. Similarly, the City of Nagpur Corporation Act, 1948 was brought out for the constitution of Nagpur Municipal Corporation. The Bombay Provincial Corporations Act, 1949 and the Maharashtra Municipalities Act, 1965 (or Maharashtra Municipal Councils Act 1965) were brought out to constitute the municipalities throughout the Maharashtra state.

**Synchronisation of 74th CAA in Maharashtra**

Maharashtra is one of the few states where the urban local bodies originated, flourished and became an important element of economic development and modernisation. The Municipal Corporations of Bombay, Nagpur and Pune are the example. Amendments for the inclusion and replacement of the required provisions have been made in the old Acts and the new Acts were brought to introduce new provisions as required time to time. The 74th CAA envisages the constitutional provisions to provide a new life to the old urban local bodies and to constitute the new bodies in a more democratic environment. To comply with the provisions of 74th CAA, Maharashtra Government has made many changes in its existing municipal laws dealing with corporations, councils and panchayats. The most concrete step in this regard was the enactment of the Maharashtra Municipal Corporations and Municipal Council (Amendment) Act, 1994 (Mah. 41 of 1994) which came into force on 31 May 1994. This is an Act further to amend the relevent parts of the Bombay Municipal Corporation Act, 1888, the city of Nagpur Corporation Act, 1948, the Bombay Provincial Corporations Act, 1949 and the Maharashtra Municipal Councils Act, 1965. To comply with all the major provisions, brought into 74th CAA, also the separate Acts are enacted to constitute the committees and appoint the officer's as required.

**Constitution and Composition of Municipal Corporations**

The section 3 of Bombay Provincial Corporation Act, 1949 has been amended to fix the uniform criteria for the constitution of new corporations and make applicable throughout the Maharashtra state. Accordingly, the minimum population of a corporation should not be less than three lakhs and a corporation should have the structure of a city with respect to its area. In fact the corporation is specified as a 'larger urban area' under clause (2) of Article 243–Q of the Constitution of India. The state government has to confirm the city status of the larger urban area by notification in the Official Gazette. The other characteristics like the density of population, revenue generated for the local administration, percentage of employment in non-agricultural activities etc. also should be considered as important factors for becoming of a city as municipal corporation.

Before the implementation of this criteria for the constitution of municipal corporation, there were 11 corporations in Maharashtra. Four new corporations, namely Nanded-Waghala Municipal Corporation, Sangli-Miraj-Kupwad Municipal Corporation, New Mumbai Municipal Corporation and Ulhasnagar

Municipal Corporation were constituted after 1993. Some more cities like Bhiwandi-Nizampur in Thane, Malegaon in Nasik and Akola in Akola district also fulfil the demographic criteria to become the corporation. The notifications have been issued in this regard. Each corporation consists of (a) the directly elected councillors and (b) nominated members (not more than five). The size of elected councillors in corporation depends upon the demographic size of the corporation. For example, the Bombay Municipal Corporation is the biggest corporation in Maharashtra comprising 221 elected and 5 nominated members. The number of councillors is fixed by section 5 of Bom. III of 1888. Similarly, section 79 of the Nagpur Corporation Act, 1948 has fixed 129 directly elected members and five nominated members in the Nagpur Municipal Corporation. Section 48 of the Provincial Corporations Act, 1949 provides the following criteria to fix the number of councillors in other corporations in the state as given in Table 2.

**TABLE 2**
**Criteria to Decide the Size of the Councillors in Corporations**

| *Demographic Size of Corporation* | *Number of Councillors* |
|---|---|
| Population between 3 to 6 lakhs | The minimum number of elected councillors is fixed as 65. For every additional population of 15,000 above three lakhs, one additional councillor is allotted but the total strength of councillors in the corporations should not exceed 85. |
| Population between 6 to 12 lakhs | The minimum number of elected councillors in this range is fixed as 85. For every additional population of 20,000, above 6 lakhs, one additional councillor is allotted but the total number of councillors should not be more than 115. |
| Population between 12 to 24 lakhs | The minimum 115 elected councillors are allotted to this range of corporations. For every additional population of 40,000 above 12 lakhs, one additional councillor should be elected but the total number of elected councillors should not exceed 145. |
| Population above 24 lakhs | The minimum number of elected councillors is fixed as 145. For every additional population of 1 lakh, one additional councillor is provided to the corporations but the total number of elected councillors should not be more than 221. |

*Source:* Mah. 41 of 1994, Government of Maharashtra Mumbai, p. 518.

**Introduction of Mayor-in-Council System in Mumbai and Nagpur Corporations**

The introduction of Mayor-in-Council system of governance in the Brihan Mumbai Corporation and the Nagpur Municipal Corporation is another step towards vesting the powers of governance in the hands of elected representatives. Earlier the post of Mayor was only the ceremonial in nature. The Maharashtra Legislative Assembly, in early 1998, enacted the Mumbai Municipal Corporation (Amendment) Act, 1998 to amend the 110 year old Bombay Municipal Corporation Act, 1888 to introduce the Mayor-in-Council system (Cabinet form of government). Similarly, on 29th January, 1998 the Governor of Maharashtra promulgated the ordinance–Maharashtra Ordinance No. 11 of 1998 (City of Nagpur Corporation (Amendment) Ordinance, 1998) to bring the amendment in the City of Nagpur Corporation Act, 1948 and partly the C.P. and Berar II of 1950 and to introduce the Mayor-in-Council form of government in Nagpur Municipal Corporation.

**Nagpur Municipal Corporation**

The system of municipal governance, in both the corporations, under new arrangement is more or less similar. The new system envisages transferring executive powers from municipal Commissioner to the 11 members council each in Bombay Municipal Corporation and Nagpur Municipal Corporation headed by the Mayor. The mayor-in-council consists of Mayor, Deputy Mayor and such number of elected councillors as determined by the state government time to time and will function for the period of two and half years. The salient features of mayor-in-council system include a full time Mayor-in-council collectively responsible to the corporation with the Mayor as its head. Mayor will be elected by and from amongst the elected councillors for a period of two years in BMC and for two and half years in NMC, charged with day-to-day administration of civic affairs. The creation of the office of the Chairperson of the corporation, elected by the councillors from among themselves for a period of one year, the provision of the reservation for SCs, STs, OBCs and of course to women by rotation for the post of Mayor and Chairperson and the replacement of standing committee and other statutory committees by the mayor-in-council and the Municipal Accounts Committee with the leader of opposition in the corporation as its ex-officio chairman along with eight member each in BMC and NMC for the period of one year, are important features of the new system.

**Constitution and Composition of Municipal Councils**

The municipal councils are 'smaller urban' areas with the characteristics like (a) the population of such area is not less than 25000, and (b) the percentage of employment in non-agricultural activities is not less than 35 per cent. Further the municipal councils, on the basis of their population size, have been classified into three types of councils: (a) the municipal councils with population of 1,00,000 or more but less than 3,00,000 have been classified as 'A' class council; (b) the municipal councils with population below 1,00,000 but not less than 40,000 have been classified as 'B' class council, and (c) the smallest municipal council is classified as 'C' class municipal council on the basis of the population of less than 40,000.

**TABLE 3**
**Municipal Corporations in Maharashtra**

| *Sl. No.* | *Municipal Corporation* | *District* | *Population (1991)* | *Percentage of Employment in non-agricultural activities* |
|---|---|---|---|---|
| 1. | Greater Mumbai Municipal Corporation | Greater Mumbai | 9925891 | 99.3 |
| 2. | Nagpur Municipal Corporation | Nagpur | 1664006 | 96.96 |
| 3. | Pune Municipal Corporation | Pune | 156651 | 98.06 |
| 4. | Kalyan-Dombivli Municipal Corporation | Thane | 1014557 | 95.71 |
| 5. | Thane Municipal Corporation | Thane | 803389 | 97.74 |
| 6. | Nashik Municipal Corporation | Nashik | 656925 | 86.76 |
| 7. | Solapur Municipal Corporation | Solapur | 604215 | 97.56 |
| 8. | Aurangabad Municipal Corporation | Aurangabad | 573273 | 91.64 |
| 9. | Pimpari-Chinchwad Municipal Corporation | Pune | 517083 | 97.74 |
| 10. | Amravati Municipal Corporation | Amravati | 421576 | 86.68 |
| 11. | Kolhapur Municipal Corporation | Kolhapur | 406370 | 91.75 |
| 12. | Ulhasnagar Municipal Corporation | Thane | 369077 | 98.22 |
| 13. | Sangli-Miraj-Kupwad Municipal Corporation | Sangli | 314790 | 91.41 |
| 14. | Nanded-Waghala Municipal Corporation | Nanded | 309316 | 99.51 |
| 15. | New Mumbai Municipal Corporation | Thane | 307724 | 84.82 |

*Source:* Government of Maharashtra, Urban Development Department, Mumbai–1999.

According to the first and the main criteria, the smallest municipal council should not be of less than 25,000 population. However, on 31st May 1994 the day of the commencement of the Mah. 41 of 1994, there were several smaller municipal councils with less than 25,000 population (Appendix-1). Section 110 (2) of Mah-41 of 1994 reiterates that this classification will remain intact and will not be changed unless such classification is duly revised by the state government under sub-section (5). The state government may review such classification after each census enumeration. The physical limit of any municipal area can be altered by addition or exclusion of any local area. Provisions have been made to amalgamate two or more than two municipal areas into one municipal area, split up any municipal area into one or more municipal areas and to cease the municipal status of any local body. Government has to have notification in the Official Gazette about it.

Under Article 243-S of the Constitution of India, the state government has fixed some guidelines for the composition of the municipalities. Accordingly, every council consists of: (a) councillors elected at ward election by direct election; and (b) nominated members with special knowledge or experience in municipal administration but the number of nominated members should not exceed ten per cent of the total number of elected councillors or five, which ever is less. Section 114 (b) of Maharashtra Municipal Councils Act, 1965 deals with the number of elected councillors for each council. Table 4 provides this criteria.

**Reservation of Seats in Corporations, Councils and Panchayats**

Article 243–T of the Constitution provides the provision of reservation of councillors in local bodies. The reservation for the councillor seats in Corporations is made under Section 5A of Bom.III of 1888, Section 49 of Provincial Corporation Act, 1949 and the Section 80 of City of Nagpur Corporation Act, 1948 and in the council under section 9 of Maharashtra Municipal Councils Act, 1965. The state follows the reservation of councillor seats in corporations and councils in the following manner: (a) the number of reserved seats for the members of Scheduled Castes (SCs) and Scheduled Tribes (STs) shall be in accordance with their proportions (separately for Scheduled Caste and Scheduled Tribe) in the total population of each municipal corporation and municipal council. It has been clarified that the one-third of the total reserved seats for the SC and ST each will be reserved for the women candidates of the same community; (b) the number of reserved seats for the members of Other Backward Classes (OBCs) would be 27 per cent of the total number of seats in the council. One-third of the total elected seats for OBCs will be reserved for the women candidates belonging to these communities; (c) one-third of the total elected seats including the number of reserved seats for the women of SCs, STs and OBCs is kept reserved for the women candidates. It is to be noted that the provision of the reservation for women and OBCs was made just before the 74th CAA. However, it came into force only after the commencement of the Mah. 41 of 1994. The State Election Commissioner has to follow the rotation system to specify the wards in order to reserve the seats for the SCs, STs, OBCs and women including the women candidates of SCs, STs and OBCs.

**TABLE 4**

**Criteria for Deciding the Number of Elected Councillors in Councils**

| *Class of Municipal Area* | *Criteria for the Number of Councillors* |
|---|---|
| 'A' Class Council | The minimum number of elected councillors shall be 38 and for every 8000 of the population above 1,00,000 there shall be one additional elected councillor, so, however, that the total number of elected councillors shall not exceed 65. |
| 'B' Class Council | The minimum number of elected councillors shall be 23, and for every 5,000 of population above 40,000 there shall be one additional elected councillors, so, however, that the total number of elected councillors shall not exceed 37. |
| 'C' Class Council | The minimum number of elected councillors shall be 17, and for every 3,000 of population above 25,000 there shall be one additional elected councillor, so, however, that the total number of elected councillors shall not exceed 23. |

*Source:* Mah. 41 of 1994, Government of Maharashtra, Mumbai, p. 539.

**Nagar Panchayats**

Nagar Panchayat is a 'transitional area' between rural and smaller urban area. For the formation of Nagar Panchayat the following criteria have been adopted by section 341 A of Mah. 40 of 1965: (a) such area should have a population of not less than 10,000 and not more than 25,000, and (b) such area should not be situated more than 25 kms. away from the territorial limits of any Municipal Corporation or an 'A' class council and the percentage of employment in non-agricultural activities in such area should not be less than 25 per cent, or (c) such area is situated more than

| Sl. No. | District | Number of Local Bodies | | | | | Number of Councillors | | | | | Nominated | Grand Total |
|---|---|---|---|---|---|---|---|---|---|---|---|---|---|
| | | Corporations | Councils | | | | Elected | | | | | | |
| | | | | | | | General | Reserved* | | | | | |
| | | | 'A' Class | 'B' Class | 'C' Class | Total | | SC | ST | Women | Total | | |
| 1. | Greater Mumbai | 1 | — | — | — | 1 | 148 | 10 | — | 63 | 73 | 5 | 226 |
| 2. | Thane** | 4 | 3 | 4 | 4 | 15 | 265 | 8 | 19 | 115 | 142 | 18 | 425 |
| 3. | Nagpur | 1 | — | 2 | 8 | 11 | 215 | 21 | 35 | 104 | 160 | 23 | 398 |
| 4. | Pune | 2 | — | 2 | 9 | 13 | 395 | 40 | 3 | 123 | 166 | 48 | 609 |
| 5. | Nashik | 1 | 1 | 1 | 7 | 10 | 247 | 18 | 24 | 113 | 113 | 47 | 449 |
| 6. | Aurangabad** | 1 | — | — | 6 | 7 | 90 | 8 | 2 | 45 | 55 | 9 | 154 |
| 7. | Amravati | 1 | — | 2 | 8 | 11 | NA | NA | NA | NA | NA | NA | NA |
| 8. | Solapur | 1 | — | 2 | 7 | 10 | 227 | 40 | — | 118 | 158 | 25 | 410 |
| 9. | Akola | — | 1 | 3 | 6 | 10 | 251 | 23 | 9 | 80 | 112 | 31 | 394 |
| 10. | Chandrapur | — | 1 | 1 | 4 | 6 | 121 | 18 | 19 | 56 | 93 | 20 | 234 |
| 11. | Jalgaon | — | 2 | 4 | 7 | 13 | 343 | 22 | 16 | 98 | 136 | 52 | 531 |
| 12. | Wardha | — | 1 | 1 | 4 | 6 | 130 | 12 | 1/6 | 64 | 92 | 20 | 242 |
| 13. | Kolhapur | 1 | 1 | — | 8 | 10 | 206 | 12 | — | 95 | 107 | 24 | 337 |
| 14. | Sangli | 1 | — | 1 | 3 | 5 | 159 | 30 | — | 73 | 103 | 24 | 286 |
| 15. | Parbhani | — | 1 | 2 | 8 | 11 | 227 | 15 | 21 | 98 | 134 | 22 | 383 |

*Contd.*

| | | | | | | | | | | | | |
|---|---|---|---|---|---|---|---|---|---|---|---|---|
| 16. Nanded | 1 | — | — | 11 | 12 | 231 | 29 | 23 | 94 | 146 | 27 | 404 |
| 17. Buldana | — | — | 4 | 7 | 11 | 231 | 15 | 2 | 103 | 120 | 28 | 379 |
| 18. Dhule | — | 1 | 2 | 4 | 7 | 162 | 14 | 24 | 80 | 118 | 25 | 305 |
| 19. Latur | — | 1 | 1 | 3 | 5 | 113 | 16 | 4 | 55 | 75 | 16 | 204 |
| 20. Raigarh | — | — | 2 | 9 | 11 | 178 | 10 | 11 | 85 | 106 | 24 | 308 |
| 21. Bid | — | 1 | 2 | 3 | 6 | 135 | 13 | — | 64 | 77 | 18 | 230 |
| 22. Yavatmal | — | 1 | 2 | 5 | 8 | 167 | 16 | 18 | 69 | 103 | 24 | 294 |
| 23. Jalna | — | 1 | — | 3 | 4 | 91 | 6 | — | 44 | 50 | 12 | 153 |
| 24. Ahmadnagar | — | 1 | 3 | 6 | 10 | 195 | 24 | 15 | 98 | 137 | 29 | 361 |
| 25. Osmanabad | — | — | 1 | 7 | 8 | 134 | 14 | 3 | 63 | 80 | 17 | 231 |
| 26. Bhandara | — | 1 | 1 | 3 | 5 | 108 | 25 | 15 | 47 | 87 | 16 | 211 |
| 27. Satara | — | — | 3 | 5 | 8 | 151 | 22 | — | 64 | 86 | 29 | 266 |
| 28. Ratnagiri | — | — | 1 | 3 | 4 | 85 | 2 | — | 39 | 41 | 11 | 137 |
| 29. Gadchiroli | — | — | — | 2 | 2 | 28 | 2 | 4 | 15 | 21 | 3 | 52 |
| 30. Sindhudurg | — | — | — | 3 | 3 | 51 | 3 | — | 24 | 27 | 6 | 84 |
| Maharashtra | 15 | 18 | 47 | 163 | 243 | 5084 | 488 | 283 | 2189 | 2960 | 648 | 8692 |

NA: Data Not Available.

* Data for OBCs were not available on March 31, 1995.

** Data for New Mumbai, Kalyan-Dombivli and Aurangabad Municipal Corporations were not available.

*Source:* Government of Maharashtra, Urban Development Department, Mumbai, 1998.

25 kms. away from the territorial limits of any Municipal Corporation or 'A' class council but the percentage of employment in non-agricultural activities in such area should not be less than 50 per cent.

Each Nagar Panchayat shall consist of 10 directly elected councillors, one each councillor from every ward. Thus every Nagar Panchayat will be divided into 10 wards for the purpose of the election of the councillors. The state government has the right to constitute a transitional area or a part thereof to be a smaller urban area or include a transitional area or any part thereof a smaller urban area. It is to be noted that not even a single Nagar Panchayat has been constituted under this provision so far. However, the process of the formation of nagar panchayats is under way and the Devrookh in Ratnagiri district will be the first duly constituted Nagar Panchayat in Maharashtra.

**Industrial Township**

By complying the provision the clause (1) of the Article 243–Q of the Constitution of India, the state government can notify and specify the location of any industrial area, developed by the Maharashtra Industrial Development Corporation (MIDC) under the Maharashtra Industrial Development Act, 1961 or by a co-operative society formed for developing a cooperative state, as industrial township. A separate chapter (No. XXVI–B) dealing with the specification and constitution of industrial township authority was incorporated in the Mah. 40 of 1965. The every industrial township shall have an industrial authority as a body corporate of that particular township. The industrial township authority shall consist of a chairperson (Non official member), nominated either by the MIDC or by the cooperative society, and five members out of which two members will be nominated either by MIDC or cooperative society, one of whom will be the Chief Executive Officer of the industrial township authority, the next two members will be nominated by the Association of Industrial Units situated in the township and the fifth member will be nominated by the collector of the district in which the township is situated. Term of office of the chairperson and the members will be five years. The industrial township authority shall meet at least once in a month to make provisions related to the collection of taxes, lighting public places, streets and buildings, matters related to public health and hygiene, drinking water and sanitation, improvement in the living conditions of the sanitary staff, maintaining the vital statistics, establishment of primary schools and any other functions and duties assigned by the state government. Industrial Township Authority may, with prior sanction of the state government make regulations for carrying out these functions. There are about 50 industrial estates in Maharashtra and the biggest among them is the industrial belt between Thane and Belapur in Thane district (New Mumbai). However, not even a single industrial township is constituted under this Act so far.

**Wards Committees**

The criteria fixed for the constitution and composition of the wards committees have been revised by Mah. 41 of 1994. Each wards committees will consist of (a) the councillors representing the wards within the territorial area of the wards committees; (b) the officer-in-charge of the territorial area of the wards committees; (c) the three nominated members of recognised Non-Government Organisations and community based organisations, engaged in social welfare activities working within the area of the wards committees, provided that the members of such organisations are registered as electors in the wards within the jurisdiction of wards committees. In Mumbai Municipal Corporation the number of wards committees is fixed as not more than 25 under section 50-TT of Bombay Corporation Act, 1888. In Nagpur Corporation there should not be more than 10 wards committees under section 38A of the concerned Act. While in other municipal corporations of the state the number of wards committees should be decided on the basis of the population size of the individual corporation in the manner as given in Table 6. So far as the number of wards committees

**TABLE 6**
**Demographic Criteria to Constitute Wards Committees in Municipal Corporations**

| *Sl. No.* | *Demographic size of Corporation* | *Minimum number of Wards Committees* | *Additional Wards Committees for additional population* | *Maximum number of Wards Committees* |
|---|---|---|---|---|
| 1. | Above 3 lakhs and upto 4.5 lakhs | 3 | — | 4 |
| 2. | Above 4.5 lakhs and upto 12 lakhs | 4 | 1,50,000 | 9 |
| 3. | Above 12 lakhs and upto 24 lakhs | 9 | 3,00,000 | 13 |
| 4. | Above 24 lakhs | 13 | 6,00,000 | 25 |

*Source:* Mah. 41 of 1994, p. 522.

in the councils is concerned the three wards committees should be constituted if the population of the council is three lakhs or more.

The nature of functions of the Wards Committees includes; (a) the speedy redressal of the common grievances of the citizens who are the consumers of the essential municipal services like water supply, drainage, sanitation and storm water disposal; (b) to consider and make recommendations on the proposals regarding estimates of expenditure pertaining to the wards under different heads of account of the budget before being forwarded to the commissioner of corporations and the president in case of council; (c) to grant administrative approval and financial sanction to the plans for municipal works to be carried out within the territorial area of the wards committees costing upto Rs. 5 lakh in corporation and Rs. 20,000 in council provided that specific provision exists therefor in the budget sanctioned by the corporation and council respectively. In other words, the functions of the wards committees include the general supervision and control of the corporation or councils as the case may be.

The duration of the wards committees would be co-terminus with the duration of the corporation or council. Elected councillors in their first meeting of the wards committees in each official year shall elect from themselves the chairperson who shall hold the office until the first meeting in the next following year. The wards committees shall meet at least once in month at the ward office.

**Duties and Responsibilities of Corporation and Council**

Maharashtra government has concluded the most comprehensive amendments in respect to the power and authority of the municipal governments in the state so as to enable them to carry out the responsibilities conferred upon them especially those matters listed in the 12th Scheduled under article 243-W of the Constitution of India. It is to be mentioned that some of the functions of 12th Schedule were already undertaken by the corporations and councils before 74th CAA came into existence. Keeping the article 243-W in view, the section 61 and 63 of Bombay Corporation Act, 1888, section 65 and 66 of Bombay Provincial Corporation Act, 1949 and the section 91 and 92 of Nagpur Corporation Act, 1948 were amended to insert (a) planning for social and economic development and (b) urban forestry, protection of the environment and promotion of ecological aspects etc. on the one hand and (a) slum improvement and upgradation; (b) urban poverty alleviation; (c) cattle pounds and prevention of cruelty to animals and (d) regulation of tanneries on the other to give due importance to clause a (ii) mentioning the matters listed under Schedule 12th of Constitution of India. Thus to comply fully with the all 18 functions mentioned in the 12th Schedule the subject number 3, 8, 10, 11, 15 and 18 were added by amending the old municipal laws. These municipal functions can be discharged and implemented either by the corporations themselves or by appointing other agency for implementation of such functions provided that the implementing agency follows the terms and conditions prescribed by the corporations consistent with the terms and conditions determined by the state government.

Section 49 of the Mah. 40 of 1965 has adopted obligatory duties and discretional functions as well as the special provisions for undertaking water supply scheme for the councils. The obligatory duties and discretional functions are basically Welfare oriented specifically for the protection and improvement of public health and environmental sanitation including the improvement in the living conditions of the sanitary staff, scheduled castes, scheduled tribes, Vimuktajatis and nomadic tribes etc. living within the limit of the municipal area. Maharashtra is one of the premier states which has made laws for the conversion of dry latrines of the municipal area into wet (water seal) latrines in 1975 and ensuring that no person shall require or compel any other person to carry and no person shall carry, night-soil as a head load for removing it from one premises or place to any other premises or place, or for disposal, in any part of the municipal area. Under, section 91A of the same Act every council shall create and maintain a special fund called the, "Dry Latrines Conversion funds". The source of this fund will be (a) the proceeds of the special latrine tax levied under clause (c) of sub-section (2) of section 105 under the chapter IX-Municipal Taxation, (b) any grants or loans received from state government for the conversion of dry latrines of which a separate account should be maintained and this amount should be utilised only for the purpose of conversion of dry latrines. The Central Government brought a comprehensive legislation in this respect as late as in 1993 when "The Employment of Manual Scavengers and Construction of Dry Latrines (Prohibition) Bill, 1993" was passed by the Parliament to enact the law to abolish inhuman practice of scavenging dry latrines (Kailash 1993).

The water supply is considered as the most essential service of the people and because of it the specific arrangement has been made through the Mah. 40 of 1965. Accordingly, within a year of its formation every council shall prepare a scheme for supply of protected drinking water to the inhabitants of its area and within five year the scheme shall be executed to draw the drinking water for the people. The people should be provided not less than 70 lped (litre per capita per day) water. Later the limit was adopted as the minimum water requirement in small towns by the National Commission on Urbanisation (1988). Every council shall have a separate fund 'The Water Supply Reserve Fund'. Council should utilise this fund to investigate, prepare plans for estimates and to execute the scheme for protected drinking water supply. If any council is unable to prepare plan and investigate and execute the scheme because of lack of the fund or the specialised manpower, the council may apply to the state government for assistance within four months from its formation. If council fails to apply to the state government it is presumed that council does not require such assistance.

**Municipal Taxation and Financial Arrangement**

In Maharashtra the state government had already adopted specific laws regarding imposition, share and distribution of the net proceeds of the taxes, duties, tolls and fees for different levels of corporations and councils. So far as the taxation is concerned the sources of municipal receipts of municipal corporations including Mumbai Municipal Corporation can be divided into four categories. The major amount of receipts comes from 'own' municipal taxes like octroi, property tax and wheel tax etc. The 'shared municipal tax' includes non-agricultural assessment and entertainment tax. The third major source is the 'user charges and fees' such as water charges, sewerage charges and building licence fee etc. Another major source of receipt is the government grants (grants-in-aid) from state government basically used for primary and secondary education.

Section 105 (1) of the Mah. 40 of 1965 has the provision of taxation separately for municipal councils and Nagar Panchayats. These include (a) consolidated property tax on lands or building or both situated within municipal area (b) Octroi (c) entertainment tax on cinema theatres, circuses and other shows (e) advertisement tax other than advertisement published in newspaper etc. The consolidated property tax includes (a) general tax (b) general water tax (c) lighting tax (d) general sanitary tax (e) special latrine tax (f) fire tax and (g) environment tax. Other taxes, which the municipal councils can impose after receiving any general or special orders of the state governments, are (a) vehicle tax (b) tax on dogs (c) special sanitary tax (d) drainage tax (e) special water tax (f) tax on pilgrims (g) special education tax. In order to make convenient to the councils to impose any other tax, the section 108 A was increased by Maharashtra 41 of 1994. Accordingly the state government may issue any general or special order to the councils to impose a parking fees and fees for the use of public streets and pavement spaces. Besides these the municipal councils also receive the grants-in-aid time to time from the state government.

Although the sources of municipal receipts of corporations and councils are more or less the same but the size of the total revenue generated differs according to their status, size and location. For example, Mumbai Corporation alone share more than half of the total municipal income and expenditure of the state (Table 7). The maximum income of municipal corporations as well as the municipal councils is channelised from their own taxation. Government grant also has a significant share in the total income of local bodies especially 'B' and 'C' class councils who are unable to collect sufficient income by imposing the taxes. So far as the expenditure is concerned, water supply, drainage, conservance and sanitation, and the public lighting have priority over other expenditure. It is important to note that the local bodies provide the maximum subsidies to their citizen through these services. After 74th CAA, the section 126G (1) was inserted in the Bombay Corporation Act, 1888, to direct the Municipal Commissioner or the General Manager of the Bombay Electric Supply and Transport Committee (BEST), as the case may be, to append a separate report indicating the source and extent of the subsidy and its beneficiary (sections or categories of local population) while submitting the budget estimates to the Standing Committee. Similarly, section 95A in the Bombay Pronvincial Act, 1949 and 86 (1A) in Nagpur Corporation Act, 1948 were inserted for the similar objective, i.e., the preparation of report on the subsidised services. In case of municipal councils, the chief officer, has to present the report on such subsidies.

The annual budget containing the statements showing the income and expenditure of the municipalities of the previous financial year will be prepared by the municipal commissioner of corporations and the chief officer in case of councils and will be placed before the Standing Committee to consider the placed budget. The Standing Committee may consider the estimates and the proposals brought out in the budget and with recommendation, if any, submit for consideration. The council shall consider the estimates prepared by the commissioner or chief officer as the case may be and the recommendations of the Standing Committee, if any, may adopt the budget estimates with or without modification.

**State Finance Commission**

To comply with the provisions made under article 243-I of Constitution of India and the Maharashtra Finance Commission (Miscellaneous Provisions) Act 1994, the Government of Maharashtra constituted the first Maharashtra Finance Commission consisting of Shri Shantaram G. Gholap as the Chairman

**TABLE 7**
**Municipal Budget in Maharashtra 1994–95 (Rs. Crore)**

*(Rs. Crore)*

| *S. No.* | *Income from* | *Income of Local Bodies** | | | *Total* | *Greater Mumbai Municipal Corporation* |
|---|---|---|---|---|---|---|
| | | *Municipal Corporation* | *Municipal Council* | *Cantonment Board* | | |
| 1. | Municipal Rates and Taxes | 1750.12 | 382.12 | 17.19 | 2149.57 | 1089.00 |
| 2. | Income from other sources | | | | | |
| | (a) Government Grants | 139.25 | 147.86 | 6.00 | 293.10 | 46.92 |
| | (b) Other sources | 1258.31 | 173.20 | 16.46 | 1447.97 | 910.40 |
| | Total Income | 3147.68 | 703.32 | 39.65 | 3890.64 | 2046.32 |
| | Opening Balance | 209.44 | 92.34 | 4.14 | 305.92 | 89.27 |
| *Sl.No.* | *Expenditure on* | *Expenditure of Local Bodies** | | | *Total* | *Greater Mumbai Municipal Corporation* |
| | | *Municipal Corporation* | *Municipal Council* | *Cantonment Board* | | |
| 1. | General Administration | 154.63 | 84.25 | 1.35 | 240.23 | 79.08 |
| 2. | Public Lighting | 78.78 | 26.44 | 1.10 | 106.32 | 41.81 |
| 3. | Water Supply | 452.61 | 82.06 | 1.78 | 536.49 | 260.79 |
| 4. | Drainage Conservance and Sanitation | 451.16 | 93.97 | 5.37 | 550.50 | 344.39 |
| 5. | Hospitals, Dispensaries and Vaccinations | 224.02 | 18.59 | 3.13 | 245.74 | 176.08 |
| 6. | Public Works | 166.64 | 111.12 | 4.86 | 282.62 | 20.98 |
| 7. | Other | 1465.02 | 253.82 | 19.91 | 1738.75 | 1009.14 |
| | Total Expenditure | 2992.86 | 670.25 | 37.50 | 3700.61 | 1932.27 |

* Excluding Greater Mumbai Municipal Corporation.

*Source:* Government of Maharashtra, Finance Department, Mumbai.

alongwith three members and a government servant as its Member Secretary on 23rd April, 1994 under government order No. SFC-1094/CR-22/Arthabal. The commission was asked to make recommendations related to the matters mentioned in clause (1) (i) to (iii) in article 243Y. Some other matters which the government expected to consider by the commission were the projected gap between the revenue receipts and the revenue expenditure (non-plan or non-developmental or both) of the municipalities for five years from 1st April 1994-95, the measures and the extent to which the municipalities have exploited the available and the potential sources of revenue and the manner and extent to which their revenue gap can be reduced, the principles of financial assistance from the state government to the municipalities and the outstanding debt position of municipalities as on 31st March, 1994.

In the beginning, the term of the commission was made up to 31st day of October, 1995. It was extended for further period of three months which ended on 31st January, 1996. In between Shri Suresh Prabhu (now Minister of Forest and Environment at the Centre) was appointed the new Chairman of the commission on 5th October, 1995. The commission was reconstituted on 1st February, 1996 and its term was extended upto 30th June, 1996. Shri Makarand K. Herwadkar was appointed as Chairman on 29th March 1996 for the period upto 31st October, 1996. After this date the term of the commission was extended twice again, i.e., upto 31st December 1996 and further upto 31st January, 1997. The report of the Commission was finally submitted to the Governor on 31st January, 1997. A cabinet sub-committee is constituted to study the recommendations of the commission. The final decision on the recommendation is expected to be taken within few months.

**State Election Commission and the Municipal Elections**

Keeping the duties and functions of the State Election Commission in view as referred in clause (1) and clause (2) of Article 243-ZA, the state government enacted an Act "The State Election Commissioner (Qualification and Appointment) Act, 1994", to be read as "Maharashtra Act No. XXII of 1994", to decide the qualifications for and the appointment of the State Election Commissioner. The first State Election Commissioner, under this Act, assumed his office on 26th April, 1994. The term of the commissioner has been decided to five year from the date of his joining the post.

The process of the preparation and finalisation of electoral rolls for conducting the municipal election of each corporation and council starts only after the government notification, regarding the constitution of individual corporation or council, is published in State Gazette. New Mumbai was the first corporation where the election was held first (14th April, 1995) among corporations. The elections of Aurangabad, Kalyan-Dombivli and Kolhapur corporations were held between 16 April to 15th October, 1995). Elections of other corporations except Nanded-Waghala and Sangli-Miraj-Kupwad, were conducted on 23rd February, 1997. Nanded-Waghala and Sangli-Miraj-Kupwad corporations were constituted recently therefore the elections were concluded on 21 September, 1997 and 26 July 1998 respectively. Among the councils Mowad in Nagpur was the first council where election was held on 22nd January, 1995. Bhadravati in Chandrapur is the last council where the election was conducted on 20 September, 1998.

**District Planning Committee**

In pursuance of clause (2) (a) and (b) of article 243-ZD, the Maharashtra Government enacted an Act the "Maharashtra District Planning Committee (constitution and functions) Act, 1998" (Maharashtra Act No. XXIV of 1998) to constitute at district level a District Planning Committee (DPC) to consolidate the plans prepared by the municipalities in the district and to prepare a draft development plan for the district as a whole.

Section 3 of this Act deals with the constitution of such committee. Accordingly, there shall be a DPC in every district of the state consisting of not less than 30 and not more than 50 members. If the population of the district is not more than 20 lakhs the number of the members of DPC shall be 30 and if district has the population between 20 to 30 lakhs, the size of the DPC shall be of 40 members. If the population of any district exceeds more than 30 lakhs, there shall be fifty members in the DPC.

Every DPC shall consist of the following types of members (1) Ex-officio Members (2) Nominated Members (3) Elected Members and (4) Special Invitees. The ex-officio members include (a) Minister-in-charge of the district (b) President of Zilla Parishad (c) one representative of the concerned Statutory Development Board for the district (d) Divisional Commissioner of the district (e) Collector of the district, and (f) Chief Executive Officer of the Zilla Parishad. The state government shall nominate the members having knoweledge in District Planning to the DPC of the concerned district. The size of the nominated members is subject to the size of the DPC of the district. If a district has the 40 member DPC, the number of the nominated member will be 4 and in case of a district having 50 members DPC, the nominated members will be 5. Four-fifth or 80 per cent of the total member of each DPC shall be filled through election from amongst the elected members of the panchayat at the district level and of the municipalities in the district in proportion to the ratio between rural and urban population in the district. The elected MPs and MLAs of district shall be special permanent invitees at the meeting of the DPC and shall have a right to take part in the deliberations of the meetings of the DPC. Minister-in-charge of the district shall be chairman of the DPC and the collector of the district as Member Secretary of the DPC. The term of the elected members of the DPC shall be co-terminus with their term of office in the respective local authority, i.e., panchayats and municipalities.

Under Section 4 of this Act, reservation of seats in DPC through direct election, is made for the members belonging to SCs, STs, OBCs and women. The number of seats to be reserved for SCs and STs in DPC shall be proportionate to their population in urban and rural areas of the concerned district. One-third of the total reserved seats will be reserved for the women candidates of these communities. Thirty per cent of the total elected seats will be reserved for the persons belonging to OBCs. One-third of such reserved seats is kept reserved for the women candidates who belong to these communities. One-third (including the number of seats reserved for the women belonging to SCs, STs and OBCs) of the total elected seats shall be reserved for the women.

The functions of the DPC includes (a) to consider and consolidate the District Annual Plans prepared by the panchayats and municipalities in the district and to prepare draft Development Plan for the district as a whole (b) to consider the Five Year Plan and perspective plans prepared by the municipalities and coordinate and prepare draft Five Year Plan and perspective development plan for the entire district (c) to review and monitor the progress of District Annual Plan, and (d) to recommend, through the chairperson, the approved draft development plan to the state government.

**Metropolitan Planning Committee**

The constitution of Metropolitan Planning Committee (MPC) in Maharashtra under Article 243-ZE of Constitution of India is in the early stage. To comply with the provision mentioned in clause (1), the state government has prepared a draft Act entitled, "Maharashtra Metropolitan Planning Committee (constitution and functions) Act, 1998", containing the provisions for the constitution of MPC in the state. The proposal is under consideration to the government.

There are three metropolitan regions namely Mumbai, Nagpur and Pune and there should be one each MPC for each region. There will be 30 members in each MPC out of which 20 will be the elected members and rest 10 as nominated. The secretaries of the Urban Development Department, Revenue Department and Water and Sanitation Department, Municipal Commissioner and the Director of the Metropolitan Region Development Authority will be nominated to MPC by the state government. Besides, two members from the voluntary organisations will also be nominated to each MPC. Duties and functions of the MPC will be the planning and coordination for the metropolitan region and the preparation of the draft development plan for the municipalities and panchayats.

**Conclusion**

The foregoing description of the various provisions of 74th CAA shows that the Act assures a better participation in the democracy at grass root level, social and gender justice, decentralisation of municipal administration and the role of urban local bodies in the planning and devlopment at local and regional level. And focuses on two kind of measures to be taken to revitalise the municipal governments viz. corrective and preparatory. The Maharashtra Government has taken steps at two levels to comply with the Act. First the changes in the old municipal laws by amending the relevant part as to insertion of new clauses and the sections and or the deletion of the irrelevant portions of Acts. A new act containing all these changes has been enacted. Secondly, the enactment of new Acts to provide the constitutional sanction to the constitution of newly created institutions like the Election Commission, Finance Commission, District Planning Committee and the Metropolitan Planning Committee etc.

The process of the constitution of the proposed 3 tier system of municipalities is yet to be completed. The delimitation exercises in context with the 'larger urban area', 'smaller urban area', and 'transitional area;' will have to be conducted with due regard to the existence of various classes and sizes of the urban settlements including 98 census towns in the state. If other factors, prescribed for the constitution of the municipalities, like the percentage of employment in non-agricultural activities, density of population and the revenue generated for the local administration are being considered, the existence of many 'C' class councils, whose existence is protected under clause 2 of section 5 of Mah. 40 of 1965, may come to an end. More than 100 councils will face the problem of declassification and will be enlisted again as the census town if the demographic and main criteria, i.e., the minimum population of 25000 is undertaken seriously. It will definitely affect the municipal map of the state. Perhaps the more serious challange may be faced while constituting the nagar panchayats whose lower limit of the population size has been fixed as 10,000.

Maharashtra state, after West Bengal, has become second state to introduce the Mayor-in-Council system of municipal governance in its two municipal corporations. This is being considered as sea change in the executive and deliberative wings of power structure in the Bombay and Nagpur corporations. In fact it has been taken as a progressive step and a commitment of the stae government to vest the real executive and decision making power in the hands of the representatives of the directly elected councillors.

By strengthening and empowering the urban local bodies the 74th CAA has specific objective to make prepare the municipal governments to face the future challenges of growth and development which will arise mainly from the problems of unemployment, poverty and the environmental degradation at local and regional level. The state government is free to assign and define the responsibilities and functions of the municipal governments mainly of the municipal corporations and big ('A' Class) councils to achieve these goals. The constitution of District Planning Committee and Metropolitan Planning Committee in this context is an an attempt to review the locally available resources, prepare strategies for their maximum utilisation and find out the priority sectors for further investment so that a better planning and development environment can be built up at local level.

## Appendix 1
## Urban Local Bodies in Maharashtra as on January 1, 1999

| Sl. No. | Local Body | District | Population (1991) |
|---|---|---|---|
| | **Municipal Corporation** | | |
| 1. | Greater Mumbai Municipal Corporation | Greater Mumbai | 9925891 |
| 2. | Nagpur Municipal Corporation | Nagpur | 1664006 |
| 3. | Pune Municipal Corporation | Pune | 1566651 |
| 4. | Kalyan-Dombivli Municipal Corporation | Thane | 1014557 |
| 5. | Thane Municipal Corporation | Thane | 803389 |
| 6. | Nashik Municipal Corporation | Nashik | 656925 |
| 7. | Solapur Municipal Corporation | Solapur | 604215 |
| 8. | Aurangabad Municipal Corporation | Aurangabad | 573273 |
| 9. | Pimpri Chinchwad Municipal Corporation | Pune | 517083 |
| 10. | Amravati Municipal Corporation | Amravati | 421576 |
| 11. | Kolhapur Municipal Corporation | Kolhapur | 406370 |
| 12. | Ulhasnagar Municipal Corporation | Thane | 369077 |
| 13. | Sangli-Miraj-Kupwad Municipal Corporation | Sangli | 314790 |
| 14. | Nanded-Waghala Municipal Corporation | Nanded | 309316 |
| 15. | New Mumbai Municipal Corporation | Thane | 307724 |
| | **Municipal Council** | | |
| | **'A' Class Municipal Council** | | |
| 1. | Bhiwandi-Nizampur Municipal Council | Thane | 379070 |
| 2. | Malegaon Municipal Council | Nashik | 342594 |
| 3. | Akola Municipal Council | Akola | 328034 |
| 4. | Dhule Municipal Council | Dhule | 278314 |
| 5. | Jalgaon Municipal Council | Jalgaon | 242193 |
| 6. | Chandrapur Municipal Council | Chandrapur | 226105 |
| 7. | Ichalkaranji Municipal Council | Kolhapur | 214950 |
| 8. | Latur Municipal Council | Latur | 197408 |

| | | | |
|---|---|---|---|
| 9. | Parbhani Municipal Council | Parbhani | 190225 |
| 10. | Ahmadnagar Municipal Council | Ahmadnagar | 181339 |
| 11. | Mira-Bhayandar Municipal Council | Thane | 175605 |
| 12. | Jalna Municipal Council | Jalna | 174985 |
| 13. | Bhusaval Municipal Council | Jalgaon | 145143 |
| 14. | Ambernath Municipal Council | Thane | 127945 |
| 15. | Bid Municipal Council | Bid | 112434 |
| 16. | Gondia Municipal Council | Bhandara | 109470 |
| 17. | Yavatmal Municipal Council | Yavatmal | 108578 |
| 18. | Wardha Municipal Council | Wardha | 102985 |
| | **'B' Class Municipal Council** | | |
| 1. | Achalpur Municipal Council | Amravati | 96229 |
| 2. | Satara Municipal Council | Satara | 95180 |
| 3. | Barsi Municipal Council | Solapur | 88810 |
| 4. | Ballarpur Municipal Council | Chandrapur | 83511 |
| 5. | Pandharpur Municipal Council | Solapur | 79902 |
| 6. | Hinganghat Municipal Council | Wardha | 78715 |
| 7. | Nandurbar Municipal Council | Dhule | 78378 |
| 8. | Chalisagaon Municipal Council | Jalgaon | 77234 |
| 9. | Kamptee Municipal Council | Nagpur | 76613 |
| 10. | Amalner Municipal Council | Jalgaon | 76462 |
| 11. | Khamgaon Municipal Council | Buldana | 73692 |
| 12. | Parli-Vaijnath Municipal Council | Bid | 72670 |
| 13. | Bhandara Municipal Council | Bhandara | 71813 |
| 14. | Shrirampur Municipal Council | Ahmadnagar | 71368 |
| 15. | Udgir Municipal Council | Latur | 70453 |
| 16. | Osmanadabad Municipal Council | Osmanabad | 68019 |
| 17. | Akot Municipal Council | Akola | 65681 |
| 18. | Nalasopara Municipal Council | Thane | 61682 |
| 19. | Manmad Municipal Council | Nashik | 61362 |
| 20. | Panvel Municipal Council | Raigarh | 58986 |
| 21. | Virar Municipal Council | Thane | 57600 |
| 22. | Ambejogai Municipal Council | Bid | 57159 |
| 23. | Karad Municipal Council | Satara | 56819 |
| 24. | Ratnagiri Municipal Council | Ratnagiri | 56529 |
| 25. | Pusad Municipal Council | Yavatmal | 55931 |

| | | | |
|---|---|---|---|
| 26. | Hingoli Municipal Council | Parbhani | 54457 |
| 27. | Buldana Municipal Council | Buldana | 52767 |
| 28. | Kulgaon-Badlapur Municipal Council | Thane | 52113 |
| 29. | Malkapur Municipal Council | Buldana | 51311 |
| 30. | Chopda Municipal Council | Jalgaon | 49234 |
| 31. | Washim Municipal Council | Akola | 49140 |
| 32. | Sangamner Municipal Council | Ahmadnagar | 49061 |
| 33. | Karnja Municipal Council | Akola | 48867 |
| 34. | Lonawala Municipal Council | Pune | 47987 |
| 35. | Kopergaon Municipal Council | Ahmadnagar | 47629 |
| 36. | Khopoli Municipal Council | Raigarh | 45039 |
| 37. | Navghar-Manikpur Municipal Council | Thane | 44953 |
| 38. | Baramati Municipal Council | Pune | 44515 |
| 39. | Phaltan Municipal Council | Satara | 44367 |
| 40. | Shirpur-Varwada Municipal Council | Dhule | 44246 |
| 41. | Umred Municipal Council | Nagpur | 43578 |
| 42. | Shegaon Municipal Council | Buldana | 42492 |
| 43. | Islampur Municipal Council | Sangli | 42459 |
| 44. | Basmatnagar Municipal Council | Parbhani | 42338 |
| 45. | Wani Municipal Council | Yavatmal | 41992 |
| 46. | Anjangaon Municipal Council | Amravati | 41674 |
| 47. | Pachora Municipal Council | Jalgaon | 41142 |
| | **'C' Class Municipal Council** | | |
| 1. | Vasai Municipal Council | Thane | 39781 |
| 2. | Pulgaon Municipal Council | Wardha | 39679 |
| 3. | Tumsar Municipal Council | Bhandara | 38518 |
| 4. | Chinkli Municipal Council | Buldana | 37862 |
| 5. | Deglur Municipal Council | Nanded | 37212 |
| 6. | Arvi Municipal Council | Wardha | 36925 |
| 7. | Akkalkot Municipal Council | Solapur | 35237 |
| 8. | Yeola Municipal Council | Nashik | 34550 |
| 9. | Manjlegaon Municipal Council | Bid | 34476 |
| 10. | Dondaicha-Varwada Municipal Council | Dhule | 34476 |
| 11. | Chiplun Municipal Council | Ratnagiri | 34294 |

| | | | |
|---|---|---|---|
| 12. | Murtizapur Municipal Council | Akola | 34014 |
| 13. | Jaysingpur Municipal Council | Kolhapur | 33766 |
| 14. | Dahanu Municipal Council | Thane | 33592 |
| 15. | Dhond Municipal Council | Pune | 33352 |
| 16. | Digras Municipal Council | Yavatmal | 33052 |
| 17. | Dharangaon Municipal Council | Jalaon | 32972 |
| 18. | Sailu Municipal Council | Parbhani | 32388 |
| 19. | Balapur Municipal Council | Akola | 32276 |
| 20. | Vita Municipal Council | Sangli | 32018 |
| 21. | Shahbad Municipal Council | Dhule | 31890 |
| 22. | Nandura Municipal Council | Buldana | 31835 |
| 23. | Talegaon Municipal Council | Pune | 31120 |
| 24. | Umerkhed Municipal Council | Yavatmal | 30750 |
| 25. | Daryapur Municipal Council | Amravati | 30596 |
| 26. | Vaijapur Municipal Council | Aurangabad | 29604 |
| 27. | Gadchiroli Municipal Council | Gadchiroli | 29565 |
| 28. | Mehkar Municipal Council | Buldana | 29546 |
| 29. | Tasgaon Municipal Council | Sangli | 29391 |
| 30. | Parola Municipal Council | Jalgaon | 29301 |
| 31. | Silled Municipal Council | Aurangabad | 28888 |
| 32. | Purna Municipal Council | Parbhani | 28836 |
| 33. | Yawal Municipal Council | Jalgaon | 28741 |
| 34. | Morshi Municipal Council | Amravati | 28523 |
| 35. | Rahuri Municipal Council | Ahmadnagar | 28408 |
| 36. | Jintur Municipal Council | Parbhani | 28345 |
| 37. | Erandol Municipal Council | Jalgaon | 27730 |
| 38. | Paithan Municipal Council | Aurangabad | 27711 |
| 39. | Satana Municipal Council | Nashik | 27666 |
| 40. | Gangakhed Municipal Council | Parbhani | 27671 |
| 41. | Ashta Municipal Council | Sangli | 27405 |
| 42. | Katol Municipal Council | Nagpur | 27332 |
| 43. | Warud Municipal Council | Amravati | 26863 |
| 44. | Brahmapuri Municipal Council | Chandrapur | 26631 |
| 45. | Wai Municipal Council | Satar | 26289 |
| 46. | Ahmedpur Muncipal Council | Latur | 25878 |

| | | | |
|---|---|---|---|
| 47. | Sinnar Municipal Council | Nashik | 25864 |
| 48. | Manwath Municipal Council | Parbhani | 25468 |
| 49. | Deolali-Pravara Municipal Council | Ahmadnagar | 25320 |
| 50. | Omerga Municipal Council | Osmanabad | 25130 |
| 51. | Nilanga Municipal Council | Latur | 24246 |
| 52. | Dharmabad Municipal Council | Nanded | 24041 |
| 53. | Nawapur Municipal Council | Dhule | 23958 |
| 54. | Raver Municipal Council | Jalgaon | 23920 |
| 55. | Darwha Municipal Council | Yavatmal | 23902 |
| 56. | Partur Municipal Council | Jalna | 23818 |
| 57. | Mangrulpir Municipal Council | Akola | 23736 |
| 58. | Georai Municipal Council | Bid | 23655 |
| 59. | Ausa Municipal Council | Latur | 23246 |
| 60. | Tuljapur Municipal Council | Osmanabad | 23012 |
| 61. | Igatpuri Municipal Council | Nashik | 22868 |
| 62. | Pandharkawda Municipal Council | Yavatmal | 22813 |
| 63. | Gandhinglaj Municipal Council | Kolhapur | 22386 |
| 64. | Jalgaon Municipal Council | Buldana | 22344 |
| 65. | Kinwat Municipal Council | Nanded | 21917 |
| 66. | Taloda Municipal Council | Dhule | 21700 |
| 67. | Shrigonda Municipal Council | Ahmadnagar | 21646 |
| 68. | Pen Municipal Council | Raigarh | 21588 |
| 69. | Kurduvadi Municipal Council | Solapur | 21555 |
| 70. | Jaunnar Municipal Council | Pune | 21416 |
| 71. | Risod Municipal Council | Akola | 21338 |
| 72. | Faizpur Municipal Council | Jalgaon | 21322 |
| 73. | Sawantwadi Municipal Council | Sindhudurg | 21305 |
| 74. | Kurumdwad Municipal Council | Kolhapur | 20917 |
| 75. | Sangole Municipal Council | Solapur | 20856 |
| 76. | Tirora Municipal Council | Bhandara | 20509 |
| 77. | Pathri Municipal Council | Parbhani | 20456 |
| 78. | Nandgaon Municipal Council | Nashik | 20434 |
| 79. | Dhamangaon Municipal Council | Amravati | 20328 |
| 80. | Pauni Municipal Council | Bhandara | 20182 |
| 81. | Karjat Municipal Council | Raigarh | 20099 |

| | | | |
|---|---|---|---|
| 82. | Ramtek Municipal Council | Nagpur | 20072 |
| 83. | Kannad Municipal Council | Aurangabad | 19679 |
| 84. | Kallam Municipal Council | Osmanabad | 19862 |
| 85. | Desaiganj Municipal Council | Gadchiroli | 19794 |
| 86. | Saoner Municipal Council | Nagpur | 19768 |
| 87. | Mangalwedhe Municipal Council | Solapur | 19658 |
| 88. | Mukhed Municipal Council | Nanded | 19646 |
| 89. | Karmala Municipal Council | Solapur | 19622 |
| 90. | Saswad Municipal Council | Pune | 19536 |
| 91. | Pathardi Municipal Council | Ahmadnagar | 19532 |
| 92. | Kagal Municipal Council | Kolhapur | 19525 |
| 93. | Narkhed Municipal Council | Nagpur | 19423 |
| 94. | Shendurjana Municipal Council | Amravati | 19278 |
| 95. | Bhadravati Municipal Council | Chandrapur | 19184 |
| 96. | Wadgaon Municipal Council | Kolhapur | 19087 |
| 97. | Rajura Municipal Council | Chandrapur | 18969 |
| 98. | Deulgaon-Raja Municipal Council | Buldana | 18896 |
| 99. | Mahad Municipal Council | Raigarh | 18602 |
| 100. | Sirur Municipal Council | Pune | 18410 |
| 101. | Mhaswad Municipal Council | Satara | 18033 |
| 102. | Mul Municipal Council | Chandrapur | 18008 |
| 103. | Ambad Municipal Council | Jalna | 18007 |
| 104. | Malwan Municipal Council | Sindhudurg | 17988 |
| 105. | Rahata-Pimplas Municipal Council | Ahmadnagar | 17953 |
| 106. | Uran Municipal Council | Raigarh | 17775 |
| 107. | Savada Municipal Council | Jalgaon | 17674 |
| 108. | Patur Municipal Council | Akola | 17398 |
| 109. | Gangapur Municipal Council | Aurangabad | 17153 |
| 110. | Hadgaon Municipal Council | Nanded | 16473 |
| 111. | Khandhar Municipal Council | Nanded | 16396 |
| 112. | Dharur Municipal Council | Bid | 16386 |
| 113. | Alibag Municipal Council | Raigarh | 16289 |
| 114. | Lonar Municipal Council | Buldana | 16002 |
| 115. | Ghatanji Municipal Council | Yavatmal | 15785 |
| 116. | Kalamnuri Municipal Council | Parbhani | 15764 |

| | | | |
|---|---|---|---|
| 117. | Shirdi Municipal Council | Ahmadnagar | 15129 |
| 118. | Bhor Municipal Council | Pune | 15065 |
| 119. | Loha Municipal Council | Nanded | 15065 |
| 120. | Bhoom Municipal Council | Osmanabad | 14845 |
| 121. | Roha Municipal Council | Raigarh | 14827 |
| 122. | Murum Municipal Council | Osmanabad | 14789 |
| 123. | Shriwardhan Municipal Council | Raigarh | 14774 |
| 124. | Chandur Bazar Municipal Council | Amravati | 14730 |
| 125. | Palghar Municipal Council | Thane | 14700 |
| 126. | Rahimatpur Municipal Council | Satara | 14585 |
| 127. | Khapa Municipal Council | Nagpur | 14278 |
| 128. | Paranda Municipal Council | Osmanabad | 14267 |
| 129. | Chandur Railway Municipal Council | Amravati | 14203 |
| 130. | Mudkhed Municipal Council | Nanded | 13956 |
| 131. | Bhokardan Municipal Council | Jalna | 13918 |
| 132. | Telhara Municipal Council | Akola | 13848 |
| 133. | Deoli Municipal Council | Wardha | 13748 |
| 134. | Kundalwadi Municipal Council | Nanded | 13148 |
| 135. | Naldurg Municipal Council | Osmanabad | 12885 |
| 136. | Maindargi Municipal Council | Solapur | 12480 |
| 137. | Kamleshwar Municipal Council | Nagpur | 12451 |
| 138. | Vengurla Municipal Council | Sindhudurg | 12257 |
| 139. | Murud Janjira Municipal Council | Raigarh | 12111 |
| 140. | Bhagpur Municipal Council | Nashik | 12078 |
| 141. | Indapur Municipal Council | Pune | 12014 |
| 142. | Sinkhed Municipal Council | Buldana | 11591 |
| 143. | Sindi Municipal Council | Wardha | 11476 |
| 144. | Khed Municipal Council | Ratnagiri | 11288 |
| 145. | Sonpeth Municipal Council | Parbhani | 10701 |
| 146. | Dudhani Municipal Council | Solapur | 10576 |
| 147. | Billoli Municipal Council | Nanded | 10392 |
| 148. | Alandi Municipal Council | Pune | 12249 |
| 149. | Rajapur Municipal Council | Ratnagiri | 9822 |
| 150. | Jawahar Municipal Council | Thane | 9325 |
| 151. | Murud Municipal Council | Kolhapur | 8598 |

| | | | |
|---|---|---|---|
| 152. | Umri Municipal Council | Nanded | 8335 |
| 153. | Trimbak Municipal Council | Nashik | 7883 |
| 154. | Mowar Municipal Council | Nagpur | 7854 |
| 155. | Jejuri Municipal Council | Pune | 7758 |
| 156. | Mohpa Municipal Council | Nagpur | 6793 |
| 157. | Malkapur Municipal Council | Kolhapur | 5238 |
| | **Hill Station Municipal Council** | | |
| 158. | Panchgiri Hill Station Municipal Council | Satara | 10569 |
| 159. | Mahabaleshwar Hill Station Municipal Council | Satara | 10564 |
| 160. | Khuldabad Hill Station Municipal Council | Aurangabad | 9192 |
| 161. | Matheran Hill Station Municipal Council | Raigarh | 4708 |
| 162. | Chikhalda Hill Station Municipal Council | Amravati | 3081 |
| 163. | Panhale Hill Station Municipal Council | Kolhapur | 2968 |

*Note:* Order of the Corporations and Councils may change as some corporations and councils were constituted after 1991 Census.
*Source:* Government of Maharashtra, Urban Development Department, Mumbai, 1999.

## REFERENCES

Government of India, 1988, Report of the National Commission on Urbanisation Vol. II. pp. 292-301.

Kailash, 1994, Cleaning the Clearners, *Quarterly Journal of All India Institute of Local Self Government,* Vol. 65, No. 3-4, July-December, pp. 149-53.

Thakore, J.M., 1957, Development of Local Self Government in Bombay and Saurashtra" *Local Self Government Institute,* Bombay, pp. 8-15.

Wacha, D.E.,1913, *Rise and Growth of Bombay Municipal Government,* G.A. Natesan & Co., Madras, pp. 1-61.

# 13

# Urban Government of Orissa After the 74th Constitution Amendment

—*Bijoyini Mohanty*

The municipal election of Orissa has suffered a long delay due to one or more factors since the amendment of Orissa Municipal Act, 1994 incorporating the contents of 74th Constitution. Amendment Act, 1992 and the dissolution of the municipal councils of Orissa by presently ruling Congress Party in August, 1994 constituted by erstwhile Janata Party rule under late Biju Patnaik. Some litigations crept in and the Supreme Court intervened in stay orders of High Court of Orissa when the Panchayati Raj elections were held urgently ignoring simultaneous election of the urban local bodies. Presence of a vast 'Scheduled Areas' in Orissa is said to be a disturbing factor in initial stages of implementation of the 74th Constitutional Amendment Act.

Incorporation of party basis in local government system in India has been suggested by GYK Rao Committee and subsequently accepted in the 73rd and 74th Constitution Amendment Acts. The expectations would have been the smooth functioning of the councils as much as the state legislative assemblies and the Lok Sabha are functioning. But today's democracy faces 'hung state' at most levels in whole of the international representative formats, more vulnerably in multiparty configurations. It is better to have a council of popular representatives than invited biased parties pulling bitterly among one another without actually going deep into developmental amenities and implementation. Let us examine the positions those have emerged out of last Municipal Election in Orissa held only in late 1997.

'*Mu-ni-cip-i-um*' is a Roman terminology referring to "*a free city where the citizens are with privileges*".[1] Archeological remains of Indus Valley civilisation dates back as far as 3000 BC and reveals clear civic patterns distinct from rural habitations. Megasthenes, the Greek ambassador to the court of Chandragupta Maurya gave a vivid description of civic bodies.

The contemporary Orissa, as inscribed in the Hathigumpha Inscriptions, portrays the existence of the capital city, Kalinganagar with social, cultural and recreational arrangements in the civic setting. Gupta and Mughal periods had civic organisation on the patronage of the authority yet with association of the prominent citizens. Local government in ancient India was widespread, real and successful.[2] The modern municipal government of India is a British creation conceived in the 17th century. By this time the indigenous urban units were losing importance on the ground of small and multiple kingdoms as well as expansionist and highly centralised administration of the British. However, growing demand of Indians and the great need for the local services led to reform which granted first the urban Municipalities.[3] In the Memorandum submitted by the Government of India to the Simon Commission, 1930 it was stated that local self government of India is, in the sense a representative organisation, responsible to a body of electors, enjoying wide powers of administration and taxation and functioning both as a school for training in responsibility and as a vital link in the chain of organisms that make up the country.[4] The municipal government under the British can be categorised into four phases[5] e.g., (i) 1687 to 1881 : Institutionalisation of municipalities—local government was viewed and utilized to ease central and provincial finances and thus to subserve Imperial needs, (ii) 1882 to 1919 : Municipalities as urban government and representation as a part of self-government; (iii) 1920 to 1937 : in this stage executive power in municipal institutions was transferred to popular control and local government came under provincial jurisdiction, (iv) 1938 to 1949 : local government was in a state of repair and reconstruction being a disturbed field in national movement in India.

The post-independent period municipal government has faced at least two phases up to present day e.g., (i) 1950 to 1991 : constitutional deficiency and non-harmonious state with rural counterpart and (ii) 1992 to continuing: constitutional amendment and urban-rural symmetry. In the phase of constitutional deficiency, no national uniformity emerged and states varied widely in handling their municipal institutions. There was no regular election and popular councils, funding and municipalities faced high-handedness of state governments with frequent supersession and dissolution of councils. There was disparity in socio-economic developments administered in Municipal and Panchayat domain and the gap between them widened deeply within 40 years. The rural local government got some impetus with establishment of Panchayati Raj. But due to some reason or other, the ethos and slogans of 1950's and 60's gradually faded away. Even the parallel attempts like Urban Community

Development Programmes did not make any significant head way. Two fundamentally different systems—a modified English local government for the urban areas and a modified French local administration for the rural areas were thus created and the twins have not since then met. The post-amendment phase witnessed a number of constructive attempts. The 74th Constitution Amendment (1992) not only ushered regular election and popular council, proportional representation, constitution of State Finance Commission for financial distribution, constitution of District Planning Committee where the municipal institutions and Panchayats proportionately represent, but initiated a uniformity and symmetry in urban-local concepts.[6]

Municipal government in Orissa has witnessed a separate development due to disintegration of the earlier greater Orissa and political disintegration of its peripheral parts, late British occupation of residual territory in 1803 from Marhattas and very late consolidation to separate Orissa province. Thus, Orissa came under British Raj 200 years after the neighbouring Bengal and much later than the neighbouring provinces, e.g., Andhra Pradesh, Madhya Pradesh (Central Province) and Bihar. Orissa became a separate province in British India only in 1938, managing administration separately for 11 years just before national Independence, that too, with punctuations by Second World War and greatest momentum of freedom struggle. The Parts of Orissa received from neighbouring states has occurred in phases and need description as they bear the initial stamps of the original Municipal Act of that province. The Sambalpur Municipality, Berhampur Municipality and Parlakhemundi Municipality are such examples.

There was difference between Orissa and West Bengal in terms of spreading English education, transport and communication, general administration and formation of local Committees. Municipal Administration in Orissa can be looked upon as Municipal administration in Orissa Division of Bengal Presidency, Municipal administration of Orissa under Bihar and Orissa Province and lastly, Municipal administration of separate Orissa Province before Independence.

Orissa was acquired by the British in 1803 from Marhattas. It was placed under Bengal Presidency until 1912. During this period, Orissa was limited to few of its coastal districts and devoid of much of present western and southern portions which were transferred in course of time before it capitalised into a separate province on linguistic basis. Jaipur and Kendrapara Municipalities were the first of its kind to be created in Orissa Division of Bengal in March-April, 1869 as per the Municipal Act, 1864[7] and Cuttack Municipality came into being with effect from 4 July 1876 and Balasore Municipality was created on 1st April, 1877. All these municipal Institutions were operated as per provisions made in newly framed Municipal Act V (B.C.) of 1876. By the year 1881-82, one Union was established at Puri—as a first class municipality with 114802 municipal citizens within the newly constituted municipality.[8] Orissa Division received Sambalpur Municipality on transfer from Central Province in 1905[9] which was created in the year 1883 under provisions of the Municipal Act prevalent in the area. Baripada municipality is the only of its kind constituted in a princely state of Orissa on 1 July 1905 under Mayurbhanj State Regulation I of 1905.

In the rudimentary stages, the Municipal functions were confined to maintenance of Municipal police for protection and its cost was defrayed by means of rates levied upon the householders and shop-keepers carrying on business within municipal limits. Initially municipal councils operated through nomination. The elective element of representation was introduced in Orissa Division initially in the district headquarter municipalities as early as 1884-85 (Cuttack, Balasore and Puri)[10] and general elections to the three district head-quarters municipalities were held successively during the years 1884-85, 1887-88, 1890-91, 1893-94, 1896-97, 1899-1900, 1902-03, 1905-06 and 1909-10. This was subsequently extended to the interior municipalities (Jaipur and Kendrapara) lately in 1913-14.[11] The municipal functions of Orissa Division have been reported as quite satisfactory from the Administrative Reports. Since election the municipal commissioners were taking part in the numerous and important discussions in the councils. Madhusudan Das, Member of Bengal Legislative Assembly for the period 1896–1911 had keen interest on municipal affairs and had discussed on certain ambiguities on taxation on musical procession within municipal area and on occupation on any municipal holding.[12]

A Proclamation dated 22nd March, 1912 created the new Bihar and Orissa Province and this province had 54 municipal towns out of 130 possessed by Bengal Province. Something qualitative in municipal functioning were taking place by this time. The Royal Commission on Decentralisation held liberal views of withdrawing all official restrictions on the working of municipalities. The Montague-Chelmsford Reforms, 1919 had widened the franchise for election to local bodies, had reduced the preponderance of bureaucracy and had entrusted the subject of municipal administration to a popular minister. The Government of Bihar and Orissa had a clear choice for an elected chairman and ordinarily did not appoint any official chairman. Madhusudan Das, the dynamic leader from Orissa and the veteran legislator became minister with portfolio of local self-government in the legislature of Bihar and Orissa from January, 1921. He had introduced the Bihar and Orissa Municipal Bill, 1921. This made some improvements in previous Municipal Act of 1864 and laid down the duties of individual commissioners and sought liberal contribution of government for sanitary improvement of municipalities.[13] The Bihar and Orissa Municipal Act, 1922 elaborated all obligatory as well as optional functions and extended to all promotional aspects like "payment on account of trust, loans and establishment, construction and maintenance of roads, bridges, gardens, tanks, drains, latrines and urinals; the establishment, maintenance and extension of drainage system, supply of water and lighting of roads; the acquiring and keeping open spaces for the promotion of physical exercise and execution; the planning and preservation of trees; the erection and maintenance of modern dwelling houses, the establishment of schools and hostels, scholarships, hospitals, dispensaries, lepper asylums, dharmasalas; employment of vaccinators, promotion of vaccination, employment of health officers, sanitary inspectors, female medical practitioners midwives, prevention of epidemics; establishment and maintenance of veterinary dispensaries, destruction of noxious animals, diseased or unclaimed dogs, establishment and maintenance of markets, dairies, fire brigades, libraries, holding of fair, exhibition, establishment of relief works during scarcity or calamity etc." The Act not only increased the number of commissioners but also enhanced the proportion of elected to officially nominated commissioners to a mark of 75 per cent Municipalities in Bihar and Orissa had encountered some degree of internal dissensions and private feuds based not on question of polity but on purely personal considerations that impeded the healthy development of municipalities. All these led to breakdown of administration and supersession by government as had happened to Cuttack Municipality from 4 December 1933 to 1st December 1937.[14]

Financial deficiencies for municipalities of Bihar and Orissa had been acute for problems inherent with taxation. It has been described as the general scale of municipal taxation throughout Orissa is by no means excessive and is lower than that which prevails in other divisions. The per cent of rate payers to the municipal population is also low and it is reported that the burden is not always equitbly distributed. The first essential is fair distribution of the incidence of municipal taxation and equally important is the organisation of an efficient collection department. The advantages of efficient municipal administration are local and if the people concerned desire these advantages, they must be preposed to pay for them. It is not reasonable for them to expect to secure these advantages at the expense of general tax payer".[15]

Orissa became a separate province on 1 April 1936. It had acquired the two new southern municipalities, e.g., Berhampur and Paralakhemundi municipalities which were constituted under the Madras Presidency operating with Madras Municipality Act, 1920. The predominant factor in post-independent phenomenon of urbanisation has been contributed greatly by the Industrialisation and formation of new townships.

Orissa has shown the slow process of extension of its municipal institutions as evidenced by existence of 11 municipal institutions in 1951, 39 in 1961, 65 in 1971, 94 in 1981 and presently in 1991 there were 102 municipal institutions.[16] This is due to its trend of urbanisation as discussed below.

### Bird's Eye View on Trend of Urbanisation and Subsequent Municipalisation in Orissa

Orissa ranks 20th among the states of Indian Union, as per the 1991 Census, and records 13.43 per cent of its total population as urban dweller against national average of 25.72. At earliest Census in 1901 when the country had urban population at the level of the 10.84, Orissa had meagre 3.47 per cent of its population living in urban areas. Such initial tardy urbanisation was confronted with apparently higher figures few decades following independence. Among the 14 major states, Orissa occupied first rank in decadal growth rate of urban population in 1971–81 and during 1981-91 it ranked 8th in the country. The trend of urbanisation revealed in Census figures of Orissa in 1991 is still slow and separate from national macro-urban scenario. The State has only 7 Class I category of towns and cities which share 44.43 per cent of total urban population, whereas 65.20 per cent of total national urban population resides in Class I cities. Despite high growth rate of particular cities like, Bhubaneswar, the state does not record a million figure of population for any of its cities to achieve the metropolitan status.[17] Orissa, in addition to the Class I towns has 10 Class II towns with 14.63 per cent of total urban population (as against 10.96) per cent for the nation); 26 Class III towns with 19.73 per cent of urban population (as against 13.33 per cent for the nation); 51 Class IV towns with 16.97 per cent of urban population (as against 7.89 per cent for the nation) and 22 Class V towns with 3.94 per cent of urban population (as against 2.62 per cent for the nation).[18] This again points to a retarded tendency for urbanisation in context to whole of the nation. Post-independent Orissa has shown growth of townships mostly related to new industrial growth from Second and Third Five Year Plans. New urban agglomerations have crystallized to municipal townships at Jaipur Road, Choudwar, Hirakud, Burla, Rourkela, Talcher, Rayagada, Sunabeda, Baragarh, etc.

In Orissa, as per last 1991 Census, urban growth has distinctly slowed down. Barring Class VI towns, a steady increase in growth rate by size class is seen which infers that bigger urban agglomerations or towns are growing faster. Class I urban agglomerations or cities, while still growing faster than other size classes of urban agglomerations or towns, seem to be losing the prime position. During 1971-81, the population of Class I urban agglomerations and cities increased by 61.65 per cent compared to 38.90 per cent in case of Class II urban agglomerations and towns. In 1981-91 the growth rate has reduced to 37.29 per cent and 30.41 per cent respectively.[19]

**Legal Municipal Structure in Orissa**

In Orissa, the legal framework of structure is provided by the Orissa Municipal Act, 1950 amended from time to time. This Act lists a structure built on three components, namely, Municipal Council, Municipal Executive and sub-ordinate staff.

The Council is the deliberative wing of the municipality. The Orissa Municipal Act provides that a council may be composed of councillors not more than 30 or not less than 11 and the Government has the power to reserve seats in the Council for Scheduled Castes and Scheduled Tribes whose number is not to exceed three.[20]

The municipal council is composed of a Chairman, a Vice-Chairman and Councillors. A municipal councillor is to be directly elected by the people residing in a particular city on the basis of universal adult franchise, and for the purpose of electing the councillors an urban area is divided by the state government into certain general wards and the wards in which seats are to be reserved for Scheduled Castes and Scheduled Tribes.[21]

The second component of the municipal government is its executive—political executive and non-political executive. The Chairman and Vice-Chairman elected by and from among the councillors constitute the political executive.

The Chairman as a political executive, exercises a number of statutory powers and functions. The Chairman looks after the proper execution of the decisions of the Council through the Executive Officer. Being responsible to the Council, he answers questions of the Councillors regarding municipal affairs. As a Chairman of the Selection Committee of the Council, he shares the power of appointing the subordinate municipal staff. As such, he enjoys the power of suspension of such staff and shares with the Council the power of dismissal. Further, in the capacity of a leader, he exercises a good deal of influence upon the state government in obtaining grants and other facilities for the development of the municipal area. The Vice-Chairman discharges the functions of the Chairman in the latter's absence. And he exercises such powers which are delegated to him.

The non-political executive of a municipality is constituted by the Executive Officer, Health Officer and the Engineer. The Executive Officer is in the position of the executive head of municipal administration. These officers are appointed on deputation from the state service cadre by the government for the municipalities in Orissa. However, all of them work under the supervision of the Chairman of the Municipality. Further, the state government, on the recommendation of the Council, can appoint an Additional or Assistant Executive Officer to assist the Executive Officer in the discharge of his duties.

The third component of municipal government is the subordinate municipal staff appointed for running the city administration. The staff include the Head Clerk, Accountant, Upper Division Clerks, Headmasters of Secondary Schools and all other ministerial posts. However, the Council is free to determine its own establishment and fix up their salary, as per the municipal laws, with the prior sanctions of the state government.

The functions of the municipality are described in the Orissa Municipal Act, 1950 as amended from time to time. These functions are both statutory and welfare function. The municipality performs statutory functions, such as administrative, executive, electoral, legislative and financial.

The principal functions of the municipality under civic or welfare services is to formulate policies in respect to obligatory and optional services such as public health and sanitation, medical relief, public works, education, development, administrative and miscellaneous. All these functions also may be called as the public utility services of Orissa municipal government.

**Orissa Municipal Finance**

Municipal Government, like the Central and state governments, prepares its annual budget. The Executive Officer, in Consultation with the Chairman, prepares budget. The Chairman then presents the budget to the Municipal Council for its approval. Then it is submitted to the state government for approval.

The sources of municipal revenue in Orissa are determined by the Orissa Municipal Act, 1950. The major revenue sources of the Orissa municipalities are three, namely, tax revenue, non-tax revenue and government grants and loans. Tax revenue includes holding tax, tax on carriage and animals, latrine tax, water tax, drainage tax, octroi tax, terminal tax, etc. Non-tax revenue of Orissa Municipalities are rents on lands, building, etc.; sale proceeds of lands and produce of lands, interest on investments, remunerative schemes like pisciculture, markets, transport services, etc.

Grants-in-aid constitute an important major source of revenue of urban local governments in Orissa. Grants provided to municipal governments can be categorised under two heads: outright grant-in-aid and shared taxes.

The state government sanctions grants to municipal bodies for non-plan schemes and plan schemes. Under the non-plan scheme, grants are provided towards the salary and dearness allowances of the municipal employees and for miscellaneous purposes including developmental works, construction and maintenance of office buildings etc. Grants are given for plan schemes which include subjects like improvement of roads, water supply, sewerage, etc. Grants in form of loan are provided by government to municipalities under the plan scheme for remunerative projects.

Municipal government derives some amount of revenue by sharing tax-revenue with state government. In Orissa, the only shared taxes are entertainment tax and motor vehicle tax.

The powers of municipalities to spend money on providing services within their respective jurisdictions are prescribed in the Orissa Municipal Act, 1950. The major heads on which a municipality in Orissa incurs expenditure are: general administration, collection of taxes and fees, repayment of loans, public health and sanitation, public safety, medical, conservancy, water supply, education, public works and other developmental functions.

### State-Municipal Relationship in Orissa and Amendments of Orissa Municipal Act, 1950

The relation between the municipality and the state government is a close one. The municipality is a creature of state government. But as a system it enjoys autonomy subject to the rules and statutes. For the realisation of grass root democracy urban bodies are expected to be autonomous having their separate jurisdiction of powers and functions. Even as early as in 1951 D.N. Chester wrote that local bodies cannot be subjected to a control like a subordinate agency of the state government.

The state government of Orissa because of its superior constitutional position exercises control over the urban bodies assumes chiefly three forms: legislative, administrative and financial control. The legislative control over municipalities may take a number of forms by enacting laws.

Orissa Municipal Act, 1950 (Orissa Act 23 of 1950)[22] came into force on 16-4-1951. Orissa Municipal Act deals with constitution of Municipalities (Section-4 to section-11) which has been amended by Orissa Act 11 of 1994 with effect from 31-5-94 incorporates mandatory provisions of 74th Constitutional Amendment Act in manner of election of councillors (Section-10), reservation of seats for Scheduled Castes, Scheduled Tribes, Women and Backward Class of citizens (Sections-11). The matters on election and election petition are dealt with in Sections 11-A to 38. The newly added Section 11-A deals with superintendence, direction and control of elections to vest in the Election Commission as envisaged in the 74th Constitution Amendment. The removal, resignation and term of councillors are dealt with in Sections 38 to 48 with clauses Inserted by Orissa Act 16 of 1968 with effect from 1-8-1968; substituted by Orissa Act 22 of 1978; deleted by Orissa Act 8 of 1984; insetted by Orissa Act 5 of 1990 and finally ruled by Orissa Act 11 of 1994 with effect from 31-5-1994. Establishment under municipality is dealt with in Sections 73-103; Budget in Sections 104-113; Municipal Fund in Sections 114-120; Municipal Property in Sections 121-130; Imposition of Taxes in Sections 131-157; Recovery of Taxes in Sections 158-195A; and other miscellaneous activities in Sections up to 417.

Orissa Municipal (Reservation of Seats and Conduct of Election) Rules, 1994 and Orissa Municipal (Delimitation of Wards, Reservation of Seats and Conduct of Election) (Amendment) Rules, 1996[23] meant for Backward Class of Citizens, meaning Backward Class of Citizens, other than Scheduled Castes and Scheduled Tribes as may be notified by the Orissa State Commissioner for Backward Classes Act, 1993. Municipal constituency for last July 1997 municipal election can be seen in Table 1.

**Municipal Election in Post 74th Constitutional Amendment in Orissa**

Municipal Councils of Orissa had faced two contrasting and alternative election strategies for the choice of Municipal Chairman in pre-amendment period. 1950-1977[24] had election from among elected councillors, changed to direct election in 1978[25] and subsequently reversed in 1983.[26] Again in 1990, the Act had been amended for direct election of chairman and election of vice-chairman by councillors from among

**TABLE 1**

**Constitution of Municipal Wards of Orissa for 1997 Municipal Election**

| *District* | *Municipal Institution* | *Reservations* | | | | | | *Total Wards* |
|---|---|---|---|---|---|---|---|---|
| | | *SC/SCW* | *ST/STW* | *BCC* | *BCCW* | *RW* | *UR* | |
| Angul | 1. Angul N | 2/1 | 1/0 | 4 | 2 | 4 | 5 | 19 |
| | 2. Athamalik N | 1/1 | 1/0 | 2 | 1 | 2 | 3 | 11 |
| | 3. Talcher M | 2/2 | 1/0 | 4 | 2 | 3 | 7 | 21 |
| Balangir | 4. Balangir M | 1/1 | 1/0 | 3 | 2 | 3 | 6 | 17 |
| | 5. Patnagarh N | 1/1 | 1/0 | 3 | 1 | 3 | 3 | 13 |
| | 6. Kantabanjhi N | 1/1 | 0/0 | 2 | 1 | 2 | 5 | 12 |
| | 7. Titilagarh N | 1/1 | 1/0 | 3 | 1 | 3 | 5 | 15 |
| Balasore | 8. Balasore M | 2/1 | 1/1 | 6 | 3 | 6 | 11 | 31 |
| | 9. Jaleswar N | 0/1 | 1/1 | 3 | 2 | 2 | 7 | 17 |
| | 10. Soro N | 2/1 | 1/0 | 4 | 2 | 4 | 5 | 19 |
| | 11. Nilagiri N | 1/1 | 2/1 | 2 | 2 | 1 | 3 | 13 |
| Baragarh | 12. Baragarh M | 1/2 | 1/0 | 3 | 2 | 2 | 6 | 17 |
| | 13. Barpali N | 1/1 | 1/1 | 1 | 0 | 2 | 4 | 11 |
| | 14. Padmapur N | 0/1 | 1/1 | 2 | 1 | 1 | 4 | 11 |
| Bhadrak | 15. Basudevpur N | 2/1 | 0/1 | 3 | 2 | 3 | 6 | 17 |
| | 16. Bhadrak M | 1/1 | 1/0 | 5 | 2 | 6 | 11 | 27 |
| Boudh Cuttack | 17. Boudha N | 2/1 | 0/0 | 4 | 0 | 4 | 3 | 14 |

| | | | | | | | | |
|---|---|---|---|---|---|---|---|---|
| | 18. Athagarh N | 2/1 | 1/0 | 3 | 1 | 3 | 3 | 14 |
| | 19. Banki N | 2/1 | 1/0 | 3 | 2 | 3 | 5 | 17 |
| | 20. Choudwar M | 1/1 | 1/0 | 3 | 2 | 3 | 6 | 17 |
| | 21. Cuttack C | 3/1 | 1/0 | 6 | 3 | 8 | 13 | 35 |
| Deogarh | 22. Deogarh | 1/1 | 1/1 | 2 | 1 | 1 | 3 | 11 |
| Dhenkanal | 23. Dhenkanal M | 2/1 | 1/0 | 4 | 2 | 4 | 7 | 21 |
| | 24. Bhuban | 1/1 | 1/0 | 3 | 1 | 3 | 5 | 15 |
| | 25. Kamakhyanagar N | 1/1 | 1/0 | 2 | 1 | 2 | 4 | 12 |
| Gujpati | 26. Kasinagar N | 2/1 | 0/1 | 3 | 1 | 2 | 3 | 13 |
| | 27. Parlakhemedi M | 1/1 | 0/1 | 3 | 2 | 2 | 6 | 16 |
| Ganjam | 28. Berhampur M | 2/1 | 1/0 | 5 | 3 | 5 | 10 | 27 |
| | 29. Chikiti N | 1/0 | 1/0 | 3 | 1 | 3 | 3 | 12 |
| | 30. Digapahandi N | 1/1 | 1/0 | 2 | 1 | 2 | 3 | 11 |
| | 31. Gopalpur N | 1/0 | 1/0 | 2 | 1 | 3 | 3 | 11 |
| | 32. Aska N | 2/1 | 1/0 | 3 | 2 | 3 | 6 | 18 |
| | 33. Belgunthan N | 1/0 | 1/0 | 3 | 1 | 3 | 3 | 12 |
| | 34. Bhanja Nagar N | 2/1 | 1/0 | 3 | 2 | 2 | 4 | 15 |
| | 35. Buguda N | 1/0 | 1/0 | 2 | 1 | 3 | 3 | 11 |
| | 36. Soroda N | 2/1 | 1/0 | 2 | 1 | 2 | 2 | 11 |
| | 37. Chhatrapur N | 1/0 | 1/0 | 3 | 1 | 3 | 3 | 12 |
| | 38. Ganjam N | 2/1 | 1/0 | 3 | 1 | 1 | 2 | 12 |

| District | Municipal Institution | Reservations | | | | | | Total Wards |
|---|---|---|---|---|---|---|---|---|
| | | SC/SCW | ST/STW | BCC | BCCW | RW | UR | |
| | 39. Hinjilicut N | 2/1 | 1/0 | 4 | 2 | 4 | 7 | 21 |
| | 40. Kabisukynagar N | 1/1 | 1/0 | 3 | 2 | 3 | 5 | 16 |
| | 41. Khalikote N | 1/0 | 1/0 | 3 | 1 | 3 | 3 | 12 |
| | 42. Kodala | 1/0 | 1/0 | 3 | 1 | 4 | 3 | 13 |
| | 43. Polsara | 1/1 | 1/0 | 3 | 1 | 3 | 3 | 13 |
| | 44. Pursotmpur N | 1/1 | 1/0 | 3 | 1 | 3 | 4 | 14 |
| | 45. Rambha N | 2/2 | 1/0 | 3 | 1 | 2 | 2 | 13 |
| Jagatsinghpur | 46. Jagatsinghpur N | 3/1 | 1/0 | 3 | 2 | 4 | 6 | 20 |
| Jajpur | 47. Jajpurroa DM | 2/2 | 2/1 | 5 | 2 | 4 | 7 | 25 |
| | 48. Jajpur | 2/1 | 0/0 | 3 | 2 | 2 | 5 | 15 |
| Jharsuguda | 49. Brajrjngr M | 3/1 | 1/1 | 3 | 2 | 2 | 4 | 17 |
| | 50. Jharsuguda M | 3/1 | 3/2 | 5 | 2 | 3 | 5 | 24 |
| Kalahandi | 51. Bhawanptnam | 1/1 | 1/0 | 3 | 1 | 3 | 5 | 15 |
| | 52. Kesinga N | 1/1 | 1/0 | 3 | 1 | 2 | 3 | 12 |
| | 53. Junagarh N | 0/1 | 0/1 | 3 | 1 | 1 | 5 | 12 |
| Kandhamal | 54. Gudaygr N | 1/1 | 2/1 | 0 | 0 | 3 | 5 | 13 |
| | 55. Phulbani | 1/2 | 1/0 | 0 | 0 | 3 | 6 | 13 |
| Kendrapara | 56. Kendrapara M | 1/1 | 1/0 | 4 | 2 | 4 | 7 | 20 |
| | 57. Pattamundai N | 4/2 | 1/0 | 4 | 2 | 3 | 4 | 20 |
| Keonjhar | 58. Anandapur N | 2/1 | 1/0 | 3 | 2 | 2 | 5 | 16 |

| | | | | | | | | |
|---|---|---|---|---|---|---|---|---|
| | 59. Barbil M | 1/1 | 3/1 | 0 | 0 | 3 | 5 | 14 |
| | 60. JODA M | 1/1 | 3/1 | 0 | 0 | 2 | 5 | 13 |
| | 61. Keonjhar M | 1/1 | 3/1 | 0 | 0 | 4 | 7 | 17 |
| Khurda | 62. Bhubanesr C | 2/1 | 1/1 | 6 | 3 | 5 | 11 | 30 |
| | 63. Jatni N | 2/1 | 0/1 | 4 | 2 | 3 | 8 | 21 |
| | 64. Balugaon | 2/1 | 1/0 | 2 | 1 | 2 | 2 | 11 |
| | 65. Banapur N | 1/1 | 1/0 | 3 | 1 | 3 | 5 | 15 |
| | 66. Khurda N | 2/1 | 0/1 | 4 | 2 | 3 | 9 | 22 |
| Koraput | 67. Kotpad N | 1/1 | 2/1 | 0 | 0 | 2 | 6 | 13 |
| | 68. Keypur M | 2/1 | 2/1 | 0 | 0 | 6 | 13 | 25 |
| | 69. Koraput N | 1/1 | 2/1 | 0 | 0 | 3 | 7 | 15 |
| Malkangiri | 70. Malkangiri N | 3/1 | 2/1 | 0 | 0 | 3 | 5 | 15 |
| Mayurbhanj | 71. Rairanagapur N | 1/0 | 1/1 | 0 | 0 | 4 | 8 | 15 |
| | 72. Baripada M | 2/1 | 2/1 | 0 | 0 | 7 | 12 | 25 |
| | 73. Udala N | 1/0 | 2/1 | 0 | 0 | 3 | 5 | 12 |
| | 74. Karanjia | 1/1 | 2/2 | 0 | 0 | 2 | 7 | 15 |
| Nabarangpur | 75. Nabarangpur M | 1/1 | 1/1 | 0 | 0 | 3 | 9 | 16 |
| | 76. Umarkot N | 3/2 | 1/1 | 0 | 0 | 2 | 4 | 13 |
| Nayagarh | 77. Khandapada N | 1/0 | 1/0 | 2 | 2 | 3 | 4 | 13 |
| | 78. Nayagarh N | 1/0 | 1/0 | 2 | 2 | 3 | 4 | 13 |
| Nuapada | 79. Khariar RD N | 2/1 | 1/0 | 3 | 2 | 3 | 5 | 17 |

| *District* | *Municipal Institution* | *Reservations* | | | | | | *Total Wards* |
|---|---|---|---|---|---|---|---|---|
| | | *SC/SCW* | *ST/STW* | *BCC* | *BCCW* | *RW* | *UR* | |
| | 80. Khariar N | 2/1 | 1/0 | 3 | 1 | 2 | 3 | 13 |
| Puri | 81. Kornak N | 2/1 | 1/0 | 3 | 1 | 2 | 3 | 13 |
| | 82. Nimapada N | 1/1 | 1/0 | 2 | 1 | 2 | 3 | 11 |
| | 83. Pipili N | 2/1 | 1/0 | 3 | 1 | 3 | 5 | 16 |
| | 84. Puri M | 2/1 | 1/0 | 5 | 3 | 6 | 12 | 30 |
| Rayagada | 85. Gudari N | 1/1 | 1/0 | 0 | 0 | 2 | 6 | 11 |
| | 86. Gunupur N | 2/1 | 1/0 | 0 | 0 | 4 | 7 | 15 |
| | 87. Rayagada N | 1/1 | 2/1 | 0 | 0 | 4 | 9 | 18 |
| Sambalpur | 88. Kuchinda N | 1/0 | 2/2 | 0 | 0 | 2 | 4 | 11 |
| | 89. Hirakud N | 2/1 | 1/1 | 3 | 2 | 2 | 5 | 17 |
| | 90. Sambalpur M | 3/1 | 2/1 | 1 | 1 | 6 | 14 | 29 |
| Subarnpur | 91. Binika N | 2/1 | 1/0 | 2 | 1 | 2 | 3 | 12 |
| | 92. Sonepur M | 2/1 | 0/0 | 3 | 1 | 3 | 4 | 14 |
| | 93. Tarbha N | 1/1 | 0/0 | 2 | 1 | 2 | 5 | 12 |
| Sundergarh | 94. Birmitrapur M | 1/1 | 2/2 | 0 | 0 | 1 | 4 | 11 |
| | 95. Rajgangpur M | 1/0 | 3/2 | 0 | 0 | 5 | 8 | 19 |
| | 96. Rourkela M | 1/1 | 2/2 | 0 | 0 | 8 | 18 | 32 |
| | 97. Sundergarh M | 1/1 | 2/2 | 0 | 0 | 3 | 7 | 16 |

| District | Municipal Institution | Reservations | | | | | | Total Wards |
|---|---|---|---|---|---|---|---|---|
| | | SC/SCW | ST/STW | BCC | BCCW | RW | UR | |
| | Councillors | 146/91 | 112/44 | 231 | 113 | 299 | 546 | 1582 |
| | Chairpersons | 8/4 | 4/2 | 14 | 7 | 19 | 39 | 97 |
| Total number of electors in 97 urban local bodies = 27,54,647 | | | | | | | | |
| List of Municipalities where election is over since 1995: | | | | | | | | |
| Jagatsinghpur | 98. Paradeep N | 1/0 | 1/0 | 0 | 0 | 5 | 8 | 15 |
| Jharsuguda | 99. Belpahar N | 1/1 | 2/2 | 0 | 0 | 3 | 7 | 16 |
| Koraput | 100. Balimela N | 2/2 | 1/0 | 0 | 0 | 2 | 5 | 12 |
| | 101. Sunabeda N | 3/2 | 3/2 | 0 | 0 | 4 | 10 | 24 |
| Sambalpur | 102. Burla N | 2/2 | 1/0 | 0 | 0 | 3 | 7 | 15 |
| | Councillors | 9/7 | 8/4 | 0 | 0 | 17 | 37 | 82 |
| | Chairpersons | 1/1 | 1/1 | 0 | 0 | 0 | 1 | 5 |

**N.B.** SC = Scheduled Caste, ST = Scheduled Tribe, SCW = SC Woman, RW = Rummit Women, UR = unreserved, M = Municipality, N = Nin, C = Corporation.

themselves at first meeting of the municipal council.[27] The 1990 amendment introduced political party in municipal elections along with reservations for women, Scheduled Tribes and Scheduled Castes. Results of Orissa Municipal Councils in 1992 had Chairpersons as follows: 44 of ruling Janata Dal, 28 Congress, 03 BJP and 15 independent, thus total 90 Councils.

**TABLE 2**
**1992 and 1997 Party Based Municipal Elections with Direct and Indirect Chairman Election**

| *Year* | *Chairperson Election* | *Ruling party* | *Result* | *Remarks* |
|---|---|---|---|---|
| 1992 | Direct | JD with Biju Patnaik as CM | 44 of ruling Janata Dal<br>28 Congress<br>03 BJP and<br>15 independent<br>90 Councils | Upper hand of Ruling party in power in direct election. |
| 1997 | Indirect | Congress with JB Patnaik as CM | 63 ruling Congress Party<br>15 Janata Party<br>06 BJP Party<br>07 Independents<br>91 Councils result available | 40 on party majority pulled 23 more Councils including Bhubaneswar corp, with 8/30 councillor |

The last 1997 municipal election has some alterations in backgrounds over that of 1992. Orissa Act 11 of 1994 introduced election of Chairperson of Municipalities by Indirect method from among the councillors. It has reservations as well as political party basis of municipal election. The results on the basis of absolute majority are as follows: 40 ruling Congress Party, 05 Janata Party, 03 BJP Party, 01 SJP. Rest 46, out of 95 Councils subjected to election in July 1997, do not have absolute majority of any political party. The dispositions after indirect chairman election has been shown in Table 2 below along with results of direct chairman election in 1992.

**Orissa State Finance Commission[29]**

Orissa State Finance Commission consisting of a Chairman and four Members was constituted by virtue of an Ordinance. The Commission shall make recommendations relating to the principles which should govern the distribution between State and Panchayati Raj Institutions and the Municipalities of the net proceeds of the taxes, duties, tolls and fees leviable by the state. The determination of taxes, duties, tolls and fees which may be assigned to, or appropriated by Panchayats, Panchayat Samitis and Zilla Parishads or, as the case may be, Municipalities is vested on the Commission. It will also consider the *grants-in-aid* to the Gram Panchayats, Panchayat Samities and Zilla Parishads or, as the case may be, Municipalities from the Consolidated Fund of the state and will adopt such measures needed to improve the financial position of the Gram Panchayats, Panchayat Samities and Zilla Parishads and Municipalities.

**District Planning Committee**

The local government system is incomplete so far as the District Planning Committee has not been constituted in any district of Orissa due to delay in Municipal election. It will consolidate all plans prepared by Panchayats and the Municipalities in the district. As the three tier Panchayati Raj institutions have completed their elections, the elections to the local bodies are not completed and the state government has to move to constitute the District Planning Committees.

**Concluding Remarks**

The election to municipal bodies in Orissa has come up very late after the 74th Constitution Amendment Act. Election to local bodies in general has faced some litigations and the election to the PRIs had been completed only in January, 1997. Still the state government is to work out its District Planning Committees and to bring out notification of Municipal Corporation Act.

## REFERENCES

1. New Concise Oxford English Dictionary, The New Edition, 1990's
2. M. Venkatarangaya and M. Pattabhiram, *Local Government in India,* Allied Publishers Pvt. Ltd., New Delhi, 1969, p.1.
3. S. Humes and E.M.Martin, *The Structures of Local Governments throughout the World (International Union of Local Authorities),* The Haugue, Martinus Nijhoff, 1961, Ch. 8, p. 242.
4. *Government of India: memorandum on the Development and Working of Representative Institutions in the sphere of Local Self Government,* Vol. V. p. 1056, Quoted in the Report of the Indian Statutory Commission; Cmd, 3568, Vol. 1, London, H.M.S.O., 1930, p. 298.
5. Maheshwari, S.R., *Local Government in India,* Lakshmi Narain Agarwal Educational Publishers, Agra, 1984, p. 14.
6. Mohanty. B., "73rd and 74th Constitution Amendments: A Predisposition to Urban-Rural Symmetry", *Nagarlok,* Urban Affairs Quarterly, IIPA, New Delhi, April-June, 1996, Vol. XXVIII. No. 2 pp. 44-54.

7. *Reports on the Administration of Bengal,* 1888-89, Bengal Secretariat Press, Calcutta, 1889, p. 62.
8. *Utkal Dipika,* Orya Weekly, 26-8-76, pp. 138-39.
9. Report on Administration of Bengal, 1905-06, Bengal Secretariat Press, Calcutta, 1906, p. 40.
10. *Report on Administration of Bengal,* 1884-85, p. 44.
11. *Report on Administration of Bihar and Orissa,* The Bihar Orissa Secretariat Book Depot, Patna, 1914, p. 35.
12. Sahu, N.K., Mishra, P.K., *Madhusudan Das: The Legislature (His Speeches),* Pragati Utkal Sangh, Rourkela, 1973, p. 334.
13. Annual administration Report of Bihar and Orissa 1921–21, pp. 227–30
14. Rai Saheb Jadunath Mohapatra, *Administration of Orissa, 1936-37 to 1938-39,* Government Press, Cuttack, 1941, p. 48.
15. Jackson, J.W.C., *Bihar and Orissa in 1927-28,* pp. 269-75.
16. Mohanty, B., *Municipal System in India: Citizens' involvement,* Ashish Publishing House, New Delhi, 1993, pp. 46-51.
17. Meher, R.K., "Growth of Urban Population, Informal Sector Economy and the Concomitant Environmental Problems: Case of Class I Towns in Orissa", *Nagarlok,* April-June, 1995, Vol. XXVII, No. 2, p. 52-55.
18. *Census of India 1991, Paper-2 of 1991, Provisional Population Totals Rural-Urban Distribution,* pp. 10-11.
19. *Ibid,* p. 61.
20. See Section-11 The Orissa Municipal Act, 1950.
21. See Section-12 *Ibid.*
22. Orissa Gazette Extraordinary 11-11-1950, for statement of objects and reasons, Orissa Gazette Extraordinary dated 25-3-1950 and for report of Select Committee, Orissa Gazette Extra ordinary dated 29-7-1950.
23. The Orissa Gazette, 12-2-1996.
24. See Section-47, The Orissa Municipal Act, 1950.
25. Orissa Municipal (Amendment) Ordinance, 1978 (Orissa Ordinance No. 5 of 1978) The Orissa Gazette, 26 July 1978.
26. Orissa Municipal (Amendment) Ordinance, 1983 The Orissa Gazette, 6 December 1983.
27. The Orissa Municipal (Amendment) Act, 1990, The Orissa Gazette, 20 April 1990.
28. *Orissa Government Notification* No. FC (10)-16/96-48704/F dated 21-10-96.

# 14

# Status of Urban Infrastructure Development in Orissa

—*Bhagabata Patro and Preyasi Nayak*

**Introduction**

The process of urbanisation helps an economy to achieve rapid economic growth. An urban area, according to 1991 census, requires a minimum population of 5,000, 75 per cent of the working male population engaged in non-agricultural activities and a population density of 400 persons per sq. kms. This indicates that urbanisation means transformation of an economy from agricultural dominated to a non-agricultural dominated. The contribution of urban sector to the gross domestic product in India has increased from 29 per cent in 1950-51 to about 47 per cent in 1980-81. With rapid urbanisation, there is a possibility of deterioration in the physical

**TABLE 1**
**Growth of Urban Population in Orissa**

*(In millions)*

| *Year* | *Urban Population* | *Percentage increase in urban population* |
|---|---|---|
| 1951 | 0.5 | — |
| 1961 | 1.1 | 120 |
| 1971 | 1.8 | 64 |
| 1981 | 3.1 | 72 |
| 1991 | 4.2 | 35 |

*Source:* Statistical outline of Orissa, Directorate of Economics and Statistics, Govt. of Orissa, Bhubaneswar, 1988.

environment and quality of life in the urban areas. This resulted in widening the gap between demand and supply in the provisioning of urban infrastructural facilities. In India, there exists wide variations in the level of urbanisation among the States and Union Territories. While the Union

Territory of Delhi (89.93 per cent) is the most urbanised in the country, the urban population is lowest in the Union Territory of Dadra and Nagar Haveli (8.47 per cent). The pace of urbanisation in Orissa is indicated in Table 1. The percentage increase in urban population is highest (120 per cent) in the decade 1951-61. In 1971-81 the increase was 72 per cent. The pressure of urbanisation slowed down in the decade 1981-91 with only 35 per cent growth in urban population. The urban local bodies in Orissa are mostly in the coastal region. The districtwise distribution of Municipalities and Notified Area Councils, according to 1991 census, is given in Table 2.

The National Commission on Urbanisation in its recommendations in August 1988, has identified National Priority Cities (NPCs) and State Priority Cities (SPCs) in the State. The NPCs in Orissa were Bhubaneswar, Rourkela, Paradeep, Koraput and Puri and the SPCs were Cuttack, Berhampur and Sambalpur. Six more cities were recommended for inclusion in the list of State Priority Cities, Cuttack, Bhubaneswar, Puri and Berhampur have been recommended for special attention as an emerging urban belt. The Commission has identified Rourkela, Sambalpur, Cuttack, Puri, Paradeep as the Spatial Priority Urban Region.

**TABLE 2**

**District-wise Urban Local Bodies in Orissa**

| *Sl. No.* | *Name of the District* | *Number of Municipalities* | *Number of NACs* | *Total* |
|---|---|---|---|---|
| 1. | Angul | 1 | 2 | 3 |
| 2. | Balasore | 1 | 3 | 4 |
| 3. | Baragarh | 1 | 2 | 3 |
| 4. | Bhadrak | 1 | 1 | 2 |
| 5. | Bolangir | 1 | 3 | 4 |
| 6. | Boudh | — | 1 | 1 |
| 7. | Cuttack | 2 | 2 | 4 |
| 8. | Deogarh | 1 | — | 1 |
| 9. | Dhenkanal | 1 | 2 | 3 |
| 10. | Gajapati | 1 | 1 | 2 |
| 11. | Ganjam | 1 | 17 | 18 |
| 12. | Jagatsinghpur | — | 2 | 2 |
| 13. | Jajpur | 2 | — | 2 |
| 14. | Jharsuguda | 2 | 1 | 3 |

*(Contd.)*

| | | | | |
|---|---|---|---|---|
| 15. | Kalahandi | 1 | 1 | 2 |
| 16. | Kandhamal | — | 2 | 2 |
| 17. | Kendrapara | 1 | 1 | 2 |
| 18. | Keonjhar | 3 | 1 | 4 |
| 19. | Khurda | 1 | 4 | 5 |
| 20. | Koraput | 1 | 3 | 4 |
| 21. | Malkangiri | — | 2 | 2 |
| 22. | Mayurbhanj | 1 | 3 | 4 |
| 23. | Nabarangpur | 1 | 1 | 2 |
| 24. | Nayagarh | — | 2 | 2 |
| 25. | Nuapada | — | 2 | 2 |
| 26. | Puri | 1 | 3 | 4 |
| 27. | Rayagada | 1 | 2 | 3 |
| 28. | Sambalpur | 1 | 3 | 4 |
| 29. | Sonepur | 1 | 2 | 3 |
| 30. | Sundargarh | 4 | — | 4 |
| | Total | 32 | 70 | 102 |

*Source:* Districts at a Glance, Directorate of Economics and Statistics, Orissa, Bhubaneswar.

**Urban Development Policy in Orissa**

The Government of Orissa, in 1990, declared that urban centres should play the role of change agent for achieving overall growth of the state economy. The state has focused on an integrated development and management of urban centres with the following objectives:

1. To provide and promote employment opportunities to meet the economic demands and needs of the region.
2. To build up indoor environment at home and at work.
3. To provide infrastructure of satisfactory level for the socio-economic activities.
4. To satisfy the housing need of different income groups.
5. To build up city environment free of population and strike an ecological balance.
6. To provide efficient services for alleviation of urban poverty.
7. To improve upon the existing organisation structure for strengthening the benefit delivery system.

8. To encourage community empowerment and self-help for increasing the effectiveness of implementation of schemes and projects.
9. To strengthen the financial base of the urban centres by plugging the linkages and loopholes and through adopting service oriented tax-structure.

To achieve the above objectives, the State Government declared that there is need to have qualitative and quantitative improvement in the civic amenities, municipal services, infrastructural facilities, wage employment measures on an increasing scale through a comprehensive approach. It is also necessary to ascertain availability of physical, financial and institutional resources and strategies to be adopted to meet the growing needs over the coming years. Efforts of different organisations like Urban Local Bodies, Development Authorities, State Undertakings and the State and Central Government departments need to be integrated and the impact shall have to converge in the urban areas to gear up urban services delivery system. It is necessary to empower communities and integrate their roles with Government and other organisations.

The State Government established State Urban Development Agency (SUDA) and District Urban Development Agency (DUDA) at the state and district levels respectively to undertake schemes and projects and play an effective role to co-ordinate the functioning of different organisations. More particularly, the DUDAs are required to advise the Urban Local Bodies in preparing an action plan to improve urban infrastructural facilities. The Urban Local Bodies in Orissa are discharging two categories of functions. The obligatory functions are construction, maintenance, improvement of roads, public health and sanitation facilities, conservancy of drainage system, promotion of education, water supply, maintenance of street lighting and cleaning the reclamation of unhealthy locality etc. The optional functions are relief work in times of flood and famine, promotion of health, establishment of markets, maintenance of schools, maintenance of parks and libraries, etc. In addition to these functions the local bodies also keep record of births and deaths, undertake remunerative commercial enterprises, etc. The sources of income of an Urban Local Body consists of taxes imposed on lands, houses and buildings, taxes on vehicles, taxes on professional and entertainment, different kinds of service related charges, octroi and Loans and aid from the State Government. The Urban Local Bodies incur expenditure on general administration, public health and medical relief, education, management of public utilities, sanitation and other amenities. The financial resources of

Urban Local Bodies in Orissa consist of own taxes, shares from some taxes and grants for special purpose schemes. In some special purpose welfare schemes the expenditure is to be shared between the local bodies and the state government on a matching basis. Some of the schemes implemented by Urban Local Bodies in Orissa are discussed below.

**Urban Development Schemes and Urban Local Bodies**

***1. I.D.S.M.T. (Integrated Development of Small and Medium Towns).*** This is a centrally sponsored plan scheme with the objective of overall development of small and medium towns with population of 5,00,000 or less. The scheme provides for construction of houses, commercial complexes, new link roads, improvement of existing roads, bus-stands and truck terminals. The Government of India assists the scheme with 48 per cent in small towns and 36 per cent in bigger towns of the estimated cost. The Urban Local Bodies receive correspondingly 32 per cent and 64 per cent respectively of the estimated cost from the State Government as grants-in-aid and the rest is to be borne by the local bodies either from their own sources or procure institutional financial assistance.

***2. Public Toilet-cum-Bath Complex.*** This is a state plan scheme aiming at providing public toilet-cum-bath complex at important places, like railway stations, bus stands, hospitals, markets, etc. to facilitate the following population coming to urban areas in pursuit of employment, official and other commercial purposes. The state government finances the scheme through grants-in-aid to the extent of 50 per cent of the estimated cost. The rest is to be met from own fund of the local bodies.

Another programme to improve public sanitation relates to conversion of dry latrines in private individual holdings into low cost pour flush water-seal latrines to make the urban areas scavenger free. Under the scheme, 45 per cent subsidy is given to individuals belonging to economically weaker sections, 25 per cent subsidy to low income group individuals and no subsidy but only loans to individuals belonging to middle income and high income groups.

***3. Urban Land Management.*** The objective of the scheme is to prevent excess lands in the hands of the individuals and to use the land for the benefit of the community in a planned manner. For category D cities the requirement is that no person shall be entitled to hold vacant land in excess of 2,000 sq. mt. The surplus land is to be distributed in order of priority for the use of State Government, Central Government, Development Authorities and other philanthropic organisations.

*4. **Environment Improvement of Urban Slums.*** Through this programme it is aimed to provide basic urban amenities like water supply, street light, roads, drains, community latrines, community bath and sewerage system to slum pockets in the Urban Local Bodies. The state government extends an aid of Rs. 300 per capita to the Urban Local Bodies under the scheme. The scheme stipulates preparation of full fledged action plan, completion of ongoing works, monthly, quarterly and annual review of achievements, community participation in the implementation process.

*5. **Other Remunerative and Non-remunerative Schemes of the ULBs.*** The Urban Local Bodies were encouraged to undertake different remunerative schemes like construction of market complexes, transport networks, exhibitions, etc. to augment their source of income. The State Government assists 25 per cent to 40 per cent of the project cost as grants-in-aid. Proper utilisation of funds and preparation of the project report well in advance are two important requirements of the schemes. The Urban Local Bodies also undertake non-remunerative projects in the interest of the general public. Under this scheme town halls, parks, bathing ghats, school buildings, office buildings, etc. are constructed. The State Government gives 50 per cent as grants-in-aids and the rest is borne by the concerned Urban Local Body.

*6. **Road Development and Maintenance.*** The Urban Local Bodies in Orissa receive grants-in-aid from the state government for improvement and construction of municipal roads, culverts and drains and also for repair and maintenance thereof. For construction of new roads the cost is shared between the state government and urban local bodies on a 50:50 basis. For maintenance purpose grant is given as per the road length of the local bodies.

*7. **Extension of Education Facilities.*** The State Government extends grants towards salaries of the secondary school teachers established by the urban local bodies. The local bodies have to bear the cost of building and other infrastructure.

*8. **Scheme for Environmental Protection.*** The State Government made a beginning to protect urban environment in the urban areas through community management. Each ward in an urban area may be divided into a number of Managable Units Area (M.U.A.) with 150 to 200 number of holdings. An environmental protection team for each M.U.A. is to be formed to look after cleaning, sweeping and maintenance of urban infrastructure.

***9. Nehru Rozgar Yojana (N.R.Y.).*** The Government of India initiated this programme to provide employment to the urban unemployed and under-employed people in urban areas. The scheme provided for setting up of micro enterprises and give training and infrastructure support for urban poor beneficiaries. Creation of socially and economically useful public assets through wage-employment programmes was another component of the scheme. While the first one was extended to all urban settlements, the second one was divided into two categories i.e.,

(a) Urban settlements below 20,000 population.
(b) Urban settlements having a population between 20,000 and 1,00,000 including new industrial towns.

The Central Government provided 100 per cent funds in case of urban micro enterprises scheme. Funding pattern in wage employment programmes was 80:10:10 by the Centre, State and urban local bodies respectively. Establishment of low cost water supply, protection of water sources, low cost sanitation, widening of streets and pathways, arrangement for garbage disposal, construction of community centres, etc. were some of the activities undertaken under this scheme.

***10. Urban Basic Services for the Poor.*** The scheme aimed at upgrading the quality of life at urban poor by reducing infant mortality and morbidity rates, enhancing learning opportunity for children, improve the capacity of the municipalities and voluntary organisations to launch child specific programmes for the urban poor. The basic services provided under the scheme were water, health, education, nutrition, environmental sanitation, recreation and shelter. The funding pattern of the scheme was Central Assistance at a rate of Rs. 175 per capita in the first year and Rs. 88 per capita from the second year on a matching basis between the Centre and State Governments. The State Government provided Rs 525 per capita for physical amenities in the first year. The programme envisaged preparation of a plan of action which was further subdivided into mini-plans. The plan of action laid down agency-wise financial commitments for each component with the stipulation of 70 per cent of the total budget to be allocated in the miniplans. The programme identified the project director of DUDA as the co-ordinator to implement this scheme. The Urban Local Body acted as the basic implementing agency.

***11. Public Health and Sewerage Disposal.*** In Orissa, the public health engineering organisation under the direct control of the State Government executes the urban water supply schemes, sewerage schemes, drainage schemes, etc. on behalf of the local bodies. There are different types of financing water supply and other schemes in vogue in Orissa. In some schemes the state and the urban local body shares the cost in the ratio of 1:2. Some other schemes are being implemented with 100 per cent government and HUDCO finance. The procedure of implementing the scheme is as follows:

1. The scheme is prepared on requisition from the urban local bodies by the public health department on a requisition from them.
2. The public health department implements the scheme after getting necessary funds from he state government and the concerned urban local body.

## Present Position of Urban Infrastructure in Orissa

In spite of the 74th Constitution Amendment relating to the functioning of Urban Local Bodies, in Orissa, there is no effort by the State Government to involve local governments administrative machinery in providing various public services. The annual report of the Housing and Urban Development Department for the year 1996-97 declared that it will take steps to have a strong infrastructure base and accelerate balanced and overall development mechanism of urban area in the state. It laid emphasis on enhancing the productive capacity of the urban economy, poverty alleviation, environment protection and development, urban infrastructure development, water supply and sanitation and urban housing. Many of these schemes are being administered by the government agencies. The achievement in the provision of public infrastructure services in the state, as per the latest available figure as shown in Table 3.

In addition to the above, certain town-specific schemes have been under implementation in the state. To meet the requirement of the tourist traffic in the pilgrim town of Puri, about 500 temporary and 50 permanent tubewells were dug up in the year 1996-97. For the Cuttack city, a polluted water treatment plant was established at Matgajpur. Similarly, with the technical collaboration of NEERI a saline water treatment plant was established at Puri.

## Pattern of Public Expenditure of Urban Local Bodies

Table 4 indicates the expenditure pattern on urban development and the role of urban local bodies in the state from 1987-88 to 1994-95. The local bodies have received specific purpose grants and block grants from the State/Centre. The Finance Accounts of the state reveals that such

## TABLE 3
## Physical Achievement of Urban Infrastructure Facilities in Orissa

| *Sl. No.* | *Items* | *Achievements* |
|---|---|---|
| 1. | Number of ULBs supplied with water supply (partially or fully) | 97 |
| 2. | Quantity of water supply available | 492 Million Litre (daily) |
| 3. | Number of population covered | 25.78 lakhs |
| | (a) piped water supply | 56 per cent |
| | (b) tube well | 16 per cent |
| 4. | Per capita water supply (daily) | 19 litres |
| 5. | Length of Urban Roads | 10280 kms. |
| 6. | Number of Towns/Cities covered under UBS | 12 numbers |
| 7. | No. of hand pump tube wells | 9104 numbers |
| 8. | Town where underground sewerage facilities available | 4 Numbers |
| 9. | No. of pollution control schemes | 4 Numbers |
| 10. | No. of towns with public toilet-cum-bath complex facilities | 96 Numbers |
| 11. | No. of sulabha complexes constructed | 164 Numbers |
| 12. | No. of towns declared scavenging free | 87 Numbers |
| 13. | No. of scavenges liberated | 159 Numbers |
| 14. | Total No. of low cost latrines constructed | 35,900 Numbers |

## TABLE 4
## Specific Purpose Expenditure on Urban Development and Assistance to Urban Local Bodies in Orissa

*(Rs. in lakh)*

| *Year* | *Asst. to ULBs* | *State Exp.* | *Total* | *Percentage* |
|---|---|---|---|---|
| *(1)* | *(2)* | *(3)* | *(4)* | *(5)* |
| 1987–88 | 8.01 | 57.05 | 65.06 | 12.3 |
| 1988–89 | 10.57 | 59.41 | 69.98 | 15.1 |
| 1990–91 | 5.40 | 58.18 | 63.58 | 8.4 |
| 1991–92 | 5.94 | 68.71 | 74.65 | 8.0 |
| 1992–93 | 7.09 | 85.51 | 92.61 | 7.7 |

| (1) | (2) | (3) | (4) | (5) |
|---|---|---|---|---|
| 1993–94 | 12.82 | 93.22 | 106.04 | 12.1 |
| 1995–96 | 21.77 | 103.47 | 125.24 | 17.4 |
| 1996–97 | 21.50 | 122.15 | 143.65 | 15.0 |

*Source:* Finance Accounts, Govt. of Orissa, Bhubaneswar (Different issues).

grants were directed to develop urban water supply, state capital development integrated development of small and medium towns, slum area development and other miscellaneous urban development schemes. Table 4 gives such assistance from 1987-88 to 1996-97.

To identify whether there is any improvement in the expenditure pattern of urban of urban local bodies for specific purposes after the 74th Constitution Amendment, we have used the method of fitting a time series trend line (using Least square techniques) for the years 1987-88 to 1994-95. Based on this, the expected spending for the years of 1995-96* and 1996-97 were obtained. This was placed against the observed figures for these two years. Thereafter a Chi-Square test is conducted to ascertain whether the difference is significant or not.

**TABLE 5**

**Testing Goodness of Fit of Specific Purpose Expenditure on Urban Development in Orissa**

*(Rs. in lakh)*

| *Year* | *Asst. to Local Bodies* | | *State spending* | | *Total* | |
|---|---|---|---|---|---|---|
| | *A.E.* | *E.E.* | *A.E.* | *E.E.* | *A.E.* | *E.E.* |
| 1995–96 | 21.77 | 9.72 | 103.47 | 97.31 | 125.24 | 107.03 |
| 1996–97 | 21.50 | 10.12 | 122.15 | 105.01 | 143.65 | 115.14 |

A.E.= Actual Expenditure
E.F.= Estimated expenditure as calculated from the regression line

Observed Chi-Square value = 37.96

Theoretical Chi-Square Value for (6–1) degrees of freedom = 11.1

This establishes that there is significant difference between expected and observed values with regard to specific purpose expenditure on urban development. This indicates rise in specific purpose expenditure significantly since 1995-96.

The other mechanism of resource flow to the urban local bodies in Orissa has been sharing of taxes and other miscellaneous assignments.

The Finance Accounts of the State have presented the total allocation to Local Bodies and Panchayati Raj Institutions. Of the two shared taxes, the importance of motor vehicle tax has not been very significant as it is linked to length of different types of roads and a fixed amount of Rs. 15 lakh per annum is given to the local bodies. The other one is the entertainment tax. The procedure of devolution is to share 50 per cent of the collection to the local bodies on the basis of origin.

**TABLE 6**

**Flow of Shared Taxes and Assignments to Local Bodies in Orissa**

*(Rs. in lakh)*

| *Year* | *Entertainment tax* | *Other miscellaneous taxes* | *Total* |
|---|---|---|---|
| 1981–82 | 60 | 341 | 401 |
| 1982–83 | 101 | 310 | 411 |
| 1983–84 | 133 | 319 | 452 |
| 1984–85 | 129 | 350 | 479 |
| 1985–86 | 133 | 342 | 475 |
| 1986–87 | 155 | 554 | 709 |
| 1987–88 | 127 | 506 | 633 |
| 1988–89 | 114 | 499 | 613 |
| 1990–91 | 100 | 1674 | 1774 |
| 1991–92 | 45 | 1247 | 1292 |
| 1992–93 | — | 1128 | 1128 |
| 1994–95 | 44 | 1246 | 1290 |
| 1995–96 | 0.3 | 1266 | 1266 |
| 1996–97 | 57 | 1305 | 1362 |

*Source* : Finance Accounts (Different Issues), Govt. of Orissa, Bhubaneswar.
*Relates to both Urban and Rural Local Bodies in Orissa.

*The year 1995–96 relates to flow of assistance in accordance with the recommendation of the 10th Finance Commission.

Table above gives the flow of grants and share of taxes from 1981–82 to 1996–97.

To examine the improvement in the allocation once again, the earlier model was adopted to see the impact of Constitution Amendment in empowering the urban and rural local bodies. The result is presented in the Table 7.

**Table 7**
**Testing Goodness of Fit of Block Assistance to Local Bodies in Orissa**

*(Rs. in lakh)*

| *Year* | *Entertainment Tax* | | *Other Miscellaneous Assignments* | | *Total* | |
|---|---|---|---|---|---|---|
| | *Actual* | *Expected* | *Actuals* | *Expected* | *Actuals* | *Expected* |
| 1995–96 | 0.3 | 79.78 | 1266 | 1425 | 1266.3 | 1462 |
| 1996–97 | 57 | 75.79 | 1305 | 1535 | 1362 | 1563 |

* Data relates to both Rural and Urban Local Bodies.

Observed Value of chi-square = 188.19
Theoretical Value of chi-square for (6–1) degrees of Freedom = 11.1

The result is that there is significant difference between expected expenditure and observed expenditure meaning thereby significant rise in assistance to the local bodies in the post Constitution Amendment period.

## Conclusions

The following conclusions emerge from the analysis conducted on the urban expenditure pattern and the availability of infrastructure services in the state economy:

1. In spite of repeated attempts, it was not possible to get any codified statistical information relating to the functioning of urban local government in the State. The office of the Director of Municipal Administration expressed its inability to provide all the information required for the purpose. The SUDA also expressed its inability to supply the information stating that they are only concerned with the poverty alleviation programmes. This indicates that the state government has not adopted any scientific formula for distributing resources among the urban areas of the states and lacks statistical information on this.
2. The appointment of the State Finance Commission only very recently under the chairmanship of Prof. Baidyanath Misra and the resignation of the earlier chairman on the ground of non-cooperation from the state government manifests state governments lack of concern for the suitable growth of urban local governments in the state.
3. A review of the functioning of the urban development department, in general, and urban development programmes implemented, in particular, reveals that most of the urban

infrastructural services are provided by the State Government directly to the urban population. Urban housing and urban water supply clearly indicate such a situation.

4. The fiscal dependence of urban local governments on the State/Central Government, even for salary purposes presents a gloomy picture of the financial position of Municipalities/NACs in the State. It appears that the municipality taxes have not been yielding adequate revenue to meet the growing challenge of providing several basic services in the urban areas.
5. The highly fluctuating figures relating to the State assistance to Municipalities/NACs indicate that such bodies are not in a position to formulate a clear and scientific budget in order of priority of demand for different services. It is necessary that a clear principle be evolved to channelise specific purpose and other grants in the State.

# 15

# Urban Local Government in Rajasthan

*—K.S. Saxena*

Political scientists are interested in the form of government a country has. In the process, they ask atleast three broad questions: (1) What are the purposes of governments, (i.e., ends of politics)? (2) What do governments do, (i.e., functions of politics)? and (3) Who exercises political power (processes of politics)? Generally speaking, democratic systems view the end of politics to be the provision, protection, or preservation of an atmosphere or social climate in which individuals may freely seek to realize their personal or collective aspirations. The special significance of cities for politics in developing countries stem from their strategic contribution to processes of economic development and modernisation and from their potential disruption. However, the research on politics and urbanism in India is still meagre and mostly exploratory. Little is known about the most basic features of urban politics in India, either about its internal structure or its external relations with state and national politics. Who are the major actors in Indian city politics? What are their goals and aspirations? How is political power distributed? On whose behalf it is used? What roles do organisations and elections play in urban political life? How do they affect decision making patterns and the content of policy? How is urban government organised institutionally, and how do its institutions work? To what extent is urban government autonomous from or penetrated by, other levels of authority? What, in short, characterizes the anatomy and functions, the behaviour and policy processes, of Indian city government and politics?

There are the questions at heart. But something more must be said to establish its terms and reference. The first problem to be considered is that of the unit of analysis, for it dictates criteria for inclusion and exclusion. The guiding questions point to 'city politics' as the subject, but what are the boundaries of city politics? Does Mayor's office serve as the focal point? Does city politics correspond to what happens within the Municipal boundaries? Or should city politics be defined more abstractly as, for example, community decision-making? The answers to these questions are not self-evident in the Indian setting. If we look at precedents, the most prominent approach assumes that city politics consists mainly of municipal politics and that the boundaries of the latter may serve, for analytic purposes, as the boundaries of the former, Rosenthal's study of Agra and Pune employed this approach. However, Municipal Government in India is far from sovereign in its own juridical domain, and its functional scope is severely limited. For example, in Jodhpur, the scope of municipal action, is restricted primarily to such services as maintenance of roads, sanitation, primary health, collection of house tax, etc. Such functions are but a small part of what urban government is all about. To determine, therefore, who exercises power in Indian city politics, one must look outside the framework of Municipal politics, i.e. why the most stimulating paradigm in the urbanisation has been the role of the city as an agent of social and cultural change.

In a case study of Jodhpur city, it is a mixture of traditional and the modern, the rural and the urban. Ascriptive bases of identification—caste, religion, language, and region—are salient in defining the lines of political cleavage, criteria of affiliation, and stakes of political competition. In same cases traditional patron-client relationships originating in rural region have been imported into Jodhpur. Caste in particular, remains important in Jodhpur society and politics, especially as a basis of group identification and mobilization, but no longer as a closed or consensual system. Same benefits are for individuals and immediate consumption, but others are shared by the group as whole elevating its position in the community at large.

Another example can be cited from the city of Ajmer, which is more or less a cosmopolitan society. No doubt, the caste or other ethnic groups are there but these are not in dominate position to affect the cosmopolitan character of the city.

However, in spite of all this, urban politics revolves round the 'municipalities' and the 'municipalities' or the urban local bodies can be treated as the Barometer of the city politics. Thus, for the first time, 74th Amendment of the Constitution added Part IX–A to the Constitution by the Constitution Act, 1992. This amendment has added 18 new articles and a new Twelfth Schedule relating to urban local bodies in the Constitution. It was implemented with effect from June 1, 1993. The

State Government, therefore, amended Rajasthan Municipality Act, 1959 (in April and Sep. 1994) accordingly. Its salient features are:

1. State Election Commission has been constituted to conduct and supervise the election to local bodies. Accordingly, the Government of Rajasthan has appointed a senior officer of Indian Administrative Service as Commissioner of State Election Commissioner in September 1994.
2. Constitution of Municipalities have been defined, vide Article 243.
3. It has been expected from the State Legislature that necessary powers will be given to these institutions to discharge their responsibilities properly and effectively.
4. Besides the elected members of the Municipalities, it has been said that members of the Parliament and State Legislature as well as experts in municipal administration may also be nominated.
5. 33 per cent reservation for SC/ST, OBCs and also for women has also been incorporated.
6. Constitution and composition of ward committees.
7. Duration of municipalities: five years and if dissolved earlier, elections shall be held within a period of six months.
8. In order to make these bodies financially self-sufficient, State Finance Commission has been constituted by the State Government under the chairmanship of Shri Krishna Kumar Goyal, former Union Minister of State for Finance.

**Elections**

In Rajasthan, there are 181 municipal bodies, out of which elections to 44 bodies were held on November 27, 1994. There are three Municipal Corporations in Jaipur, Jodhpur and Kota, nine Municipal Councils in Sriganganagar, Bikaner, Sikar, Alwar, Bharatpur, Tonk, Beawar, Udaipur and Pali, and 32 municipalities in Pushkar, Banswar, Chabra, Mangrole, Balotra, Barmer, Chittorgarh, Nimbahera, Churu, Rajgarh, Suratgarh, Hanumangarh, Jaiselmare, Bheenmal, Jalore, Jhunghunn, Bisan, Pilani, Phalodi, Kaithoon, Sangod, Didwana, Makrana, Sumerpur, Amet, Nathdwara, Neem-ka-Thana, Mt. Abu, Pindwara, Shivganj, Sirohi and Kanod (Udaipur). In all, there were 1425 wards and the reservation for SCs, STs and OBCs were made as per Constitutional positions, as evident from the following Table 15.1.

**Table 15.1**
**Distribution of Wards**

| *Category* | *Male* | *Female* | *Total* |
|---|---|---|---|
| General | 641 | 331 | 972 |
| Scheduled Castes | 134 | 63 | 197 |
| Scheduled Tribes | 28 | 09 | 37 |
| OBCs | 145 | 74 | 219 |
| Total | 948 | 477 | 1425 |

The State Government vide its notification dated November 8, 1994, has implemented reservation for the chairman of these bodies also. The following Table 15.2 shows the position:

**Table 15.2**
**Reservation for Chairman**

| *Category* | *Male* | *Female* | *Total* |
|---|---|---|---|
| General | 79 | 41 | 120 |
| Scheduled Castes | 19 | 08 | 27 |
| Scheduled Tribes | 04 | 01 | 05 |
| OBCs | 19 | 10 | 29 |
| Total | 121 | 60 | 181 |

(*Note:* Out of three Municipal Corporations, Mayor for Kota Corporation is reserved for woman, (in general category) and Jodhpur Corporation for OBC. Mayor for the Municipal Corporation, Jaipur, can be any elected member from any ward).

Rajasthan Municipalities Elections Rules, 1994, have incorporated an important provision that rotation through lottery system would be there after every five years for Mayor of the Ward members, the result has been that the same ward members cannot contest elections for the second term from the same ward.

However, elections to aforesaid 44 local bodies held on November 27, 1994 were contested on party basis. The Bharatiya Janata Party (BJP) captured 33 municipalities including three municipal corporations. Besides, elections to 129 out of 137 urban bodies, which had completed their term of five years, elections were held on August 27, 1995. (Due to natural calamities elections to eight local bodies were postponed and later held on 17 December 1995). The party-wise position is indicated in the following table 15.3:

**Table 15.3**
**Party-wise Chairman**

| Name of the party | BJP | Cong-ress | Janata-Dal | Indepe-ndents | CPM | Total |
|---|---|---|---|---|---|---|
| Number | 73 | 34 | 02 | 19 | 01 | 129 |

Disqualification for membership: Rajasthan State Government is perhaps, has made an important provision for the disqualification of membership to the local bodies by incorporating that any person who has two or more than two children shall not be eligible to contest the election to these bodies.

Consequent to the application of the 74th Constitution Amendment and the State Government Act of 1993, the municipalities have been given a Constitutional status. With 33 per cent reservation for women, it is clearly evident, that the State Government is serious about uplifting the status of women in Rajasthan, which is considered a backward state in the country. But as a result of this, one problem is being faced almost in all the districts. Most of the woman candidates who are occupying the position of Mayor or members of the ward, are almost illiterate, have no experience and are the prisoners of age-old social traditions of 'Parda Pratha'. The result has been that the menfolk, may be their husband, brother or brother-in-law, virtually run the administration. But this is a passing phase, and it is hoped that in the coming years, women will realise their hidden strength and will come out with more courage and vigour.

The other important impact has been that since the elections to these bodies were held on party basis, the whole scenario has been politicised. The inner fighting in the parties has also contributed to the political confusion. Therefore, it would be better, if elections are held on non-party basis. However, one may hope that in the coming years these bodies will be more strengthened by giving them more financial powers and would contribute in strengthening the roots of democracy in our country.

# 16

# Impact of the Constitution (Seventy Fourth Amendment) Act, 1992 on Urban Administration in Tamil Nadu

*—K.P. Subramanian*

**Background**

Tamil Nadu has a long history of local self-government since mediaeval period. However, Tamil Nadu has no qualms in not conducting local body polls for many decades. Even after the Constitution Act. Tamil Nadu was one of the four states the other three being, Orissa, Bihar and eight hill districts of U.P., where local body polls were not held within the stipulated time, though the elections were held belatedly and popular councils installed in all local bodies. In the wake of Constitution (Seventy Fourth Amendment) Act, a task force consisting of senior officials, to examine in detail the amendments that are required to be undertaken in the state Acts, was set up on 4.6.93, with the Director of Town and Country Planning as convener. The task force was of the opinion that as far as the urban planning and development was concerned the *status quo* would continue. That means powers would not be transferred to the local governments in respect of urban development. Hence based on the recommendations of the task force, amendments were made only to the Tamil Nadu Municipal Corporation Acts, Tamil Nadu District Municipalities Act and Tamil Nadu Panchayats Act.

**Amendments to the Tamil Nadu Acts**

As per the amendments made in 1993 by the then AIADMK government, the State Government may entrust to the corporation, such powers and responsibilities with respect to preparation of plans for economic development and social justice and also with such powers and authority to enable them to carry out the matters listed in Schedule XI. The the Schedule XI included 15 out of 18 matters listed in the Twelfth Schedule of the Constitution (74th Amendment) Act. The three excluded functions were:

1. Urban planning including Town planning.
2. Regulation of land use and construction of building and
3. Fire fighting.

This implied that the functions and powers of Chennai Metropolitan Development Authority (CMDA) would be intact. But the present DMK government, through a subsequent amendment to the local authorities Acts, in 1996, transferred these three functions also to the Madras City Municipal Corporation and other local bodies. Thus, the urban planning has become the domain of the local bodies ranging from Nagar Panchayats to Municipal Corporations. Until then the Urban Planning functions were derived from the Tamil Nadu Town and Country Planning Act 1971, under which the CMDA, and other Local Planning Authorities and New Town Development Authorities were constituted. After the amendments in 1996, the planning function is the primary responsibility of the local bodies. As they are now expected to plan, implement, enforce, and manage, it is only logical that functions like urban planning, including Town Planning, Regulation of land uses and construction of buildings, water supply, slum improvements and upgradation, protection of environment and promotion of ecological aspects, and planning for economic and social development, should form part of the urban local bodies. In the changed context, the role of specialised functional agencies vis-a-vis the local bodies has to be redefined and realigned.

### Amendments to Chennai City Municipal Corporation Act 1919 (CCMC)

***Ward Committees.*** Provision has been made for constitution of ten ward committees in Chennai Municipal Corporation. For each one of the ten zones within the limits of Chennai city, there shall be a ward committee which shall consist of all the councillors elected from the divisions comprised in that zone and the person, if any, nominated by the State Government if his name is registered as an elector within the territorial limits of the zone concerned. The ward committees will have powers to sanction estimates, plans for municipal works within the zone costing up to rupees ten lakh call for any report or plan pertaining to the municipal administration in the zone from the commissioner, scrutinise monthly statements of receipts and disbursements and of the progress reports in the collection revenue in the zone and consider and make recommendations for the zonal budget. In general, the ward committee may exercise all such municipal powers and functions of the corporation as are to be performed exclusively in the zone concerned, other than those relating to Chennai as a whole or involving two or more zones.

***Metropolitan Planning Committee (MPC).*** The amended CCMC Act provides to constitution of MPC to prepare a draft development plan for the Metropolitan area as a whole. The State Government may by rules provide for the composition of Metropolitan Planning Committee. The MPC shall prepare draft development plan for the Metropolitan area and the chairperson of the MPC shall forward the development plan, as recommended by the committee, to the state government. The composition and the manner of filling up the seats in the MPC is to be determined by the State Government. It is expected that the Tamil Nadu Government would issue separate rules governing the constitution of the MPC, which has not been constituted so far.

**Amendment to Tamil Nadu District Municipalities Act**

***District Planning Committee.*** The Tamil Nadu District Municipalities Act, 1920 has been amended to provide for the constitution of District Planning Committees (DPC) for every district for consolidating the development plan of the district as a whole. The district level setup has been revived nearly after four decades. The District Development Councils (DDC), with collectors as the chairman, were at the districts level as hitherto as advisory bodies. The DDCs replaced the erstwhile statutory District Boards which were similar to the DPCs in late 1950s. While the Central statute wants the handing over of executive functions to the DPCs, the State Act has assigned them only an advisory role. Functions given to them are essentially those entrusted to the DDCs. Whether the elected heads of the DPCs will remain content with the advisory role is a most point.

In the meantime, in a meeting held on 4.11.98, the Tamil Nadu District Panchayats Councillors have urged the government to accord executive powers to the district panchayats to enable them to implement development schemes utilising the funds allotted to the DPCs. The meeting felt that though the DPCs have been given power under 31 heads, they are only of supervisory nature. The resolution demanded that the DPCs be vested with powers enjoyed by the erstwhile District Boards. It also pleaded that the Powers to implement the District Decentralisation plan should be vested with the DPCs and the District Rural Development Agencies should form the secretariat for the DPCs.

**Interface between Functional Agencies and CCMC**

A large number of functional agencies whose functions have, after the amendments, become the primary responsibility of the Chennai City Municipal Corporation, have been operating within the jurisdiction of Chennai Corporation. They are:

1. Chennai Metropolitan Development Authority.
2. Chennai Metropolitan Water Supply and Sewerage Board.
3. Tamil Nadu Housing Board.
4. Tamil Nadu Slum Clearance Board.
5. Tamil Nadu Pollution Control Board.
6. Transport Corporations.

A bizarre situation prevails in the Chennai Metropolitan Area wherein, provision in the local bodies Act have been made to restore with them all the functions hitherto performed by the functional agencies. In view of this, the Acts under which the functional agencies derive their powers and functions have become redundant. The local bodies clamour for more powers and in the process try to assert their constitutional right. This has created an air of uncertainty and acrimony.

**Interface between CCMC and CMDA**

Some time back, the CMDA and the CCMC were at logger-heads on the question of giving sanctions for construction of multistoried buildings and special buildings in the city. While the CMDA claimed that it was its prerogative to issue planning permission for such buildings, the CCMC asserted that the planning permission was of no significance unless the civic body granted building permits. "Not a brick can be moved in the city" without its permission, asserted CCMC authorities. The "tug-of-war" between the two government bodies followed the refusal of building permits to more than 100 multistoried residential buildings in the city by the CCMC for which the CMDA had already issued planning permission on the ground that the builders had not provided sufficient parking space. The CMDA was very furious about the contention of the CCMC and had proposed to issue planning permission directly to the builders by-passing the corporation and had decided to apprise the government of the situation. With a powerful Mayor in the Chief Minister's son, the CCMC is trying to usurp the powers for planning permission from the CMDA. As per the Tamil Nadu Urban Local Bodies Bill 1998, all the urban local bodies in Tamil Nadu ranging from town panchayats to municipal corporations have been vested with absolute powers on issue of permission/licence to all developments on lands or buildings. Hitherto, the appeal powers are exercised by the Government, Directorate of Town and Country Planning or the CMDA as the case may be.

**Interface Between CCMC and CMWSSB**

The system of CMWSSB controlling the sewerage system, the CCMC looking after the drains had on many occasions, led to each body accusing the other of not maintaining the system. Passing the buck was acute during heavy rains, when many areas in the city report stagnation of either rain water or sewage. It was in this context that the State Government accepted a proposal of the CMWSSB and directed the CCMC in September 1996, to hand over maintenance of storm water drains including the staff to the CMWSSB. This was considered as the most controversial and conflicting decision at the time when the entire nation was echoed with the slogan, "devolution and democratisation, and power to the people". However, the decision became abortive in the wake of elections to local bodies and installation of popular council. As a counter move the CCMC proposed merger of CMWSSB with the CCMC and necessary papers were submitted to the Government.

**Interface between CCMC and TNSCB**

Besides the development control and water supply and sewerage, slum is another sensitive area which the CCMC wants to keep close to its chest. Even though there was no open conflict between the TNSCB and the CCMC, the TNSCB hitherto functioned on its own, independently without any co-ordination with the CCMC. In the changed context, the CCMC wanted to bring the TNSCB into its ambit. So also the Tamil Nadu Housing Board, and the Tamil Nadu Pollution Control Board.

**Balancing Acts by the Tamil Nadu Government**

***Devolution and Democratisation.*** In this situation, the Government is on the horns of a dilemma and is not willing to tilt the 'Apple Cart', and tries to do some balancing act. On one hand, power has to be transferred to the local bodies, the cradle of democracy and through them to the people. On the other hand, technical expertise is available only with the functional agencies which are only nominated bodies, of bureaucrats. In a recently held local bodies 'meet' when a long list of suggestions regarding devolution of powers was put forth, the Chief Minister assured that all their demands would be taken up at the state cabinet and state planning commission. As a follow up, the government have taken series of steps for democratisation and devaluation of planning functions at grass root level. The Government have ordered setting up of Joint Administration

Committees to bring Chennai Metropolitan Water Supply and Sewerage Board and the Slum Clearance Board under the purview of the Chennai Corporation. The Chennai Mayor will be the chairman of the committees and the councillors will be made members, which literally means that water supply and slum improvement will become the functions of municipal corporation, though indirectly. However, urban planning and development control which are very vital and sensitive are continued to be performed by the CMDA, which is not an elected body and hence, is not accountable to the people. This goes against the letter and spirit of the Constitution Amendment Act.

***Fiscal Devolution.*** Based on the recommendations of the State Finance Commission, the Tamil Nadu Government announced more grants to the local bodies in the budget for the year 1997-98. It proposed to step up the allocation of funds to the local bodies on revenue accounts from Rs. 646 crore, in 1996-97, to Rs. 1174 crore, in 1997-98. What is important is the involvement of the local bodies in the implementation of the development projects. The decision to allocate 90 per cent of the receipts under the entertainment tax and 8 per cent of the total tax revenue receipts to the local bodies is hailed as a path breaking initiative. As per the government's decision, the local bodies shall have a larger share of responsibilities with minimum bureaucratic intervention in the implementation and supervision of poverty alleviation and infrastructural development programmes. However, the elected representatives of the urban local bodies and various political parties clamour for a 29 per cent hike in the state allotment of tax revenue from the present eight per cent. Consequently, the urban local bodies got a huge increase in their share of the assigned revenues, mainly for implementing new schemes.

A major chunk of the shared finance has come as a devaluation package as per the State Finance Commission's recommendations:

1997-98—Rs. 114.75 Cr.

1998-99—Rs. 146.00 Cr.

Besides the increases in assigned finances, the local bodies have been given more financial powers to take up schemes on their own, without Government approval. Earlier the municipalities could give administrative sanction for works costing only between Rs. 20,000 (for third grade municipalities) and Rs. 2.00 lakh (for top grade). Now, that the third grade municipalities have been abolished, the second grade municipalities can sanction works up to Rs. 3.00 lakh; for the first grade upto Rs. 4.00 lakh, the special and selection grade upto Rs. 5.00 Lakh. This has paved the way for not only devolving more powers to the elected local bodies but also in helping faster implementation of projects and schemes.

**Tamil Nadu Urban Local Bodies Bill, 1998**

Currently the urban administration derives its legal sanction, from a large number of Acts such as, Tamil Nadu Panchayat Act 1958, Tamil Nadu District Municipalities Act, 1920, Chennai City Municipal Corporation Act 1919, and separate Municipal Corporation Acts for Madurai, Coimbatore, Salem, Tiruchi and Tirunelveli. The Tamil Nadu Urban Local Bodies Bill 1998, which was approved by the Tamil Nadu Legislative Assembly on 28-11-98, replaces all the existing legislations for urban local bodies. Enacted in the post-Constitution (Seventy Fourth Amendment) Act, era, it vests more functional autonomy with higher accountability for the urban administration. The bill seeks to remove needless government intervention in crucial decision making areas like budget preparation.

As per the new provision, the councils shall consider and approve the budget proposals. Only a copy of the approved budget proposals needs to be sent to the Director of Municipal Administration (DMA)/the Government. This is a significant departure from the earlier legislation, where the DMA/Government have to approve the budget of each one of the local bodies. At the same time, the local bodies are made accountable for water supply, sewerage disposal, scavenging, solid waste management, and street lights.

The bill gives a free hand to mobilise resources through collection of taxes, tolls, and licence fee. Under the new legislation, the local bodies can take stringent action against unauthorised and violated developments. They can cut off water supply and impose penalty up to Rs. 10,000, if such developments remain unaltered even after issue of notice. Besides, the encroachers will also face stiff sentence of one to three years of imprisonment and/or fine up to Rs. 20,000.

**Perception of the People**

Chennai being the prime city, it is considered as the barometer for the perception of the people. Hence it is considered that the perception of the people in Chennai reflects that of whole Tamil Nadu on the performance of the elected local bodies. When the elected council assumed office, lot of hopes were raised. The worshipful Mayor assured that he would strive to convert the city into 'Singara' Chennai (a pleasant place to live in). However now, two years since then, the hopes are belled. People have more complaints against the councillors, a strange case of remedy turning worse than the malady. It is alleged that no activity of the municipal corporation is spared of the councillors' interference. It is said that they exert maximum pressure on flat promoters and hawkers and those who satisfy them can escape procedures and formalities. The Tamil Nadu Metalware Manufacturers Association, few months back, took out a procession in Chennai, protesting against humiliation, and harassment by a councillor who destroyed material worth lakhs of rupees without prior notice to the traders. On the whole, people were disenchanted with the performance of the elected councils and they strongly believed that the situations have not improved much.

**Conclusion**

***Urban Government Need More Powers.*** Even though the Tamil Nadu Government has made a beginning, the real devaluation and democratisation demand radical restructuring and redefinition of the role of local bodies and functional agencies. Most important among the errors of the past which have to be made good is the exclusion of local authorities from functions which ought to be fundamentally their charge. Now the local authorities have only the status of interested witnesses in planning, urban development and housing.

There may be administrative compulsions against handing over planning and urban development to the municipal authorities. But no other deprival has offended the concept of urban local government at this one. The urban government will not be worth its name if it is to have only the witness status.

In Tamil Nadu, until 1973, when the Tamil Nadu Town and Country Planning Act, 1971 came into effect, urban planning and the development control functions were performed by the local authorities. Until 1960, housing was also their domain.

***Bold Decisions Needed.*** The action of the Government of Tamil Nadu in constituting 'Joint Administration Committees' and giving absolute powers in approving layout and building plan, taking into consideration of even the Master Plan and Detailed Development Plan is welcome. But the Joint Administrative Committees have no statutory footing. Secondly, when the local authorities are empowered under the Tamil Nadu Urban Local Bodies Bill to sanction plans in consonance with the Development Plans, there is no need to issue planning permission under the Tamil Nadu Town and Country Planning Act, 1971, which will amount to duplication and is unnecessary. Hence a firm decision is needed to repeal the other Acts, such as the Tamil Nadu Town and Country Planning Act, 1971. Tamil Nadu Slum Areas Act, 1970, etc. and incorporate the important provisions of those Acts into the Tamil Nadu Urban Local Bodies Act.

***Proposed Restructure for Chennai Metropolitan Area.*** The Metropolitan Planning Committee, the constitution of which is mandatory take over the position of the present CMDA, which is a nominated body constituted under the State Town and Country Planning Act. Since the primary function of the MPC is only to dovetail the plans prepared by various local bodies within the metropolitan area. MPC may have only a minimum manpower, and the remaining expertise now available with the CMDA may be deployed to CCMC and other local bodies within the Chennai Metropolitan Area.

***Proposed Restructuring for Other Cities.*** As Water Supply and Sewerage, Housing and Slum Housing will be the obligatory functions of local bodies, the Tamil Nadu Water Supply and Sewerage Board, the Tamil Nadu Housing Board and Tamil Nadu Slum Clearance Board may have to carry out their functions on behalf and in accordance with the directions of the municipal councils. They may not be able to take up schemes on their own without the concurrence of local bodies as they have done all along these years. As the protection of the environment has become the domain of the local bodies the pollution control board has to work in close co-ordination and in tandem with the local governments. The transport undertakings have to decide the bus routes and locate the bus stops as decided by the local governments.

In the case of major cities other than Chennai, wherever there were outgrowth beyond the municipal boundary, compositive Local Planning Authorities (LPA) were constituted under the Tamil Nadu Town and Country Planning Act 1971 with the respective collectors as chairman and deputy directors of town and country planning as member secretaries. The composite LPAs have only skeleton staff. These LPAs in respect of Coimbatore, Madurai, Tiruchi, Salem and Tirunelveli can be upgraded as MPCs and the technical and managerial capability of these five municipal corporations and all other municipalities may be augmented so that they themselves can take care of the urban planning, landuse regulation, water supply and other functions. The Regional Directorate of Town and Country Planning can provide the supporting staff to the DPCs.

The initiative taken by the Government of Tamil Nadu for devaluation of powers to local bodies may not be complete. Nevertheless, Tamil Nadu has made a beginning, for others to emulate.

## REFERENCES

1. Legislations enacted by the Government of Tamil Nadu.
2. News items *The Hindu, Indian Express,* 'National Dailies'.

# 17

# Urban Local Governance in Tamil Nadu: Retrospect and Prospects

*—Subramaniam Chandran*

Urban governance in India was envisaged by the British as a way of colonial appropriation and systematic exploitation of resources. From the modest collection of land revenue to decide petty cases, the municipal administration was begun by the East India Company. In Tamil Nadu, a system of local self-government existed during the reign of Pallavas and Pandyas in the eighth and ninth centuries, and it was well developed under the Cholas. In the modern era, a municipal corporation came to be formed in Madras by a Charter granted in 1687. Set up on the British model of a town council, this body was empowered to levy taxes for building a guild hall and schools. In the course, the activities of this corporation were expanded and similar bodies were set up in other major towns and their taxation powers were widened.[1] After Independence, in the sphere of urban governance, Tamil Nadu has experienced both problems and prospects in terms of reorganisation of structure as well as the functions of the urban local bodies, regular elections to local bodies, and the administration of municipalities. On the basis of the 74th Constitution Amendment, the Tamil Nadu Municipalities Act, 1994 endeavours to provide effective urban governance in Tamil Nadu.

**Foundations and Growth**

Since 1641 Madras became a prosperous commercial city owing to the efforts of East India Company. Elihu Yale, Governor of Madras Presidency (1687-1692) was responsible for the development of Madras Municipality and for the creation of the office of Mayor for the Corporation of Madras[2] along with Aldermen and Burgesses. In 1690, representation of different communities in the composition of the corporation emerged. The body of Alderman included Armenians, Hebrews, Portuguese, Hindu and Moors. The Charter of 1726 was given to the East India Company in order to bring about an effective judicial administration in the name of

'Mayor and Aldermen of Madraspatnam'. In 1727, the Corporation was reorganised with a Court of Record to try civil cases. The office of Sheriff was also instituted.

The Third Charter of 1753 provided for the revival of the Mayor and the Aldermen. Robert Clive was included in the list of the first Aldermen. The Charter had curtailed the corporation's autonomy in choosing the Mayor and made him the nominee of Fort St. George. The vacancies in the office of the Aldermen were to be filled by the President and Council of Fort St. George. This Charter was the last Royal Charter granted directly to the Company and all subsequents were based on the Acts of Parliament.

In 1792, an Act of Parliament gave powers to levy municipal taxes in Madras. Clause 151 of this Act provided for the appointment of Justices of the Peace. The Act further provided for the collection of the assessment and for licensing the sale of spirituous liquors in the Presidency town. This was the commencement of the Madras municipality as much, differing from the Mayor and corporation who were almost purely judicial functionaries. A member of the council presided over the meeting of Justices for municipal purposes.

The 1841 Act provided for a voluntary system of self-government, permitting the collection and management of the rates of their respective decisions.[3] The Act of 1856 abolished the Justices of the Peace in the Madras Presidency along with other Presidencies and appointed three commissioners for each city. The Madras Act IX of 1863 empowered the addition of 3 honorary members selected from among the inhabitants of the city to assist the 3 commissioners. Under the Act of 1867, the management and supervision of the city municipality were vested in a paid President and 30 Honorary commissioners. In 1878, an Act of the Legislature provided that 16 out of the 32 commissioners should be elected from among the rate-payers, it created two new officers known as the vice-presidents, who along with the president, exercised all the executive powers and control. The City of Madras Municipal Act of 1884 defined the purposes for which the Municipal funds might be spent. These purposes were divided into four categories, public health, public safety, elementary education and poor schools and public convenience. The Act of 1904 further raised the number of commissioners from 32 to 36 and allowed the representation of institutions on the council of commissioners.[4]

In 1885, the position of Mayor was renamed as President. It was only in 1913 that the Corporation moved its officers from Errabalu Chetty Street to Ripon building. The Madras City Municipality Act of 1919 gave the city municipal council, full control over taxation and the budget.[5] I our standing committees were constituted for taxation and finance, works, health, and education. According to the 1919 Act, at their first meeting in November, the council was empowered to elect one of their members to be their president.

The Madras City Municipal Amendment Act of 1933 changed the designation of the 'President' into the previous title 'Mayor'. Raja Sir Muthiah Chettiar became the first Indian Mayor. The Madras City Municipal Amendment Act 1936 divided the city into 40 divisions, raised the number of councillors from 50 to 60 and provided for election of five Aldermen of whom were one should be a women. A deputy mayor was also to be elected by the councillors. The Act also increased the standing committees from 4 to 6 and Taxation Appeal Committee was formed.

The Act of 1947 further amended the 1919 Act and increased the Divisions to 50 and the strength of the council was increased to 85, reserving seats for women, certain communities, and trade and industry. The term of the councillors was fixed at 3 years. Under this Act, first election was held in 1948. In 1961, the name of the city Municipality was changed to the Madras City Municipal Corporation by an amendment. In 1965, the state government took power under an amending Act to dissolve or supersede the corporation. The Act of 1967 increased the Divisions further to 120. An amendment in 1971 abolished the circle committees and revived the functional standing committees. The Act of 1979 increased the number of Divisions to 150 with 15 men and 6 women to be coopted from the SCs and STs, if there were no elected members from these communities.

**Municipal Administration**

In principle, municipal administration in Tamil Nadu was begun from the Town Improvement Act 1850, but this Act was actually not implemented. Later, the Town Improvement Act 1865 created the municipalities. The District Magistrate acted as the President of the municipalities and appointed the Vice-President of various municipalities within his district. The normal sources of revenue for the municipalities were profession-tax, the house-tax, the vehicles tax and tolls and license fees. Bulk of the revenues were spent on the maintenance of the police and the remainder was distributed on repairs of roads and drains, and on sanitation.

With the Town Improvement Act of 1871, the municipalities were given the additional functions of maintenance of hospitals and dispensaries, schools, birth and death registration and vaccination. The tenure of office for the councillors was raised from one to three years. The municipalities were also no longer required to contribute towards police charges. However, owing to financial pressure, the Act of 1878 directed the municipalities to bear 75 per cent of the police charges. The Madras District Municipalities Act of 1884, laid down that the municipal council would consist of not less than 12 members holding office for three years. The concerned revenue divisional officer was made an ex-officio councillor of the municipality. Rest of the councillors were appointed by the government. According to this Act, the Chairman was nominated by the government or it permitted the councillors to elect a chairman. The Chairman was considered to be the executive officer of the council and was held responsible for due discharge of all activities. The Government had the right to remove any Chairman or Councillor at any time. The District Collector was given emergency Powers under this Act.

Based on the recommendations of the Royal Commission on Decentralisation, the Madras District Municipalities Act of 1920 was passed for repealing the Act of 1884. The Act increased the elected proportion of the municipal council as well as the resources and powers of municipalities. An Inspector of Municipal Councils and Local Boards was also appointed. Under this Act, detailed provisions with regard to the constitution and abolition of municipalities and for fixing the strength of the municipal council were made.

The municipalities levied property tax, profession tax, vehicle tax and tolls on vehicles and animals entering the municipality. The government also appointed auditors to audit municipal funds. The council was given full control over streets, public water courses, wells, tanks etc. It maintained a register of vital statistics and arrange for prevention of diseases and for compulsory vaccination. It provided for expansion of elementary education and levied education tax for the purpose. The amending Act of 1930 did away with the system of nomination of councillors fully, but provided for the reservation of seats to minority communities. The disqualification of women to stand for elections was removed. The amending Act of 1933 introduced the system of appointing commissioners. In 1957 and 1973, amending Acts were also passed to regulate the service conditions of the employees of the municipalities, the councillors and municipal activities.

**Electoral Politics**

The electoral competition between the DMK and the Congress in the municipal corporation of Madras and municipalities was sharp. It was believed that the pattern of Madras Municipal Corporation elections would influence the voting pattern in the general elections for the state. The Congress was in power in the corporation till 1959. In the 1959 municipal corporation elections, the DMK securing 49 seats out of 100 captured power. The Congress which was in power both at the Centre and the State secured 40 seats. In the 1968 elections, the DMK captured 68 out of 120 seats. In the 1971 elections also, the DMK came to power. In 1973, the Madras Municipal Corporation was dissolved for the cause of 'Muster Roll Case' by the government of Tamil Nadu.[6] After dissolving Madras Municipal Corporation in 1973, the corporation was administered by the special officer who was appointed by the government till 1996.

**The 74th Constitution Amendment**

The 74th Constitution Amendment Act 1992 factually placed greater responsibilities in the hands of the urban local bodies. It provides the following features for urban local bodies: devolution of more functions and taxation powers; revenue sharing with state government funds; regular conduct of elections; reservation of seats for SCs, STs and for women; uniform composition of the urban bodies throughout the country; prescription of criteria for categorising urban local bodies like Town Panchayats, Municipalities, City Municipal Corporations; restriction on the formation of Townships only to industrial areas where the entire municipal services are provided or proposed to be provided by the industry; and formation of District Planning and Metropolitan Planning Committees.

**Tamil Nadu District Municipalities Act, 1994**

In accordance with the 74th Amendment, the Tamil Nadu District Municipalities Act 1994 came into existence. The new Act states that a town panchayat shall be constituted for each panchayat town and the administration of the town panchayat town shall vest in the town panchayat. The office of chairperson of the town panchayat is also reserved for women, SC and ST. Next comes municipalities and municipal authorities charged with carrying out the provisions of this Act are a council, a chairman and an executive authority. The chairman shall be elected by the persons whose names appear in the electoral rolls relating to the municipality. The council shall elect one of its members other than the chairman to be its vice-chairman. They shall nominate a panel of not more than three members any one of who shall perform the functions of the chairman in the absence of both chairman and vice-chairman. A commissioner shall be appointed by the state government.[7]

For the purpose of election of councillors to town panchayat, the inspector shall after consulting the town into wards, determine the number of members to be elected. The chairman of the municipal council shall make arrangements for the election of the vice-chairman, convene meetings of the council, and perform all the duties and exercise all the powers specially conferred by the Act. The executive authority of the municipal council shall carry into effect the resolutions of the council. It shall furnish to the council such periodical reports regarding the progress made in carrying out the resolutions of that body in the collection of taxes, and perform duties conferred by the Act. The chairman shall, by virtue of his office, be a member of council and of every committee for the purpose of exercising such powers, and functions. Every municipality shall have a taxation appeal committee and other committees. The council shall submit every year to the state government through the district collector a report on the administration.

The district collector can inspect any immovable property or any work in progress under the control of any municipal authority in his district. If the executive authority of a municipality has made default in carrying out any resolution of the council, the district collector after giving the executive authority a reasonable opportunity of explanation shall send a report to the state government. The state government has the power to suspend or cancel any resolution passed by the council. The district collector has emergency powers as well to direct the executive authority to suspend or change any work. The state government can also appoint officers for the purpose of inspecting any municipalities and their work. The state government can also appoint officers for the purpose of inspecting any municipalities and their work. The state government can by notification remove any vice-chairman who omits or refuses to carry out or disobeys the provision of this Act.[8] The councillors constituted one-third of the sanctioned strength of the council can write to the collector for the removal of the chairman if he willfully omits or refuse to carry out or disobeys any provisions of the Act.[9] There is also a provision for recall of chairman or councillors from their office by voters through referendum.[10] When the state government comes to know that the municipality is not competent to perform or persistently makes default in performing the duties imposed on it by law or abuses its power, the state government can dissolve the municipality and direct that the municipality be reconstituted.

The urban local bodies *viz.* town panchayats, municipalities and city municipal corporations are individual units themselves and each one is in charge of the civic needs of their own area. In Tamil Nadu, there are

10173 wards in town panchayats, 3392 wards in municipalities and 474 wards in corporations apart from the office of chairpersons numbering 13736.

The chairpersons and the councillors of these urban bodies are elected directly by the voters themselves. Hence in the urban areas just two elections one for councillor or ward and the other for chairperson or mayor as the case may be, are held. Apart from these direct elections the indirect elections are also held for the post of deputy mayor/vice-chairman of city municipal corporation, municipalities and town panchayats respectively, by and from among the elected councillors of every concerned local body; for chairpersons of the wards committees in city municipal corporation areas and municipalities having a population of three lakhs and above by and from among the elected councillors of every concerned local body and for the members of the various statutory and standing committees of the respective urban local bodies by and form among the elected councillors of every concerned local body.

**TABLE 1**
**Seats Won by Political Parties in the Urban Local Elections 1996**

| *Party* | *Mayors* | *Corporation Councillors* | *Municipal Chairman* | *Municipal Councillors* | *Town Pan. Chairman* | *Town Pan. Ward Members* |
|---|---|---|---|---|---|---|
| DMK | 4 | 234 | 48 | 1117 | 208 | 2210 |
| TMC | 2 | 135 | 28 | 536 | 108 | 1140 |
| AIADMK | — | 37 | 9 | 456 | 85 | 1028 |
| MDMK | — | 4 | 5 | 109 | 21 | 209 |
| CPI | — | 12 | 2 | 57 | 5 | 98 |
| BJP | — | 1 | 1 | 49 | 14 | 163 |
| PMK | — | 1 | — | 43 | 4 | 81 |
| CPI (M) | — | 12 | 1 | 42 | 16 | 200 |
| INC | — | 1 | — | 32 | 6 | 85 |
| Janata Dal | — | 1 | — | 20 | 4 | 47 |
| Samata | — | — | | 7 | — | 1 |
| Janata | — | — | — | 1 | — | 2 |
| Independents | — | 37 | 7 | 922 | 163 | 4487 |
| Total | 6 | 474 | 102 | 3389 | 634 | 10151 |

**Election Scenario**

It was one of the promises made by Shri M. Karunanidhi at the time of general elections that the elections to the local bodies would be conducted within six months. Accordingly, the elections were held during October 1996. The Mayors for municipal corporations have been directly elected by the people for the first time. The elections were held for municipal corporations, municipalities and town panchayats in the state. The election of mayors and the councillors of the city municipal corporations was direct on the party basis. The following tables show the seats and percentage of votes won by different parties in the election of mayors, corporation councillors, municipal chairman, municipal councillors, town panchayat chairmen, and town panchayat ward members.[11]

**TABLE 2**
**Percentage of Votes got by Political Parties in the Urban Local Body Elections**

| *Party* | *Mayors* | *Corporation Councillors* | *Municipal Chairman* | *Municipal Councillors* | *Town Pan. Chairman* | *Town Pan. Ward Members* |
|---|---|---|---|---|---|---|
| DMK | 44.91 | 27.18 | 31.99 | 22.60 | 23.94 | 19.59 |
| TMC | 13.20 | 13.90 | 13.29 | 11.18 | 11.92 | 10.34 |
| AIADMK | 12.69 | 19.95 | 24.94 | 18.50 | 20.48 | 13.44 |
| MDMK | 5.99 | 5.43 | 7.54 | 5.42 | 5.16 | 3.04 |
| CPI | — | 1.10 | 0.82 | 1.45 | 1.25 | 1.21 |
| BJP | 1.37 | 1.83 | 2.34 | 1.57 | 3.03 | 1.81 |
| PMK | 0.04 | 1.09 | 1.87 | 1.66 | 1.23 | 0.99 |
| CPI (M) | 1.79 | 3.93 | 3.54 | 2.28 | 4.20 | 3.12 |
| INC | 2.36 | 3.95 | 3.79 | 2.43 | 2.86 | 1.29 |
| Janata Dal | 0.19 | 1.59 | 1.02 | 0.90 | 0.89 | 0.71 |
| Samata | — | 0.39 | 0.37 | 0.15 | — | 0.01 |
| Janata | 14.12 | — | 0.06 | 0.14 | 0.04 | 0.03 |
| Independents | 3.33 | 19.65 | 8.42 | 31.73 | 24.99 | 44.43 |

**Emerging Trends**

Many municipalities in Tamil Nadu have to meet the infrastructure needs of rapidly increasing population. They must contemplate on how the financial resources and administrative competence can be effectively utilised. The 74th Constitution Amendment has placed greater responsibilities of urban governance in the hands of the urban local bodies. The urban governance increasingly involves town planning, land use planning, socio-economic development planning, poverty alleviation programmes, development of roads and bridges, water supply, sanitation and solid waste, and the provision of various other services and amenities. It is obvious that certain vagueness imbedded in the Nagarpalika Act identifies the many municipal tasks as 'discretionary' instead of 'mandatory'. This adds to certain doubts about the strength of this legislation.[12] The urban local bodies will be required to improve and strengthen their governance. In the absence of elections to local bodies for a long time in Tamil Nadu, the estrangement of people from the public realm was very much visualised. After the elections, the elected members provide an expansion of public realm for interaction and in one way the proples' participation is strengthened.

## REFERENCES


1. Venkatarangaiya, M. and Pattabhiram, M. eds. *Local Government in India: Select Readings.* Allied, Bombay, 1969; Tinker. Hugh. *The Foundations of Local Self-Government in India. Pakistan and Burma,* Athlone Press, London, 1954.
2. Smith, Vincent A. *The Oxford History of India,* Oxford University Press, London, 1958, p. 390 and p. 460; see also Nayudu, W.S. Krishnaswami. *Old Madras,* Madras, 1965, pp. 48-50. Also see, Penny. *Fort St. George,m Madras,* London, 1900; Foster, W. *The Founding of Fort St. George,* Eyre and Spottiswoode, 1902; Love, H.D. *Vestiges of Old Madras 1640-1800,* Murray, 1913; Lawson, Charles. *Memories of Madras,* London, 1905; Barlow, Glyn. *The Story of Madras,* Oxford University Press, London, 1921; Srinivaschari, C.S. *History of the City of Madras,* Madras, 1939; Maclean, *Manual of the Administration of the Madras Presidency,* Madras, 1885.
3. *The Madras Tercentenary Commemoration Volume,* Oxford University Press, Madras, 1989, p. 177.
4. Rao, J.V. Satchidananda. "Madras City and its Corporation" *Independence Day Silver Jubilee Special Issue,* Madras, 1972, p. 4.
5. The taxes levied are; property tax, profession tax, company tax, vehicle tax and animal tax, timber tax, advertisement tax and duty on transfer of property and entertainment.
6. The Muster Roll case was relating to the employment of temporary Labours in the Electrical Department. In this case allegedly cheating and defrauding the corporation of large sums of money about Rs. 1.26 crores during 1969 to 1973.
7. See the Tamil Nadu District Municipalities Act (Act 25 of 1994), Government of Tamil Nadu.

8. These provisions were originally included by the Act 10 of 1930; Act 4 of 1933; and Act 11 of 1939.
9. This provision was originally included by Act 23 of 1978.
10. Referendum was included by the Act 16 of 1987.
11. Compiled from the *Statistical Report on Election to Local Bodies 1996,* State Election Commission, Government of Tamil Nadu.
12. Singh, K. and Steinberg, F. (eds), *Urban India in Crisis,* New Age, Delhi, 1996.

# 18

# Empowerment of Women in Local Self Government: A Critical Analysis

*—H.D. Dwarkanath*

**Focus**

The participation of women in the Panchayati Raj Institutions (PRIs) and urban local bodies is considered essential not only for ensuring political participation in the democratic process but also for realising the developmental goals for women. During freedom movement, Indian women played a vital role under the leadership of Gandhiji in every walk of life. In a contemporary political system, women played a crucial role in the socio-economic and political front when compared to other western democracies. The participation of women in Indian politics was high, both qualitatively and quantitatively.[1]

The document on women's development (1985) recognised that despite the rapid growth of informal political activity by women, their role in political power structure had virtually remained unchanged.[2] The fourth Global Conference of Women Empowerment held in Beijing on September 4, 1995 highlighted women as parterners of development. The UN sponsored conference set an agenda for the advancement of women at the National and International levels to move into the 21st century with a sharpened focus on removal of gender discrimination.[3] The Human Development Report for 1995, presents a gloomy picture on the status of women in the world. The most striking point the report has made is that, there is not a single country where women enjoy equality and freedom with men. Another finding is that of the total burden of work women carry 53 per cent and men 47 per cent in developing countries and the figures are 51 per cent and 49 per cent respectively for developed countries.[4]

The Eighth Plan document in India recommended that women have to be empowered by raising their socio-economic status.

Gender equality continues to be a distant dream in case of developing countries today. The wide gap between male female literacy ratio, the disproportionate representation of women in various political institutions is widely observed. As Swamy Vivekananda said "Nation would not march forward if women are left behind". While writing in *Young India,* Gandhiji stated that "as long as the women of India do not take part in public life there can be no salvation for the country".[5] In fact the Gandhian struggle marked by the non-violent political battle succeeded in involving women in the modern form of political struggle, thus freedom movement provided equal space for women along with men.

The Constitution of India has guaranteed to all women the fundamental rights, equality of political participation, but in practice, these rights have no meaning because their voice is hardly given any weightage. This is definitely due to ignorance, illiteracy and poor representation. The oppressed situation of Hindu women was regarded by the British administration as an example of backwardness. Several political parties including the Congress were therefore committed to include women in almost every aspect of their programmes to demonstrate the progressiveness and moral superiority of all Indians.

**Status of Women in India**

It is needless to say that women all over the world are discriminated against their urge and effort to achieve equality in all spheres of life. In India, 74 per cent of women of the 900 million population are working in the unorganised sector. Approximately ¾ of them are engaged in agriculture, animal husbandry, farm labour, crafts and cottage industries and construction works etc. The remaining 26 per cent of them have managed to encroach on teaching, health, professional, services, commerce and communications.

The UNICEF report reveals that nearly 61 per cent women in India are illiterate and 40 per cent of them live below the poverty line. In fact, rural women who work 14 hours a day and remain engaged in different domestic activities from dawn to dusk and one may heard her as unsung heroine of our country. The socio-economic and political innovations in recent years have not benefited women. The needs and aspirations of women have long been neglected. Their basic need for health care, child welfare, water, sanitation, roadways, illiteracy and employment have not been translated into action.[6]

**Low Literacy Rate**

With 50 per cent of population consisting of women, it is a matter of concern that female literacy rates in India are very low. According to 1991

Census, the number of female literacy rate is 39.42 per cent as against 63.68 per cent for males. Between 1981-91 the number of literate female rose from 182.91 millions to 202.14 millions against of 19.23 millions, i.e., two millions a year. Total literacy ratio in 1991 recorded only 11 per cent for women compared with 52 per cent for men. Though the rate has progressively increased from 8.86 per cent in 1951, 15.34 in 1961, 21.97 in 1971, 29.15 in 1981 to 39.42 in 1991, this is still below the designed level in absolute terms. Out of a total population of over 840 millions, only 130 million women are literate. Further, the pace of increase in literacy among females has been less than that of males. During the last eighty years that increase in literacy among the males has been 37 per cent, whereas for female it is 24 per cent only.[7]

However, the education of women in Indian political scenario is directly linked to the status in society. Down the ages, the Indian women have been treated as second class citizen.

**Women's Entry into Politics**

Ever since the beginning of the present century, the educated women started getting restless about the empowerment of political structure. Their struggle to get the franchise started in earnest in 1917. Three women organisations viz., (1) Women's Indian Association (WIA), (2) National Council of Women in India (NCWI), (3) All India Women's Conference (AIWC), spearheaded the movement for women voting rights. Finally, women gained access to franchise on the same basis as men, in 1929. During this period, women made social issues their plank for contesting elections.[8]

It was a decade after Independence that the Balwant Rai Mehta Committee, set up on January 7, 1957, was regarded as the pioneering step to recognise and recreate Panchayati Raj Institutions in modern India. The committee laid the foundation for a three tier system of local self government. One of the salient features of the committee report was the provision to coopt two women members in all the three tiers of Panchayati Raj administration. The committee also specified that the selection of these two women should be based on the interest they took in activities relating to welfare of women and children. This indeed was the first step when women were enabled to have a specific role in the Panchayati Raj administration. However, it was in 1974 that a committee on the status of women in India came out with the recommendation of establishing a statutory women's Panchayat at the grassroot level to look after the welfare programmes for women and children and also to ensure greater political participation in the developmental administration.[9]

Later the Committee on Panchayati Raj (1978) recommended the reservation of two seats for women in Panchayat through direct elections. The central government asked the states to take measure for increasing effective representation of women in Panchayati Raj Institutions. The examples of Orissa, Karnataka and Andhra Pradesh were cited where 25 to 30 per cent seats had been reserved for women. This representation was likely to remove the isolation of women and give them visibility and strength to be more assertive and to take part in decision making. Unfortunately, several states, including Uttar Pradesh, did not implement the recommendations in true spirit.[10] However the National Perspective Plan for Women (1988), recommended the following measures for effective empowerment of women and political participation at the grass root level in the democratic Institutions:[11]

(A) Reservation should be made of 30 per cent seats from Panchayat to Zilla Parishad level and local Municipal bodies for women. Wherever possible, higher representation of Dalit/ Tribal women of weaker sections should be ensured.

(B) 30 per cent of executive heads of all bodies, from village to district level and certain percentage of Chief Executives of Panchayati Raj bodies at the lower, middle and higher levels must be reserved for women.

(C) A more effective step would be to declare a certain percentage of constituencies in the lower tier of Panchayati Raj as exclusively women's constituencies and all executive positions in a certain number of territorial juridictions reserved for women candidates.

(D) All women members of Panchayats and other executive bodies must be trained and empowered to exercise their authority. Conscious efforts are needed to elicit participation of women through establishing links between the elected representatives and the developmental functionaries.

(E) Women's development programmes must also be linked with Panchayati Raj bodies for more effective participation of women at the grass root democracy.

However, all the attempts, discussed earlier, confined themselves, to strengthen and empower the women in rural India, where illiteracy prevailed, traditions and customs dominated. The propagators of women empowerment, probably had conceived of a better position of urban women, majority of whom were on the same social footing on which their rural counterparts were. A selected core of urban women were enjoying the same powers and recognition as the menfolk did.

**Promoting Women's Participation**

The 73rd and 74th Amendments to Indian Constitution have been looked upon as epoch making events in the Indian Constitutional history. It promises not only "decentralised administration and local self government" but also participation in the process by those groups of persons, hitherto considered "weaker sections" namely, scheduled castes/ scheduled tribes and women. These amendments first time dealt the women irrespective of their regional habitation, with the uniform standards.

The political and economic reservation of seats provided by these amendments to the Constitution is to pull women from the back rows and bring them on the main stream of national life, to manage the resources and govern the local community. The process of empowerment is expected to open the whole vista of human resource development to them. Viewed from this long term, perspective, these Amendments are powerful instruments of empowerment which women need to grab and wield skilfully.[12]

Thus, these Amendments have stipulated a significant percentage of reservation for SCs/STs and women candidates, which on becoming operative, is likely to throw up altogether new power structure in India. Thus, a very significant formidable force of newly elected leadership from these categories will be in the field. According to a rough estimate, as many as one lakh women alone including those belonging to weaker sections will be taking up leadership roles. It is not only a question of merely getting into the leadership but also responding to the Amendment in a positive manner in which both the society and the newly elected leaders have to prove their capacity both as partners in development and also as the key decision makers.[13]

**Representation of Women in Politics**

Since the adoption of the Republic Constitution, several legal measures were taken by the Government of India, which in turn, improved the status of women in the country. The Constitution guaranteed to all women equal rights of participation in the political process of the country along with equal opportunities and rights in education, voting, politics and employment.

The Inter-Parliament Union Chart published recently (1997) reveals that the empowerment of women parliamentarians is very high in countries like Sweden (40.4), Newzealand (29.2), Argentina (25.3), China (21.0), Asia (13.1), USA (12.7), Pacific (11.6), Europe (12.6), Syria (9.6), Africa (10.4), India (7.01) and Arabian countries (3.3). The percentage of participation of women parliamentarians in countries like India, Africa, Syria and Arabian countries is considerably very low.[14]

The political empowerment of women has made considerable strides with only 2.8 per cent women being represented in the Parliament of 1952-57 to 7.2 per cent in the present Lok Sabha (1996). The women representation in the Rajya Sabha has, however, shown greater improvement having increased from 7.7 per cent in 1952 to 15.5 in 1991. It is however felt that these amendments to the Constitution Constitutional Amendments Acts will empower women politically at the grassroots level in a revolutionary fashion. This will enable them to take interest at the local level and energise and improve the situation of women in areas like educations, health and employment which is essential for their basic existence.[15]

Despite being very few in number, the women members, especially in Rajya Sabha, have always a constant presence in Parliament. Most of the earlier women members of Parliament within a short span of time introduced not only many but important private members' bill like the dowry restraint bill, Indian adoption of children bill, etc.

The role played by women parliamentarians in contemporary political system underwent a qualitative change, from the third Lok Sabha onwards, largely due to Indira Gandhi's becoming India's First Woman Prime Minister. They participated in the deliberations on Foreign Policy and economic issues which, by and large, are not favourites among all women members of Parliament.[16]

The geminisation of women's entry into the political process of the country made social issues their major plank for contesting Assembly and Lok Sabha elections. But the major political parties were not at all inclined to field women candidate nor support any one, who is willing to contest elections. At this point the reservation for women's group remained opposed to this idea just as Gandhiji was opposed to special favours and concession to women. He was convinced of women's capability from their widespread participation in the movements led by him. This issue of reservation is of special significance in the present context with the empowerment of women in grass root level local institutions.[17] The successful implementation of reservation at local level institutions, the Union Government has introduced in the Lok Sabha a Bill containing one-third of seats to be reserved in Parliament and the States Legislature. Only the next few months can show the moral of male politicians to grant reservation to their female counterpart or not.

**Panchayats and Women Reservation**

The participation of women in local self institutions is considered essential not only for ensuring political participation in the democratic process but also for realising the developmental goals of urban and rural development. Participation of women in these grassroot institutions involves (1) women as voters (2) women as member of political parties (3) women as candidates (4) women as member of panchayati Raj Institutions and urban local bodies and taking part in decision making, planning, implementation and evaluation (5) women as members of Mahila Mandals and their association with voluntary organisations.[18]

It was, in 1974, that a committee on the status of women in India suggested statutory women's Panchayats at village level. The purpose of these bodies was to look after development and welfare programmes for women and children with resources of their own. Women's empowerment is one of the objective of the third generation of Panchayats in India. Women, as in many other countries, are awfully under represented in political Institutions. The question of women's participation in National politics in general and rural/urban politics in particular has assumed importance following the formulation of National Perspective Plan for Women in 1988. The 73rd and 74th Constitution Amendments have become the milestones by stipulating 33 per cent, a significant percentage, of reservation for women in operation. It has paved the way for altogether a new power structure in India. The class which was earlier confined to domestic and household affairs now empowered to solve their local problems with locally available resources and manpower. The following discussion shows the Reservation of Seats for Women in Panchayati Raj Institutions in different states after the 73rd amendment.[19] The data relating to municipalities are not available. The following pages attempt to analyse the level and scope of empowering rural women. It may help in understanding the situation in urban India.

With the implementation of the 73rd Amendment Act Orissa was probably the first state in the country to implement 33 per cent reservation of seats for women in Panchayati Raj Institutions. The state has now 25000 women representatives in about 5236 Gram Panchayats and 314 Panchayat Samities. The second state to follow suit was West Bengal in which 36 per cent of the total members in the Panchayat bodies are women. The position of women in the present

Panchayat setup of West Bengal can be seen (after 1993 elections) in the table given as follows:

**TABLE 1**

| *Panchayati Raj Bodies* | *Total Strength* | *Women Representation* | *Percentage of the Women* |
|---|---|---|---|
| 1. Gram Pradhan | 3324 | 196 | 6 |
| 2. Panchayati Samiti Sabhapati | 340 | 08 | 2.5 |
| 3. Zilla Parishad Sabhapati | 16 | Nil | NA |

In southern States like Karnataka, Andhra Pradesh and Kerala, the women representation has been quite encouraging, where elections to grassroots tier were held in 1994. Karnataka had 25 per cent reservation for women at the Zilla Parishad level, whereas Kerala District Councils Act of 1984 represented 30 per cent of seats in the district council for women. In the elections held in 1991, 31 per cent women were elected in which 5 per cent of them did not have any agriculture land of their own in Kerala state. In Karnataka, it is reported that out of 80,627 of seats in 5,640 Gram Panchayats 43.77 per cent are women.[20]

Surprisingly, for the first time in the history of Panchayati Raj elections in Andhra Pradesh, about 6864 women representatives have become sarpanchas to improve the socio-economic conditions of the rural poor. Women's entry into politics at the grassroot level through reservation is certainly a positive development in the process of political decision making. The major challenges before the elected women representatives of the reserved class is to setup a new system of functioning in the intricacies of the process of decision making and in the administration.[21]

The outcome of these elections in terms of women's participation has been very much encouraging. Panchayati Raj elections in Karnataka, Orissa, West Bengal and Andhra Pradesh earlier had witnessed appreciable number of women turnout as voters as well as candidates for local self government. In many states the percentage of women who got elected to PRI's exceeded the reserved positions. Thus it can be said that in all these above instances the participation of women went beyond expectations.[22]

**TABLE 2**

**Reservation for Women in the Panchayat Raj Bodies in Andhra Pradesh after the 73rd Constitution Amendment (1994)**

| *Sl. No.* | *Panchayati Raj Institutions* | *Total Strength* | *Women Representatives* | *Percentage of the Women* |
|---|---|---|---|---|
| 1. | Gram Panchayat Sarpanchas | 21934 | 6846 | 31.21 |
| 2. | MPTC Members | 14604 | 4766 | 32.63 |
| 3. | Mandal Parishad Presidents | 1091 | 364 | 33.36 |
| 4. | ZPTC Members | 1091 | 364 | 33.36 |
| 5. | XP Chairpersons | 22 | 7 | 31.80 |

## Training Women in tiie Art of Polity

Stressing the vital role of education and training in moulding effective and dynamic women leaders, the political women leadership at the grassroot level is the need of hour. Women should be given fair knowledge about the functioning of political system. The trainer has a dual role of an education and a catalyst in the process of empowering women. A new leadership of women would provide constructive thinking in administration and ensure financial management.

The new local self government systems give the country a whooping 22.5 lakhs elected representatives with reserved seats in all the three tier systems in Panchayat Raj and about 10 lakhs women in Urban administration areas of development have been identified in which the elected members have a free hand in planning and disbursement of funds. Obviously, all these are the activities in which the women have a crucial role to play despite several handicaps they are confronted with. The objective of enhanced representation in the executive bodies of local self grassroot Institutions is to remove isolation of women from development and political process of the polity.

It may be recalled that in earlier years of community development programme, Mahila Mandals were set up in villages with the help of women social education organisation. Similarly, the community based organisations of women are being formed in urban areas also. Today there is a crying need for a platform where the women may interact among themselves for their own socialisation and upliftment.

It is argued that for any meaningful participation of women in administration, gender equality is a pre-requisite. The women need to be trained in the art of administration, polity, finance and the cybernetics of development. Here the role of voluntary agencies must come into prominance. Local self-government and co-operatives are like twin sisters and they can be nourished equally well by our women folk. Planning from below should be stimulated and put in shape by simultaneous development of a powerful co-operative structure.[23]

In the matter of making Panchayati Raj Institutions and municipalities viable financially, women should take much interest and see that funds are not frittered away. They can serve as watch-dogs in spending money and keeping accounts. The women vested with power have to function with great objectivity keeping in mind the overall interest of economic and social development of the area, where they live.

Decentralisation of structures and decision making certainly has the potential and relevance in increasing response to grassroots initiatives, of poor women. Panchayati Raj Institutions and municipalities are not minor political bodies. They constitute the first base to ensure that the voice of the women is heared. Women's views which are increasingly articulated through grassroot organizations and movements on issues such as environmental pollution, forestry, water management, land reforms, planning, slum improvement etc. have been virtually headed by men in local units of self-government and the bureaucracy.

It is observed that due to rapid industrial transformation, empowerment of women in Panchayati Raj and municipalities cannot be sufficient device for development of women. After all, empowerment of women is accomplished if they acquire necessary skills to initiate the changes, and not by calculating how much benefit they can earn for themselves from ongoing transformation process. In a country, like India, this is formidable challenge to be faced because majority of the people reside in rural areas and more than half of them are illiterate.[24]

**Evaluation**

The emergence of women power structure into Panchayati Raj and Municipal Institutions is a milestone in achieving socio-economic development with a positive direction but to make it work, needs sincere efforts from different quarters. The framers of the legislation have to ensure that undue difficulties are not created for women that may discourage them from participating in the political process of decision making judiciously.

It is due to absence of effective intent, commitment and sensibility, the programmes meant for women, and financial allocations made for them remain unutilized or wrongly utilized. This can be stopped if there is adequate number of women participation in various implementing agencies, see to it that policies and programme are implemented according to the prescribed manner within the specified time frame.

After entering into local grassroot administration women become more confident that they can save the country from corruption, criminalisation of politics and other kinds of maladies. Women at large are more and more convinced that men have failed in governance specially in areas of education, health, environment, food production and development programmes.

Empowerment of political power to women is extremely important for making progress. Once women get opportunity to participate in decision making bodies, there would be spectacular change in the social status of backward communities.

Much of the effectiveness of these grassroot local self-government would depend on the functions assigned to them by the states. The role of the women members would be important in identifying various resources and assessing various needs of the community so as to optimally use the scarce resources for the benefit of the people.

In this regard, the short-term training programmes, refresher courses, workshops, seminars etc., are sure to help them to understand and appreciate their responsibilities and obligations under the changed setup. Much would depend on the attitudinal and behavioural overtones of the varied functionaries involved in the functioning of these Institutions because it is not the system but empowerment of women that really matters. This, in fact is the trust of decentralised administration.

## REFERENCES


1. Nirmala Deshpande, Participation of women in political system, Kurukshetra, p. 56, Feb., 1989.
2. Plan document on women's development (1985) Government of India, Hyderabad.
3. The fourth world conference on women, held at Beijing on 4th September, 1995.
4. UN Human Development Report document published by UNDP, p. 10., 1995.
5. *Young India,* 25 November, 1925.
6. UNO's UNICEF Report, 1991.
7. Anjana Maitrasinha, Women's education needs new approach-*The Hindu* Education page-8th February, 1994.

8. Forbes Geraldine H. 1979, "Votes for women the demand for women's Franchise in India 1917-1937" symbols of poor studies on the political status of women in India-Allied Publishers, Bombay, p. l.
9. KA Rolin EDAVIS, Representation of women through reservation and Panchayati Raj Women's like Vol. 3, No. 2 April-June, 1997.
10. The Committee on Panchayati Raj (1978), Ministry of Rural Development, Government of India, New Delhi, 1978.
11. K.B. Saxena, Panchayats and women, Kurukshetra, Feb. 1989 Vol. XXXVII No. 5. p. 59.
12. Dr. Sarala Gopalan, Joint Secretary, Ministry of Rural Development, Government of India, New Delhi, Paper presented in workshop entitled Women and Panchayati Raj organised by structural Commission for women from October, 19-018-97.
13. Ministry of Rural development, Gramin Vikas, *Newsletter,* January, 1993. p. 3.
14. Susheela Kaushik, Women and political participation women in politics-Forms and processes 1992, p. 40.
15. Miraseth, Women's development: Indian initiatives-Kurukshetra August, 1995, p. 35.
16. Bhargava B.S. and Vidya K.C., Position of women in Political Institutions, *Journal of Rural Development* Vol. 11 No. 5, September 1992, p. 603.
17. Sukla Deb kanango Panchayati Raj and Emerging Women Leadership: An overview Social Action, New Delhi, Vol. 46., No. I, Jan-Mar, 1996, pp. 79-80.
18. Bhargava B.S. and Vidya K.C., *op. cit*, p. 618.
19. South Link, South-South Solidarity, *Newsletter* Special issue, Vol. VI, No. I and II, April/June, 1995.
20. Parvatamma "Ground to Halt": Elections to the Karnataka's Local Bodies, 1994, *Frontline,* April 1, 1-22, 1994.
21. Dr. S.P. Ranga Rao The Mandal Panchayas of Andhra Pradesh: A Critical Analysis, Kurukshetra, December, 1996, p. 132.
22. P. Manikyamba, *Women in Panchayati Raj Structure,* Gyan Publishing House, New Delhi, 1989, pp. 17-24.
23 Uma Joshi, Rural women in National development, Kurukshetra, Special Number, Aug. 1995, p. 37.
24. Swati Chakraborthy, Rethinking on Reservation for women in legislatures women's link, April-June, 1997, p. 30.

# 19

# The Octroi Debate: The Case of Punjab

*—Gagan Deep*

Octroi, the biggest source of revenue to urban local bodies, in the Indian context is derivative of the Persian term meaning a "handful". Octroi, in its present form, can be described as a tax levied on the entry of goods into local areas for consumption, use or sale therein. It has a long history and is one of the ancient sources of revenue of local bodies. During the Mughal period it was called "Chungi", "Dhart" during Sikh regime and in Maratha towns it was known as "Mustarfa". In its present structure it is found in the Regulation of 1805 framed by East India Company. In 1920, an alternative to octroi called terminal tax was introduced in some towns under the rules framed under the Government of India Act, 1919. In the Indian Constitution, octroi and terminal taxes are included in the Union List and in the State List vide entries 89, 52 and 56 respectively.

There are provisions in the Punjab Municipal Act, 1911 and the Punjab Municipal Corporation Act, 1976 relating to levy of octroi including power to examine articles liable to octroi, power to search where octroi is leviable, penalty for evasion of tax and recovery of octroi by the Municipal officials.

Rate of octroi varies from item to item (listed in octroi schedule of the state). Some of the items such as food grains, military and police canteen goods, election material etc. are exempted from levy of octroi.

Presently octroi constitutes one-fourth of the total tax revenue of local bodies in the country. It occupies an important place in the tax structure of the Municipalities of various states like, Haryana, Orissa, Punjab, Rajasthan, Gujarat and Maharashtra. One of the most remarkable features of octroi is that, it can be treated as an indicator of economic dynamism of a particular municipality.

Octroi which is the important source of income of local bodies has been the subject of debate among all sections of society. Over the years, there have been repeated demands to discontinue this major source of revenue of urban local bodies. Traders view this tax as obstructant. A number of committees constituted by the government, to consider the issue of octroi, surprisingly gave a unanimous verdict against this tax. All this is causing great confusion regarding the future of octroi.

A number of states, keeping in view the recommendations of these committees, have scrapped octroi but without proper alternative for the revenue loss, leading to a crisis situation for urban local bodies. Recently, issue of abolition of octroi was in news in Punjab too, because of political commitment of government to the certain sections of the society. Despite objections and criticism from traders, Punjab has decided to continue with octroi.

The objective of the present study is to deliberate over the role of octroi in the total tax structure of urban local bodies in state of Punjab and the desirability of continuing it and secondly, to assess the case for privatisation of its collection with a view to checking its massive leakage. Its impact on different sections of society shall also be evaluated.

The paper is divided into three parts. First part would deal with the existing structure of octroi in the state, i.e., contribution and growth of octroi income and variations in octroi income in terms of administrative status of local bodies and their distribution in different parts of the state. The second part examines the controversies arising out of continuation of octroi in the state and issues involved in it. The third part deliberates on the issue of involving the private sector in the collection of octroi.

**Situation in Punjab**

At present there are some states, namely Punjab, Haryana, Gujarat, Maharashtra, Orissa and Rajasthan, which allow the levy of this tax and it is of considerable fiscal importance to these states. Not only that it is the chief contributor to the municipal sources, it is also the most steady and reliable source. Moreover it has been found to be highly elastic and over the years, there has been a consistent increase in the total revenue yielded by this source. As indicated by Table 1, revenue from octroi in 1994-95 was to the order of Rs. 9193 lakh, which constituted more than half (54.68 per cent) of total income of local bodies of the state.

**TABLE 1**
**Income from Octroi in Punjab Municipal Councils**

| *Year* | *Income from Octroi (Rs. in lakh)* | *Total Income (Rs. in lakh)* | *Percentage of Octroi Income* |
|---|---|---|---|
| 1991–92 | 5433.36 | 8,911.65 | 60.42 |
| 1992–93 | 5978.21 | 10,315.96 | 57.95 |
| 1993–94 | 7261.61 | 13,038.59 | 55.89 |
| 1994–95 | 9193.34 | 16,811.41 | 54.88 |

*Source:* Directorate of local self Government, Punjab.

Figures of octroi in the above table establish the importance of octroi as a major contributor to the municipal income. Despite the declining trend in octroi income, it continues to play an important role in generating adequate source of revenue. A close and detailed examination of individual municipal councils reveals that more than one-fourth of Municipal Councils receive more than three-fourths of their revenue from octroi only. In some Municipal Councils, namely Gobindgarh, Nangal, Kotkapura, Bathinda, Rajpura, and Dinanagar, income from this tax is as high as 65 per cent of total revenue. In other municipalities, where octroi income is not as high as in such places but still constitutes the major source of income.

Octroi income has been found to have the positive co-relation with economic/commercial activities of the town/city. Table 2 shows that contribution of this tax was greater in case of those municipalities, which were larger in size or enjoyed higher municipal status. For lower categories of municipalities, the revenue generated by octroi was also of the lower order.

Further study of data from individual municipal councils has revealed that municipalities falling in South-West and Central region of the State have higher proportion of octroi than those in the submountaineous areas of the state. The most remarkable feature of this tax is its higher growth rate, as compared to all other sources of municipal income. Octroi continues to be the most important source of revenue in the State and has shown a higher growth rate during the period of 1989-90 to1993-94. It has been as high as 21.23 per cent as against 15.41 per cent in case of property tax during the same period.

**TABLE 2**
**Municipal Status–wise Income from Octroi (Punjab)**

*(Percentage distribution)*

| *Status of Municipalities* | *1991–92* | *1992–93* | *1993–94* | *1994–95* |
|---|---|---|---|---|
| Class I | 65.34 | 63.92 | 59.94 | 62.06 |
| Class II | 49.58 | 47.08 | 43.92 | 44.62 |
| Class III | 44.53 | 42.08 | 45.42 | 40.12 |

*Source:* Directorate of Local Self Government, Punjab.

## The Issue of Octroi Abolition

Octroi as a tax has always been criticised by scholars, politicians, traders and transporters. It has been termed as the most regressive in nature because it hampers growth of trade as well as industrial activities and leads to waste of considerable amount of time and fuel. The main irritant of this tax is corruption and manipulations by municipal staff at octroi barriers which hinder the smooth flow of normal traffic. The Indian Texation Inquiry Committee (1924), The Local Finance Inquiry Committee (1949), Motor Vehicle Texation Inquiry Committee (1950), The Texation Enquiry Commission (1953), The Road Transport Reorganisation Committee (1959), The Committee on Augmentation of Financial Resources of Urban Local Bodies (1963), Zakaria Committee (1965), Committee on Transport Policy and Coordination (1966), Road Transport Texation Committee (1967), Rural-Urban Relationship Committee constituted to look into various facets of municipal resources have described octroi as meaningless and vexatious source and recommended its gradual replacement by some other suitable alternative free from the aforesaid evils of octroi.

The history of the demand for abolition of octroi is not new. It was abolished in the provinces of Bengal and Madras as early as 1835-1842.

## Strengths and Weaknesses of Octroi

Abolition of octroi has a number of implications for various functionaries in the state and others, which *inter-alia* would include:

(i) The major beneficiary of the abolition of octroi will be traders, businessmen and transporters. They would save a lot of their time, energy and money which they have to waste at octroi barriers.

(ii) State Government will both gain and lose in the process of octroi abolition. They will gain by way of acquiring better administrative control over municipal bodies. Critics of the octroi most of the time suggest the abolition of octroi and its replacement with grants by State Government to compensate the Local Bodies for their revenue loss. However, State Government will have to bear an additional financial burden.

(iii) Local Bodies in this process will be major loser because of the loss of their major source of revenue. Most of the daily expenditure that municipalities incur generally comes from octroi collection. Moreover, they will lose their financial autonomy and they have to depend more and more on grants by the State Government in order to render municipal service.

(iv) Development activities, in the local areas would suffer considerably due to lack of resources with local bodies. In the provision of basic services/infrastructures, it will be difficult for these organisations to do justice to the inhabitants in terms of satisfactory municipal services if octroi revenue is not available.

(v) If octroi is abolished without finding suitable alternative, State Government will have to compensate local bodies. This additional financial liability/burden on the State Government will obviously call for imposing more direct taxes on the people which would lead to inflation and increase in prices of daily utility goods. In the total process, common man will be adversely affected.

**Necessary Reforms in Octroi Collection**

Despite the fact that octroi is the most promising source of revenue of the municipal bodies, there are a number of problems faced by local bodies in collection of this tax. Following are a few problems in the collection of octroi:

(i) A good number of traders/business house have set up their stores/warehouses outside municipal limits avoiding payment of octroi.

(ii) Large scale leakage of octroi has been noticed due to malpractices adopted by the staff involved in the collection and management of octroi.

(iii) Lack of motivation, prevailing work-culture and negative attitudes of employees, contribute largely to the loss in the octroi collection.

Though it is difficult to make accurate guess of evasion due to above reasons, it is commonly believed that evasion ranges anything from 30 to 40 per cent of the total collection. Therefore, under these circumstances, there is a need to bring necessary changes. For this purpose, necessary amendments in the Municipal Acts need to be made so as to minimise evasion of octroi. Provisions should also be made in the municipal acts to check the organised evasion by the traders by locating their stores and warehouses outside the municipal limits.

**Privatisation of Octroi Collection**

In order to minimise evasion of octroi and to make its management more effective, there is increasing demand of involvement of private sector in collection of taxes and other activities of local bodies. There is no doubt that primary function of private sector is to earn more money/profit with less emphasis on social service. However past experience of privatisation shows that it is helpful in creating a work culture that ultimately leads to faster growth.

As it has happened in most of the states where octroi is levied, Punjab also experienced wide spread leakage in octroi collection in the state which requires immediate action. Although octroi rates were revised during 1993-94, yet the amount of increase in collection of octroi was not commensurate with the increase in the rates. (Source Directorate Local Self Government Punjab). It was therefore, a clear case of massive evasion of octroi. This led to a rethinking on the part of government to substitute the traditional system of octroi collection with some other system. Accordingly, private collection of octroi was resorted to. Privatisation of octroi collection was introduced in the state on selected basis in selected municipalities and it was found that privatisation of the octroi had positive effect on the overall revenue collection of local bodies in the State.

The overall growth of revenue due to privatisation in the whole state is around Rs. 50 crore approximately. There has been an increase of 30 per cent in octroi collection of municipal bodies. Accordingly, it will be in the interest of the state that more and more local bodies adopt this system of octroi collection. In the beginning when this system was introduced in some of the municipal councils, the per cent increase recorded was very high and it ranged between 20 to 45 per cent of total octroi collection.

**Strengths and Weaknesses of Privatisation**

The system of privatisation of octroi collection has been adopted by the Government, keeping in view the inherent weaknesses of the existing system.

However, there are number of the related issues which need to be closely looked into. They may be:

1. Due to privatisation of octroi, municipal bodies will have more staff available which can be spared for the task of managing the maintenance and development activities.
2. Due to reduction in leakage of octroi, there will be considerable increase in income from octroi. As a result, there will be more resources with local bodies to ensure proper development of their area.
3. It would help in promoting better work culture among the employees.

Apart from above merits, there can be a number of pitfalls in this system which are mentioned below:

1. With this change, many things have gone in the hands of private persons. In order to generate more octroi and gain more profit they have tried to misuse the existing source. Norms and octroi schedules laid down by government/civic bodies have been violated by the contractors.
2. Due to misbehaviour of the private contractors incidences of strike and agitation of employees have been noticed affecting adversely the collection of octroi.
3. If everything goes into the hands of a private contractor, he will exploit the system.
4. Incidences of harassment to common man at octroi barriers have been noticed.

**Conclusion**

As a result of foregone discussions, the following conclusions can be drawn from the understanding of the Punjab experience:

(i) Octroi as a chief, reliable and regular source of revenue from urban local bodies needs to be treated as an integral part of the revenue base of the municipal bodies. Its abolition will further deteriorate their financial health. It will have an adverse effect on their autonomy.

(ii) Large scale leakage of octroi and evasion of this tax, requires to be checked, through reforms in the existing set-up or changing traditional system of octroi collection through privatisation.

(iii) In 74th Constitution Amendment Act, there is a specific thrust on more powers and autonomous status to local bodies. So keeping in view this latest amendment and importance of octroi, no step in haste should be taken to abolish the octroi.

The State Finance Commissions, while recommending the assignment of taxes and sharing of state taxes to local bodies should keep in mind the reliability of this flexible source of revenue. As advocated by most of the earlier committees and commissions, octroi should not be compensated but replaced by a suitable source.

# 20
# Urban Poverty Alleviation in North-Eastern States

*—A.C. Mohapatra*

**Background**

Poverty is the single most important issue besetting the Indian polity and society. Nearly a quarter of the world's poorest of the poor live here (250 mn.). Despite the half-a-century of planning and efforts, nationally and through international assistance, the proportion of those afflicted by abject poverty has come down (from 70-80 per cent at the time of Independence) to about 30 per cent by current estimates—the sheer size of the population below the poverty line is still mind boggling. There are also wide differences in the share of poverty between different states from 12.3 per cent in Manipur to 49.1 per cent in Bihar[1]. By and large, the larger states like U.P., Bihar, Madhya Pradesh, Orissa, West Bengal etc. have a larger share of population below the poverty line than the smaller states. However, there is wide difference in estimates of poverty by different organisations. In its 38th Round report (84-85) while NSSO puts the poverty component at around 28 per cent (at Rs. 122 per capita consumption expenditure), CSO estimates it over 53 per cent (at 136.75).

It may however, be mentioned that while talking of poverty line, we are essentially concerned about the absolute physiological deprivation only, by whatever methods of estimation employed. But once secondary characteristics like basic services of health, education, housing and sanitation are used, a very large population, particularly those marginally above the poverty line would come under this category and then, the proportion could be a staggering 40-50 per cent or so, or about 400-450 mn. in absolute terms. It is an undeniable fact that it is a long and arduous journey to complete removal of poverty in country.

**Urban Poverty and its Dimensions**

Poverty in Urban areas is defined by the consumptions expenditure equivalent of 2100 calories of food intake and other essentials for physiological survival of an individual, equivalent of monthly income per capita of Rs. 198 (1990-91 prices of Rs. 11,850 per year per family of average size of five). As per the Seventh Five Year Plan, urban poverty has been estimated at about 27.7 per cent of the population or 50.5 mn.[2] On the basis of 1991 census estimates of urban population of 217.18 million (provisional estimates), with the same ratio the population under the poverty line would be 60 mn. plus. However, assuming that various urban poverty alleviation programmes of the Central and State Governments and activities of NGOs and the general economic improvements made during the Seventh Five Year Plan (1985-90) having reduced the content of poverty in urban areas by 2-3 percentage points, the overall absolute population below the poverty line would still remain around 50 million or so (42 million by the Eighth Plan estimates). It may be mentioned that while poverty as such, whether in rural and urban areas is degrading itself, apart from being a constant physical threat to survival, the urban poor, in certain respects, are greatly disadvantaged due to the extremely threatening environmental conditions they live in, i.e., poor shelter conditions, low-lying areas of shanties and water logging, unhygienic sanitary conditions, lack of potable water and often degrading social situation of alcoholism, drug addiction, prostitution, etc. While rural poverty is equally degrading but some of the specific environmental and social situation which the urban poor are placed are not normally encountered in rural areas. Table-1 provides that state-wise share of population classified as urban poor.[3]

Traditionally, the largest concentration of urban are found in metro-cities. Exodus from far flung rural areas, especially those affected by frequent droughts and floods, population pressure on land (decline in *land-man ratio*), lack of opportunities of employment and earning in the rural areas at one hand, and the attractions of some (perceived) avenues of earning in the urban *informal sector,* have been the reasons for migration from rural areas

**TABLE 1**
**Poverty Levels in India**

| *States* | *Percentage Living Below the Poverty Line, 1983-84* | |
|---|---|---|
| | *Urban* | *Total* |
| Uttar Pradesh | 40.3 | 45.3 |
| Bihar | 37.0 | 49.1 |
| Maharashtra | 23.3 | 49.1 |
| West Bengal | 26.5 | 39.2 |

| | | |
|---|---|---|
| Andhra Pradesh | 29.5 | 36.4 |
| Madhya Pradesh | 31.1 | 46.2 |
| Tamil Nadu | 30.9 | 39.6 |
| Karnataka | 29.2 | 35.0 |
| Rajasthan | 26.1 | 34.3 |
| Gujarat | 17.3 | 24.3 |
| Orissa | 29.5 | 42.8 |
| Kerala | 30.1 | 26.8 |
| Assam | 21.6 | 23.5 |
| Punjab | 21.0 | 30.8 |
| Haryana | 16.9 | 15.6 |
| Jammu & Kashmir | 15.8 | 16.3 |
| Himachal Pradesh | 8.0 | 13.5 |
| Tripura** | 50.0 | 73.50 |
| Manipur | 13.8 | 12.3 |
| Meghalaya** | 25.0 | 40.00 |
| Nagaland* | 17.7 | 27.1 |
| Sikkim* | 17.7 | 27.1 |

* Averages have been used in the case of Nagaland and Sikkim.

** Recent estimates as per Planning Commission (1993), Expert Group on Estimation of Poverty, New Delhi.

*Source:* NIUA, New Delhi, *Urban Data Sheet,* 1986.

to large cities. They are then relocated in the sprawling slums of these cities. Poverty in small and medium size towns and cities, though prevalent were rarely encounted in slums as such, or if at all, only in small pockets. Lastly, this situation appears to be changing and in Class I Cities of sizes 1-5 lakhs, slums are becoming a common phenomenon. However, the metro-cities still have the largest chunk of the urban poor living in the slums. Table-2 provides a break up of slum population in the twelve million plus cities (1981 census) where the estimate of slum population was 19.87 mn. out of a projected population of 61.87 mn., i.e. constituting 32.12 per cent of the population[4]). The total estimated slum population of the four largest metropolitan cities (Calcutta, Bombay, Delhi and Madras) was 14 million.

Among this large poor population living in the towns and cities of the country, 68 per cent are women and children, a dependent population with limited avenues or access to employment and earning. The urban poor live in appalling conditions. Forty per cent of the urban population lives in just one room and 75 per cent of these one room tenements have no windows. Eighty per cent of the households have no private latrines and of the rest two-thirds get water-logged during the rains. The situation of women and children is especially difficult. High mortality among women due to poor living condition and deficiency of nutrition have led to a decline in sex-ratio from 972 (1971) to 933 (1981) and 893 (1991)[5]. The literacy rate of women in urban areas is only 54.01 per cent compared to 68.71 per cent for men, nearly 15 percentage points below the male literacy (1991)[6]. The situation among the urban poor and slum dwellers could be far worse only. In the employment front, compared to 48.18 per cent males classified as main workers only 7.7 per cent of the women are so classified (1981)[7]. Of the estimated 13 million slum children (by the lowest estimate), 28 per cent are below 4 years of age, the most vulnerable. About 300,000 urban children die each year due to diarrhoeal dehydration, the largest segment of which belongs to the slum and poor population in the city. There is severe nutritional and vitamin deficiencies (Vitamin A and iron). Fifty per cent of the infant deaths are neo-natal and due to premature births, tetanus, maternal malnutrition and lack of sanitation. Only a fraction of this child population is protected against preventable but crippling diseases (like 53 per cent BCG, 24 per cent Triple Vaccine and 11 per cent Polio)[8].

**Urban Poverty Alleviation Programmes**

Amid this dismal urban scenario of India, when one evaluates the governmental efforts in poverty alleviation, the picture emerges equally dismal. By and large, the approach to urban poverty alleviation in the first two decades of independent India was marked by elitism, lack of imagination, reluctance in employing social overheads for the poor and grasp on the issues needing attention. This phase was marked by the *Improvement and Clearance Act, 1956, (Delhi)* with emphasis on relocating the slum population by provision of housing sites or even housing at outlying areas, to which the slum population was reluctant to move which could affect their livelihood and earning the areas of which lied closer to the city centres. Many simply disposed of the sites or houses earning a little fortune and lived where they were. The government found the relocation scheme unattractive to the beneficiaries and capital intensive with the little money available with the municipal bodies and corporations. This programme was a non-starter.

**TABLE 2**
**Estimated Slum Population in Metropolitan Cities**

| *Cities* | *Identified slum population* | *Percentage to total population* | *Estimated population 1990* | *Estimated slum popula-ation 1990* |
|---|---|---|---|---|
| 1. Calcutta | 30.280 | 32.9 | 125.33 | 43.86 |
| 2. Bombay | 28.314 | 34.3 | 117.89 | 41.26 |
| 3. Delhi | 18.000 | 31.4 | 97.67 | 32.08 |
| 4. Madras | 13.630 | 32.1 | 60.22 | 21.08 |
| 5. Bangalore | 3.050 | 10.4 | 51.86 | 10.37 |
| 6. Hyderabad | 5.000 | 19.6 | 37.07 | 11.12 |
| 7. Ahmedabad | 5.363 | 20.3 | 37.76 | 11.33 |
| 8. Kanpur | 6.140 | 37.5 | 22.84 | 8.00 |
| 9. Pune | 2.743 | 16.3 | 25.73 | 5.15 |
| 10. Nagpur | 4.161 | 31.9 | 18.82 | 5.64 |
| 11. Lucknow | 2.850 | 28.3 | 13.12 | 3.94 |
| 12. Jaipur | 2.960 | 29.1 | 16.34 | 4.90 |
| Total | 122.491 | 29.1 | 618.65 | 198.73 |

*Source:* A Compendium of Indian Slums, TCPO, 1985.

In the seventies, the approach to urban poor and slum changed from *relocation to on-site rehabilitation* with the beginning of the central sector scheme of Environmental Improvement of Urban Slums (EIUS, 1972), since transferred to the state sector. Along with this, the experiments on Urban Community Development Scheme (UCD, Delhi 1958) was extended to additional towns/cities with the assistance of UNICEF and World Bank. Some successes of UCD in cities like Hyderabad, Visakhapatnam and Delhi etc. led to change in the approach to urban poverty alleviation from physical infrastructure based to social inputs orientation and from *directive system to participatory system,* with the objective that the state intervention could be only catalytic in poverty alleviation, whereas the tangible result could come from community-based efforts of the urban poor and their efforts to stand on their own legs and improve the *quality of life of their communities.* Apart from other subsidiary schemes like IDSMT, ICDS, MNP SNP/MDM programmes, the Government of India with the assistance of UNICEF launched the Urban Basic Services (UBS) Programme as a Central Sector Scheme at the beginning of the Seventh Five Year Plan (1985) with a coverage of 168 towns/cities with fund allocation ratio of 20:40:40 between the Central Government, the State Government and the UNICEF. This programme got strong endorsement from the National Commission on Urbanisation (NCU, 1988)[9]. The key concepts were *community participation, convergence (of service delivery), cost effectiveness* etc. From 1990, the UBS was further extended to about 500 cities/towns (currently 247 towns and cities, 1994) in all the States and UTs with the ultimate aim of 100 per cent coverage of the country with change in the nomenclature to Urban Basic Services for the Poor (UBSP). The launching of Nehru Rozgar Yojna (NRY) from 1989 in the entire country, principally with the three schemes of SUWE, SUME and SHASU, with the objective of employment generation, the Urban Poverty Alleviation programmes were expected to get a fuller impetus. The latest in the service is Swarna Jayanti Shahri Rozgar Yojana, launched in late 1997.

**Urbanisation and Urban Poverty in the North Eastern States of India**

The seven states of India's North East, i.e., Assam, Arunachal Pradesh, Manipur, Meghalaya, Mizoram, Nagaland and Tripura (often also called the *Seven Sisters*) constitute of approximately 7.7 per cent of the geographical area of the country and about 4 per cent of the population (31.39 mn., 1991). The region being long neglected and underdeveloped, has lower level of urbanisation (4.36 mn., being only 13.88 per cent compared to the national level of 25.72 per cent, 1991). Of the 4689 towns/ cities of the country, the region has 184, i.e., 3.92 per cent only (1991). Of the 300 class I cities (100,000 +) the region has only 8, i.e., 2.7 per cent, the largest being Guwahati (577, 591) followed by Shillong UA (222, 273). Assam alone has 85 per cent of the Urban population of the Region—but there exist wide difference in the level of urbanisation of the constituent states of the region Table 3.

**TABLE 3**

**Percentage of Urban to Total Population (1961-91)**

| *States* | *1961* | *1971* | *1981* | *1991* | *% deca. var 1981–91* |
|---|---|---|---|---|---|
| 1. Arunachal Pradesh | 0.0 | 3.7 | 6.6 | 12.2 | 12.2 |
| 2. Assam | 8.4 | 8.9 | 10.3 | 11.1 | 2.7 |
| 3. Manipur | 8.7 | 13.2 | 26.4 | 27.4 | 19.0 |
| 4. Meghalaya | 15.3 | 14.6 | 18.1 | 18.7 | 3.4 |
| 5. Mizoram | 5.4 | 11.4 | 24.7 | 46.2 | 40.8 |
| 6. Nagaland | 5.2 | 10.0 | 15.5 | 17.3 | 12.1 |

| | | | | | |
|---|---|---|---|---|---|
| 7. Tripura | 9.0 | 10.4 | 11.0 | 15.3 | 6.3 |
| 8. N.E. | | | | 13.88 | |
| India | 18.4 | 19.9 | 23.3 | 25.7 | 7.3 |

*Source:* Census of India, 1981, (Final)[10] and 1991 (Provisional) Tables.

As is discernible, the State of Mizoram and Manipur have levels of urbanisation significantly higher than the national average. Except for the state of Assam, Meghalaya and Tripura that enjoy traditionally a higher level of urbanisation and a low rate of growth, the other four states experienced a quantum jump in the level urbanisation, particularly Mizoram from 5 per cent to 46 per cent during the 3 decades, Arunachal from 0 to 12.2 per cent, Nagaland from 5 to 17 per cent and Manipur from 9 to 27 per cent[11]. These states also recorded a very large increase in these states increased substantially. This has the following implications:

(1) While the 1991 census indicates that the growth of urban population has somewhat slowed down in the country as a whole, i.e., compared to a decadal growth of 46 per cent between 1971–81 decade, the growth between 19981–91 has been only 36.19 per cent, the growth in the North Eastern States has been fairly high, i.e. five states, out of the seven recorded an annual exponential rate of growth of urban population growth higher than the national average of 3.09 per cent, though the growth rate in case of four states was lower than the 1971–81 decade Table 4. It may be noted that in the hill states of the region, the high growth has been due to a substantial rural to urban migration and also establishment of new administrative towns–in the plains, particularly of Assam, Manipur Valley and Tripura, it is due to inclusions of new towns due to re-classification of emerging rural market centres into urban area category. The Class I towns like Guwahati, Jorhat, Silchar, Imphal and Agartala had a large percentage of decadal growth.

**TABLE 4**
**Exponential Annual Growth Rate of Urban Population (1971–81 and 1981–91)**

| *States* | *1971–81* | *1981–91* |
|---|---|---|
| 1. Arunachal Pradesh | 8.74 | 9.28 |
| 2. Manipur | 9.76 | 2.98 |
| 3. Meghalaya | 4.95 | 2.74 |

| | | | | |
|---|---|---|---|---|
| 4. Mizoram | | 11.71 | | 9.57 |
| 5. Nagaland | | 8.50 | | 5.58 |
| 6. Tripura | 3.29 | | 6.19 | |
| 7. Assam[12] | | 2.23 | | 2.37 |
| All India | | 3.83 | | 3.09 |

*Source:* Census of India, Provisional Population Totals, Paper–2, 1991.

(2) The North-Eastern States being by and large agricultural with low level of industrial development, the level of urbanisation has been traditionally low. It was from 1970s that the region has been enjoying a high growth in its urban population due to a low base share. The region also enjoys a low density of population. This process of large increase in urban population is likely to continue for at least a couple of decades. It may be noted that although the North-Eastern States record a relatively low level of poverty in general and urban migration, low level of industrial development and therefore, low opportunities of employment and earning is likely to aggravate the situation. The major portion of urban employment comes from either the service sector, the trade sector and the informal sectors.

(3) The situation of women in general and in the urban areas of N.E. in particular, is qualitatively different than rest of the country due to higher female literacy, the egalitarian social ethos of a large segment of Scheduled Tribe population and a matrilineal society in states like Meghalaya. Table 5 provides the state-wise female literacy status in urban areas of N.E. India in 1991. It could be noted that with the exception of Arunachal Pradesh and Manipur, all other states enjoy a higher female literacy (urban) compared to the all India average.

It could also be mentioned that unlike the overall Indian situation, the differentiation between the male and female literacy is fairly narrow in case of the North-Eastern States. However, with a growing impetus on urbanisation, the situation of urban poverty may dramatically change for the worse, the indication of which

**TABLE 5**

**Female Literacy in Urban Population, 1991**

| *States* | *Overall literacy* | *Female literacy* |
|---|---|---|
| 1. Arunachal Pradesh | 57.73 | 49.20 |
| 2. Assam | 69.92 | 63.26 |
| 3. Manipur | 60.08 | 49.80 |

| | | |
|---|---|---|
| 4. Meghalaya | 67.78 | 64.74 |
| 5. Mizoram | 77.82 | 75.82 |
| 6. Nagaland | 67.62 | 64.42 |
| 7. Tripura | 72.32 | 67.76 |
| All India | 61.75 | 53.92 |

*Source:* Census 1991, Provisional Totals, Paper-2, 91.

are already visible in the larger Class I towns/cities like . Guwahati, Shillong, Silchar, Imphal or Agartala, where large slum areas are a common sight now.

(4) However, the situation of urban poverty in the region could not be viewed with the incidence of primary poverty along—the situation of urban basic services like drinking water, sanitation, roads, housing and other urban infrastructure in the region is woefully inadequate. If one considers the situation, then the overall urban poverty content in the region is likely to go up substantially.

**UPA Programmes in the Three States of Meghalaya, Mizoram and Tripura**

The various UPA activities operative in the three above mentioned states have been summarized in Table 6. The main focus of these programmes are in the three Class I, capital cities of Shillong, Aizawl and Agartala. These cities have larger poverty segments and also locational features more akin to slums. In very small towns, the population is comparatively mixed with no typical slums but not necessarily exhibiting any lesser degree of poverty.

The UBSP programme (strategy) is aimed at providing a community structure (organisation) which can be crucial to the success of other UPA activities. The Tables VII (a), (b) and (c) provide nature and coverage of UBSP in the 3 states under review. The largest coverage is in Aizawl with about 8-10,000 households under the programme. Tripura has 5 towns and cities covered along with the capital city of Agartala having been taken up recently (1993). The fulcrum of UBSP is the *community structure* that collectively responds to *public service delivery system*—the community identifies its critical problem areas, plans with assistance of the project staff and otherwise makes the participatory planning and implementation possible. A key element is also the convergence of services from various levels and programmes. Such a community structure could be programme independent, i.e., once built, is expected to sustain over a longer duration with minimal government support. It is in this area the real performance of UBSP and other UPA activities could be tested.

**TABLE 6**
**Towns Covered Under Various UPA Activities**
**(in three States of Meghalaya, Mizoram and Tripura)**

| *UPA/States* | *Meghalaya* | *Mizoram* | *Tripura* |
|---|---|---|---|
| 1. UBSP | Shillong (M), Tura Jowai, Williamnagar and Baghmara[13] | Aizawl | Udaipur, Belonia, Amarpur, Sabroom, Agartala (93) |
| 2. NRY | Shillong Tura | Aizwal | All towns |
| 3. IDSMT | do | do | Agartala, Udaipur, Amarpur, Belonia, Dharamnagar, Kailasahar |
| 4. EIUS | do | do | do |
| 5. LCS | Shillong | Aizawl | Agartala, Khowai, Sona-mura, Dharamnagar, Kailasahar, Udaipur, Amarpur, Belonia, Sabroom |

**Issues for discussion**

(a) Problems related to establishing the community structure:

- RCV selection
- Neighbourhood groups and Neighbourhood Committees
- Registering Societies
- Net working the community.

(b) Training of community leaders (RCVs), CBOs and UBSP grass-root functionaries.

(c) Community Empowerment:

- Community Plans (Mini-Plans)
- Operation of Community Revolving Funds.
- Community Action Projects: Education, Health Awareness campaigns, and citizens rights.

(d) Convergence of service delivery: What to converge?

Level of Convergence :

- Within UBSP activities
- Within UPA programmes
- Regular Government Departments and UBSP
- Tapping community resources

Other related questions to be answered are as follows:

1. How to bring about convergence of basic services?
2. Where and whom to deliver services?
3. Community participation in convergence.

**Urban Infrastructure and Basic Services in the North Eastern States**

A study by NIUA[14] has the following to say about the situation of urban infrastructure of the region :

> "Urban centres of the NER have been registering disproportionately high population growth rates, and consequently the demand for essential urban services has increased much faster than their supply, leading to the emergence of imbalance and critical gaps in urban infrastructure. The major aspects include:
>
> 1. An inequitable distribution of basic services among different sections of the urban population;
> 2. an inequitable access to basic services particularly for the vulnerable segments; and
> 3. Wide-inter-urban centre differentials in the availability of major urban infrastructure facilities.

The study on infrastructure is based on 22 major urban centres of the region. Some of the main features of the infrastructural situation is outlined as follows:

*(a) Water Supply.* Availability of safe water in adequate quantities is a basic necessity for the urban dweller since his access to other free sources is limited by locational factors. Sixty to seventy per cent of the urban population of the region have no access to safe drinking water. Except for two cities, i.e., Karimganj and Guwahati, the rest of the 20 towns and cities are deficit in water availability varying from 5 to 34 per cent. The figure against Guwahati appears to be a grossly over-stated Table 6, since it is widely known that GMC could hardly meet 10–15 per cent of the water requirement of the city. The Greater Guwahati is completely beyond the reach of municipal supply. Moreover, 90 per cent of the water supplied by municipality are unsuitable for consumption. For example, Shillong being the second largest city of the region has no facility of water treatment for supply to consumers[15]. Due to high capital intensity of modern water treatment for supply to consumers[15]. Due to high capital intensity of moder water treatment plants, high storage and distribution cost, due to rugged nature of topography and little municipal finances available to the

LSGs, treated water supply in the region remains a far city against a situation where water availability barring a few areas is no constraint at all.

**TABLE 6**
**Water Supply Capacity and Gap, 1981**
**(Selected Urban Centres)**

| *Selected Urban Centres*[16] | *Capacity (mgd)* | *Availability (gpcd)*[17] | *Standard (gpcd)* | *Water Supply (mgd)* | *Total deficit/gap surplus (gpcd)* |
|---|---|---|---|---|---|
| Karimganj | 2.73 | 78.49 | 15 | (+) 63.49 | (+) 2.21 |
| Silchar | 1.00 | 19.31 | 25 | (–) 5.69 | (–) 0.41 |
| Tezpur | 0.06 | 0.84 | 25 | (–) 24.16 | (–) 1.59 |
| Bongaigaon | 0.08 | 1.56 | 25 | (–) 23.44 | (–) 1.17 |
| Kokrajhar | — | — | 15 | — | — |
| Dhubri | 0.06 | 1.19 | 15 | (–) 13.81 | (–) 0.65 |
| Guwahati | 10.10 | 66.40 | 35 | (+) 31.40 | (+) 4.78 |
| Barpeta | — | — | 15 | — | — |
| Tinsukia | 0.03 | 0.28 | 35 | (–) 34.72 | (–) 3.72 |
| Dibrugarh | — | — | 35 | — | — |
| North Lakhimpur | — | — | 15 | — | — |
| Nagaon | — | — | 25 | — | — |
| Lumding | 0.18 | 4.87 | 15 | (–) 10.13 | (–) 0.37 |
| Hojai | — | — | 15 | — | — |
| Jorhat | 0.33 | 8.98 | 15 | (–) 6.02 | (–) 0.22 |
| Sibsagar | 0.06 | 1.34 | 15 | (–) 13.76 | (–) 0.64 |
| Imphal | 1.56 | 9.93 | 35 | (–) 25.07 | (–) 3.93 |
| Agartala | 0.11 | 0.94 | 35 | (–) 34.16 | (–) 4.52 |
| Shillong | 0.20 | 1.14 | 35 | (–) 33.86 | (–) 5.92 |
| Kohima | 0.05 | 1.54 | 15 | (–) 13.46 | (–) 0.46 |
| Dimapur | 0.10 | 0.17 | 15 | (+) 11.93 | (–) 0.39 |
| Aizawl | 0.20 | 2.68 | 25 | (–) 22.32 | (–) 1.66 |

*Source:* NIUA, New Delhi, NEC Report, 1988.

*(b) Roads.* The average road length per sq.km. of city area for the selected 22 towns/cities in 3.96 kms. including both surfaced and unsurfaced roads Table 7. It varies from 2 km./sq km. in case of Guwahati, North Lakhimpur and Sibsagar to more than 10 in kms. of Dibrugarh, Nagaon, Agartala and

Shillong. In the hill towns like Aizawl, Kohima and Shillong, the roads are often narrow and with high density of motorised vehicle the traffic snare ups are common. Shillong, for example, has a vehicular density of over 1:10, i.e., more than 1 registered vehicle for 10 persons.

**TABLE 7**
**Road Development: Length and Density, 1981**
**(Selected Urban Centres)**

| *Selected Urban Centres* | *Area sq. km.* | *Total road length per $km^2$ area* | *Total road length per $km^2$* | *Surfaced road length $km^2$* | *Unsurd. road length $km^2$* |
|---|---|---|---|---|---|
| *(1)* | *(2)* | *(3)* | *(4)* | *(5)* | *(6)* |
| Karimganj | 5.93 | 29.33 | 4.95 | 9.00 | 20.33 |
| Silchar | 13.35 | 35.59 | 2.69 | 14.32 | 21.27 |
| Tezpur | 7.10 | 30.72 | 4.33 | 20.60 | 10.12 |
| Bongaigaon | 4.79 | 25.58 | 5.34 | 14.13 | 11.45 |
| Kokrajhar | 8.34 | 48.50 | 5.82 | 10.00 | 32.50 |
| Dhubri | 7.21 | 32.53 | 4.51 | 13.07 | 19.46 |
| Guwahati | 215.00 | 288.78 | 1.34 | 125.01 | 163.77 |
| Barpeta | 3.86 | 37.67 | 9.76 | 19.13 | 18.54 |
| Tinsukia | 13.16 | 56.09 | 4.36 | 20.60 | 35.19 |
| Dibrugarh | 13.72 | 196.08 | 14.29 | 38.08 | 158.00 |
| North Lakhimpur | 13.74 | 20.21 | 1.47 | 6.86 | 13.25 |
| Nagaon | 7.93 | 119.77 | 15.10 | 88.40 | 31.37 |
| Lumding | 5.20 | 115.00 | 22.01 | 97.00 | 18.00 |
| Hojai | 5.28 | 77.59 | 14.70 | 37.00 | 40.59 |
| Jorhat | 17.12 | 107.50 | 6.28 | 38.50 | 69.00 |
| Sibsagar | 10.95 | 21.88 | 1.99 | 11.63 | 10.25 |
| Imphal | 29.57 | 122.00 | 4.13 | 46.00 | 76.00 |
| Agartala | 15.81 | 222.59 | 14.08 | 49.66 | 172.93 |
| Shilong | 10.36 | 131.80 | 12.72 | 26.36 | 105.44 |
| Kohima | 23.00 | 151.69 | 6.59 | 28.52 | 123.17 |
| Deemapur | 18.13 | 127.00 | 7.00 | 47.00 | 80.00 |
| Aizawl | 110.00 | 220.09 | 2.03 | 88.00 | 132.00 |
| All urban centres | 559.45 | 2217.09 | 3.96 | 854.87 | 1363.03 |

*Source:* Census of India (Town Directory) 1981 and NIUA Survey.

*(c) Street lighting.* A well designed lighting system for urban roads is considered as an essential municipal service. The norm worked out by the Planning Commission was lighting point at distances of 100 ft. By such norm 9 towns/cities (of the 22) are adequately lighted or surplus. Moreover, the region (except Meghalaya) being chronically power deficit (the overall peak time load gap being around 300 MW or about 35-40 per cent), power cuts are frequent which severely restricts a peak evening hour activities of the towns and cities in the region. Table 8 summarises the overall street lighting situations of the selected 22 urban centres of the region.

**TABLE 8**
**Street Lighting Capacity and Gaps**
**(Selected Urban Centres)**

| *Selected urban Centres* | *Street-lighting Points (Nos)* | *Number of Points as per COPP Norms* | *Infrastructure Gap (Nos) (Surplus/ Deficit ±)* |
|---|---|---|---|
| *(1)* | *(2)* | *(3)* | *(4)* |
| Karimganj | 709 | 295 | (+) 414 |
| Silchar | 1963 | 470 | (+) 1493 |
| Tezpur | 803 | 676 | (+) 127 |
| Bongaigoan | 2192 | 463 | (+) 1729 |
| Kokrajhar | 316 | 525 | (–) 209 |
| Dhubri | 390 | 429 | (–) 39 |
| Guwahati | 2294 | 4100 | (–) 1806 |
| Barpeta | 156 | 627 | (–) 471 |
| Tinsukia | 738 | 676 | (+) 62 |
| Dibrugarh | 862 | 1249 | (–) 387 |
| North Lakhimpur | 819 | 225 | (+) 594 |
| Nagoan | 98 | 2899 | (–) 2801 |
| Lumding | 1202 | 3182 | (–) 1980 |
| Hojai | 208 | 1214 | (–) 1006 |
| Jorhat | 544 | 1263 | (–) 719 |
| Sibsagar | 579 | 382 | (+) 187 |
| Imphal | 1120 | 1509 | (–) 389 |

*(contd)*

| | | | |
|---|---|---|---|
| Agartala | 2575 | 1629 | (+) 946 |
| Shillong | 2039 | 865 | (+) 1174 |
| Kohima | 815 | 936 | (–) 121 |
| Dimapur | 809 | 1542 | (–) 733 |
| Aizawl | 567 | 2886 | (–) 2319 |
| All Urban Centres | 22063 | 28501 | (–) 6438 |

*Source:* Same as Table 7.

By and large the inadequate finances with urban local bodies, faulty tax structure, collections, weak organisational structure has led to a constant decline in management of the municipalities and corporations leading to a sharp fall in urban infrastructure available in the urban centres of the region and decline in services is likely to affect more the weaker sections of the population who are even more dependent on such services than the rich.

**Urban Basic Services Programme**

The fulcrum of UBS Programme (strategy) is building a *community structure* which collectively responds to the *public service delivery system,* identifies their critical problem areas, plans with assistance of the programme staff and otherwise makes participatory planning and implementation possible. As it appears, barring exceptions, building a community structure (i.e. organising the poor into small interesting groups like the NHG) in the UBS/UBSP towns has been a failure. There are the following reasons which may explain the situation:

(i) The response of the state Governments to the UBSP/UBS has been lacklustre after the initial bouts of enthusiasm, because actual fund component of the programme for the small states is rather small.

(ii) While the bureaucracy is by and large is conversant with programme implementation with physical inputs, it is rather hesitant in the sphere of social inputs. It fails to relate to the people directly, compared to file decisions and physical plan implementation by the project staff. This perhaps, happened with the UBS (old) in which the initial physical inputs like Mark–II hand pumps, water filters or certain sanitation schemes could be easily undertaken.

(iii) The community leader (RCV) is not very often elected by the community, but is appointed with some honorarium or quasi-salary arrangement. It is often argued that RCVs are difficult to locate. If this is correct, then of course, the whole idea of UBS is defeated and no tangible gains could be achieved.

(iv) In the urban centres of the N.E. states though poverty is identifiable, these households are very often interspersed with the non-poverty segments, except in the larger cities where slum pockets are visible. Therefore, the area based community organisation is difficult to operationalise.

(v) Finally, in many states of the region, particularly those in the hilly and tribal belts, there are strong traditional institutions of community structure often referred to as village *durbars* (as in Khasi Hills) or village councils of Nagaland with a headman and a council of members sanctified and protected under the provisions of the Sixth Schedule of the Constitution of India[18]. Creation of a different community organisation may impinge upon the jurisdiction of the traditional councils. Therefore, in certain states like in Meghalaya a flexible approach was adopted, i.e., a marriage of the old and the new institutions by putting a certain number of RCVs under the charge of the existing village durbar. The results have been rather mixed. While patronage of the village council/durbar provides legitimacy in operationalising the scheme, the durbars often are dominated by the well-to-do among the community that might deprive the real beneficiaries. Moreover, the poor among the community have no effective voice in ameliorating their conditions—the active participation.

The progress in the areas of physical inputs of basic services like drinking water, sanitation and other infrastructures has been a mixed one. By and large, such infrastructural inputs last till the project funds are available. Very little efforts are made to actually involve the community both at the state of creating the community assets or in their maintenance. Sanitational measures relate to individual facilities—a few and for between, due to the a really scattered nature of the beneficiaries. In many cases the funds have come from other schemes like the LCS, the funds under physical inputs in UBSP is limited to 25-30 per cent only as need-based interventions. In any case, without building a true community structure, there are problems of maintenance of the community assets, that include the tube wells and many such small inputs at the community level that have telling impact on their well-being.

In the sphere of social inputs the main areas emphasised in the said states have been immunisation, supplementary nutrition programme (SNP) and Creche/Balwadi/Anganwadi (either under ICDS or UBSP) and Non-Formal Education (NFE). While the first few years in in Meghalaya was practically devoted to the immunisation programmes with other ante-natal, neo-natal, mother and child care programmes with mixed results, in Tripura the emphasis was on NFE (North Tripura district was under UBS) resulting in eradication of illiteracy from the 3 towns of Dharamnagar, Kailasahr and Kamalpur by the middle of 1991. The progress NFE in UBSP (new) towns in the South Tripura district (Udaipur, Belonia, Amarpur and Sabroom) has been quite successful and all the towns have been declared as fully literate (90 per cent plus coverage). The progress in large cities like Guwahati or Imphal are rather sketchy without definite information. Moreover, it is difficult to accurately assess the impact of UBSP on health and education areas since, concurrent programmes are being run under MH and FW and HRD (NLM). However, critical areas remain specific to different cities. For example, when drug addiction (and AIDS) remain a major problem in Manipur, alcoholism is a problem in Shillong, Kohima or Dimapur. Sanitation and basic civic amenities of water, housing, sanitation etc. remain critical areas in cities like Guwahati, Silchar and Agartala (non-UBSP).

In the areas of community organisation and social inputs, the role of NGOs is considered indispensable. Unfortunately, the number and quality of NGOs involved in the sphere of poverty alleviation in urban areas is a minuscule. Moreover, they are small and inexperienced organisations without sufficient motivation, training and experience. The Government support to this thin NGO activity has been also non-committal.

In the sphere of training infrastructure and training of UBSP nodal officers, project staff and NGOs, the progress is rather unsatisfactory, which perhaps, is an important reason for motivational deficiency and lack of organisational effectiveness of the programme in the Region.[19]

**Issues and Perspectives**

Some of the major issues raised in the paper could be summarised in the following manner :

(1) The North Eastern Region comprising of seven states have a low level of urbanisation but a very high growth of urban population observed in the last couple of decades. Therefore, though the overall incidence of urban poverty is somewhat low, this is likely to aggravate further due to the poor economic base of the urban centres, high level of educated unemployed

and inadequate urban infrastructure per capita as is absorbed now. Therefore, a nominally low poverty component need not lead to complacency.

(2) The implementation of the (old) UBS and the UBSP schemes have been sketchy, without a proper organisational structure and lackadaisical, resulting in poor implementation with the sole exception of the state of Tripura where success in certain areas is discernible.

(3) The most critical problem has been the failure to build a community structure that could stand on its own even after the state interventions are withdrawn. In fact, this is perhaps the reason that not only the programme is not sufficiently effective in UBS/UBSP towns but they have perhaps fallen back in old UBS towns from which state support was withdrawn around 1990–91. It may be important to study a couple of such towns to evaluate if UBS/UBSP await the same fate as the myriad of other government schemes.

(4) Another critical issue related to community structure is the apparent conflict between the new structure to be established and the traditional institutions. An innovative approach to flexibility and effectiveness of these institutions under the scheme needs attention.

(5) In the entire region while NFE and literacy drive has been doing fairly well, critical areas in health, particularly of the mother and child needs additional impetus. Fertility levels in the region are still high, so also IMR and U5MR and MMR.

(6) Finally, the issue of employment and earning remains a critical question with organised sector employment being saturated and informal sector or wage sector employments in urban areas are fraught with the ethnic rivalries and violence. In the ultimate analysis the poor (and also the urban poor) remains at the receiving end with an uncertain future.

## REFERENCES

1. NIUA (1986), *Dimensions of Urban Poverty,* New Delhi (Mimeo).
2. NIUA (1988), *Approach to Urban Poverty: A Position Note,* RSS No. 27, New Delhi (Mimeo).
3. 1983–84 estimates, NIUA, 1986.
4. TCPO, MOUD, GOI(1985), *A Compedium on Indian Slums,* New Delhi.

5. Registration General of Census of India (1991), *Provisional Population Totals: Rural-Urban Distribution.* Paper-2.
6. *Ibid.*
7. NIUA, *UBS Reference Manual,* 1989, pp. 7–8.
8. *Ibid.*
9. National Commission on Urbanisation, MOUD, GOI (1988), *Report,* Vol. II, New Delhi.
10. Registrar General of Census of India (1981), *Primary Census Abstract, General Population,* Part-II, B(i), New Delhi.
11. The case of Manipur is somewhat peculiar due to constant classification and declassification of some towns as towns, from census to census with modifications in definition of urban areas.
12. In case of Assam, the projected figures were taken since there was no census enumerations during 1981.
13. The latter three included in 1996 after notification of municipal boards.
14. NIUA (1988), *Urbanisation and Urban Development: Policy Issues of the North Eastern Region,* Tech. Report on project sponsored by NEC, New Delhi, pp. 58–59 (Mimeo).
15. Recently, partially treated water in limited quantities is being made available from the Greater Shillong Water Supply Scheme (GSWSS), a project under implementation over two decades with no immediate hope of alleviating the sufferings of city dwellers.
16. Estimated on the basis of 1981 population data, Census of India.
17. Standard (gpcd) norm is as per the Zakaria Committee.
18. U/s 3(e) & (i) of Sixth Schedule [Article 244(2) and 275(1)], the District Councils shall administered as under 3(e) the establishment of village and town administration, including village and town police and public health and sanitation; Constitution of India, GOI, New Delhi, (Rev. ed) 1994, pp. 153–54.
19. In 1991, MOUD, GOI identified NEHU, Shillong as a nodal training institution and subsequently was joined by the Assam Administrative Training Institute for UNICEF support in capacity building activities for the seven states plus Sikkim.

# 21

# Financing of Municipal Corporations in U.P. : Functional Realities and Prospects

*—Awadhesh Kumar Singh*

Uttar Pradesh is one of the leading states after Maharashtra in terms of absolute number of people living in urban areas. However, the proportion of the urban population in state of Uttar Pradesh (19.89 per cent) is below the national average (25.71 per cent). The state had high urban growth rate during 1981–91, i.e., 38.69 per cent and has a sizable number of urban settlements (702 towns and urban agglomerations). Again, out of total urban population of the state, 55.51 per cent were in class I towns as per 1991 census and out of total population of class I towns, 34 per cent were in eleven Nagar Nigams (Municipal Corporations) including urban agglomerations. There are 684 urban local bodies comprising of 11 Nagar Nigams, 226 Nagar Palika Parishads, and 447 Nagar Panchayats. The total population of urban local bodies was reported to be 262.40 lakh and population of Nagar Nigams constituted 35.83 per cent. Similarly, total area of urban local bodies in U.P. was reported 5578.14 sq. km. and area of Nagar Nigams constituted 24.74 per cent (1380.24 sq. km. in absolute term).

It is almost well accepted fact that financial position of urban local bodies in the country has not been very satisfactory. Their sources of income are limited as compared to their assigned responsibilities. Despite steps taken by the governments at different levels, the situation in this sphere has not shown any marked change. It is to be noted that financial position of Nagar Nigams (Municipal Corporations) in the state of Uttar Pradesh is far from satisfactory. The gap between the income and expenditure is widening. Moreover, they depend upon the grants and aid from state as well as Central government and also on loans from state governments or foreign agencies. Again, their financial deficit as well as their financial liabilities are gradually increasing.

In the present paper, an overview of financial position of municipal corporations in the state of Uttar Pradesh has been presented, ensuring analysis of time series data. Interestingly, sources of municipal revenue, growth of revenue, pattern of revenue and capital expenditure has been critically analysed. Moreover, devolution of funds to municipal corporations as per recommendations of State Finance Commission, financial powers, and recommendations of State Finance Commission regarding resource mobilization have also been reviewed in the present paper. The paper is based on available literature, secondary data and information available from Directorate of Urban Local Bodies, U.P. and other academic and research institutions.

**Sources of Municipal Revenues**

The local bodies, although autonomous in character are, by and large, subordinate to state governments which create them. Their revenues are also limited to the sources assigned to them under the state law. Their income is derived from local taxation, enterprises, services, or the wealth of the citizen inhibated within the limits of municipal body. The local revenue is taxable from the residents within the area of the local bodies. Direct taxation is common in municipal fiscal administration. Besides, they impose special levies, commonly termed as betterment levies charged for improvements on property made by them. They also receive assistance from state and Central governments for discharging their obligatory duties. At times, international agencies also provide financial assistance through state governments for projects of urban development, like housing, water supply, sanitation, roads, etc. In short, the local revenue may be classified as follows: tax revenue, non-tax revenue, grants-in-aid and loans and borrowings. The taxes are broadly grouped as:

(i) Property taxes;
(ii) Octroi (abolished in U.P.), terminal and toll and;
(iii) Other taxes.

The property taxes include:

(a) general tax,
(b) water tax,
(c) conservancy tax; and
(d) drainage tax, market tax, house tax etc.

Under the group of other taxes, following have been included:

(i) tax on trades, callings, and vocations;
(ii) theatre tax,

(iii) tax on dogs;
(iv) toll on vehicles and other conveyances and animals;
(v) tax on circumstances and property;
(vi) tax on deeds of transfer of immovable property;
(vii) betterment tax;
(viii) tax on advertisement (excluding newspapers);
(ix) tax on vehicles and other conveyance placing for hire.

Interestingly, non-tax sources include the following:

(i) license fees;
(ii) sale and rent of municipal properties;
(iii) fees from educational institutions;
(iv) fees from hospitals and dispensaries;
(v) fees from cattle pounds;
(vi) fees from slaughtering of animals;
(vii) tehbazari;
(viii) copying charges;
(ix) building materials on roads and streets;
(x) removal charges of encroachments and fprojections;
(xi) sale of forms;
(xii) Sale of compost and manure;
(xiii) income from silage forms;
(xiv) income from sale of water;
(xv) meter rents;
(xvi) conservancy services;
(xvii) fees from fines under other enactments;
(xviii) miscellaneous income.

Under section 172 of the U.P. Nagar Nigam Act, 1959, imposition of every type of taxes are obligatory. At present every municipal corporation has levied the house tax @ 10 per cent to 18.5 per cent and water tax @ 4 per cent to 14 per cent of he Annual Rental Value of the Property. Secondly, taxes are shared by the municipal corporations; thirdly, every municipal corporation has been assigned to levy 2 per cent extra stamp duty on the transfer of immovable property, located in their limit. They have to frame their own bye laws for this purpose and serve the copy of such bye laws to the Sub-Registrar of Registration Department of the concerned area. Fourthly, after the acceptance of the State Finance Commission's recommendations by the state government, no grant is admissible to the urban local bodies including municipal corporations. Before 74th

Amendment, grants-in-aid were given to municipal corporations for general purpose like grants for the maintenance of roads, street light, sanitation, storm water drains or nalas were given. Specific purpose grants were given for pay, which included pay subsidy, octroi and toll compensation.

As per the recommendations of the State Finance Commission, the funds are devolved by the state government directly to the municipal corporation. Interestingly, before the 74th Amendment of the Constitution, no share of taxes, duties of fees was transferred to municipal corporation. But after the 74th Amendment the State Finance Commission was constituted in April 1994. It submitted its final report before the government in December 1996, which was accepted by the state government from April, 1997. As per the recommendation of State Finance Commission, 7 per cent of the net proceeds of state revenue (taxes, duties and fees) is being transferred to urban local bodies through direct devolution. Out of this 7 per cent, 3.12 per cent has been earmarked to Nagar Nigams (Municipal Corporations), 3.12 per cent to the Nagar Palika Parishads (Municipalities) and 0.76 per cent to the Town Panchayats. Out of this 3.12 per cent State Finance Commission has also determined the share of each municipal corporation separately on the basis of 80 per cent population and 20 per cent area of every municipal corporation. It is to be noted that after the acceptance of SFC's recommendations no grants in non plan is admissible to the urban local bodies including municipal corporations.

Rate structure of taxes, user charges and fees etc. of municipal corporations may be understood under the following points:

(i) property tax levied on the basis of 10 per cent to 18.5 per cent of Annual Rental Value of the Property. After every five years, the reassessment of the property is made and a fresh Annual Rental Value is determined;

(ii) vehicle tax is levied on vehicles and other conveyances placing for hire or kept with in the corporation or on boats moored therein. But it cannot be levied in respect of any motor vehicles. It is realised on the basis of Rs. 10 to 50 per vehicle per day;

(iii) the rates of trade license fees has been revised in 1997. License fee is levied on yearly basis @ Rs. 10 to 12000 per annum on different types of trades and callings;

(iv) show tax or cinema house fee is levied on the basis of per show of the cinema house @ 10 to 50 per show;

(v) rate of water charges has been revised in 1997. At present it is levied @ Rs. 40 to 75 per connection per month.

Revenue receipts of municipal corporations from own sources (tax and non-tax revenue), grants-in-aid, TFC grants and loans for the period 1990-91 to 1999-2000 has been shown in the annexed tables:

(i) figures shown under the other tax heading, i.e., under own taxes include revenue receipts from other taxes, e.g. vehicle tax, advertisement tax, projection tax, conservancy tax etc.;

(ii) figures shown under the other sources, i.e., under non-tax user charges include non-tax revenue or fees realized from fairs and festivals, tourist bus, fishery rental, bus stand, ferry services, etc. for the year 1998-99 and 1999-2000, the estimation has been made on the basis of 10 per cent per year increase in the income of 1997-98. It is to be noted that in the year 1998-99 and 1999-2000 the total revenue receipts is more than expenditure (revenue + capital). It is supposed that the balance amount will be utilized into the payment of arrears of revised payscale. Moreover, projected revenue of municipal corporations for the period 2000-01 to 2004-05 has been also given in annexed tables.

The following steps were taken by the government:

(i) that every municipal corporation will have levy the taxes and fees minimum Rs. 120 per capita, by assessing new house/colonies constructed within their limits, revising the age old rates of licensing fees on various trade and calling and also revising the water charges;

(ii) instructions have been issued to municipal corporations to increase the parking fees.

**Constitution of State Finance Commission (SFC)**

Consequent to the 73rd and 74th amendments in the Constitution of India, and in exercise of the powers conferred by Articles 243 (i) and (x), the Governer vide Finance Departments Notification dated October 22, 1994 constituted the State Finance Commission (Panchayati Raj and Local Bodies). The SFC was required to study and recommend among other things the distribution between state, gram/kshetra/zila panchayats and urban local bodies, of the net proceeds of taxes, duties, toll and fees leviable by the state which may be divided amongst them under part IX and IX-A of the Constitution and the allocation between Panchayats at all levels and urban local bodies of their respective shares of such proceeds. The SFC submitted its final report of recommendations on 31st December 1996, which was accepted by the government in January 1998. The recommendations of the SFC were made effective since 1st April 1997. There are in all 61 recommendations of the SFC which deals with the urban local bodies. Salient and the foremost amongst them are as follows:

(i) Devolution of the 7 per cent of the net proceeds of the local tax revenue of the state government to the urban local bodies;

(ii) The inter-se distribution of the 7 per cent of net proceeds is 3.12 per cent each of municipal corporation and municipalities and the remaining 0.76 per cent for Town Panchayats;

(iii) SFC has recommended the criteria of 80 per cent population and 20 per cent area for devolution of net proceeds of states tax revenue to the three categories of urban local bodies and determine their percentage share accordingly in 3.12 per cent of net proceeds earmarked each for municipal corporation and municipalities and 0.76 per cent of net proceeds earmarked for town panchayats. The amount of 7 per cent devolution was Rs. 445.78 crore in 1997-98, while in 1998-99, it swelled up to the tune of Rs. 525.00 crore;

(iv) Unpaid electric bills (upto 31st March 1997) of the local bodies which is about Rs. 550 crore has been waived off. State Government is paying the same amount to the U.P. State Electricity Board on behalf of the urban local bodies;

(v) Loans sanctioned to the urban local bodies which was overdue on 31st March 1997 under water supply schemes, integrated city development schemes, Special Component Plan for scheduled castes and scheduled tribes, schemes for beautification of the cities has been converted into grants by the state government;

(vi) Rates of non-tax revenue has been revised and as mentioned earlier the power to further revise these rates in future by framing or amending the bye laws has been delegated to urban local bodies;

(vii) To increase the own source of tax revenue of urban local bodies the target has been fixed to fix the demand as per the estimated population of 1997, minimum per capita Rs. 120 for municipal corporation and Rs. 40 to 90 per capita in Nagar Palika Parishad (depending upon the population) and Rs. 20 per capita in town panchayats;

(viii) Imposition of all type of taxes enumerated in the Act, has been made compulsory.

**Revenue Receipts**

A comparative picture of 11 states in respect of the revenue composition of their municipalities demonstrated that in the octroi collecting states the relative importance of tax revenue in the revenue composition of municipalities is much higher than that of in the non-octroi collecting states. In Gujarat, Maharashtra, Rajasthan and Uttar Pradesh 53 to 75 per cent of total municipal revenue is composed of taxes alone. Among the non-octroi collecting states, however, Karnataka, Kerala and Orissa stand apart as regards the percentage of tax revenue (55 to 63 per cent to total revenue). The revenue composition of municipal bodies in Uttar Pradesh during 1986-87 presents 62 per cent own sources, while 38 per cent accounts transferred revenue. Moreover, during 1990-91 share of own tax constituted just 10.30 per cent in total revenue of municipal corporations in the state of Uttar Pradesh. Non-tax revenue accounted 25.41 per cent, while grants-in-aid had a lion's share in total revenue generated by municipal corporations in the state. During 1999-2000, it is estimated that own tax revenue will have a share of 11.44 per cent as compared to non-tax revenue user charges of 12.86 per cent in total revenue of municipal corporations in the state. Significantly, the share of SFC funds will account 72.05 per cent in total revenue generated among the municipal corporations, the same pattern is discernible of course, with some exceptions. Among the octroi collecting corporations, the tax revenue accounted for between 62 to 84 per cent of total revenue as compared to 20 to 57 per cent in non-octroi corporations with the exception of Cochin (84 per cent) and Madras (67 per cent).

Transfer of revenue from state to urban local bodies is being increasingly used as a fiscal instrument by the states for meeting the budgetary gaps of the urban local bodies. The extent and composition of the transferred revenue reflect the respective state. Policy orientation in sharing of resource bases with the urban local bodies. Three modalities of state local transfer of revenue are commonly in practice; (1) shared tax; (2) assigned tax; and grant-specific purpose grant and block grant. It is to be noted that no grant-in-aid is admissible under the norm of financial devolution in the state.

**Growth of Revenue**

The total ordinary revenues of Nagar Palikas increased from Rs. 480.27 lakh in 1959–60 to Rs. 1150.95 lakh in 1971–72, registering growth of 139.65 per cent. The growth of tax receipts during this period indicated 148.66 per cent while growth of non-tax revenue during this period indicated

83.50 per cent. It is worth to note that the grants during this period increased from Rs. 81.63 lakh in 1959–60 to Rs. 230.53 lakh in 1971–72, registering increase of 182.41 per cent. This composition of revenue during same period indicates, an increase in grants and tax revenue by 3 percentage points and 2.2 percentage points while 5.2 percentage points decline was reported in case of non-tax revenue. During 1971–72, composition of revenue accounted 60.3 per cent tax revenue, 20 per cent state grants and 19.7 per cent non-tax revenue. However, growth of revenue during 1980–81 to 1993-94 in Uttar Pradesh accounted 432.68 per cent, showing increase from Rs. 3129.25 lakh in 1980-81 to Rs. 16669.07 lakh in 1993–94. Tax revenue during the said period increased from Rs. 2006.84 lakh in 1980–81 to Rs. 4060.19 lakh, registering growth of 102.32 per cent. Non-tax revenue of municipal corporations during the said period showed an increase of 16.70 per cent only. Moreover, composition of revenue indicated decline in tax revenue (39.77 percentage points) and non-tax revenue (10.97 percentage points) and growth in grants (51.43 percentage points). The compound annual growth rates computed during the periods of 1960–61 to 1970–71, 1970–71 to 1980–81, 1980–81 to 1990–91 and 1990–91 to 1998–99 demonstrate some positive trends as far as growth of revenue of municipal corporations of state is concerned. During the period of 1960–61 to 1970–71 revenue grew by 16.46 per cent per annum while non-tax revenue grew by 6.91 per cent per annum followed by tax revenue (6.68 per cent). During the period grants grew by 5.26 per cent per annum. Moreover, during 1970–71 to 1980–81 revenue recorded comparatively high growth (11.69 per cent per annum), while tax revenue grew by slightly higher rate, i.e., 12.12 per cent annum. During the period non-tax revenue grew by 8.69 per cent per annum. Interestingly, during 1980–81 to 1990–91 revenue of municipal corporations in the state grew by just 2.97 per cent per annum, while non-tax revenue (-6.80 per cent per annum) and tax revenue (4.88 per cent) declined sharply. During the period of 1990–91 to 1998–99 revenue of municipal corporations recorded growth rate of 9.59 per cent per annum while tax revenue grew by 11.48 per cent per annum. Non-tax revenue recorded a nominal growth rates (2.94 per cent per annum) during the said period. Information from 10th State Finance Commission Report, tax and non-tax revenue receipts of 5 Nagar Nigams, 5 Nagar Palika Parishads and 5 Nagar Panchayats during 1990–91 to 1993–94 has been analysed to present an overview of fiscal administration of urban local bodies in the state of Uttar Pradesh. Tax receipts of 1992–93 over 1991–92 show a growth rate of 9.7 per cent, whereas receipts of 1993–94 over 1992–93 exhibit a growth rate of 19.7 per cent. Thus, the average annual growth of tax revenue comes to 15.7 per cent. Against this, growth of tax receipts in case of Nagar Nigams show 30.20 per cent over 1991–92 to 1993–94 while highest growth of tax receipts was recorded in the case of Nagar Panchayats (103.68 per cent) during the said period. Non–tax revenue receipts during 1991–92 to 1993–94 indicated highest growth in Nagar Panchayats (54.97 per cent) followed by Nagar Palika Parishad (37.67 per cent) and Nagar Nigams accounted just 20.05 per cent growth. Overall non–tax revenue of local bodies recorded the growth rate of 35.3 per cent which is slightly less than growth rate of tax receipts (31.5 per cent) during the said period. Moreover the non-tax revenue receipts during 1992–93 shows a growth rate of 28.2 per cent over the reeipts of 1991–92. However, in 1993–94, the growth rate of non-tax revenue as compared to 1992-93 came down to 5.5 per cent. Since the local bodies are able to recover only 40 to 50 per cent of their current demand, it is apparent that substantial arrears of tax and non-tax revenues are accumulating over the years.

During 1990–91 to 1997–98 revenue growth in the state recorded 100.34 per cent while tax revenue recorded growth of 141.89 per cent, whereas grants to municipal corporations recorded growth of 140.97 per cent. However, non-tax revenue recorded nominal growth (10.28 per cent). Interestingly, revenue composition during 1990–91 showed comparatively higher share of grants (53.76 per cent), while own tax constituted share of 10.31 per cent and non-tax revenue comprises share of 25.41 per cent. against this, during 1997-98 grant component in total revenue receipts of municipal corporations of state recorded 10.91 per centage points increase over the period while 11.42 percentage points decline was noticed in non-tax revenue. Moreover, situation appears to be changed in the post 74th Amendment Act period. During 1999-2000, it is expected revenue will comprise share of 72.05 per cent of S.F.C. devolution while non-tax revenue user charges will account 12.86 per cent in total revenue while own tax revenue will comprise 11.44 per cent share. Interestingly, during 1990-91 to 1999-2000 growth in revenue was recorded 163.62 per cent while tax revenue has recorded 192.72 per cent whereas non-tax revenue user charges recorded growth rate of 33.44 per cent. It is expected during 2000-01 to 2004-05 revenue will grow 46.41 per cent, comprising largest share of SFC devolution funds (65.73 per cent).

**Expenditure Pattern**

The performance of local body in the discharge of its various functions tends to be judged by the ways its revenues are spent, the tendencies of increase or decrease in expenditure. It is also to be noted that in present time, rapid urbanisation has resulted in more stress on municipal corporations in terms of meeting out the raising expectations of urban people. The civic services are gradually declining its quality. The process of urbanization and the problems arising out of it has awaken a national consensus and a quite number of civic problems are being not tackled at local as well as they have become a national phenomenon. Housing, education, water supply, environmental pollution, sanitation and drainage, transport, slum clearance, social and welfare activities, employment opportunities, industrialization etc. can be effectively dealt with at a national level.

In respect of a number of services, therefore, the state is either taking upon itself the responsibility of implementing these programmes by setting up its own statutory agencies or providing finance to local bodies for implementation by way of loans and grants. This is another aspect which has widened the scope of civic services and has considerably increased the expenditure of urban local bodies. Moreover, after execution of the capital projects the burden of maintenance, operational cost and debt services gradually fall on local bodies thereby increasing their expenditure. These are some of the important factors which have influenced the expenditure pattern of local bodies. An attempt has been made to analyse the existing expenditure pattern of Nagar Nigams and discussion to this a review of the debt position has been ensured.

The discussion that follows is based on the classification of services according to the budget heads as prescribed in the budgetary proforma of municipal corporations in Uttar Pradesh. The major heads are as follows: (i) General administration and collection of revenues; (ii) Water supply, drainage and conservancy, (iii) Medical and Public Health, (iv) Public Works, (v) Public Safety and Convenience, (vi) Education and (vii) Miscellaneous.

It is evident from available statistics that total expenditure of all Mahapalikas in the state of Uttar Pradesh increased Rs. 495.70 lakh in 1959-60 to Rs. 1196.55 lakh in 1971-72 registering an increase of 141.4 per cent. Increase in services was reported highest in expenditure. It was reported highest increase in public safety and convenience (193.0 per cent) followed by education (170.7 per cent), water supply, drainage and conservancy (169.1 per cent). In case of medical and public health, the increase was 139.6 per cent. The increase in expenditure on public works was less than 100 per cent. Increase in general administration and collection charges and miscellaneous expenditure was 105.5 per cent and 82.9 per cent respectively. A comparison of the expenditure on different heads in 1960–61, i.e., from the year of formations of Mahapalikas and 1971–72 reveal that water supply, drainage and conservancy accounted for 42.7 per cent of total expenditure in 1960-61 which increased to 48.5 per cent in 1971–72. Thus, this service done consumed nearly half of the total ordinary expenditure of all Mahapalikas. The next was education accounting for 14.4 per cent of total expenditure in 1960–61. This percentage increased to 15.9 per cent in 1971–72.

During 1992-93, out of total expenditure of municipal corporations in state of Uttar Pradesh, establishment expenditure was reported highest (57.60 per cent) while development expenditure accounted 42.40 per cent. Again, out of total expenditure, highest expenditure was reported in road construction (11.35 per cent). This percentage share sharply declined in 1993–94. It is to be noted that expenditure on water supply and drainage cleaning were reported with less percentage share against total expenditure. It seems that these services are in the agenda of state and national government therefore, expenditure on these heads were reported comparatively low.

Information available from State Finance Commission report. Government of Uttar Pradesh an attempt has been made to assess the non–plan revenue expenditure of the urban local bodies keeping in view the past trends in the growth of normal expenditure and of a few urban local bodies present interesting scene. It shows that the non-plan revenue expenditure on pay and allowances during the year 1992–93 registered an increase of 2.4 per cent over the expenditure of 1991–92. But during 1993–94, the non–plan revenue expenditure on this item registered an increase of 11.7 per cent over the year of 1992–93. Highest growth in non-plan revenue expenditure in 1993-94 was primarily due to payment of arrears of pay of employees. Even the average annual growth that of non-plan revenue expenditure comes to 7.2 per cent only which has an in built element of payment of arrears of dues of employees. Normally a growth rate of 3 per cent is more than adequate for normal annual increment of employees.

During 1990–91 to 1997–98 expenditure of municipal corporations in U.P. registered growth of 108.58 per cent while developmental expenditure showed a growth of 151.38 per cent and establishment expenditure accounted 119.81 per cent growth. It is to be noted establishment expenditure in total expenditure accounted comparatively higher share of 77.07 per cent in 1990–91 and 4.15 percentage points increase in 1997–98.

Moreover, revenue expenditure during the corresponding period registered 101.27 per cent growth accounting 81.65 and 89.17 per cent share of general administration in 1990–91 and 1997–98, respectively in total revenue expenditure. Interestingly, capital expenditure during the corresponding period showed growth of 157.17 per cent. The largest share accounted sanitation heads (67.64 per cent) while expenditure on roads accounted 32.36 per cent in 1997–98. There has been decline of 22.81 percentage points in expenditure on roads during 1990–91 to 1997–98. During 1990–91 to 1998–99, expenditure of municipal corporations increased by 146.20 per cent while highest growth was recorded in case of developmental expenditure (172.30 per cent) followed by establishment expenditure (163.19 per cent). Moreover, during 1990–91 expenditure on development heads accounted highest share of expenditure on roads (55.17 per cent) while sanitation accounted 31.56 per cent. Against this there has been decline of 22.81 percentage points on roads while 23.17 percentage points growth in expenditure on drainage during 1997–98. Similarly, highest expenditure under maintenance heads accounted roads (61.88 per cent), and street light (26.95 per cent). Against this there has been 8.01 percentage points increase in expenditure on roads and 15.12 percentage points decline in expenditure on street light.

During 2000–01 AD projected revenue expenditure of municipal corporations in the state of Uttar Pradesh showed Rs. 396 per capita expenditure and general administration accounted largest share as compared to expenditure on obligatory services. It is expected that during 2004–05 AD per capita revenue expenditure of municipal corporations will be Rs. 536 accounting higher share of general administration. Similarly projected per capita expenditure of municipal corporations of state during the corresponding years will be Rs. 433 and Rs. 433 respectively.

The projected revenue of the urban local bodies of state (2000–01 to 2004–05) is Rs. 6150.89 crore. It is estimated that the expenditure required on the maintenance of the civic services in the aforesaid period will be Rs. 1293.17 crore and the salary of the staff will be Rs. 3417.12 crore out of total revenue receipts of Rs. 6150.89 crore. It is expected that Rs. 1440.60 crore will be the balance in the hands of the local bodies. As per norms and provisions of civic services Rs. 8311.12 crore amount will be required in the aforesaid period. The net requirement will be Rs. 6870.52 crore to meet out the expenses of urban local bodies of state during the aforesaid period. Interestingly, net requirement of amount in the corresponding period will be Rs. 1806.40 crore for meeting expenses of municipal corporations of state.

**Review of Debt Position**

The loans are being given by the state government for a number of purposes by and large. They can be grouped broadly into five categories as follows: (1) Loans for water supply schemes, (2) Loans for urban development including integrated urban development schemes, (3) Loans given under special and general component plan for scheduled castes, scheduled tribes etc. (4) Loans advanced for integrated development of small and medium towns. (5) Other related developmental schemes.

Information available from Finance Department, government of Uttar Pradesh, collected by State Finance Commission, details upto March 1994, urban local bodies in the state had loans amounting Rs. 77.05 crore out of which a sum of Rs. 76.20 crore by the way of principal and a sum of Rs. 52.16 crore by the way of interest therein were outstanding. It is to be noted that State Finance Commission has recommended waiving off loans and advances to urban local bodies in the state due upto March, 1997.

**Conclusion and Prospects**

The urban local bodies including municipal corporations have in general been unable to keep pace with the growing demand for civic services to their budgetary difficulties. There is a growing trend towards: (1) transferring major functional responsibilities from the municipal domain to state administered special purpose authorities; (2) increasing use of transfer as fiscal instrument for bridging budgetary gaps of the local bodies and (3) provincialization of local tax basis. This trend complied with the absence of a constitutional base has brought about ambiguity and uncertainty in the municipal functional domain and fiscal management. Moreover encroaching on major functional areas of urban local bodies and centralisation of local tax together reflect the state policy orientation which is tendency to be skewed towards centralisation than local government autonomy.

This trend at the state level is perhaps grounded on the following policy myths: (1) the urban local bodies are in capable of managing major functions like water, sewerage and drainage, (2) the tax administration of the urban local bodies is less efficient than that of the state and their efforts for tax collection are for less than adequate; (3) the scheme that entails collection of taxes by the state and balancing the budget largely by transferred revenue, works much better.

The provisions of 73rd and 74th Amendments to the Constitution do not specifically indicate any sources of revenue exclusively for the use of either Panchayati Raj Institutions or urban local bodies. The following suggestions can be easily made to activate resource mobilization and effective fiscal management:

1. Resurrecting of property taxes should be ensured and strong mechanism should be developed for assessing or evaluating of property taxes and its effective collection or recovery of taxes;
2. Recovery of user charges should be ensured on the part of municipal corporations. Moreover, these charges should be properly assessed and its effective collection should be ensured;
3. Reassessment of property after every five years should be ensured and exemption from property tax should be given a go-by;
4. License fees should be affectively implemented and collected by urban local bodies·
5. State government should pass a law for imposing and collection of property tax, water tax, latrine or sewerage tax by urban local bodies. Since U.P. Jal Sansthan (Nigam) and Housing Development Authorities have implemented schemes of water supply, sewerage and housing development therefore, it is required to avoid future tensions or conflicts. It is also suggested to enhance coordinated efforts under harmonious environment among these bodies or departments for effective collection of user charges such as water, sewerage and property taxes;
6. Tax collection may be made on self assessment and a sufficient penalty be fixed for default and willful concealment of information;
7. Municipal commercial ventures should be further promoted and strengthened through financial support and coordinated efforts. These ventures have a strong possibility of generating revenue surplus.
8. Fiscal administration should be reassessed and efforts should be towards minimising non-plan and non-developmental expenditure. Moreover, there should be strong mechanism to collect taxes and minimising establishment expenditure.

# ANNEXURE I

## Total Revenue of Municipal Corporations (1990–91 to 1999–2000)

*(Rs. thousand)*

| | *1990–91* | *1991–92* | *1992–93* | *1993–94* | *1994–95* | *1995–96* | *1996–97* | *1997–98* | *1998–99* | *1999–2000* |
|---|---|---|---|---|---|---|---|---|---|---|
| **(A) Own Tax** | | | | | | | | | | |
| | 132806 | 192042 | 190710 | 239463 | 254481 | 252152 | 272431 | 299674 | 329675 | 362643 |
| 2. Water Tax | 6278 | 8708 | 10103 | 6569 | 35607 | 41323 | 43113 | 47424 | 52166 | 57383 |
| | 12046 | 8538 | 9622 | 10559 | 12995 | 14526 | 16791 | 18471 | 20318 | 22350 |
| **(B) Non Tax Revenue User Charges** | | | | | | | | | | |
| (a) Trade Licence Fees | 1235 | 875 | 986 | 1083 | 1333 | 1490 | 25015 | 27415 | 2030 | 2233 |
| (b) Water Charges | 7335 | 8443 | 11637 | 15931 | 23861 | 22218 | 32227 | 35450 | 30157 | 33173 |
| (c) Tahbazari | 10731 | 11507 | 11698 | 18800 | 19363 | 13052 | 37592 | 40592 | 38995 | 42896 |
| (d) Rent | 27696 | 19631 | 22121 | 24276 | 29877 | 33398 | 4523 | 4921 | 44651 | 49116 |
| (e) Parking | 3332 | 2361 | 2661 | 2920 | 3594 | 4018 | 1677 | 1845 | 5413 | 5954 |
| (f) Other Sources | 322311 | 119143 | 158792 | 139486 | 183904 | 249404 | 273378 | 300716 | 330788 | 363867 |
| **(C) Assigned Revenue** | | | | | | | | | | |
| (a) Surcharges on Stamp duty | | | | | | | 4138 | 4651 | 5116 | 5628 |
| **(D) Grants Aid** | | | | | | | | | | |
| | 100402 | 121130 | 119126 | 115876 | 128748 | 114335 | 131897 | 216240 | — | — |
| | 584246 | 819118 | 891338 | 996232 | 1129500 | 1359324 | 1591441 | 1422797 | — | — |
| Purpose grants | | | | | | | | | | |

*(Contd.)*

| | *1990–91* | *1991–92* | *1992–93* | *1993–94* | *1994–95* | *1995–96* | *1996–97* | *1997–98* | *1998–99* | *1999–2000* |
|---|---|---|---|---|---|---|---|---|---|---|
| **T.F.C.** | — | — | — | — | — | — | 135000 | 135000 | 135000 | 135000 |
| **(E) Loans from Govt.** | 154304 | 50349 | 127068 | 36500 | 55910 | 38500 | — | — | — | — |
| **(F) Loans from Financial Inst.** | — | 400 | 1508 | 10000 | 9920 | 20934 | 7363 | — | — | — |
| **(G) SFC Devolution** | — | — | — | — | — | — | — | 121900 | 2339925 | 2785625 |
| **Total** | **1466444** | **1484319** | **1672186** | **1727198** | **2056790** | **2293034** | **2823983** | **2937837** | **3334234** | **3865868** |

*Source:* Directorate of Urban Local Bodies, Govt. of U.P. Lucknow.

## ANNEXURE II

### Projected Revenue of Municipal Corporation (2000–01 to 2004–05)

*(Rs. thousand)*

| | 2000–01 | | 2001–02 | | 2002–03 | | 2003–04 | | 2004–05 | |
|---|---|---|---|---|---|---|---|---|---|---|
| | *Amt.* | *PC (Rs.)* | *Amt.* | *PC (Rs.)* | *Amt.* | *PC (Rs.)* | *Amt.* | *PC (Rs.)* | *Amt.* | *PC (Rs.)* |
| **(A) Taxes and User Charges** | | | | | | | | | | |
| 1. Lands (Non. Agri) | 624078 | 53.1 | 686486 | 57.3 | 755134 | 61.8 | 830648 | 66.7 | 913713 | 72 |
| 2. Water tax | 112014 | 9.53 | 123215 | 10.3 | 135537 | 11.1 | 149091 | 12 | 164000 | 12.9 |
| 3. Any other tax | 40005 | 3.4 | 44006 | 3.67 | 48406 | 3.96 | 53247 | 4.27 | 58571 | 4.61 |
| **(B) Non Tax Revenue User Charges** | | | | | | | | | | |
| 1. Trade Licence Fees | 8001 | 0.68 | 8801 | 0.73 | 9681 | 0.79 | 10649 | 0.85 | 11714 | 0.92 |
| 2. Water Charges | 64008 | 5.45 | 70409 | 5.87 | 77450 | 6.34 | 85195 | 6.84 | 93714 | 7.38 |
| 3. Tahbazari | 96012 | 8.17 | 105613 | 8.81 | 116175 | 9.51 | 127792 | 10.3 | 140571 | 11.1 |
| 4. Rent | 96012 | 8.17 | 105613 | 8.81 | 116175 | 9.51 | 127792 | 10.3 | 140571 | 11.1 |
| 5. Parking | 16002 | 1.36 | 17602 | 1.47 | 19362 | 1.58 | 21299 | 1.71 | 23429 | 1.85 |
| 6. Other Sources | 528066 | 44.9 | 580873 | 48.5 | 638960 | 52.3 | 702856 | 56.4 | 773141 | 60.9 |

*(contd.)*

| | *2000–01* | | *2001–02* | | *2002–03* | | *2003–04* | | *2004–05* | |
|---|---|---|---|---|---|---|---|---|---|---|
| | *Amt.* | *PC (Rs.)* | *Amt.* | *PC (Rs.)* | *Amt.* | *PC (Rs.)* | *Amt.* | *PC (Rs.)* | *Amt.* | *PC (Rs.)* |
| **(C) Additional Resource Mobilisation** | | | | | | | | | | |
| **(D) Assigned Revenue** | | | | | | | | | | |
| 1. Surcharge on stamp | 16002 | 1.36 | 17602 | 1.47 | 19362 | 1.58 | 21299 | 1.71 | 23429 | 1.85 |
| **(E) Shared Revenue** | | | | | | | | | | |
| **(F) Grants in Aid from State** | | | | | | | | | | |
| **(G) T.F.C. Grants** | | | | | | | | | | |
| **(H) Centrally Spon.,** | | | | | | | | | | |
| **1. SFC Devolution** | 3064188 | 261 | 3370607 | 281 | 3707667 | 303 | 4078434 | 327 | 4486278 | 353 |
| **Total** | **4664388** | **397** | **5130827** | **428** | **5643909** | **462** | **6208301** | **498** | **6829131** | **538** |

*Source: Directorate of Urban Local Bodies, Govt. of UP Lucknow.*

# ANNEXURE III

## Expenditure of Municipal Corporations in U.P.

*(Rs. thousand)*

| | *1990–91* | *1991–92* | *1992–93* | *1993–94* | *1994–95* | *1995–96* | *1996–97* | *1997–98* | *1998–99 (Est.)* |
|---|---|---|---|---|---|---|---|---|---|
| **Expenditure** | | | | | | | | | |
| (a) Salary and Other | 742216 | 873654 | 922913 | 1177442 | 1329961 | 1428288 | 1593718 | 1753084 | 2191355 |
| (b) Other Expen. | 331972 | 333604 | 362390 | 4423732 | 435663 | 406552 | 552847 | 608132 | 635774 |
| **(A) Establishment** | — | — | — | — | — | — | — | — | — |
| **(B) Core** | — | — | — | — | — | — | — | — | — |
| **(C) Development** | | | | | | | | | |
| 1. Water Supply | 2167 | 1079 | 1254 | 1504 | 3514 | 2672 | 2795 | 3080 | 3214 |
| 2. Roads | 57225 | 40449 | 54572 | 46885 | 76446 | 49591 | 76706 | 84376 | 97033 |
| 3. Drainage | 11595 | 16006 | 8082 | 5623 | 19900 | 29246 | 88762 | 89563 | 90998 |
| | 32735 | 64542 | 50908 | 55491 | 67837 | 46851 | 79134 | 83722 | 91293 |
| | — | — | — | — | — | — | — | — | — |

*(Contd.)*

| | *1990–91* | *1991–92* | *1992–93* | *1993–94* | *1994–95* | *1995–96* | *1996–97* | *1997–98* | *1998–99 (Est.)* |
|---|---|---|---|---|---|---|---|---|---|
| **(D) Maintenance** | | | | | | | | | |
| | 133526 | 94382 | 127336 | 109197 | 178374 | 115713 | 178980 | 196878 | 226409 |
| | — | — | — | — | — | — | — | — | — |
| | 58147 | 35289 | 38965 | 40622 | 32780 | 38392 | 30625 | 33727 | 38786 |
| 4. Water Supply | 19502 | 9708 | 11281 | 13537 | 31627 | 24049 | 25158 | 27723 | 28932 |
| | 1723 | 3397 | 2679 | 2921 | 3570 | 2466 | 4165 | 4407 | 4805 |
| | 2899 | 4002 | 2020 | 1406 | 4975 | 7311 | 22190 | 22391 | 22749 |
| **Total** | **1393707** | **1476112** | **1582400** | **5878360** | **2184647** | **2151131** | **2655080** | **2907085** | **3431348** |

*Source:* Directorate of the Local Bodies, Govt. of U.P., Lucknow

# ANNEXURE IV

## Revenue Expenditure of Municipal Corporations (1990–91 to 1999–2000)

*(Rs. thousand)*

| *Expenditure Head* | *1990–91* | *1991–92* | *1992–93* | *1993–94* | *1994–95* | *1995–96* | *1996–97* | *1997–98* | *1998–99* | *1999–00* |
|---|---|---|---|---|---|---|---|---|---|---|
| **(A) General Administration** | | | | | | | | | | |
| 1. Salary of Municipal | 742216 | 873654 | 922913 | 1177442 | 1329961 | 1428288 | 1593718 | 1753084 | 2191355 | 2410470 |
| 2. Maintenance of Assets and others | 331972 | 333604 | 362390 | 442373 | 435663 | 406552 | 552847 | 608132 | 635774 | 699351 |
| **(B) Expenditure of Services** | | | | | | | | | | |
| 1. Water Supply | 19502 | 9708 | 11281 | 13537 | 31627 | 24049 | 25158 | 27723 | 28932 | 31824 |
| 2. Street Lighting | 58147 | 32289 | 38965 | 40622 | 32780 | 38392 | 30625 | 33727 | 38786 | 42665 |
| 3. Solid Waste Disposal | 1723 | 3397 | 2679 | 2921 | 3570 | 2466 | 4165 | 4407 | 4805 | 5110 |
| 4. Storm Water Drainage | 2899 | 4002 | 2020 | 1406 | 4975 | 7311 | 22190 | 22391 | 22749 | 23024 |
| 5. Roads | 133536 | 94382 | 127336 | 109197 | 178374 | 115713 | 178980 | 196878 | 226409 | 249050 |
| 6. Burial Burning Grounds | | | | | | | | | | |
| **(C) Expenditure on Discreptionary Services** | | | | | | | | | | |
| **(D) Expenditure on Development Grants** | | | | | | | | | | |
| **(E) Repayment of Loans** | 25572 | 25392 | 29990 | 3220 | 782 | 10979 | 1413 | 1554 | 1625 | 1778 |
| **(F) Any Other Expenditure** | | | | | | | | | | |
| **Total** | **1315567** | **1376428** | **1497574** | **1790718** | **2017732** | **2033750** | **2409096** | **2647896** | **3150435** | **3463282** |

*Source:* Directorate of Urban Local Bodies, Govt. of UP, Lucknow.

# ANNEXURE V

## Capital Expenditure of Municipal Corporations (1990–91 to 1999–2000)

*(Rs. Crore)*

| Expenditure Head | *1990–91* | *1991–92* | *1892–93* | *1993–94* | *1994–95* | *1995–96* | *1996–97* | *1997–98* | *1998–99* | *1999–2000* |
|---|---|---|---|---|---|---|---|---|---|---|
| **(A) General Administration** | | | | | | | | | | |
| 1. Salary of municipal corps. Staff | — | — | — | — | — | — | — | — | — | — |
| (2) Maintenance of Assets and others | — | — | — | — | — | — | — | — | — | — |
| **(B) Expenditure on Obligatory Services** | — | — | — | — | — | — | — | — | — | |
| 1. Water Supply | 2167 | 1079 | 1254 | 1504 | 3514 | 2672 | 2795 | 3080 | 3214 | 3535 |
| 2. Solid Waste Disposal | 327357 | 64542 | 50908 | 55491 | 67837 | 46851 | 79134 | 83722 | 91293 | 100422 |
| 3. Storm Water Drainage | 11595 | 16006 | 8082 | 5623 | 19900 | 29246 | 88762 | 89563 | 90998 | 100098 |
| 4. Roads | 57225 | 40449 | 54572 | 46885 | 76446 | 49591 | 76706 | 84376 | 97033 | 106736 |
| 5. Others | — | — | — | — | — | — | — | — | — | |
| **(C) Expenditure on Discretionary Services** | — | — | — | — | — | — | — | — | — | — |
| **(D) Expenditure on** | — | — | — | — | — | — | — | — | — | — |
| **(E) Repayment of Loans** | — | — | — | — | — | — | — | — | — | — |
| **(F) Any Other** | — | — | — | — | — | — | — | — | — | — |
| **Total** | **103722** | **122076** | **114816** | **109503** | **167697** | **128360** | **247397** | **260741** | **282538** | **310791** |

*Source:* Directorate of Urban Local Bodies, UP Govt., Lucknow.

# ANNEXURE VI

## Projected Revenue Expenditure of Municipal Corporations (2000–01 to 2004–2005)

*(Rs. thousand)*

| | *2000–01* | | *2001–02* | | *2002–03* | | *2003–04* | | *2004–05* | |
|---|---|---|---|---|---|---|---|---|---|---|
| | *Amt.* | *PC (Rs.)* | *Amt.* | *PC (Rs.)* | *Amt.* | *PC (Rs.)* | *Amt.* | *PC (Rs.)* | *Amt.* | *PC (Rs.)* |
| **(A) General Administration** | | | | | | | | | | |
| 1. Salary of Municipal | 2651517 | 226 | 2916669 | 243 | 3208336 | 263 | 3529169 | 283 | 3882086 | 306 |
| 2. Terminal Benefits | — | — | — | — | — | — | — | — | — | — |
| 3. Maintenance of Assets and Others | 769286 | 65 | 846215 | 71 | 930836 | 76 | 1023920 | 82 | 1126312 | 89 |
| **(B) Expenditure on Obligatory Services** | | | | | | | | | | |
| 1. Water Supply | 43138 | 3.7 | 47452 | 4 | 52197 | 4.3 | 57417 | 4.6 | 63158 | 5 |
| 2. Street Lighting | 52051 | 4.4 | 57256 | 4.8 | 62982 | 4.8 | 69280 | 5.6 | 76208 | 6 |
| 3. Solid Waste Disposal | 12875 | 1.1 | 14162 | 1.2 | 15579 | 1.3 | 17136 | 1.4 | 18850 | 1.5 |
| 4. Education | | | | | | | | | | |
| 5. Public Health | | | | | | | | | | |

| | | | | | | | | | | |
|---|---|---|---|---|---|---|---|---|---|---|
| 6. Sanitation/Sewage | 115874 | 9.9 | 127462 | 11 | 140207 | 11 | 154229 | 12 | 169651 | 13 |
| 7. Storm Water Drainage | 150209 | 13 | 165230 | 14 | 181753 | 15 | 199928 | 16 | 219921 | 17 |
| 8. Roads | 434059 | 37 | 477465 | 40 | 525211 | 43 | 577733 | 46 | 635506 | 50 |
| 9. Burial & Burning Grounds | | | | | | | | | | |
| 10. Other/Electric Bill | 419466 | 36 | 461413 | 38 | 507554 | 42 | 558309 | 45 | 614140 | 48 |
| **C. Expenditure on** | | | | | | | | | | |
| **D. Expenditure on** | | | | | | | | | | |
| **E. Repayment of Loans** | | | | | | | | | | |
| **F. Any Other Expenditure** | | | | | | | | | | |
| **Total** | 4688475 | 396 | 5113323 | 427 | 5624655 | 460 | 6187120 | 497 | 6605832 | 536 |

*Source*: Directorate of Urban Local Bodies, Govt. of UP, Lucknow.

# ANNEXURE VII

## Projected Capital Expenditure of Municipal Corporations (2000–01 to 2004–05)

*(Rs. thousand)*

| | 2000–01 | | 2001–02 | | 2002–03 | | 2003–04 | | 2004–05 | |
|---|---|---|---|---|---|---|---|---|---|---|
| | *Amt.* | *PC (Rs.)* | *Amt.* | *PC (Rs.)* | *Amt.* | *PC (Rs.)* | *Amt.* | *PC (Rs.)* | *Amt.* | *PC (Rs.)* |
| **(A) General Administration** | | | | | | | | | | |
| **(B) Expenditure on Obligatory Services** | | | | | | | | | | |
| 1. Water Supply | 1500000 | 128 | 1500000 | 128 | 1500000 | 128 | 1500000 | 128 | 1500000 | 128 |
| 2. Street Lighting | 106060 | 9 | 106060 | 9 | 106060 | 9 | 106060 | 9 | 106060 | 9 |
| 3. Solid Waste Disposal | 47960 | 4.1 | 47960 | 4.1 | 47960 | 4.1 | 47960 | 4.1 | 47960 | 4.1 |
| 4. Education | | | | | | | | | | |
| 5. Public Health | | | | | | | | | | |
| 6. Sanitation/Sewage | 2141377 | 182 | 2141377 | 182 | 2141377 | 182 | 2141377 | 182 | 2141377 | 182 |
| 7. Storm Water Drainage | 483120 | 41 | 483120 | 41 | 483120 | 41 | 483120 | 41 | 483120 | 41 |
| 8. Roads | 805200 | 69 | 805200 | 69 | 805200 | 69 | 805200 | 69 | 805200 | 69 |
| 9. Burial & Burning Grounds | | | | | | | | | | |
| 10. Others | | | | | | | | | | |
| **(C) Expenditure on** | | | | | | | | | | |
| **(D) Expenditure on** | | | | | | | | | | |
| **(E) Repayment Expenditure** | | | | | | | | | | |
| **Total** | **5083717** | **433** | **5083717** | **433** | **5083717** | **433** | **5083717** | **433** | **5083717** | **433** |

*Source*: Directorate of Urban Local Bodies, Govt. of UP, Lucknow.

# ANNEXURE VIII

## Headwise Total Capital Requirement of Urban Local Bodies in U.P. (2001 to 2005)

*(Rs. Crore)*

| *Head* | *Municipal Corps.* | | *Municipalities* | | *Town Panchayats* | | *Total* | |
|---|---|---|---|---|---|---|---|---|
| Water Suply | 750.00 | (29.50) | 1359.00 | (28.90) | 441.00 | (41.30) | 2550.00 | (30.68) |
| Sewerage/Sanitation | 1070.69 | (42.12) | 2434.35 | (51.78) | 205.51 | (19.25) | 3710.55 | (44.65) |
| Roads | 402.60 | (15.83) | 508.70 | (10.82) | 228.92 | (21.44) | 1140.22 | (13.72) |
| Street Light | 53.03 | (2.09) | 63.03 | (1.34) | 29.01 | (2.72) | 145.07 | (1.75) |
| Solid Waste Disposal | 23.98 | (0.94) | 31.13 | (0.67) | 26.65 | (2.50) | 81.76 | (0.98) |
| Drainage | 241.56 | (9.50) | 305.22 | (6.49) | 136.74 | (12.81) | 632.52 | (8.22) |
| **Total** | **2541.86** | **(100.00)** | **4701.43** | **(100.00)** | **(1067.83)** | **100.00** | **8311.12** | **(100.00)** |
| Total Capital Requirement | 2541.86 | | 4701.43 | | 1067.83 | | 8311.12 | |
| Projected Balance | 735.46 | | 587.28 | | 117.86 | | 1440.60 | |
| Net Requirement | 180640 | | 4114.15 | | 949.97 | | 6870.52 | |

*Source:* Directorate of Local Bodies, Govt. of UP, Lucknow.

# 22

# Tirupati Urban Development Authority (TUDA) on way to Develop Holy Tirupati Town

*—S. Srikrishna, S. Anil Kumar*

Population migration from rural to urban areas in search of better living conditions is the crux of the problem in urbanisation. This has created complexities of problems in urban areas like demand for shelter, pressure on the existing transport network and infrastructure facilities which ultimately lead to haphazard development. Owing to rapid industrialisation and increase in population in urban areas, it was called for to create organisations/authorities which can promote and co-ordinate the development in these urban areas in a planned way. For this purpose, Andhra Pradesh Urban Areas (Development) Act, 1975 was enacted with an object to promote and secure the development of all or any of the areas comprised in the development area concerned according to plan.

**Constitution of the Authority**

The government in November, 1981 declared Tirupati town and 89 villages around as development area for Tirupati Urban Development Authority. In February, 1982 the Government appointed an officer on Special Duty to take all necessary steps for establishing Tirupati Urban Development Authority as well as to maintain liaison with all the departments of the Government with a view to expedite formulation of policies and implementation of programmes of Urban Development Authority. As per Section 3 (3) of A.P. Urban Areas (Development) Act, 1975 he Government constituted the first Authority in August, 1982.

**Objectives of the Authority**

The objective of the Authority is to promote and secure the development of all or any of the areas comprised in the development area concerned according to plan. For the purpose, the authority has the power to acquire, by way of purchase or otherwise, dispose of land and other property, to carry out by or on its behalf building, engineering, mining and other operations to execute works in connection with supply of water and electricity, disposal of sewage and control of pollution, other services and amenities and generally to do anything necessary or expedient for purposes incidental thereto.

**Functions Envisaged in the Act**

The following are the main functions that have been envisaged in the Act:

(a) To promote and secure development of areas constituted in the development area according to Master Plan and Zonal Development Plan;

(b) To control the use of lands for various purposes, acquisition, development and disposal of lands; and

(c) To carry out the development works such as roads, buildings, water supply, sewerage and other schemes within the development area and also coordination and regulating the activities of various agencies of the state and Central governments and other local authorities.

**Organisational Set Up**

For carrying out the day-to-day functions of the Authority, the Development Authority has been divided into 6 wings, with the Vice-Chairman as the Chief Executive as follows:

(a) Administrative wing
(b) Planning wing
(c) Development wing
(d) Horticulture wing
(e) Accounts wing
(f) Land Acquisition wing

**Activities taken up by Tirupati Urban Development Authority**

To fulfil the objectives laid down in the Act, Tirupati Urban Development Authority has made attempts in all spheres to find out solutions for emerging problems posed by the rapid increase in urban population and expansion of areas.

To provide shelter to different income categories of people, Tirupati Urban Development Authority has identified major chunks of lands which is located on all different directions of Tirupati Town. The concept is to create impulse for planned development and to relieve congestion in the town. And also it was decided to generate resources for the organisation which can be utilised for the phased balanced development of the area.

**Housing Programmes**

As a common fact, much of the lands in and around the Tirupati Town is held up within a few hands. As a result, the real estate value of the land shot up beyond the reach of a common man. Most of the lands were sub-divided and disposed off to the public without providing amenities which resulted in haphazard development. The real estate developers have reaped the benefits but providing the amenities to these areas has become the organisational responsibility.

In order to promote planned development, to curb the illicit transaction of the real estate developers to provide developed house sites to the needy people of different income categories at a reasonable price and to raise the financial resources of the authority, a number of programmes to develop house sites have been taken up.

In order to solve the above problem, Tirupati Urban Development Authority has developed three pockets of land in three different directions to an extent of 165.79 acres with all infrastructure facilities like W.B.M., roads, drains, water supply, parks and avenue plantation. In these areas provisions were also made for educational, transportation and commercial activities so as to make the areas self-sufficient. The plots were allotted to the public falling under different income groups viz., Higher Income Group (284), Middle Income Group (575) and Lower Income Group (354).

Apart from the above scheme, Tirupati Urban Development Authority has also taken up construction of houses for low income category of people. The Authority has constructed 386 units of LIG houses with the financial assistance of HUDCO and has allotted to the public.

The land for the above schemes was provided by the Government.

**Construction of Residential Flats**

Tirupati Urban Development Authority has launched a pilot scheme for construction of residential flats. The scheme was aimed at promoting multi-storied development and to reduce pressure on demand for land. The scheme consists of 6 flats and was taken up on self-financing basis with a project cost of Rs. 8.10 lakh.

**Transportation**

To develop integrated network to Tirupati town with the surrounding region, to promote the development along the arteries of the new roads in a planned way and also to relieve traffic problem within the town, Tirupati Urban Development Authority has laid new roads and widened the existing roads to a length of 20.00 kms. as a part of integrated network development. For this purpose, land to the tune of 60.10 acres has been acquired and an amount of Rs. 238.40 lakh has already been spent.

In order to solve the traffic problems within the Tirupati town, the Authority has taken up a number of junction improvement programmes by spending Rs. 22.50 lakh. Finance for the above schemes was met from the internal resources generated from the housing programmes.

**Park Development**

Time has economic value. To enable the children to spend their leisure time in good spirit and to boost their morale, to create lung spaces in the town, to maintain the ecological balance and to reduce the pollution effects, the Tirupati Urban Development Authority has developed a number of parks in the town at a cost of Rs. 6.81 lakhs.

In addition to the above programmes, the Authority has developed avenue plantation on all the roads formed with 11,533 plants.

**Miscellaneous Works**

Under environmental improvement of scheme, the Authority has laid roads and drains in Channa Reddy Colony at a cost of Rs. 0.601 lakh.

Tirupati Urban Development Authority has taken up improvement of water supply scheme at Renigunta at a cost of Rs. 0.20 lakh.

**Proposed Action Plan**

*1. Master Plan.* Tirupati Development Area is growing rapidly in an unplanned way which needs to be developed in a planned manner. To promote orderly development, the Authority has prepared a Master Plan for its development area as per Sec. 6 of A.P. Urban Areas (Dev.) Act, 1975. After conducting surveys and analysing the potentials of development, an outline plan has been drawn which would serve as a basic pattern of framework for the development area. In the plan it is indicated the manner in which the land in the development area is proposed to be used. For the purpose of development, the entire area has been divided into 10 development zones. The Plan still awaits government sanction even after a decade of submission.

In the development area many proposals for development are being submitted to this authority for clearance in contravention to the Master Plan proposals. If these activities are allowed, the basic objective of Master Plan will be defeated. Hence, the Government is requested to approve the Master Plan at an early date.

***2. Seshachalam Hill View Layout Phase–II.*** Owing to rapid growth of development area, the population of the development area is expected to reach 6.17 lakhs by 2001 A.D. It is also estimated that by 2001 A.D. there will be a net housing demand for 17640 housing units. In order to meet the housing shortage and also to promote planned development, the Authority has taken up sites and services programme.

For this purpose, an extent of 117.53 acres of land has been identified. In this project, it is proposed to develop 1211 plots for HIG (559), MIG (700) and EWS (252) groups of income.

To make the above project viable and effective, a demand survey has been conducted in different Government organisations. From different organisations 400 persons have positively responded for purchase of plots.

The Authority has proposed to develop the layout at an estimated cost of Rs. 182.52 lakh which includes formation of B.T. Roads, storm water drains, water supply, street lighting, avenue plantation and park development. It is contemplated to allot plots for Economically Weaker Section on no profit no loss basis. The receipts accrued from the scheme is to be utilised for other developmental activities. The entire project was submitted to the Government for approval of sale price of plots and for developing the scheme in November 1990 but the final clearance is awaited. Such a delay may mar the basic objectives of the scheme. The Government is requested to issue orders for developing the scheme at an early date.

**Commercial Complex**

Tirupati town with a population of 1.89 lakhs, as per 1991 census, is expected to reach a limit of Rs. 2.98 lakhs by 2001 A.D. At present, the town does not have any planned commercial centres to serve the residents. The commercial areas have developed in a haphazard way causing congestion and lack of infrastructure facilities leading to traffic problems. In order to promote planned commercial activities, to serve the residents in a better way and to solve the problems of congestion and other traffic problems, Tirupati Urban Development Authority has proposed to elevelop a commercial complex. But the shops could not be allotted to the public for want of rental regulations. Early orders are solicited.

Since the town is fast growing, there is a heavy demand of office spaces. In order to bring all the private and public organisations together so as to improve the public convenience, Tirupati Urban Development Authority conducted a demand survey for office spaces. Based on demand, Tirupati Urban Development Authority has proposed to develop an integrated commercial complex with all infrastructure facilities. The scheme comprises of 5 blocks which shall accommodate shopping in the ground floor and the upper floors are meant for Government offices, commercial ventures, restaurants etc. The scheme is divided into 5 phases. The total cost of the project is Rs. 549.95 lakh with a total plinth area of 25,472 sq. mts. As per the demand survey conducted, the demand from Government offices itself is 10,000 sq. mts. Of the total plinth area the rentable area is worked out to 18,214 sq. mts. which is estimated to fetch a recurring income of Rs. 85,00 lakh approximately per annum. The project is to be taken up by raising loans from financial institutions.

After completion of this scheme, it will be a new focal point for Tirupati town containing shops and all government offices and disperses the commercial activity from the existing core of the Tirupati town.

TUDA office building is located in the heart of the town, and there is acute demand for office space in Tirupati town. To provide office space in one central area, it is proposed to construct 2nd and 3rd floors over TUDA building to be leased on rent to other Government Agencies. The project is to be taken up with the loan assistance. Its clearance is awaited.

**Group Housing Schemes**

Construction of 16 Nos of flats in Tirupati South Extension layout has been proposed by the Authority. All the plots belong to HIG group of people. The plot area is about 0.28 acres and the estimated cost is about Rs. 33 lakh.

A plot of size 0.28 acres has been earmarked in T.S.E. layout (a TUDA developed layout) for group housing scheme as it is located in the heart of the town. The detailed architectural drawings, estimates have been submitted to government for administrative sanction.

The scheme will be taken up (subject to approval of government) on self financing basis.

**Potential for Development**

There is immense potential for development of Tirupati Development area in near future by rapid growth of population. Economic activities and other service activities besides increase in pilgrim population. It is also estimated that pilgrim trend will be around 50,000 persons per day by 2001 A.D. As per the 1991 census the population of Tirupati town was 1,89,000 and present population (1998) is around 2,50,000 persons in view of the increasing demand of workers in non/agricultural activities like institutional and industrial sectors. To ease the congestion in Tirupati, Tirupati Urban Development Authority has already prepared draft Master Plan for Tirupati Development has been submitted to the Government for approval. The main objective of the Master Plan is to keep the organised growth of Tirupati as mother city and the other important centres like Renigunta, Chandragiri, Tiruchanur and Gajulamandyam as counter magnets. Satellite township development has already been taken up by Tirupati Urban Development Authority by formulating the sites and services programme in Chennaiahgunta village with an area of 241.00 acres with all amenities as self-contained neighbourhood to meet the housing demand in Tirupati town and pave for planned development.

Transport network plays an important role for overall development of area/region. In this regard, Tirupati Urban Development Authority has laid 21.3 kms. road network in and around Tirupati town which has opened new avenues for movement and development of new areas with organised growth conceived by Tirupati Urban Development Authority. Effective steps have been taken to achieve optimum circulation in the area keeping the Ropeway proposal to T.T.D. near Sreevarimettu and linking of all the villages of the southernside of Swarnamukhi with transport links like Tirupati–Madras road and Tirupati–Banglore road.

**Improvement and Beautification of Tirupati**

The Hon'ble Chief Minister of Andhra Pradesh, during his visit to Tirupati on 16-9-91, desired to improve and develop the Tirupati town and instructed the Tirupati Urban Development Authority to suggest the ways to improve the town. In order to give top priority to improve Tirupati town, Tirupati Urban Development Authority has prepared a project report on "Improvement and Beautification" of Tirupati town. By ascertaining information and by conducting meetings with various Government departments and other voluntary agencies under the direction of vice-chairman, Tirupati Urban Development Authority has evolved various schemes ongoing and proposed in the programmes.

**Development of Growth Centres—Need of the Housing Programme**

The population of Tirupati Development area is about 4.00 lakhs, as per 1991 census. Based on the trend of the past decadel growth, it is estimated that the population of development area shall be 6.17 lakhs by 2001 A.D. besides migration from the surrounding region.

The housing demand survey conducted by the Authority in recent past shows that there is a demand for 13277 housing units/plots from residents of Tirupati and a demand for 6305 houses/flats from outsiders but within the development area. Taking the decadeal population growth rate as basis it is estimated that the total housing requirement by 2001 A.D. shall be about 30,000 units.

To meet the above requirements of future, planning at this stage is essential. The consequence of various economic activities that shall be generated within the development area needs to be thought of well in advance. By the end of the decade, before attaining the metropolitan character, the profelling effect of these economic activities induce inward migration. The impact of this migration factor on the land, a limited resource needs careful consideration. This situation calls for alternative strategies to mitigate the migration effect on the mother town and development of various potential centres for accommodating the inflow population nearer to the work centres and promoting the development in a planned and predetermined path.

For the above purpose the Authority has identified the following lands at different locations to develop as a self-contained townships. The details of the schemes are given hereunder:

***(a) Seshachalam Hill View Extension Layout.*** The Authority has developed an extent of 135.80 acres of land abutting 150 feet wide Karakambadi road at a distance of about 5 ms, away from the town by name "Seshachalam Hill View Layout". About 887 house plots and 386 nos. of houses were developed with all infrastructure facilities.

In continuation to the above layout, the Authority has proposed to develop anextent of land under sites and service programme with all infrastrúcture facilities. It is proposed to develop the layout at an approximate cost of Rs. 182.52 lakh. Provision has been made for facilities like school, bus stand, commercial centres, parks and other facilities. This new townships is accessible by 150 feet wide road and is nearer to their work centres located at the eastern side of the Tirupati Town.

***(b) Sites and Services Programme Around Tirupati Towns.*** To ease out traffic congestion in the town and to promote planned development at the fringe of the town and also to decentralise commercial activities, the Authority has identified certain lands for plotted development and commercial centres within the same.

***(c) Sites and Services Programmes at Tiruchanur and Daminedu.*** Tiruchanur is an important pilgrim centre. Besides pilgrimage, many of the industrial units are coming up along Renigunta-Tiruchanur Road. Tiruchanur is connected to Tirupati with high frequency of transportation facilities. To promote planned development around Tiruchanur and to reduce the time distance to the work centres, the Authority has identified lands to the extent of 64.38 acres for plotted development with the total cost to be above Rs. 350 lakh.

***(d) Sites and Services Programme at Veelantapuram*** To create an impulse for rapidly expanding southern side of the Tirupati Town, the Authority has identified certain lands at Vendantapuram and Mallamgunta village to an extent of 40.73 acres. The cost of land acquisition is estimated at Rs. 145.00 lakh and the cost of development is about Rs. 102.00 lakh.

It is proposed to develop the above areas as residential-cum-commercial centres with all infrastructure facilities like WBH roads, drainage, water supply and park development. Development of the areas shall act as modal centres for planned development and relieve the mother town from traffic congestion and reduce the pressure on the infrastructure like water supply, drainage and other facilities.

**Transportation**

The Tirupati town is well connected by road to major cities like Chennai, Bangalore and Hyderabad. The narrow roads and carriage widths is already over-burdened with heavy traffic movement. The major roads connecting Bangalore and Chennai are passing through thickly built up areas like Chandragiri and Renigunta. The recent traffic studies conducted by the Authority show the major roads connecting Tirupati with other cities are heavily burdened with traffic. In addition to this, the T.T.D. has proposed to construct rope-way from Sreevarimettu to Tirumala. This proposal calls for a revision in the network pattern. To meet the above proposals and also to solve the traffic problems on the existing major roads, the Authority has proposed the following new roads.

***(a) Brahmanapatu-Kaluru Bye-pass Road*** Keeping in view of the rope-way proposals made by the Tirumala Tirupati Devasthanams, the Authority has proposed a 100 feet bye-pass road running on the southern side of the development area. This proposed road connects the pilgrim traffic coming from Chennai and Southern parts of the country. This road runs a length of 16 kms. connecting Puthalaput-Naidupet road at Kaluru village. This road also helps the sugarcane growers of the region in transporting the product direct to the Gajulamandyam mill. As it is a major material road, it shall promote economic activity in the large rural tract all along the road. This road bye-passes and relieves the traffic congestion on the thickly built up areas of Renigunta and Tirupati town. Land to an extent of 120 acres is to be acquired for the above purpose. The total cost of development of the road is about Rs. 480.00 lakh.

***(b) Road Connecting Sreevarimettu—Outer Ringroad.*** To facilitate the pilgrim traffic reach the base camp of rope way at Sreevarimettu, the Authority has proposed a 100 feet road running on the northern side railway line connecting the 150 feet wide outer ring road. This proposed road bye–passes the Tirupati town for the traffic coming from the eastern side of the town. The total length of the road is about 4 kms. An extent of 30 acres of land is to be acquired for the above purpose. The cost of road development shall be about Rs. 120.00 lakh.

***(c) Bye-pass Road at Chandragiri.*** The existing Tirupati Bangalore road passes through the thickly built up parts of Chandragiri Town. To relieve the traffic congestion within the Chandragiri town, it is proposed to develop a 100 feet bye-pass road running on southern side of the town. Total length of the road is about 3 kms. An extent of 22 acres of land is to be acquired for the above purpose. The cost of road formation is worked out to be Rs. 90.00 lakh.

***(d) Bye–pass road at Renigunta.*** To solve the traffic problems in Renigunta town, it is proposed to develop 80 feet wide bye-pass road deviating the Puthalput-Naidupet road at Railway over bridge and joining at railway level crossing. The total length of the proposed road is 4.5 kms. The total cost of the development shall be about Rs. 70.00 lakh.

**Water Supply**

In Tirupati town water supply is found to be quite inadequate to meet the requirements of growing population and the floating pilgrim population besides industrial requirements.

At present, the Kalyani Dam is the only source of protected water supply since 1978 with a capacity of 25 lakh gallons daily. In addition to the above quantity, five lakh gallons of water is being added to the public water supply system from 450 bore wells in the town. Presently, the Municipality is able to supply nine gallons per person per day only as against the required standard of 30 gallons per capita per day. The situation is bound to worsen in near future unless additional sources are identified. One of such schemes is Mallimadugu reservoir.

***(A) Mallimadugu Reservoir.*** Mallimadugu reservoir is an irrigation scheme for storing water coming from Rallakalva. The site is located about 14 kms. away from Tirupati town. The reservoir consist of an earthen bund for a length of 1385.46 mts. The present capacity of the reservoir is $4.98 \times 10^6$ million cu. mts. It is a convenient source for lifting ten lakh gallons per day drinking water for Tirupati town.

The cost of the scheme works out to be Rs. 670.00 lakh and the Tirupati Municipality has proposed to raise Rs. 150.00 lakh by way of donations from the public who seek individual water tap connections and remaining balance of Rs. 520.00 lakh is proposed to be obtained by way of loan from financing agencies like L.I.C., HUDCO. The principal component of the repayment amount may be borne by the Government/Tirumala Tirupati Devasthanams as the Municipality financial position is weak and interest shall be borne by the Municipality from the water charges collected.

***(B) Lifting of Water from Telugu Ganga Project.*** The population of Tirupati town by 2011, i.e., in another 20 years time may cross be five lakhs mark and the water requirement for this population and pilgrims will be 160 lakhs gallons per day. The water requirement after completion of the above proposals will still be about 90 lakh gallons per day. Hence, it is proposed to lift 90 lakh gallons per day from Telugu Ganga Project from Srikalahasti point at a cost of Rs. 1970 lakh. The scheme consists of construction of offtake chamber at Telugu Ganga Project, installation of raw water chambers, laying of pumping main, construction of treatment plant and remodelling of distribution system.

**Proposals to the Government for Financial Assistance**

The rapid growth and expansion of Tirupati town and neighbouring areas has called for strengthening of the Authority. Apart from the natural growth of the area, the proposed activities generate more traffic and generate demand for accommodation. These future growing activities are to be properly planned by allocating appropriate location of housing and other amenities like educational, recreational, commercial, etc. A suitable network has to be developed so as to reduce the time distance from the place of work to place of residence. In order to carry out these programmes the financial position of the Authority needs to be strengthened.

To raise the financial position of the Authority, the following proposals are submitted to the governmen for consideration:

(a) The major source of internal income generation to this Authority is by developing the house sites and allotting to the public taking into consideration the development cost. By doing this, the Authority is promoting planned development and providing developed house sites to different income category people at reasonable price with a thrust on the LIG section of the society.

To take up the above mentioned sites and services programme, the government has been requested to provide Rs. 10.00 crore interest free loan with a moratorium period of 5 years. The Authority proposes to repay the loans as and when the amount is realised from the schemes.

(b) The infrastructure developed by the authority is being largely utilised by the pilgrims visiting Tirumala in one way or the other. The Government have issued directions to the Tirumala Tirupati Devasthanams to contribute Rs. 10.00 lakh, per annum to the Authority. The Tirumala Tirupati Devasthanams has not released the amount so far. The Government is requested to issue orders to Tirumala Tirupati Devasthanams to pay the annual contribution of Rs. 10.00 lakh from 1982 onwards. This will improve the financial position of the Authority.

(c) Tirumala Tirupati Devasthanams is taking up number of constructions both at Tirumala and in Tirupati. As per the provisions made under section 14 of A.P.U.A. (Dev.) Act, 1975, the T.T.D. has to pay the development charges to the Authority. The Authority has resolved that unless the development charges in arrears are paid to it, the powers shall not be delegated to T.T.D. The same has been initiated to T.T.D. but so far the development charges due to Tirupati Urban Development Authority have not been paid. The matter has been brought to the notice of the Government. Hence the Government is requested to issue necessary instructions to T.T.D. to remit the development charges due to the Authority since 1982.

(d) At present, the pilgrim tax collected by railways is being shared equally by the Municipality and the T.T.D. which have limited jurisdiction. The pilgrim coverage into the town from different directions and by different modes of transport. As the town is already congested, arterial roads are to be planned and implemented at regional level for easy flow of pilgrim traffic. The Authority is the only competent body for this purpose. As the Authority has taken many schemes and proposes to do many, the Government is requested to issue orders for payment of one-third share of pilgrim tax to it. This will help in augmenting the resources of the Authority for taking up the development activities for the benefit of pilgrims.

# 23

# Some Perspectives of Rural-Urban Interface in Planning

*—U.C. Dasgupta*

## Introduction

The much talked about 74th Amendment to the Constitution brings, in addition to other provisions, a revolutionary change in the planning process. Planning in India is first time being placed in the Constitution through inserting the 73rd and 74th Amendments therein. The Constitution provides for constituting a District Planning Committee in every district and a Metropolitan Planning Committee for a city having population of ten lakhs or more. Both these committees have to consist of the representatives of urban and rural local bodies besides officials. These Committees have to prepare a draft development plan of the district by consolidating the plans prepared by the respective grassroot level institutions. An integration in planning and development is the main aim of these Committees. The paper attempts to present a rural urban interfacial scenario in the most populated state of the country. The planners, policy makers and administrators have to appreciate the problems while talking of integrated planning through District Planning and Metropolitan Committees.

Uttar Pradesh is the most populous State in India accounting for a total population of about 139.11 million (16.5 per cent of total population in the country) during 1991. Nearly 19.8 per cent or 27.61 million of this resided in the urban areas. It had a total geographical area of 244416 sq. kms. and the density of population in the State was 473 persons per sq. m. There were 702 town–groups and towns (in all 784 urban centres) in the State in 1991, 41 of these belonged to Class–I, 46 to Class–II, 130 Class–III, 236 Class–IV, 209 Class–V and 40 Class–VI categories. The State is divided into five economic regions, viz., Western, Central, Eastern, Bundelkhand and Hill. Nearly 47.28 per cent of the total urban population in the State was concentrated in the Western region (21 districts), 22.8 per cent in Eastern region (19 districts),

20.78 per cent in the Central region (10 districts), 5.20 per cent in the Bundelkhand region (5 districts) and 4.66 per cent in the Hill region (8 districts). There were three metropolitan cities in the State as per 1991 Census viz. Kanpur, Lucknow and Varanasi. By the year 2001 this number is likely to rise to six as Agra, Allahabad and Meerut cities are expected to achieve this category.

Growth in urban population in the State has been quite rapid during the last 2 decades. Between 1971–81, this growth was about 4.9 per cent per annum. Between 1981–91 this growth has been at about 3.4 per cent per annum. In both these decades the growth was more than that at the All India level. With the average growth trend as perceived between 1971–91, the urban population in the State is likely to reach about 40.9 million by the year 2001. During 1971–81, 379 new urban areas centres were added in the State. During 1981–91, 43 new urban centres were again added. The recent spurt in the State's urbanization is a reflection of major structural movements in the economy. The indications are that, with agricultural growth as income increases subsequently and further productivity changes as occur the rate of urbanisation is expected to be high.

**State of Economy**

The economy of the State is primarily based on agriculture with as much as 75 per cent of the workers in 1987–88 dependent on the primary sector (agriculture and allied) for livelihood. However per capita availability of land (reporting area) has over time declined from 0.29 hectare in 1970–71 to 0.27 hectare in 1980–81 and to 0.23 hectare in 1988–89. Agriculture is also characterised by the preponderance of marginal holdings on one hand, and by the abundance of small villages according to population size. The number of sub-marginal and marginal holdings of less than one hectare in the State rose from 125.72 lac in 1980–81 to 137.82 lac in 1985–86. The share of these holdings in the total number of operational holdings also moved up from 70.6 per cent in 1980–81 to 72.6 per cent in 1985–86. In terms of area in 1985–86, these huge number of marginal holdings covered only 28.3 per cent of the total area under operational holdings. In 1985–86 the average size of operational holdings in the State was 0.93 hectare only which is lower than the national average of 1.68 hectare and also lowest amongst all the major States but for West Bengal (0.92 ha.) Bihar (0.87 ha.) and Kerala (8.36 ha.).

The abundance of small villages (population size adds to the magnitude of efforts required for development. The number of villages with population less than 500 constitute 47.3 per cent in the State. The share of population in these villages is only 14.1 per cent. The share of villages in the population size of 500–1999 in 44.8 per cent which is 54.6 per cent of the population. Thus, nearly 92.1 per cent of the total number of villages in the State contain only 68.7 per cent of the rural population. Table 1 gives broad view of the distribution of villages by size and population served.

**TABLE 1**

| *Range of Population* | *Per cent of total number* | *Per cent of total rural population* |
|---|---|---|
| Less than 500 | 47.3 | 14.1 |
| 500 to 1999 | 44.8 | 54.6 |
| 2000 to 4999 | 7.2 | 25.4 |
| 5000 and above | 0.7 | 5.9 |
| Total | 100.0 | 100.0 |

*Source:* Draft Eighth Five Year Plan U.P. Vol. I.

The economy of the State is also characterised by high incidence of unemployment and poverty which are symptoms of backwardness. More than open unemployment, it is the incidence of severe under-employment or disguised unemployment which lies at the root of high incidence of poverty. This is particularly very high amongst agricultural workers. It is worthwhile to mention therefore that neither a higher growth in the overall economy nor adhoc measures without creating avenues of gainful and self-sustaining employment for the poor and unemployed can be a sufficient guarantee for mitigating these problems.

**Structure of State Economy**

The State income, both at current prices and in real terms, i.e., at constant prices shows a continuous rising trend. The total State income at current prices rose from Rs. 14102 crore (1980–81) to Rs. 21658 crore (1984–85) and to Rs. 40719 crore (1989–90), recording an increase of 53.6 per cent (1981–85) and 88.0 per cent (1985–90). Likewise, in real terms, i.e., at constant prices of 1980–81, it moved up from Rs. 14102 crore to Rs. 16486 crore and further to Rs. 20838 crore during the same periods, registering an increase of 16.9 per cent (1981–85) and 26.4 per cent (1985–90). Despite these increases, the share of the State in total national income (current prices) declined from 12.7 per cent in 1980–81 to 11.7 per cent in 1984–85 and remained at this level in 1989–90 also, while at constant prices (1980–

81), it receded from 12.7 per cent to 12.4 per cent and to 11.9 per cent respectively in the same period. In other words after making adjustment for inflation, the share of State income declined in 1989–90 also over 1984–85.

Like the total State income, per capita income (current prices) in the State also registered an increasing trend. It increased from Rs. 1286 in 1980–81 to Rs. 1812 in 1984–85, and to Rs. 3072 in 1989–90, the increases being 40.9 per cent (1981–85) and 69.5 per cent (1985–90). However, the gap between the per capita income of the country and of the State increased from Rs. 344 in 1980–81 to Rs. 683 in 1984–85 and to Rs. 1180 in 1989–90. Thus, in spite of the State's economy performing better during the latter half of the decade ending 1989–90 in comparison to the first four years of the decade, the gap in per capita income became still higher. This was due to the fact that the growth in the country's economy, as a whole was much better than this State and the growth in State's population higher than that of the country.

The average annual growth in rural growth in total income and in per capita income of the State vis-a-vis the country is given in Table 2.

**TABLE 2**

*(In percentages)*

| *Period* | *Annual growth in total Income* | | *Annual growth in per capital income* | |
|---|---|---|---|---|
| | *U.P.* | *All India* | *U.P.* | *All India* |
| 1. 1951–52 to 1955–56 | 2.0 | 3.6 | 0.5 | 1.7 |
| 2. 1956–57 to 1960–61 | 1.9 | 4.0 | 0.3 | 1.9 |
| 3. 1961–62 to 1965–66 | 1.6 | 2.2 | –0.2 | 0.0 |
| 4. 1966–67 to 1968–69 | 0.3 | 4.0 | –1.5 | 1.8 |
| 5. 1969–70 to 1973–74 | 2.3 | 3.3 | 0.4 | 1.1 |
| 6. 1974–75 to 1978–79 | 5.7 | 5.3 | 3.3 | 2.9 |
| 7. 1981–82 to 1984–85* | 4.0 | 4.8 | 1.8 | 2.6 |
| 8. 1985–86 to 1989–90* | 4.8 | 5.6 | 2.7 | 2.6 |
| 9. 1981–82 to 1989–90* | 4.4 | 5.2 | 2.3 | 3.1 |

*Note:* Based on new series with 1980–81 as a base.

*Source:* Draft Eighth Five Year U.P. Vol. 1.

It will be seen from the above that from the very inception of planning in the country, the annual growth rates in total and per capita income of the State have always remained lower than the national averages during different Plan periods except in Fifth Plan period from 1974–75 to 1978–79, when the per capita income in this State registered an annual growth rate of 3.3 per cent against the national average of 2.9 per cent. Prior to this, owing to a comparatively higher growth in population in comparison with income, the State's per capita income registered e.g., native growth during the period 1961–62 to 1968–69. In the remaining period of 1951–74 also the annual growth rates in State's per capita income were nominal (0.3 per cent to 0.5 per cent). It will also be seen that during the period 1981–82 to 1989–90, the gap between growth rates in per capita income of the State and the country remained more or less constant at 0.8 percentage point. This only shows that whatever growth in State income took place during the period 1981–90 was absorbed by the growth in its population.

The contribution of primary sector to total State income slipped down from 60.2 per cent in 1970–71 to 52.0 per cent in 1980–81 and further 41.5 per cent in 1989–90, indicating a decline of 8.2 percentage points during 1980–81 over 1970–71 and of 10.5 percentage points during 1989–90 over 1980–81. On the other hand, the share of secondary sector moved up by 1.4 percentage points from 14.9 per cent in 1970–71 to 16.3 per cent in 1980–81 and further by 4.2 per cent in 20.5 in 1989–90, while the contribution of tertiary sector in the total State income stood at 24.9 per cent in 1970–71, 31.7 per cent in 1980–81 and 38.0 per cent in 1989–90. Thus, amongst these sectors, the tertiary sector recorded the highest increase in its share, having absorbed a major part of the decline which took place in the shares of primary sector. The structural pattern of the State's economy can be depicted as below:

**TABLE 3**

**Structure of State Income (Current Prices)**

| *Sectors* | *According to old series (1970–71)* | *Accordin to new series (1980–81)* | |
|---|---|---|---|
| | *1970–71* | *1980–81* | *1989–81* |
| 1. Primary | 60.2 | 52.0 | 41.5 |
| 2. Secondary | 14:9 | 16.3 | 20.5 |
| 3. Tertiary | 24.9 | 31.7 | 38.0 |
| Total | 100.00 | 100.00 | 100.00 |

*Source:* Draft Eighth Year Plan U.P. Vol. I.

The average annual growth in agriculture (including animal husbandry) remained stagnant at 2.7 per cent during the period 1981–85 and 1985–90. The Annual growth in secondary sector declined from 6.7 per cent in the first four years to 5.8 per cent in the latter five years of 1981–90. Similarly the annual growth rate in manufacturing sector fell down from 9.0 per cent to 6.4 per cent during the same period. The two components of this sub–sector, viz., the registered and unregistered manufacturing receded from 14.2 per cent to 7.8 per cent per annum and from 5.1 per cent to 5.0 per cent per annum respectively. The trends are indicative of the fact that the unregistered manufacturing component, comprising mainly the entire village industries and a bulk of small industries grew at a slower pace than the registered manufacturing. Thus, deployment of large funds in unorganized sector for promotion of these industries mainly for employment generation did not yield satisfactory results in terms of value added in this sector. The annual growth rate in tertiary sector increased from 5.2 per cent (1981–85) to 7.1 per cent (1985–90). During the period 1971–81 and 1981–90, the tertiary sector registered a growth rate of 3.6 per cent and 6.3 per cent per annum respectively. During the same period the three constituent subsectors of "Transport, Communication and Trade". "Finance and Real Estates" and "Community and Personal Services" recorded annual growth rates of 3.7 per cent and 4.3 per cent, 5.3 per cent and 7.5 per cent and 2.4 per cent and 4.3 per cent, 5.3 per cent and 7.5 per cent and 2.4 per cent and 8.7 per cent respectively. The low growth rate in the "Transport, Communication and Trade" sub-sector is a disquieting feature in so far as it represents a lower growth in commodity producing activities.

The variations in growth rates of different sectors and their weightage in State's economy lead to overall growth of 4.0 per cent during 1971–81 and 4.4 per cent during 1981–90, as against the corresponding national averages of 4.8 per cent, 5.6 per cent, 3.3 per cent and 5.2 per cent respectively.

The structure of State income and its workforce in 1970–71 and 1987–88 in term 2 per cent can be broadly stated in Table 4.

**TABLE 4**

| *Sector* | *1970* | | *1987–88* | |
|---|---|---|---|---|
| | *Income** | *Workers*** | *Income** | *Workers*** |
| Primary (Agri and Allied) | 60 | 78 | 40 | 75 |
| Secondary (industry and Allied) | 15 | 8 | 22 | 10 |
| Tertiary (others | 25 | 14 | 38 | 15 |
| Total | 100 | 100 | 100 | 100 |

* at current prices

** Census

It is evident from Table 4 that decline in income from primary sector was matched by a fall of only 3 per cent in its workforce. It implies therefore that the income of workers in this sector were reduced which constituted the largest segment of workers. The table also makes it clear that growth in secondary sector was largely capital intensive as income increased by 7 per cent against a 2 per cent rise in number of workers. In a similar way income gains in the tertiary sector was still larger and the situation was much better for the workers of this sector.

The situation which emerges from the above is that the distribution of gains from development has not been only spread. The growth has been more capital intensive than labour intensive more urban based than rural based (thereby widening rural urban dichotomy) and the shift in income from primary to other sectors has not been accompanied by a corresponding shift in workers.

In order to determine comparative position of the regions (economic) and the districts in the State economy the UPDESCO had carried out a study of the value of sectorwise net output from commodity producing sectors from 1977–78 to 1986–87 which were based on secondary sources obtained from Bulletin of Economic and Statistic department, State Planning Institute. The community producing sectors identified were as follows:

1. Agriculture and Animal Husbandry
2. Forestry and Logging
3. Fishing
4. Mining and Quarrying
5. Manufacturing (registered)
6. Manufacturing (unregistered)

The total output (in Rs. crore) and per capita output (in Rs.) was derived for each of the 5 regions and the State as a whole for the different years from 1981–82 to 1986–87. A similar figure was obtained for each of the districts and then compared with the State average. It was found that the Western region accounted for 40 per cent of the State output followed by Eastern, Central, Hill and Bundelkhand region.

On the basis of the net output and the rate of growth in total output the districts in the State were divided into 4 categories as per Table 5.

**TABLE 5**

| *Categories* | *Name of district* |
|---|---|
| 1. Districts having per capita net output and rate of growth in total output more than the State average. | Ghaziabad, Shaharanpur, Budayun, Etah, Shahjahanpur, Mathura, Meerut, Rampur, (Western Region), Rae Bareilly, Kheri, |

| | | |
|---|---|---|
| | | Barabanki (Central region), Jhansi (Bundelkhand region), Nainital (Hill region), Mirzapur (Eastern) |
| 2. | Districts having per capita net output above the states average and rate of growth in total output below the state average | Alligarh, Bulandshahr, Bareilly, Pilibhit, Moradabad, Muzzaffar-nagar, Mainpuri, Bijnor (Western region, Hamirpur, Banda (Bundel-khand region), Garhwal, Chamoli, Pithoragarh, Uttar Kashi (Hill region). |
| 3. | Districts having per capita net output below but rate of growth in total output above the State average. | Etawah, Farrukhabad (Western region, Lucknow (Central), Allahabad, Ghazipur, Azamgarh, Ballia, Faizabad (Eastern region). |
| 4. | Districts having both per Capita net output and rate of growth in total output below the state average | Agra (Western region), Hardoi, Sitapur, Unnao, Pratapgarh, Fatehpur, Kanpur, (Central region) jalaun, Dalitpur (Bundelkhand region), Tehri Garhwal, Dehradun, Almora, (Hill Region), Gonda, Basti, Sutampur, Varanasi, Jaunpur, Gorakhpur, Bahraich, Deoria (Eastern region). |

**Link between Town Development and Rural Growth Strategies**

Given the undeveloped nature of rural infrastructure in general and the dispersed nature of the rural population, small cities and towns needs to be critical hubs of local economic development. Hence more efforts are needed to identify.

1. Which cities and towns have development potential in support of agriculture?
2. Which policies and institutions help or hinder the efficient symbiosis between town and country? and
3. What bottlenecks exist that prevent the more efficient functioning of these towns in support of rural areas, especially with regard to infrastructure and services?

A review of macro economic implications of urban growth in the developing countries reveal that as economies develop, the interdependence between rural and urban growth increases. It has been observed that a subsistence (marginal) farmer has no need of markets. For the others, the production and sale of agricultural products are not ends in themselves. They are means of earning money to buy consumer goods, to save, or to invest. Much of what the farmer might want to buy should be produced or made available in local urban centres. Savings and investment opportunities tend to be found in these centres. The towns can also provide access to public services. Urban-based schools, health facilities and communication networks can effectively service a large number of farms and villages. The degree to which urban areas perform these tasks efficiently is likely to have significant implications for the success of rural growth strategies.

In turn, successful agricultural development programmes can be expected to generate greater rural demand for the goods and services that are provided in local cities and towns. The effect is likely to be more business activity, more jobs, and more people in these urban centres.

### Macro Perspective

***Spatial Distribution of Urban Population*** A comparison of urban growth and trends with that at the national level shows that the proportion of urban population to the total population was higher at the national level (26.13 per cent) during 1991 against a corresponding proportion of 19.84 per cent at the State level. Urban growth, however, was higher at the State level (38.73 per cent) than at the national level (36.47 per cent) during 1981–91. Another striking feature is that the structure of urban population by class-size shows a higher percentage (65.20 per cent) being covered by class I towns at the National level than at the State level (55.51 per cent). Barring these, the overall growth rates for each of the class-sizes of towns from Class–I to Class IV were higher at the State level than at the national level.

The distribution of urban population as yet do not exhibit much polarisation. The three metropolitan centres in the State cover about 17.13 of the total urban population in contrast to nearly 32.54 per cent covered by 23 metropolitan cities at the country level. Despite this, there is a growing trend of population shift towards the larger urban centres. At 41 Class–I towns in the State accounted for nearly 66.13 of the total increase in urban population between 1981–91 in contrast to 78.48 per cent at the country level. In terms of population growth also, the Class–I towns in the State show a high figure of 49.83 per cent between 1981–91. Apart from this, the other group of towns that have shown high growth is the Class–III towns (population between 20000 to 49999) with a growth of 54.00 per cent between 1981–91. The following tables give a broad picture of the urban scenario at both national and State levels.

**TABLE 6**
**Proportion of Urban Population and Growth Rate**

| | *U/T* | | *Growth in Urban population* | |
|---|---|---|---|---|
| | *1981* | *1991* | *1971–81* | *1981–91* |
| India | 23.73 | 26.13 | (+) 46.14 | (+) 36.47 |
| Uttar Pradesh | 17.95 | 19.84 | (+) 60.62 | (+) 38.73 |

**TABLE 7**
**Distribution of Urban Population and Growth by Class-Size of Urban Centres–1991**

| | *India* | | *U.P.* | |
|---|---|---|---|---|
| | *Percentage to total* | *Growth 1981–91* | *Percentage to total* | *Growth 1981–91* |
| Class – I | 65.20 | (+) 16.87 | 55.51 | (+) 49.83 |
| Class – II | 10.95 | (+) 28.14 | 11.83 | (+) 32.03 |
| Class – III | 13.19 | (+) 25.30 | 14.04 | (+) 54.00 |
| Class – IV | 7.77 | (+) 10.72 | 12.26 | (+) 25.91 |
| Class –V | 2.60 | (–) 1.27 | 5.85 | (–) 5.29 |
| Class – VI | 0.29 | (–) 21.70 | 0.51 | (–) 51.40 |

**TABLE 8**
**Distribution of Urban Population by Million Plus Cities**

| | *No. of Urban Centres* | *Percentage of Population to* | |
|---|---|---|---|
| | | *Total population* | *Total Urban Population* |
| | 23 | 8.37 | 32.54 |
| | 3 | 3.40 | 17.13 |

**TABLE 9**
**Distribution of Urban Population by Class of Urban Centres U.P.**

| *Class of Centres* | *Population 1971* | *Per cent to Total* | *Population 1981* | *Per cent to total* | *Population 1991* | *per cent to total* |
|---|---|---|---|---|---|---|
| Class I | 706893 | 57.06 | 10227410 | 51.40 | 15324059 | 55.5 |
| Class II | 1341436 | 10.83 | 2474296 | 12.43 | 3266884 | 11.8 |

| | | | | | | |
|---|---|---|---|---|---|---|
| Class III | 2069104 | 16.70 | 2516433 | 12.65 | 3875188 | 14.0 |
| Class IV | 1292753 | 10.44 | 268946 | 13.51 | 3385980 | 12.2 |
| Class V | 587608 | 4.74 | 1704090 | 8.56 | 1614003 | 5.8 |
| Class VI | 28803 | 0.23 | 287640 | 1.45 | 139801 | 0.5 |
| Total | 12388596 | 100 | 19899115 | 100 | 27605915 | 100 |

**TABLE 10**

**Increase/Decrease of Population in Each Size Class During 1981–91**

| | *India* | | *U.P.* | |
|---|---|---|---|---|
| | *Population Increase/ Decrease 1981–91* | *Percentage* | *Population Increase/ Decrease 1981–91* | *Percentage* |
| All Classes | 56447569 | 100.00 | 7706800 | 100.00 |
| Class I | 44298200 | (+) 78.48 | 509649 | (+) 66.13 |
| Class II | 5119439 | (+) 9.07 | (+) 792588 | (+) 10.28 |
| Class III | 5670186 | (+) 10.04 | 1358755 | (+) 17.63 |
| Class IV | 1600797 | (+) 2.84 | 696734 | (+) 9.04 |
| Class V | (–) 70982 | (–) 0.13 | (–) 90087 | (–) 1.17 |
| Class VI | (–) 170071 | (–) 0.30 | (–) 147839 | (–) 1.91 |

***Urban Population Classified by Economic Regions***

Studies in regional urbanisation trends suggest that the western region contained about 47.28 per cent of the total urban population in the State followed by 22.08 per cent in the Eastern region and 20.78 per cent in the Central region. Western region also contained nearly 45.37 per cent of all urban centres in the State in 1991. Following tables illustrates the regional distribution of urban population in the State.

Interestingly however the proportion of urban population to the total population works out fairly uniform in all the Economic Regions excepting for the Eastern Region which had a low proportion of 11.56 per cent of urban population to the total population in the region. Regionally, the trend of urban population growth in all the economic regions were fairly uniform except for the Hill region where growth has been much higher than the State average.

Nearly 78.94 per cent of the State urban population was contained within the municipal jurisdiction which constituted roughly 32.73 per cent of all urban centres in the State. In the Central Region, more than fourth-fifth of the urban population was concentrated in the municipal areas, which was about 30.56 per cent of all urban centres in this region. It is worthwhile to note in this connection that out of 41 Class-I towns in the State (population one lakh and above) 24 are located in the Western region. Geographically the Western region is also more numerously served by urban centres. The following table illustrates the position of distribution of urban population and urban centres region-wise.

**TABLE 11**

**Growth in Urban Population Classified by Economic Region**

| *Name of Region* | *Urban Population (lac)* | | | | *Total Population (lac)* | | | *Percentage of Population to total Population* | |
|---|---|---|---|---|---|---|---|---|---|
| | *1981* | *1991* | *percent to total* | *percentage to total growth* | *1981* | *1991* | *percent growth in 1991* | | |
| Hill | 8.8 | 12.9 | 4.7 | 45.3 | 48.7 | 59.3 | 22.5 | 18.3 | 21.7 |
| Western | 93.3 | 130.5 | 47.3 | 39.9 | 393.5 | 495.5 | 25.9 | 23.7 | 26.3 |
| Central | 41.8 | 57.8 | 20.8 | 38.3 | 196.0 | 241.9 | 23.4 | 21.2 | 23.7 |
| Eastern | 44.5 | 61.0 | 22.1 | 37.0 | 416.5 | 527.2 | 26.6 | 10.7 | 11.6 |
| Bundelkhand | 10.8 | 14.4 | 5.2 | 32.4 | 54.3 | 67.3 | 24.0 | 20.0 | 21.3 |
| U.P. Urban | 199.0 | 276.1 | 100.0 | 38.7 | 1108.6 | 1391.1 | 25.5 | 18.0 | 19.8 |

Although polarisation has not yet been perceived in the State owing largely to a fair distribution of large urban centres geographically, nevertheless wide disparities persist in the distribution of urban population regionally. Nearly 40 districts out of a total of 63 districts in the State have an urban context lower than the state average. Geographically these 40 districts occupied an area of about 233524 sq. km. which was 79.32 per cent of the total area under the State. Districts with lower urban content were more numerous in the Eastern Region and Central Region. About 17 districts out of a total of 19 districts in the Eastern Region and 8 districts out of a total of 10 districts in the Central Region had an urban content less than the State average. Table 15 gives in nutshell the broad spectrum of regional urbanisation within the State in 1991.

**TABLE 12**

**Some Salient Features of Regional Distribution of Urban Population 1981**

| *Name of Region* | *Total urban population* | *Total population in MC and MB/CB (Lac)* | *Per cent of 2 over 3* | *Total No. of Urban Centres* | *No. of MC and MB* | *Per cent of 6 over 6* |
|---|---|---|---|---|---|---|
| *1* | *2* | *3* | *4* | *5* | *6* | *7* |
| Hill | 8.9 | 6.22 | 70.3 | 62 | 21 | 33.9 |
| Western | 93.3 | 74.74 | 90.1 | 326 | 94 | 28.8 |
| Central | 41.5 | 32.34 | 78.0 | 106 | 25 | 23.6 |
| Eastern | 44.5 | 30.60 | 68.8 | 180 | 33 | 18.31 |
| Bundelkh-and | 10.8 | 7.94 | 73.3 | 52 | 18 | 34.6 |
| Total | 199.0 | 151.84 | 76.3 | 726 | 189 | 26.3 |

**TABLE 13**

**Some Salient Features of Regional Distribution of Urban Population 1991**

| *Name of Region* | *Total urban population* | *Total population in MC and MB/CB (Lac)* | *Per cent of 2 over 3* | *Total No. of Urban Centres* | *No. of MC and MB* | *Per cent of 6 over 6* |
|---|---|---|---|---|---|---|
| *1* | *2* | *3* | *4* | *5* | *6* | *7* |
| Hill | 12.86 | 10.26 | 79.8 | 75 | 29 | 38.7 |
| Western | 130.52 | 101.70 | 77.9 | 353 | 113 | 32.0 |
| Central | 57.37 | 49.84 | 86.8 | 108 | 31 | 28.7 |
| Eastern | 60.96 | 45.10 | 73.9 | 189 | 44 | 23.3 |
| Bundelkh-and | 14.35 | 11.02 | 76.8 | 59 | 19 | 32.3 |
| Total | 276.06 | 217.92 | 78.9 | 784 | 236 | 30.1k |

MC: Municipal Corporation, MB: Municipal Board, CB: City Board

**TABLE 14**

**Geographical Distribution of Urban Centres by Regions in U.P. 1991**

| *Name of Regions* | *Geographical Area (sq. km)* | *No. of Urban Centres* | *Geographical Area per Centre (sq. km)* |
|---|---|---|---|
| Hill | 51125 | 75 | 681.67 |
| Western | 82196 | 353 | 232.85 |

| | | | |
|---|---|---|---|
| Central | 45834 | 108 | 424.39 |
| Eastern | 85844 | 189 | 454.20 |
| Bundelkhand | 29417 | 59 | 498.59 |
| Total | 294416 | 784 | 375.53 |

**TABLE 15**

**Economic Regions Classified According to Proportion of Urban to Total Population in U.P.–1991**

| *Percentage* | *Hill* | *Western* | *Central* | *Eastern* | *Bundelkhand* | *Grand total* |
|---|---|---|---|---|---|---|
| 00–05 | – | – | – | 3 | – | 3 |
| 05–10 | 5 | – | 4 | 9 | – | 18 |
| 10–15 | 1 | 1 | 4 | 3 | 2 | 11 |
| 15–20 | – | 5 | – | 2 | 1 | 8 |
| 20–25 | – | 4 | – | 1 | 1 | 6 |
| 25–30 | – | 6 | – | 1 | – | 7 |
| 30–35 | 1 | 2 | – | – | – | 3 |
| 35–40 | – | 1 | – | – | 1 | 2 |
| 40 and above | 1 | 2 | 2 | – | – | 5 |
| Total | 8 | 21 | 10 | 19 | 5 | 63 |

*Note:* Percentage of urban population to total population for the State of U.P. was 19.84 in 1991.

The foregone discussion clearly indicates the areas wherein special attention is required at the District Planning and Metropolitan Planning Committees level. The problems arising from the complexities of rural urban continuum in areas, population, culture, aesthetic and environment. The insertion of provisions is not going to help a balanced development in that taking care of the gram realities.

# 24

# One Hundred Fifty Years of Civic Administration in Shimla City—Tiny Bits of England

*—P.K. Banta*

Barely two centuries ago, the area occupied by the modern day Shimla was dense forest. Only the Jakhu temple which has stood the test of time, and a few scattered house comprised the sign of civilisation. For a lack of contemporary history, opinion is divided even over the origin of the name while some asserts that the name is derived from a solitary house called 'Shamley', others believe that the name is a derivative from the name of a village called 'Shimlah' or 'Shumlah'. A few others believe that the temple of goddess 'Shamli' gave birth to the modern name but other asserts that its original name was 'Shyamalaya'. Indeed very little is known about its early history. The earliest available records reveal that the area formed a part of Keonthal State at the dawn of the 18th Century.[1]

**City in Making**

Shimla was born out of storm and turmoils of war. Prior to the arrival of British, the inhabitants of the area were growing under iron rule of Gurkha Chieftains. The British conquered this area in 1815. "Shimla was a familiar name in the British in nineteenth century India. It was called Mount Olympus, the Viceroy's shooting box, India Capna, the abode of little tin gods, etc.[2]

Shimla, one time Summer Capital of Government of India and Headquarters of Indian Army, and now that of Government of Himachal Pradesh is picturesquely "situated on several small suburbs of lower Himalayas at the mean elevation of about 7100 feet above the sea level.[3] Easily accessible by road and rail, it has bracing climate, cool, bright, refreshing days and crisp nights. Annual rainfall is 55 inches. It is one of the finest hill stations of the country—with an area of 7.55 square miles. It provides varied opportunities for sports like ice-skating near Rivoli Cinema,

Skiting at Kufri, Gold at Naldehra and riding all around the city. Game is found in abundance.

It was a dream of coolness in a very hotlands, a hope of healthy rest from the burden of imperial office, a heaven of familiarity pinnacled above the alien dust of the plains, a solace of wounded and the desolate, the ill and the bored, a promise of fun and flirtation above all, a bitter-sweet memory of home-cockoos and thrushes, pines in the mist, honey-suckle and roses in the rain.[4]

The possibilities of the health resort were realised after the close of the campaign of 1815. The first mention of 'Semla middling sized village' comes in 1817 from the 'diary of two Scottish officers, Lieutenants Patrick and Alexander Gerard, and they surveyed and mapped the newly-subjugated hill state where a Fakir resided to give water to travellers.[5] The land-upon which the station stands formerly belonged jointly to the Maharaja of Patiala, Rana of Keonthal and Rana of Koti. It was Lord Kennedy, who in 1822, erected the first General who stayed at Kennedy House with Major Kennedy, the then political agent.[6]

Shimla's first Settlement Report recounts that from 1824 onwards, 'European gentleman, chiefly involves form plains, built many of earliest houses' Land for house constructions was leased 'free of rent' from the rulers of Keonthal or Patiala, depending on the sight chosen.[7] Begarees, building material and wood were also secured from them, and the transactions recorded in Kennedy's office.[8] The first cottage of wood, and thatch was built in 1819 by Lt. Ross, Assistant Political Agent in Hill States. Simla was chosen, in 1827, by Amherst, the Governor-General, for summer trip. He came with his entourage and 1700 coolies in attendance.[9] Amherst spent an uneventful summer at Kennedy House, leaving Simla after two months—apprehending that it would be unhealthy after the middle of June, once monsoon set in. The visit creates a precedent. It also left six large houses that had been built for his entourage. In 1824, Europeans had established themselves in the Hills.

By 1830, a township of thirty British-owned houses scattered over the Simla tract had come up. It was then acquired by the Fast India Company. Patiala was asked to part with four villages (Kainthu, Paghog, Cheog and Aindari) which came within Simla. They spread from Bharari, across Kainthu to Prospect Hill, including the plague post on the Cart Road, upto Jutogh railway station. The Maharaja was compensated with seven villages in Bharauli. The Rana of Keonthal was given the area near Ravin, mimus the fortress Raingarh, in exchange for twelve villages of Panjar, Sirian, Dharma, Phagli, Dillen, Kiar, Bamnoi, Pagawag, Dhar, Kanlog,

Kilian, and Khalini-villages that lay between Tara Devi across Simla upto Kasumpati. Simla town now comprised an area of about six square miles. It was surrounded by princely states, Patiala lay on the north and west; Keonthal on the south and the east; and Koti, which included the suburbs of Sanjauli, Mashobra, Kufri and Naldehra on the north-east. A chain of hill states lay along the route from Kalka via Simla to Bushahr and on towards Tibet.[10]

Once Simla had passed under the direct jurisdiction of Government, the first civic rules were formulated in the year 1829.[11] The earliest houses, paths and water reservoirs built by individuals were now brought within the general scheme of improvement of the town. Bentick, the Governor-General, suggested that two hundred square yards be utmost allowed an individual for construction of a house. As a first step, the boundaries of houses and the land attached to them were demarcated. A graduated ground tax, ranging from twenty to forty rupees, depending on the built up area, was fixed. The proceeds from the Chowkidari were meant to defray the cost of policing.[12]

In 1832, Bentick appointed a three-man committee to suggest measures for improvement of the town. The main problems which confronted the three members, Captain Kennedy, Colonel C.B. Stevenson, the Quarter-Master General of Subathu, and MacSween, a house owner, were how to improve the water supply and roads in Simla. Since springs were the only source of supply, water was a perennial problem and a few reservoirs had been built in 1828 and 1830. One of the first instructions to the committee was that 'every spring that can be turned to account for the purpose, with the roads and pathways leading to it, must of course be considered public property. Narrow, but clearly marked tracks linked the various houses. The first 'fine broad' level road around Mount Jakhu, about three miles in length, was built in 1828 under the supervision of Combermere, the Commander-in-Chief.[13] This was beginning of Simla's greatness. Lord William Bentick, who succeeded Lord Amherst in 1829 had a house built for himself which was known as 'Bentick Castle', the site of existing Grand Hotel.[14] During last year of Lord Bentick's stay in Simla, Sir Edward Barnes, the Commander-in-Chief came to Simla and resided for two years at "Barnes Court".

**Municipal Administration**

"Simla's Municipal Committee was first introduced in December 1851 under the provision of Act XXVI of 1850.[16] Simla municipality shares the distinction of being the oldest in Punjab. All the members were elected originally. The chairman was also elected but afterwards the Deputy Commissioner was nominated ex-officio President and some other ex-officio members were added, and some other changes were made". It was first constituted in 1852 according to the Government of India notification on December 15, 1851.

According to the Government of India Act of December, 1850, the Government of any province was given power to setup a municipal committee in any town where it was satisfied that the inhabitant of the town wanted one. Government was, in that case, authorised to appoint the magistrate and the requisite number of local inhabitants on the municipal committee. The Act conferred large powers for making civic regulations and levying taxes upon the committee.

At a meeting of house owners held in July 1852, seven were elected commissioners while the Deputy Commissioner was nominated ex-officio Chairman, when other ex-officio members were added, out numbering the private house owners, there were protests over the official infiltration into the committee, which had altered the representative character of the municipality.

Thirty-six house owners submitted a memorandum with an alternative code of rules and regulations decided at meeting convened on 18 September 1854. In view of pressure from house owners, a new constitution was framed in 1855. According to this, although the Deputy Commissioner was an ex-officio member of committee, the Municipal Commissioners were all elected by house owners. In 1864, when the offices of the Government of India moved formally to Simla, membership was increased. Three ex-officio members were added—an Executive Commissioner, a Medical Officer and a Senior Commissioner—all nominated to represent the interests of the Government.

During 1871, it was given the status of first class municipality, one of the six categories created by an Act of 1867. A first class municipality was to enjoy independence with regard to expenditure, subject only to a Government audit. The committee was reconstituted again to consist of seventeen to twenty members. Seven of these were officials, nominated to the committee. Between seven to ten house owners, of whom three were to be Indian, were to be elected. Three representative of the summer visitors were chosen by the committee from a list of six submitted by the Deputy Commissioner. The newly constituted committee was weighted so that the house owners of Simla could exercise a prepondering influence.

Under the arrangements, which existed in 1874, there were 17 to 20 non-officials including three house owners being the native residence of the place. Three members to represent visitors from officials or non-officials were nominated. The representatives of visitors were appointed by Local Government from a list of six names recommended to the Deputy Commissioner at the beginning of each season. The representatives of the house owners were popularly elected. The elections were held every second year. The voting qualification was the possession of house property in Simla of an estimated yearly rental value of Rs. 300 or upwards, on which all the assessments have been paid up. The house proprietors, qualified as above, were entitled to vote or votes on a graduated scale, based on the estimated yearly value of their property, the proprietor of a house of the minimum yearly rental value had one vote. A person having property rental yield of Rs. 10,000 and upwards have five votes.

The first municipal board for Simla was constituted by the Punjab Government in 1876 vide Punjab Government Notification No. 457 dated 4th July 1876. It consisted of 19 members, 7 of whom were officials and 12 non-officials. Out of 12 non-officials, three were appointed by notification. The remaining were appointed by selection from property owners. Out of later 9, two were to be Indians.[17]

In 1876, the committee was once again reconstituted to ensure official control. The Deputy Commissioner served as ex-officio President, and committee was limited to five nominated members, two salaried government officials and two house owners. Simla's private house owners rekindled the controversy on the unrepresentative constitution of the municipality in 1881. The attack on the 'despotic and arbitrary tendencies' of the Simla Municipal Committee was launched by Allan Octavian Hume and some other house owners. Between 1876 to 1883 the strength of the Committee was same as reconstituted in the year 1876. Hume felt that an elected element in the Simla Municipal Committee would act as a break on such arbitrary tendencies. To achieve this, he organised a Reform Committee of which he was Secretary.

A Committee was formed to enquire about the desirability of having an elected Municipality. The Committee, by a majority decision, recommended a wholly elected Municipal Committee though Hume favoured a gradual process towards that aim. The Committee's recommendation were based, predictably, on the concept of enfranchising interests and classes rather than individuals. Difference arose on the extent to which these different groups should be given right to vote. The overriding idea was that the votes were apportioned to house owners/proprietors and tenants not in proportions to their intelligence, but in proportion to the amount of taxes which they pay. Hume in his dissenting note, cautioned against the sudden introduction of a purely elective system, since successful institutions are generally the growth of time, they develop slowly—evolution is the law of entire universe. Hume preferred a committee of which only two-third was elected, raised to three-fifth of the total within five years.

Hume advocated enfranchising a mixed bag of six interests. These included the Government of India and Punjab as landlords and tenants, Europeans and Indian landlords and tenants; European professionals such as barristers, doctors, dentists, photographers, brewers, Indian lawyers and traders including stall keepers and all clerks drawing salary upwards of thirty rupees per month. After careful reflection, he added to the list of magistrates of Jutogh Cantonment and Vakils of ruling princes whose territories adjoined Simla. The controversy affected another major interest-government officers resident in Simla. Thirty officials held a meeting to protest against the recommendations of the Reform Committee. The officers disliked the idea of playing at politics and submitting themselves to the indignity of the election. Charles Aitchison, the Lieutenant-Governor, was enthusiastic about local self government in Simla, and a nucleus of officials held a meeting to lend support to new constitution.

Ripon's Resolution of 18th May 1882, on local self-government paved the way to a fresh experiment in municipal government in Simla. Since Simla was considered an English town where the electors and municipal commissioners would largely be British; it was assumed that there were a few problems in actualising the ideal. In Simla, in June 1882, a memorandum of fourteen points spelled out the basis on which the new municipal constitution was framed. It included issues of membership, the manner of election or nomination, qualification for holding office, qualification for voters, conditions for voting if a voter had more than one vote, division of the town into wards for the purpose of election, the election and position of President, the role of elected municipality, and the special precautions necessary to ensure representation and protection of interests of the Government.

A seven member committee which included A.O. Hume, Edward Cullin, a lawyer and J. Elston, a house owner, was appointed by the government to draft a suitable constitution for the Simla Municipal Committee. By September 1882, the committee had submitted its recommendations. Despite four dissenting notes, the Committee favoured a wholly elected Municipal Committee. The Municipal Committee was to consist of thirteen honorary members, including the President, who was elected by the Committee. Members of the Committee had a three year term, but one-third were to retire each year. All the voters had to be residents at Simla for five months.

There were two categories of voters: Property owners and tenants. Different qualifications were prescribed for the station and Bazar wards. The first consisted of house-owners: male or female; resident or non-resident. In Station ward they had one vote for every 1,000 rupees of rent on which house tax had been paid. In Bazar ward, one vote was allotted for every twenty-five rupees of house tax or frontage tax paid. Male Tenants in Station Ward had one vote for every 500 rupees of bonafide rental paid and in the Bazar ward one vote for every quarter of it. A house owner living in his own house qualified for voting as both house owner and tenant. The government voting power in Simla was measured in proportion to the taxes it paid to the municipality as property owner or tenant. Such votes were exercised through persons nominated by Government from time to time on its behalf. Persons residing in government houses qualified as tenants. The Government vote was divided into three: the votes of the Government of India; the Punjab Government; and the Viceregal Establishment.

In 1882, for the purpose of the Municipal elections, the town was divided into two wards—Station ward and Bazar ward signifying not only the residential and commercial areas of Simla, but also the European and Indian Bazar ward covered all the five bazars of Simla—Lower, Chotta, Boileauganj, Lakkar and Kainthu. Shops on the Mall were until 1900, included in Bazar ward, thereafter in Station Ward. The interest of each ward in municipal affairs was established on the basis of income they yielded to the municipality. The first elections held in 1883, changed the complexion of Municipal Committee. A.O. Hume elected Vice-president and James Walker a wealthy banker became Committee's President.

In September 1884, Government permitted the municipality to issue debentures bearing an interest of 6 per cent per annum and repayable at a periods varying between three to eighteen years, to part finance the project of Town Hall. It was to cover an area of 1602 square yards and cost 1,50,000 rupees.[18] A tramway was laid from Lakkar Bazar to Sanjauli to carry away the rubble masonry. According to Act XIII of 1884 of the municipal bye laws the management, control and administration of every public institution maintained out of municipal funds vested in the Committee. The Ripon Hospital was declared opened by Dufferin on 14th May 1885. The dominance of government interest in Simla mirrored in the subsequent reconstitution of the municipality, the elected municipality of the previous decade having been declared by official opinion to inadequate. The man who had conceived the set-up in the Ripon era as a model of local-self Government in India were no longer at the helm of affairs and many ardent supporters of the experiment had resigned or retired. There were sharp exchanges between officials and non-officials. There is a playing off of element against element, and when cliquism sets in fraternity and with it, usefulness takes flight. For this the constitution of the committee, combining officials and non-official members, was held mainly accountable; on the other hand a municipal committee dominated by the non-official British-estate agents, bankers, house owners and traders in a predominantly official town, seems untenable and unworkable.

In 1890, the Punjab Government after consulting the Government of India by its notification dated 18th December, 1890, decided to fix the number of the members of the board at 10 instead of 13 and it was stated that in the future out of those 10 members, 6 members to be elected and 4 nominated. The four nominated members were to represent the interest of government and one of these seats was to be reserved for civil surgeon and one for Executive Engineer, Simla Provincial Division. The Other seats were reserved for the representative of Central Government. Out of six, three were to represent the station ward and three the bazar ward.

In 1891, the committee was reconstituted to consist of four nominated and six elected members. Of the latter, the two wards were represented by three seats each. As before, the nominations of Government Officers and redistribution of seats tended to erode the influence of the British non-officials. The Indian representatives from Bazar ward were non-controversial, virtually ciphers who did not understand English. In 1883, the Municipal committee passed a resolution saying that, "with a view to the expeditious dispatch of business a majority of the committee shall decide what matter are proper and necessary to be explained in the vernacular to the Indian members". However, it seemed 'inexpedient' to appoint Indian members to a subcommittee even for the special inspection of the Bazar, and they were doubtlessly induced to cast their votes in favour of Government resolutions. With such a composition it was not possible for Government to effectively control municipal functioning.

The 1880's had however laid a precedent, the committee met weekly to confirm proceedings and take fresh decisions. In 1884, two permanent sub-committees, one for finance and the other for executive and general affairs, were appointed. From time to time various adhoc committees were set up to inquire into complaints, the construction of large buildings, etc. Each Municipal Commissioner was given field duties in one of the four wards into which town is divided. The ward commissioners were authorised to grant permission on the spot for routine or trivial matters, reporting them for formal confirmation by the Municipal Committee.

Subsequently during 1900, the elected seats were reduced to five and again in 1907 it was reconstituted with just seven members. Its misfortunes never looked up and it remained dominated by the government officials since then. The nominations were also made on pick and choose basis and managed a large number of services. In 1908, the facade of elections was removed and for reasons affecting the 'Public interest' the Municipal Committee was reconstituted to consist of seven nominated members, of whom only four were ex-officio Government nominees. The Deputy Commissioner served as President. Three 'interests', those of house owners, traders and the Indian communities were represented by three nominated members. Each municipal commissioner was given field duties, one of the four wards into which town was divided. The Ward Commissioners were authorised to grant permission on the spot for routine or trivial matters, reporting them for formal confirmation by Municipal Committee. The experiment with a whole elected municipality bequeathed a lasting mistrust of democratisation.

Several representations were received by the government regarding the unsatisfactory constitution of committee. Suffice is to say that as a result of prolonged parley, it was decided that Municipal Committee should consist of 12 members including the President, all of whom were to be elected. The right of election of President was given to the members of the committee alone.

Local government made the following rules:

1. Every adult rate payer who resided in Simla for 5 months, had not been convicted of a non-bailable offences and was not under contrast as regard works to be done for the municipality was eligible for the office of the members of the committee;
2. There were two classes of voters 'A' and 'B'.

***Class–A.*** House proprietors, male or female, residents or non-residents, shall have, for houses outside the bazars, one vote for every Rs. 1000 of rent on which house tax is bonafide paid by them and within bazar limits the vote for every Rs. 25 of house tax paid by them.

***Class–B.*** Male tenants outside the bazar shall have one vote for every Rs. 500 of bonafide rental value paid and within bazar limits one vote for every Rs. 125 of rent paid. Votes of these scales may be given for each house by either one or more bonafide tenants, shops or offices and partly for other such purposes, the total votes for any house shall not exceed the number allowed on the Gross rental on which house tax is paid by proprietor.

By the Punjab Government Notification of June 1908, the Constitution of Simla Municipal Board was again changed and it consisted of the seven members, all of whom were to be nominated. Subsequently by a Notification of June 1917, the number of the members of Municipal Committee, Simla was raised from seven to eight, all of whom to be appointed. Further, in November 1922 the committee was constituted with ten members—three (Deputy Commissioner, Health Officer and Provincial Executive Engineer), as ex-officio, two (one of whom might be the Superintending Engineer, Imperial Circle) nominated by the Government of India, three nominated non-officials and two (one by upper ward and one by lower ward) elected.

The Punjab Government vide their Notification of the 9th December, 1936 increased the number of members further to 12, of whom three to be elected and nine appointed by name of office. Out of these, four members continued to be ex-officio. They were Deputy Commissioner, Simla, Executive Engineer, Simla Provincial Division, Executive Engineer, Simla Central Division, and Civil Surgeon, Simla.

This system continued upto 1953. Elections during 1953 to 1960 were held on the basis of this system. During 1962 the Punjab Government raised the number of members to 19 (13 single and 3 double members constituencies) according to the population of the town. Out of these 19 members, three members were to be from scheduled castes.

The general elections to the Municipal Committee, Simla were held on 6th November, 1960 and notified by the Punjab Government on 25th November 1960. The committee took oath of allegiance on 8th December 1960.

In addition to 16 elected members, four persons were appointed as advisors to Municipal Committee. They included Civil Surgeon, Shimla; Executive Engineer, Simla Central Division; Executive Engineer, Simla Provincial, Divisional; and Adjutant General Western Command, Simla. The last one was however, substituted by the Station Officer, Station Head Quarters, Simla vide Punjab Government Notification of June 1961.

As a result of reorganisation of Punjab with effect from 1st November, 1966, Simla along with other hilly areas was merged in Himachal Pradesh and became permanent capital of the Himachal Pradesh. The development of this town and its suburbs and for management of municipal affairs therefore, engaged the attention of Himachal Pradesh Government. The Government felt that the concrete steps were necessary and this could only be done if there was a separate legislation for this purpose. As a result, the Capital of Himachal Pradesh (Development and Regulations) Act was passed by the State Legislative Assembly, which received the assent of the President of India on 20th June, 1969.[19] Consequently, the erstwhile Municipal Committee was dissolved on 27th June 1969 and replaced by a Corporation consisting of one administrator and ten nominated members, out of which, one was to be a women and one scheduled caste. Upto the constitution of the Corporation, the Deputy Commissioner, Mahasu, was appointed as officer-in-charge to perforn the functions of the corporation from 27th June, 1969. The Municipal Corporation came into being from first September 1970 vide Himachal Pradesh Government Notification of the 1st September, 1970. Shri R.K. Anand, I.A.S. was appointed as Administrator and ten other members were nominated. The members included one women and one person from the scheduled caste besides eight officers inclusive of the Director of Tourism; Inspector General of Police; Director, Health Services; Chief Engineer, P.W.D. (B & R); Chief Engineer, M.P.P. and Power; Chief Conservator of Forest Liaison Officer, Western Command; and Under Secretary (LSG). The Chief Engineer, M.P.P. and Power was later on substituted by the Superintending Engineer, H.P. State Electricity Board; the Director of Tourism was replaced by Managing Director, H.P. Tourism Development Corporation and the Liaison Officer of the Western Command was substituted by Director, Re-Settlement and Employment Western Command.

Shimla Municipal Corporation had its election after 25 years on May 14, 1986. These elections were held due to the judgement of Supreme Court, to hold elections.[20] On the petition filed by Shri Om Prakash Sood and Shri Yoginder Lal Sharma, the enlightened citizens of Shimla Municipal Corporation, Shimla, shall have to wait for no less than twenty five years in Independent India to have an affected and elected body. This too was done on the intervention of courts. The elections were held in 1986 after successive Governments avoided to get themselves involved in the institution of local self-government.[21]

The Himachal Pradesh Government divided in December 1985 Municipal Corporation area into twenty-one wards and of which three wards were reserved for scheduled castes. Himachal Pradesh Government on April 3rd, 1986 decided to hold election to Municipal Corporation, Shimla on May 14th, 1986.

The Governor of Himachal Pradesh under section 6 of Himachal Pradesh Municipal Corporation Act, 1979 had nominated Smt. Ram Piari and three persons to the Municipal Corporation.

Elections schedules for 1963 did not take place, and in 1966, the Punjab Government superseded the committee on the charge of incompetence, misappropriation of powers and nepotism. A court order reinstated the committee in 1976, however fresh elections were not held as the Capital of Himachal Pradesh (Development and Regulations) Act, 1968, was passed and the Committee was converted into Corporation totally manned by nominated members. In 1986, elections were again held, and a band of councillors with a mayor, shared power with the Corporation,[22] does not enjoy a majority support.[23]

After the expiry of first term of Shri Adarsh Kumar and Shri Narinder Singh Thakur as the Mayor and the Deputy Mayor respectively, Shri Adarsh Kumar was again elected as Mayor and Shri Shiv Kumar Dogra replaced Shri Narinder Singh Thakur as Deputy Mayor for the second term of two years and six months.

Election to the next municipal corporation was due by the month of May, 1991. However, the Government could not conduct the election on schedule, Citizen Forum on 24th May, 1991, thus approached the Hon'ble High Court, Shimla to ask the Government of Himachal Pradesh to conduct the election. The Hon'ble High Court ordered the Government of Himachal Pradesh to conduct the election by 30th November, 1991. The State Government wanted some more time for the revision of electoral rolls and for delimitation of the wards in view of new census figures. Ultimately the High Court ordered for the conduct of election by May, 1992. As a result of this order of Hon'ble High Court, the elections to the Municipal Corporation, Shimla were held on 24th May, 1992. The election was conducted in 20 wards only. In one ward, i.e., ward no. 6, the election could not be conducted due to the death of one of the candidates.[24] Three wards were reserved for Scheduled Castes. The Government of Himachal Pradesh under sub-section (3) of section 4 of Himachal Pradesh Municipal Corporation Act, 1979, notified the name of 21 elected councillors from various wards of Municipal Corporation.

Shri Adarsh Kumar and Smt. Kamal Walta were elected as the Mayor and the Deputy Mayor for two and a half years respectively. But due to death of Smt. Kamal Walta in the year 1993, the post of Deputy Mayor fell vacant to which Smt. Jenny Prem was elected for the remaining term. After the expiry of first term of the Mayor and the Deputy Mayor, Shri Adarsh Kumar and Smt. Jeany Prem were again elected as the Mayor and the Deputy Mayor. As in the month of August 1996, Shri Adarsh Kumar was elected as M.L.A. to Himachal Pradesh Legislative Assembly, he resigned from the post of Mayor and Shri Manoj Kumar was elected as the Mayor in the month of October, 1996 for the remaining term.

The State Government under section 6 of Himachal Pradesh Municipal Corporation Act, 1979 nominated Shri Umer Abdullah Khan, Shri Shadi Ram and S. Kesar Singh to the Municipal Corporation, Shimla. After the death of S. Kesar Singh, the Himachal Pradesh Government nominated S. Nirmal Singh in his place.

In the year 1996, the State Government extended the municipal limits to adjoining rural areas, which includes Tara Devi Chakker, Ghora Chowki, Tutoo, Dhalli, Kasumpati, Vikas Nagar, New Dhimla, etc. in order to provide better civic amenities and planned development. After delimitation of wards and area of the Municipal Corporation, Shimla, the number of wards was increased to be from 21. The old Himachal Pradesh Municipal Corporation, Act, 1979, was replaced by new Himachal Pradesh Municipal Corporation Act, 1994 after the enforcement of 74th Constitution Amendment.

Under the provision of section 10 of Himachal Pradesh Municipal Corporation Act, 1994, it is made mandatory to reserve the wards for scheduled castes, scheduled tribes and women. One-third out of total number of seats are reserved for women and scheduled castes and scheduled tribes. The seats reserved for women, scheduled castes and scheduled tribes are allocated by rotation.

According to the section 36 (1) of Himachal Pradesh Municipal Corporation Act, 1994, the office of the Mayor is reserved for the scheduled caste, scheduled tribes and women, by rotation or by lots in the manner prescribed, and its term has been made to one year.

The last elections of the Corporation were held on 22 May, 1997, and 25 councillors were elected. The Governor under section 4 sub-section 3 of Himachal Pradesh Municipal Corporation Act, 1994 nominated Shri Adarsh Kumar M.L.A. from Shimla assembly constituency and Shri Charanjiv Lal Kashyap, M.L.A. from Kasumpti assembly constituency as associated members of the Municipal Corporation, Shimla and later on when the new assembly was constituted in year 1998, they were replaced by new M.L.A.'s, Shri Narinder Bragta and Shri Roop Dass Kashyap, new M.L.A.'s from Shimla and Kasumpti respectively. The Governor also nominated Shri Deepak Sharma, S. Baldev Singh and Smt. Bimla Kashyap, as Councillors without voting right. The Government notified the election of Shri Manoj Kumar and Shri Durga Singh Verma as the Mayor and the Deputy Mayor.

**Municipal Laws**

Himachal Pradesh Government enacted two new Acts, as a sequal to the 74th Amendment Act, i.e., (i) Himachal Pradesh Municipal Act 1994 and (ii) Himachal Pradesh Municipal Corporation Act, 1994. Accordingly the government constituted the Nagar Panchayats and the Municipal Councils, and Municipal Corporation of Shimla respectively.

**Himachal Pradesh Municipal Corporation Act**

Main feature of the Himachal Pradesh Municipal Corporation Act, 1994 is that the members of Municipal Corporation, Shimla are directly elected and other person who is not directly elected has no right to vote. As regards reservation of seats, the Act provides:

(i) The reservation to Scheduled Castes/Scheduled Tribes is directly in proportion to their population in a municipal area;

(ii) 1/3 seats reserved out of SC/STs wards are reserved for SC/ST women;

(iii) 1/3 seats reserved for women out of total seats of general including SC/ST categories.

Now, let us first compile and evaluate the provisions in the conformity legislations regarding three of the most important aspects of municipal decentralization, namely functional decentralisation, financial decentralisation and popular participation in the provision and monitoring of affairs of Municipal Corporation, Shimla.

**Functional Decentralisation**

On assignment of functions to urban local bodies, the 12th Schedule of the Constitution provides an illustrative list of municipal functions. In view of the 74th amendment, the State Government has legalised all the functions listed in the 12th Schedule as legitimate municipal functions. The Act provides for obligatory and discretionary functions to be performed by the Municipal Corporation, Shimla. The Act further empowers the State Government to issue notification to determine the various additional functions of the Corporation on the subject itself and 12th Schedule. Therefore, apart from obligatory functions and discretionary functions of the Municipal Corporation, Shimla, some additional functions are bestowed on the Corporation.

The rationale behind the inclusion of new responsibilities such as: (i) urban forestry, protection of the environment and promotion of ecological aspects, and (ii) urban poverty alleviation under the 12th Schedule is that these functions which are of tremendous social importance are best handled locally. The conformity legislation indicate that there are tremendous difference in views regarding whether the above mentioned functions ought to be local, obligatory or discretionary. Perhaps there is doubt whether the Municipal Corporation, Shimla will be able to shoulder these onerous responsibilities or not. It may, however, be mentioned here that while some functions are appropriate for municipal corporation, it is not necessary that they be financed by Corporation's collected revenue. There may be valid reasons to link them to inter-governmental transfers.

Table 1, 2 and 3 show the functions performed by the Municipal Corporation, Shimla at present (inclusive of pre and post 74th Amendment to the Constitution of India).

Table 1 depicts that out of three functions relating to the general administration one was obligatory and remaining were discretionary before the promulgation of the 74th CAA. Four core functions were mandatory and one was discretionary. All the developmental functions were optional and maintenance functions as obligatory. In addition, a number of miscellaneous functions were also performed by the Corporation. Table 2 clearly indicates that the Shimla Municipal Corporation is already vested with nine functions out of the ones enumerated in the Twelfth Schedule. The present functional areas are earmarked in Table 3.

**Obligatory Functions of Municipal Corporation**

It is incumbent on the corporation to make adequate provision by any means or measures which it may lawfully use or take for each of the following matters, namely:[25]

(a) the construction, maintenance and cleaning of drains and drainage works and of public latrines, urinals and similar conveniences;

(b) the construction of works and means for providing supply of water for public and private purposes;

(c) the scavenging, removal and disposal of fifth, rubbish and other obnoxious or polluted matters;

(d) the reclamation of unhealthy localities, the removal of noxious vegetation and generally the abatement of all nuisances;

(e) the regulation of places for the disposal of the dead and the provision and maintenance of places for the said purpose;

(f) the construction and maintenance of cattle pond;

(g) measures for preventing and checking the spread of dangerous diseases;

(h) the construction and maintenance of municipal markets and the regulation thereof;

(i) the regulation and abatement of offensive or dangerous trades or practices;

(j) the securing or removal of dangerous buildings and places;

(k) the construction, maintenance, alteration, and improvement of public streets, bridges, culverts, cause ways and the like;

(l) the lighting, watering and cleaning of public streets and other public places;

(m) the removal of obstructions and projections in or upon streets, bridges and other public places;

(n) the naming and numbering of streets and premises;

(o) the maintenance of municipal offices;

(p) the laying out of the maintenance of public parks, gardens or recreation grounds;

(q) the maintenance of monuments and memorials vested in a local authority in the municipal area immediately before the commencement of this Act or which may be vested in the Corporation after such commencement;

(r) the maintenance and development of the value of all properties vested in or entrusted to the management of the Corporation;

(s) the fulfilment of any other obligation imposed by or under this Act or any other law for the time being in force;

(t) planting and care of trees on road sides etc. and

(u) survey of buildings and lands.

**Discretionary Functions of Municipal Corporation**

The corporation may in its discretion provide either wholly or in part for all or any of the following matters[26]:

(a) the furtherance of education including cultural and physical education;

(b) the establishment and maintenance of, and aid to, libraries, museums art galleries, botanical or zoological collections;

(c) the establishments and maintenance of, aid to stadia, gymnasia, akharas and places for sports and games;

(d) the civic reception to persons of distinction;

(e) the providing of music or other entertainment's in public places or places of public resort and the establishment of theatres and cinemas;

(f) the organisation and management of fairs and exhibitions;

(g) the construction and maintenance of
  - (i) rest houses
  - (ii) poor houses
  - (iii) infirmaries
  - (iv) children's houses
  - (v) house for the deaf and dumb and for disabled and handicapped children
  - (vi) shelters for destitute and disabled persons
  - (vii) asylums for persons of unsound mind.

(h) the building or purchase and maintenance of dwelling houses for corporation officers and other corporation employees;

(i) any measures for the welfare of the corporation officers and other corporation employees or any class of them, including the sanctioning of loans to such officers and employees or any class of them for construction of houses and purchase of vehicles;

(j) the organisation or management of chemical or bacteriological laboratories for the examination or analysis of water, food and drugs for the detection of diseases or research connected with the public health medical relief;

(k) the provision for relief to destitute and disabled persons;

(l) public vaccination and inoculation;

(m) the organisation, construction, maintenance and management of swimming pools, public wash houses, bathing place and other institution designed for improvement of public health;

(n) the organisation and management of farms and diaries within or outside the municipal area for the supply, distribution and processing of milk and products for the benefits of the residents of the municipal area;

(o) the organisation and management of cottage industries, handicraft centres and sales emporium;

(p) the construction and maintenance of warehouses and godowns;

(q) the construction and maintenance of garages, sheds and stands for vehicles and cattle biers;

(r) the provision for unfiltered water-supply;

(s) the improvement of municipal areas in accordance with the rules laid down in the Municipal Act.

(t) improvement schemes approved by the corporation; the provision of housing accommodation for the inhabitants of any area or for class of inhabitants;

(u) the establishment and maintenance of hospitals, dispensaries and maternity and child welfare centre and carrying out of the other measures necessary for medical relief; and

(v) any measure not hereinbefore specifically mentioned, likely to promote public safety, health, convenience or general welfare.

**Additional Functions**

In view of the spirit of 74th Constitution. Amendment, the sphere of functions of the Municipal Corporation, Shimla have been enlarged to a greater extent so as to achieve greater democratic decentralisation at the grass root level. The 74th Amendment to the Constitution and the consequential changes enacted in the Himachal Pradesh Municipal Corporation Act, 1994 has considerably widen and assigned comprehensive function and responsibilities—statutory and obligatory, solid waste management, abatement of slum degradation, protection of environment and promotion of ecological aspects.

Himachal Pradesh Municipal Corporation Act, 1994 empower the state government to issue notification to determine the various additional functions of the corporation on the subject itself indicated in section 42 (1) (a) and (b) and further heads (i) to (xviii) and the twelfth schedule of the constitution corresponding to Article 243 W. Therefore, apart from obligatory and discretionary functions of the corporation, the some additional functions are bestowed on the corporation.

(a) the preparation of plans for economic development and social justice;

(b) the performance of functions and implementation of schemes which be entrusted to it including the functions in respect of the following matters, namely:—

***(i) Urban Planning Including Town Planning***

(a) Implementation of land use map notified by the government; Provided that where no such map is notified, the concerned, local body, will prepare and implement the local land use map;

***(ii) Planning for Economic and Social Development***

(a) Formulation of schemes for the up-liftment of poor

(b) Generation of employment

(c) Implementation of poverty alleviation programmes.

***(iii) Roads and Bridges***

(a) Construction and maintenance of roads and bridges except the roads and bridges on National Highway and State Highway within municipal areas.

***(iv) Water-Supply***

(a) Planning, provision for construction and maintenance of water supply for domestic, commercial and industrial purposes in this the municipal area; Provided that execution of really new schemes will be in accordance with decision of government in each case.

***(v) Public Health***

(a) Provision of drain and sewerage, and sewerage disposal and nallahs.

***(vi) Urban Forestry, Protection of the Environment and Promotion of Ecological Aspects***

(a) Creation maintenance and regulating the use of urban forest blocks;
(b) Plantation, maintenance and preservation of trees both ornamental and economic within the municipal areas;
(c) Regulating the plantation preservation and felling of trees;
(d) To establish and maintain refuse disposal sites and apparatus;
(e) To regulate the polluting trades, callings and occupations causing airwater pollution;
(f) Establishment and maintenance of electric crematoriums.

***(vii) Safeguarding the Interests of Weaker Section of Society, Including the Handicapped and Mentally Retarded***

(a) Establishment of orphanage, mental hospital, administration and care of mentally retarded children and women homes.

***(viii) Slum Improvement and Upgradation***

(a) Identification of slum areas, formulation of schemes for the rehabilitation of the people living in slums.

***(ix) Urban Poverty Alleviation***

(a) Identification of urban poor localities pre-dominantly occupied by them;
(b) Formulation and execution of schemes for the upliftment;

***(x) Promotion of Cultural, Educational and Asthetic Aspects***

***(xi) Burial and Burial Grounds, Cremation-Cremation Grounds and Electric Crematoriums***

(a) To establish and maintain electric crematorium

***(xii) Cattle Ponds, Prevention of Cruelty to Animals***

(a) To provide for a care and upkeep of old and injured cattles;
(b) To establish and maintain veterinary hospitals;
(c) To take action against persons causing cruelty to animals.

***(xiii) Vital Statistics including Registration of Births and Deaths***

(a) To keep the population record of the municipal areas and annual publications of population statistic including male, female, schedule caste, schedule tribe, and handicapped persons living below poverty line.

***(xiv) Public Amenities Including Street lighting, Parking Lots, Bus stop and Public Conveniences***

(a) Bus Stand, bus stop, rain shelters loading and unloading points.

***(xv) Regulation of Slaughter Houses and Tanneries***

(a) Establishment, maintenance, regulation and control of slaughter houses and tanneries.

In India, there has been an increasing tendency on the part of governments to take over more and more local functions, either directly or indirectly or by creating special purpose agencies. This has been justified mainly on the growth of poor performance and inefficiency of the local bodies in the discharge of their functions, inadequacy of efficient staff, want of financial resourcs, factionalism and maladministration and indifference of citizens to civic-affairs...the remedy lies not in depriving the local bodies functions but in improving and strengthening their organisational and administrative set-up, allocating to them adequate resources and giving expert and technical help in the discharge of their functions.

The particulars furnished in Table 1 shows the functional domain of the Shimla Municipal Corporation in pre-74th CAA era. Table 2 mentions that half of the functions listed in the Twelfth Schedule are still not entrusted to the Municipal Corporation. The present functional domain is shown in Table 3.

**Financial Decentralisation**

One of the most important features of the 74th Amendment is the devolution of financial resources and autonomy to the local bodies. Article 243–x lays down mandatory directions to the State Government to give powers to impose taxes to the local bodies as well as to share the consolidated fund of the State with local bodies. Accordingly, to determine the share of urban local bodies in various taxes, duties, tolls and fees levied and collected by the State Government and also to provide grants-in-aid to municipalities from the consolidated fund of the state, the Constitution further provides the constitution of State Finance Commission. This is very important constitutional provision as it is binding on the State Government to implement the award of the State Finance Commission. Even the State Finance Commission's recommendations shall form guiding principles for the Finance Commission of India. In article 280 (3) new sub-clauses (bb) and (c) have been added wherein recommendations of the State Finance Commission will be taken as the basis by the Finance Commission of India, in order to augment the consolidated fund of the State to supplement the resources of the municipalities.

The 74th Constitution Amendment Act, in addition to providing State Finance Commission, requires that State Government specify "bye laws" regarding:

(1) taxes, duties, tolls and fees levied and collected by the municipalities;
(2) taxes, duties, tolls and fees levied and collected by the State government, which are to be assigned to or shared with the municipalities; and
(3) Grants-in-aid to be given to the municipalities from Consolidated Fund of the State.

The conformity legislations of Himachal Pradesh show that even where additional functional responsibilities have been enthrusted to Municipal Corporation Shimla, 'no provision' has been made as to how finances will be mobilised to discharge these new responsibilities. Regarding setting up of State Finance Commission, the State of Himachal Pradesh have adopted the provisions prescribed by the 74th Constitution Amendment Act in full. Detailed terms of reference for such commission are attempted to the amended legislations. Consequently, the Government constituted the State Finance Commission on 23rd April, 1994. The recommendations are still awaited.

**Finances**

Municipal Corporation, Shimla enjoys tax powers and functional competence as conferred on it by the Himachal Pradesh Municipal Corporation Act, 1994. The Act provides powers to levy taxes (tax-revenue and non-tax revenue) to perform its functions in order to achieve the organisational goals and to raise its efficiency. Municipal Corporation is a self-financing institution, the State government also provides grants-in-aids to it. The source of income of Municipal Corporation, Shimla is of two types:

(1) Tax Revenue; and
(2) Non-Tax Revenue.

***Tax Revenue***

Under section 84 of Himachal Pradesh Municipal Corporation Act, 1994, the Corporation:

(a) taxes on building and lands;
(b) tax on profession, trades, calling and employment;
(c) tax on vehicles other than motor vehicles and animals;
(d) tax on the increase in urban land values caused by the execution of development or improvement work;
(e) show tax;
(f) tax on consumption of energy at a rate of not exceeding 02 paise for every unit of electricity consumed by any person within municipal area;
(g) sewerage tax on commercial buildings;
(h) a duty on the transfer of immovable properties situated within the limits of the municipal area in addition to the duty imposed under the Indian Stamp Act, 1899. (The amount of the duty so collected shall be paid to the Corporation)
(i) House Tax;
(j) Sanitation Tax;
(k) Water Tax;
(l) Ground Tax and;
(m) General Tax (levied on a graduated scale, if the government so determines)

***Non Tax Revenue***

Under section 85 of Himachal Pradesh Municipal Corporation Act, 1994, the Municipal Corporation, Shimla, Subject to prior approval of the State government, may in the manner prescribed, levy a fee with regard to the following:—

(a) Fee on advertisement other than advertisements in the newspapers;
(b) Fee on building applications;
(c) Development fee for providing and maintaining civic amenities in certain areas;
(d) Fee with regard to lighting;
(e) Fee with regard to scavenging;
(f) Fee in nature of costs for providing internal services in a building scheme or town planning scheme; and
(g) Teh-Bazari fee.

### *Conclusion*

In a nutshell, the Himachal Pradesh Municipal Corporation Act, 1994, under which Municipal Corporation, Shimla functions suffer from the following general drawbacks in the areas of functional and financial decentralisation and popular participation in civic affairs;

(1) The Himachal Pradesh Municipal Corporation Act, 1994, does not provide clarity to the package of functions to be handled by Municipal Corporation's Planning Committees. The possibilities of overlapping of functions between Municipal Corporation, Shimla and State Government are not overruled.
(2) No distinction is made between essential functions of Municipal Corporation, and the functions 'assigned' by State Government and those discharged as the 'agents' of higher levels of Government.

A reference has already been made in preceding pages to 'essential' 'assigned' and 'agency' functions of municipal corporation. Essential functions are those which are 'local' in nature in the sense that the benefits and costs associated with them are largely confined to local jurisdictions. Assigned functions include those which are not strictly local but assigned by the state government under municipal laws. Agency functions are those of State and central governments but entrusted to municipal corporation for reason of convenience. The general prescription is that 'assigned' municipal functions should be financed out of specific inter-government transfers, 'agency' functions and 'essential' functions with, municipal corporation's 'own' and 'assigned' revenue sources.

(3) Municipal Corporation, Shimla is not differentiated in term of capacity. Differentiation of functions is important since revenue base is likely to differ. In the absence of corrective

transfer mechanisms from above, a municipality can not normally be expected to perform the same functions effectively.

(4) In the light of 74th Amendment, the State have made addition to the list of local functions in view of the 12th Schedule, but without earmarking additional resources to the Municipal Corporation. This may lead to the worsening of municipal problems.

(5) Little attempt has been made to improve the revenue base of the corporation. A practice of waiting for the State Finance Commission to recommend municipal fiscal reforms may not be healthy. The newly created local political structure will lose credibility in the absence of financial capability to perform.

(6) The issue of alternative mechanisms to produce and deliver local public services have not been addressed by the conformity legislation. The provisions have not been addressed by the conformity legislation. The provisions have not been made in Himachal Pradesh Municipal Corporation Act, 1994 for institutional arrangements, such as public-private partnership, privatisation etc. It is important to note that discharging of municipal functions through the official municipal machinery is only one of the options available to a municipality. If efficient public service is 'the mandate of local self-government, then the municipality should be made able to choose the most appropriate production and delivery mechanism. Thus, the 74th Amendment which is for urban local bodies have incorporated establishment of some constitutional norms in order to provide some uniformity and respectability to the system of local self-government. Despite these amendments, functioning and powers of local bodies will still depend on the State Government to a larger extent yet the amendments created some legal enforceable rights and obligations which cannot be ignored beyond a limit by the State Government. It is a binding on the State Government to constitute local bodies and to ensure elections at regular intervals. It is also mandatory to transfer powers and functions to act them as institute of local self government

and to involve them in planning and development and to ensure financial resources and autonomy to these bodies. The State Government must first be willing to decentralize their powers, functions and finances to politically responsible Municipal Corporation, Shimla.

Functional clarity and strengthening of Municipal Corporation, Shimla, its finance and management should occupy the centre-stage of the follow up action on the conformity legislation. The ways to improve municipal functioning will have to include among other things, the rational allocation of responsibilities and finances between level of government, incentive-penality structures to enhance local efforts to raise revenue and improve the responsiveness of service providers, minimisation of waste, adoption of efficient and cost effective practices and promotion of policies that enhance local initiative Municipal reforms need to address these issues systematically.

**TABLE 1**

**Functions Performed by Municipal Corporation, Shimla before 74th Amendment**

| *Sl. No.* | | *Functions* | |
|---|---|---|---|
| | | *Obligatory* | *Discretionary* |
| **(A)** | **General Administration** | | |
| (i) | Information and Publicity | | # |
| (ii) | Maintenance of Houses | # | # |
| (iii) | Numbering of Houses | | # |
| **(B)** | **Core functions** | | |
| (i) | Street Lighting | # | |
| (ii) | Water Supply | # | |
| (iii) | Sanitation | # | |
| (iv) | Drainage and Sewerage | # | |
| (v) | Town Planning | | # |
| **(C)** | **Development Functions** | | |
| (i) | Housing | | # |
| (ii) | Education | | # |
| (iii) | Public Health | | # |
| (iv) | Social Welfare | | # |
| **(D)** | **Maintenance Functions** | | |
| (i) | Sanitation | # | |
| (ii) | Roads | # | |
| **(E)** | **Miscellaneous Functions** | | |
| | # # # # | | |

## TABLE 2

### Functions Performed by Municipal Corporation, Shimla After 74th Amendment (As Per 12th Schedule of Constitution)

| *Sl. No.* | *Functions* | *Whether transferred or not* |
|---|---|---|
| 1. | Urban Planning including Town Planning | Not yet |
| 2. | Regulation of land use and construction of buildings | Already vested in M.C., Shimla |
| 3. | Planning for economic ans social development | Not yet |
| 4. | Roads and Bridges | Already vested in M.C., Shimla |
| 5. | Water Supply for Domestic, Industrial and Commercial purposes | Already vested in M.C., Shimla |
| 6. | Public Health, Sanitation, Conservancy and Solid Waste Management | Already vested in M.C. Shimla |
| 7. | Fire Services | Not yet |
| 8. | Urban Forestry Protection of Environment and Protection of Ecological aspects | Not yet |
| 9. | Safeguarding the interests of weaker sections of society including the handicapped and mentally retarded | Not yet |
| 10. | Slum improvement and upgradation | Not yet |
| 11. | Urban Poverty alleviation | Not yet |
| 12. | Provision of Urban Amenitiesa and facilities such as parks, gardens, playgrounds | Not yet |
| 13. | Promotion of Cultural Educational and aesthetic aspects | Not yet |
| 14. | Burials and burial grounds, cremations, cremation grounds and electric crematiums | Already vested in M.C., Shimla |
| 15. | Cattle ponds, preention of cruelty to animals | do |
| 16. | Vital statistics including registration of Births and Deaths | Already vested in M.C., Shimla |
| 17. | Public amenities including street lightening, parking lots, Bus-stops and Public conveniences | M.C., Shimla |
| 18. | Regulation of slaughter houses and tanneries | do |

## Table 3

### Functions Performed by Municipal Corporation, Shimla at Present (Inclusive of Pre and Post 74 Amendment)

| S. No. | Functions |
|---|---|

**I General Administration**

(i) Maintenance of Records

**II Core Functions**

(i) Street Lighting

(ii) Water Supply

(iii) Sanitation
(iv) Drainage/Sewerage

**III Development Functions**
(i) Maintenance/Development Activities
(ii) Construction of Parking spaces, public amenities
(iii) Conversion of dry latrines to handflush and rehabilitation
(iv) Implementation of (SJSRY)

**IV Maintenance Functions**
(i) Sanitation
(ii) Roads
(iii) Drains
(iv) Water supply system

**V Miscellaneous Functions**
(i) Erection and Maintenance of Parking Places
(ii) Parks, etc.
(iii) Markets and Slaughter House
(iv) Maintenane of Municipal Properties and offices
(v) Assessment and Collection of Taxes/fees, etc.
(vi) Sweeping and Public Streets and drains
(viii) Running and maintenance of labour hostels and working women hostels, etc.

## REFRENCES

1. Vipin Pubby, *Shimla Then and Now,* (New Delhi: Indus Publishing Company, 1997), p. 17.
2. H.T.S. Forrest, *Indian Municipality,* Thaekes: Spintand Company, 1925), p. 3.
3. Edward Buck, *Shimla Past and Present,* (Delhi: Sumeet Publication, 1979), p. 7.
4. Barr, Patand and Dermos Ray, *Simla-A Hill station in British India,* (Delhi: B. R. Publishing Corporation, 1978), p. 7.
5. Alexander Gerrard, *Account of Koonawur in Himalaya,* (London: Oxford University Press, 1941), p. 197.
6. Pawan Kumar Banta, "Historical Background of Simla Municipal Corporation," *Civic Affairs,* Vol. 40, No. 15, October-1993, p. 34.
7. Pamela Kanwar, *Imperial Simla, The Political Culture of Raj.* (Delhi: Oxford University Press, 1990), p. 16.
8. *Ibid.,* p. 16.
9. Hunter (ed), *Lord Amherst and the British Advance Eastwards to Burma,* (London: Oxford University Press, 1889), pp. 198–200.
10. Pamela Kanwar, *op. cit,* p. 18.
11. *Ibid.*
12. Pawan Kumar Banta, "Personnel Administration of Shimla Municipal Corporation," (Unpublished dissertation). (Shimla: Himachal Pradesh University, Department of Public Administration, 1987), p. 102.
13. Edward Buck, *op. cit,* pp. 144–46.
14. Pawan Kumar Banta, "Lesser Himalayas–Shimla", in cultural *Heritage of Himachal,* (New Delhi: Indian Environmental Society, 1998), p. 31.

15. Sharda Thakur, "Organisation and Working of Simla Municipal Corporation", (Shimla: Department of Public Administration, H.P. University, 1985), p. 18.
16. Act–XXVI of 1850 of Punjab Government.
17. Padam Nabh Gautam, *Administrative History of Shimla Municipal Corporation,* Mimeo, July, 1981, p. 3.
18. Pamela Kanwar, *op. cit.,* p.112.
19. Padam Nabh Gautam, *Municipal Corporation of Shimla a Monograph.* (Patiala: Punjabi University, 1983), p. 8.
20. Sarita Sharda, *Finances of Shimla Municipal Corporation–An Analytical Study.* (Shimla: Department of Public Administration, H.P. University, 1983) p. 55.
21. Pawan Kumar Banta, "Municipal Corporation, Shimla", (Lucknow: *Journal of Institute of Public Administration,* Vol. 6, No. 1 to 4, April 90-March 91), p. 12.
22. Vipin Pubby, *op. cit.,* 96.
23. Raja Bhasin, *Simla: The Summer Capital of British India,* (New Delhi Penguin Books India Pvt. Ltd, 1992), pp. 166–67.
24. Vipin Pubby, *op. cit.,* p. 119.
25. Padam Nabh Gautam, *Participation and Development–A Study of Municipal Corporation, Shimla,* Mimeo, 1995, p. 5.
26. M.P. Municipal Corporation Act 1994, 27–28.
27. "Report of the Rural–Urban Relationship Committee", Vol. 1 (New Delhi), Ministry of Health and Family Welfare Planning, Government of India 1966), pp. 16–17.

# INDEX